Big Data Science & Analytics

A Hands-On Approach

Arshdeep Bahga · **Vijay Madisetti**

Big Data Science & Analytics: A Hands-On Approach

Copyright © 2016 by Arshdeep Bahga & Vijay Madisetti

Published by Arshdeep Bahga & Vijay Madisetti

ISBN: 978-0996025539

Book Website: www.big-data-analytics-book.com

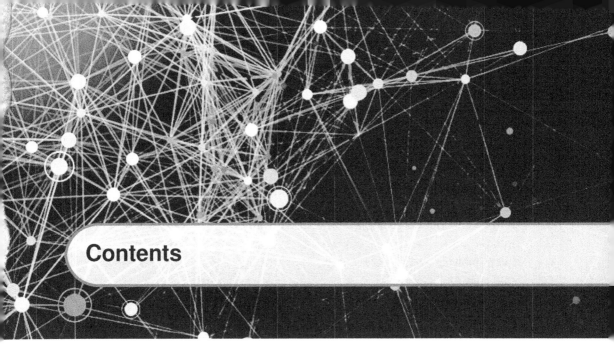

Contents

Preface

About the Book

We are living in the dawn of what has been termed as the "Fourth Industrial Revolution" by the World Economic Forum (WEF) in 2016. The Fourth Industrial Revolution is marked through the emergence of "cyber-physical systems" where software interfaces seamlessly over networks with physical systems, such as sensors, smartphones, vehicles, power grids or buildings, to create a new world of Internet of Things (IoT). Data and information are fuel of this new age where powerful analytics algorithms burn this fuel to generate decisions that are expected to create a smarter and more efficient world for all of us to live in. This new area of technology has been defined as Big Data Science and Analytics, and the industrial and academic communities are realizing this as a competitive technology that can generate significant new wealth and opportunity.

Big data is defined as collections of datasets whose volume, velocity or variety is so large that it is difficult to store, manage, process and analyze the data using traditional databases and data processing tools. In the recent years, there has been an exponential growth in the both structured and unstructured data generated by information technology, industrial, healthcare, retail, web, and other systems. Big data science and analytics deals with collection, storage, processing and analysis of massive-scale data on cloud-based computing systems. Industry surveys, by Gartner and e-Skills, for instance, predict that there will be over 2 million job openings for engineers and scientists trained in the area of data science and analytics alone, and that the job market is in this area is growing at a 150 percent year-over-year growth rate.

There are very few books that can serve as a foundational textbook for colleges looking to create new educational programs in these areas of big data science and analytics. Existing books are primarily focused on the business side of analytics, or describing vendor-specific offerings for certain types of analytics applications, or implementation of certain analytics algorithms in specialized languages, such as R.

We have written this textbook, as part of our expanding "A Hands-On Approach"™

series, to meet this need at colleges and universities, and also for big data service providers who may be interested in offering a broader perspective of this emerging field to accompany their customer and developer training programs. The typical reader is expected to have completed a couple of courses in programming using traditional high-level languages at the college-level, and is either a senior or a beginning graduate student in one of the science, technology, engineering or mathematics (STEM) fields. The reader is provided the necessary guidance and knowledge to develop working code for real-world big data applications. Concurrent development of practical applications that accompanies traditional instructional material within the book further enhances the learning process, in our opinion. Furthermore, an accompanying website for this book contains additional support for instruction and learning (www.big-data-analytics-book.com)

The book is organized into three main parts, comprising a total of twelve chapters. Part I provides an introduction to big data, applications of big data, and big data science and analytics patterns and architectures. A novel data science and analytics application system design methodology is proposed and its realization through use of open-source big data frameworks is described. This methodology describes big data analytics applications as realization of the proposed Alpha, Beta, Gamma and Delta models, that comprise tools and frameworks for collecting and ingesting data from various sources into the big data analytics infrastructure, distributed filesystems and non-relational (NoSQL) databases for data storage, processing frameworks for batch and real-time analytics, serving databases, web and visualization frameworks. This new methodology forms the pedagogical foundation of this book.

Part II introduces the reader to various tools and frameworks for big data analytics, and the architectural and programming aspects of these frameworks as used in the proposed design methodology. We chose Python as the primary programming language for this book. Other languages, besides Python, may also be easily used within the Big Data stack described in this book. We describe tools and frameworks for Data Acquisition including Publish-subscribe messaging frameworks such as Apache Kafka and Amazon Kinesis, Source-Sink connectors such as Apache Flume, Database Connectors such as Apache Sqoop, Messaging Queues such as RabbitMQ, ZeroMQ, RestMQ, Amazon SQS and custom REST-based connectors and WebSocket-based connectors. The reader is introduced to Hadoop Distributed File System (HDFS) and HBase non-relational database. The batch analysis chapter provides an in-depth study of frameworks such as Hadoop-MapReduce, Pig, Oozie, Spark and Solr. The real-time analysis chapter focuses on Apache Storm and Spark Streaming frameworks. In the chapter on interactive querying, we describe with the help of examples, the use of frameworks and services such as Spark SQL, Hive, Amazon Redshift and Google BigQuery. The chapter on serving databases and web frameworks provide an introduction to popular relational and non-relational databases (such as MySQL, Amazon DynamoDB, Cassandra, and MongoDB) and the Django Python web framework.

Part III focuses advanced topics on big data including analytics algorithms and data visualization tools. The chapter on analytics algorithms introduces the reader to machine learning algorithms for clustering, classification, regression and recommendation systems, with examples using the Spark MLlib and H2O frameworks. The chapter on data visualization describes examples of creating various types of visualizations using frameworks such as Lightning, pygal and Seaborn.

Through generous use of hundreds of figures and tested code samples, we have attempted to provide a rigorous "no hype" guide to big data science and analytics. It is expected that diligent readers of this book can use the canonical realizations of Alpha, Beta, Delta, and Gamma models for analytics systems to develop their own big data applications. We adopted an informal approach to describing well-known concepts primarily because these topics are covered well in existing textbooks, and our focus instead is on getting the reader firmly on track to developing robust big data applications as opposed to more theory.

While we frequently refer to offerings from commercial vendors, such as Amazon, Google and Microsoft, this book is not an endorsement of their products or services, nor is any portion of our work supported financially (or otherwise) by these vendors. All trademarks and products belong to their respective owners and the underlying principles and approaches, we believe, are applicable to other vendors as well. The opinions in this book are those of the authors alone.

Please also refer to our books "Internet of Things: A Hands-On Approach^{TM}" and "Cloud Computing: A Hands-On Approach^{TM}" that provide additional and complementary information on these topics. We are grateful to the Association of Computing Surveys (ACM) for recognizing our book on cloud computing as a "Notable Book of 2014" as part of their annual literature survey, and also to the 50+ universities worldwide that have adopted these textbooks as part of their program offerings.

Proposed Course Outline

The book can serve as a textbook for senior-level and graduate-level courses in Big Data Analytics and Data Science offered in Computer Science, Mathematics and Business Schools.

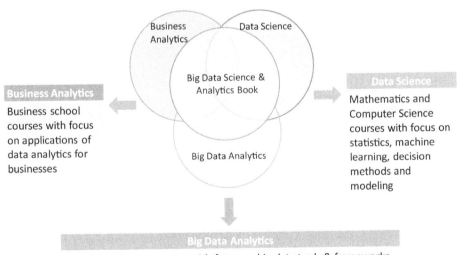

We propose the following outline for a 16-week senior level/graduate-level course based on the book.

Week	Topics
1	Introduction to Big Data • Types of analytics • Big Data characteristics • Data analysis flow • Big data examples, applications & case studies
2	Big Data stack setup and examples • HDP • Cloudera CDH • EMR • Azure HDInsights
3	MapReduce • Programming model • Examples • MapReduce patterns
4	Big Data architectures & patterns
5	NoSQL Databases • Key-value databases • Document databases • Column Family databases • Graph databases
6	Data acquisition • Publish - Subscribe Messaging Frameworks • Big Data Collection Systems • Messaging queues • Custom connectors • Implementation examples
7	Big Data storage • HDFS • HBase
8	Batch Data analysis • Hadoop & YARN • MapReduce & Pig • Spark core • Batch data analysis examples & case studies
9	Real-time Analysis • Stream processing with Storm • In-memory processing with Spark Streaming • Real-time analysis examples & case studies
10	Interactive querying • Hive • Spark SQL • Interactive querying examples & case studies

Week	Topics
11	Web Frameworks & Serving Databases • Django - Python web framework • Using different serving databases with Django • Implementation examples
12	Big Data analytics algorithms • Spark MLib • H2O • Clustering algorithms
13	Big Data analytics algorithms • Classification algorithms • Regression algorithms
14	Big Data analytics algorithms • Recommendation systems
15	Big Data analytics case studies with implementations
16	Data Visualization • Building visualizations with Lightning, pyGal & Seaborn

Book Website

For more information on the book, copyrighted source code of all examples in the book, lab exercises, and instructor material, visit the book website: www.big-data-analytics-book.com

Acknowledgments

From Arshdeep Bahga
I would like to thank my father, Sarbjit Bahga, for inspiring me to write a book and sharing his valuable insights and experiences on authoring books. This book could not have been completed without the support of my mother Gurdeep Kaur, wife Navsangeet Kaur, son Navroz Bahga and brother Supreet Bahga, who have always motivated me and encouraged me to explore my interests.

From Vijay Madisetti
I thank my family, especially Anitha and Jerry (Raj), and my parents (Prof. M. A. Ramlu and Mrs. Madhavi Ramlu) for their support.

From the Authors
We would like to acknowledge the instructors who have adopted our earlier books in the "A Hands-On Approach"[TM] series, for their constructive feedback.
A subset of case studies in the areas of weather data analysis, smart parking, music recommendation, news analytics, movie recommendation, and sentiment analysis were tested in our class on Cloud Computing at Georgia Tech. We thank the following students for contributing to the development of some of the case studies based on the code templates for the Alpha, Beta, Gamma and Delta patterns that we provided to them: Christopher Roberts, Tyler Lisowski, Gina Holden, Julie Freeman, Srikar Durbha, Sachin D. Shylaja, Nikhil Bharat, Rahul Kayala, Harsha Manivannan, Chenyu Li, Pratheek M. Cheluvakumar, Daniel Morton, Akshay Phadke, Dylan Slack, Monodeep Kar, Vinish Chamrani, Zeheng Chen, Azim Ali, Kamran Fardanesh, Ryan Pickren, Ashutosh Singh, Paul Wilson, Liuxizi Xu, Thomas Barnes, Rohit Belapurkar, Baishen Huang, Zeeshan Khan, Rashmi Mehere, Nishant Shah, David Ehrlich, Raj Patel, Ryan Williams, Prachi Kulkarni, Kendra Dodson and Aditya Garg.

About the Authors

Arshdeep Bahga

Arshdeep Bahga is a Research Scientist with Georgia Institute of Technology. His research interests include cloud computing and big data analytics. Arshdeep has authored several scientific publications in peer-reviewed journals in the areas of cloud computing and big data. Arshdeep received the 2014 Roger P. Webb - Research Spotlight Award from the School of Electrical and Computer Engineering, Georgia Tech.

Vijay Madisetti

Vijay Madisetti is a Professor of Electrical and Computer Engineering at Georgia Institute of Technology. Vijay is a Fellow of the IEEE, and received the 2006 Terman Medal from the American Society of Engineering Education and HP Corporation.

Companion Books from the Authors

Cloud Computing: A Hands-On Approach

Recent industry surveys expect the cloud computing services market to be in excess of $20 billion and cloud computing jobs to be in excess of 10 million worldwide in 2014 alone. In addition, since a majority of existing information technology (IT) jobs is focused on maintaining legacy in-house systems, the demand for these kinds of jobs is likely to drop rapidly if cloud computing continues to take hold of the industry. However, there are very few educational options available in the area of cloud computing beyond vendor-specific training by cloud providers themselves. Cloud computing courses have not found their way (yet) into mainstream college curricula. This book is written as a textbook on cloud computing for educational programs at colleges. It can also be used by cloud service providers who may be interested in offering a broader perspective of cloud computing to accompany their customer and employee training programs.

Additional support is available at the book's website: www.cloudcomputingbook.info

Internet of Things: A Hands-On Approach

Internet of Things (IoT) refers to physical and virtual objects that have unique identities and are connected to the Internet to facilitate intelligent applications that make energy, logistics, industrial control, retail, agriculture and many other domains "smarter". Internet of Things is a new revolution of the Internet that is rapidly gathering momentum driven by the advancements in sensor networks, mobile devices, wireless communications, networking and cloud technologies. Experts forecast that by the year 2020 there will be a total of 50 billion devices/things connected to the Internet. This book is written as a textbook on Internet of Things for educational programs at colleges and universities, and also for IoT vendors and service providers who may be interested in offering a broader perspective of Internet of Things to accompany their customer and developer training programs.

Additional support is available at the book's website: www.internet-of-things-book.com/

Part I

BIG DATA ANALYTICS CONCEPTS

1 - Introduction to Big Data

This chapter covers

- What is Analytics?
- What is Big Data?
- Characteristics of Big Data
- Domain Specific Examples of Big Data
- Analytics Flow for Big Data
- Big Data Stack
- Mapping Analytics Flow to Big Data Stack
- Analytics Patterns

1.1   What is Analytics?

Analytics is a broad term that encompasses the processes, technologies, frameworks and algorithms to extract meaningful insights from data. Raw data in itself does not have a meaning until it is contextualized and processed into useful information. Analytics is this process of extracting and creating information from raw data by filtering, processing, categorizing, condensing and contextualizing the data. This information obtained is then organized and structured to infer knowledge about the system and/or its users, its environment, and its operations and progress towards its objectives, thus making the systems smarter and more efficient.

The choice of the technologies, algorithms, and frameworks for analytics is driven by the analytics goals of the application. For example, the goals of the analytics task may be: (1) to predict something (for example whether a transaction is a fraud or not, whether it will rain on a particular day, or whether a tumor is benign or malignant), (2) to find patterns in the data (for example, finding the top 10 coldest days in the year, finding which pages are visited the most on a particular website, or finding the most searched celebrity in a particular year), (3) finding relationships in the data (for example, finding similar news articles, finding similar patients in an electronic health record system, finding related products on an eCommerce website, finding similar images, or finding correlation between news items and stock prices).

The National Research Council [1] has done a characterization of computational tasks for massive data analysis (called the seven "giants"). These computational tasks include: (1) Basis Statistics, (2) Generalized N-Body Problems, (3) Linear Algebraic Computations, (4) Graph-Theoretic Computations, (5) Optimization, (6) Integration and (7) Alignment Problems. This characterization of computational tasks aims to provide a taxonomy of tasks that have proved to be useful in data analysis and grouping them roughly according to mathematical structure and computational strategy.

We will also establish a mapping between the analytics types the seven computational giants. Figure 1.1 shows the mapping between analytics types and the seven computational giants.

1.1.1   Descriptive Analytics

Descriptive analytics comprises analyzing past data to present it in a summarized form which can be easily interpreted. Descriptive analytics aims to answer - *What has happened?* A major portion of analytics done today is descriptive analytics through use of statistics functions such as counts, maximum, minimum, mean, top-N, percentage, for instance. These statistics help in describing patterns in the data and present the data in a summarized form. For example, computing the total number of likes for a particular post, computing the average monthly rainfall or finding the average number of visitors per month on a website. Descriptive analytics is useful to summarize the data. In Chapter-3, we describe implementations of various MapReduce patterns for descriptive analytics (such as Count, Max/Min, Average, Distinct, and Top-N).

Among the seven computational tasks as shown in Figure 1.1, tasks such as Basic Statistics and Linear Algebraic Computations can be used for descriptive analytics.

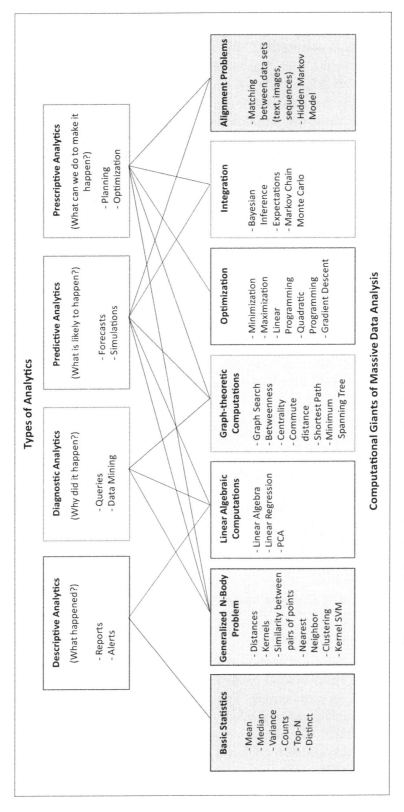

Figure 1.1: Mapping between types of analytics and computational tasks or 'giants'

1.1.2 Diagnostic Analytics

Diagnostic analytics comprises analysis of past data to diagnose the reasons as to why certain events happened. Diagnostic analytics aims to answer - *Why did it happen?* Let us consider an example of a system that collects and analyzes sensor data from machines for monitoring their health and predicting failures. While descriptive analytics can be useful for summarizing the data by computing various statistics (such as mean, minimum, maximum, variance, or top-N), diagnostic analytics can provide more insights into why certain a fault has occurred based on the patterns in the sensor data for previous faults.

Among the seven computational tasks, the computational tasks such as Linear Algebraic Computations, General N-Body Problems, and Graph-theoretic Computations can be used for diagnostic analytics.

1.1.3 Predictive Analytics

Predictive analytics comprises predicting the occurrence of an event or the likely outcome of an event or forecasting the future values using prediction models. Predictive analytics aims to answer - *What is likely to happen?* For example, predictive analytics can be used for predicting when a fault will occur in a machine, predicting whether a tumor is benign or malignant, predicting the occurrence of natural emergency (events such as forest fires or river floods) or forecasting the pollution levels. Predictive Analytics is done using predictive models which are trained by existing data. These models learn patterns and trends from the existing data and predict the occurrence of an event or the likely outcome of an event (classification models) or forecast numbers (regression models). The accuracy of prediction models depends on the quality and volume of the existing data available for training the models, such that all the patterns and trends in the existing data can be learned accurately. Before a model is used for prediction, it must be validated with existing data. The typical approach adopted while developing prediction models is to divide the existing data into training and test data sets (for example 75% of the data is used for training and 25% data is used for testing the prediction model). In Chapter-11, we provide implementations of various algorithms for predictive analytics (including clustering, classification and regression algorithms) using frameworks such as Spark MLlib and H2O.

Among the seven computational tasks, tasks such as Linear Algebraic Computations, General N-Body Problems, Graph-theoretic Computations, Integration and Alignment Problems can be used for predictive analytics.

1.1.4 Prescriptive Analytics

While predictive analytics uses prediction models to predict the likely outcome of an event, prescriptive analytics uses multiple prediction models to predict various outcomes and the best course of action for each outcome. Prescriptive analytics aims to answer - *What can we do to make it happen?* Prescriptive Analytics can predict the possible outcomes based on the current choice of actions. We can consider prescriptive analytics as a type of analytics that uses different prediction models for different inputs. Prescriptive analytics prescribes actions or the best option to follow from the available options. For example, prescriptive analytics can be used to prescribe the best medicine for treatment of a patient based on the outcomes of various medicines for similar patients. Another example of prescriptive analytics would be to suggest the best mobile data plan for a customer based on the customer's browsing patterns.

Among the seven computational tasks, tasks such as General N-Body Problems, Graph-theoretic Computations, Optimization and Alignment Problems can be used for prescriptive analytics.

1.2 What is Big Data?

Big data is defined as collections of datasets whose volume, velocity or variety is so large that it is difficult to store, manage, process and analyze the data using traditional databases and data processing tools. In the recent years, there has been an exponential growth in the both structured and unstructured data generated by information technology, industrial, healthcare, Internet of Things, and other systems.

According to an estimate by IBM, 2.5 quintillion bytes of data is created every day [9]. A recent report by DOMO estimates the amount of data generated every minute on popular online platforms [10]. Below are some key pieces of data from the report:

- Facebook users share nearly 4.16 million pieces of content
- Twitter users send nearly 300,000 tweets
- Instagram users like nearly 1.73 million photos
- YouTube users upload 300 hours of new video content
- Apple users download nearly 51,000 apps
- Skype users make nearly 110,000 new calls
- Amazon receives 4300 new visitors
- Uber passengers take 694 rides
- Netflix subscribers stream nearly 77,000 hours of video

Big Data has the potential to power next generation of smart applications that will leverage the power of the data to make the applications intelligent. Applications of big data span a wide range of domains such as web, retail and marketing, banking and financial, industrial, healthcare, environmental, Internet of Things and cyber-physical systems.

Big Data analytics deals with collection, storage, processing and analysis of this massive-scale data. Specialized tools and frameworks are required for big data analysis when: (1) the volume of data involved is so large that it is difficult to store, process and analyze data on a single machine, (2) the velocity of data is very high and the data needs to be analyzed in real-time, (3) there is variety of data involved, which can be structured, unstructured or semi-structured, and is collected from multiple data sources, (5) various types of analytics need to be performed to extract value from the data such as descriptive, diagnostic, predictive and prescriptive analytics. Big Data tools and frameworks have distributed and parallel processing architectures and can leverage the storage and computational resources of a large cluster of machines.

Big data analytics involves several steps starting from data cleansing, data munging (or wrangling), data processing and visualization. Big data analytics life-cycle starts from the collection of data from multiple data sources. Specialized tools and frameworks are required to ingest the data from different sources into the dig data analytics backend. The data is stored in specialized storage solutions (such as distributed filesystems and non-relational databases) which are designed to scale. Based on the analysis requirements (batch or real-time), and type of analysis to be performed (descriptive, diagnostic, predictive, or predictive) specialized frameworks are used. Big data analytics is enabled by several technologies such as cloud computing, distributed and parallel processing frameworks, non-relational databases, in-memory computing, for instance.

Some examples of big data are listed as follows:

- Data generated by social networks including text, images, audio and video data
- Click-stream data generated by web applications such as e-Commerce to analyze user behavior
- Machine sensor data collected from sensors embedded in industrial and energy systems for monitoring their health and detecting failures
- Healthcare data collected in electronic health record (EHR) systems
- Logs generated by web applications
- Stock markets data
- Transactional data generated by banking and financial applications

1.3   Characteristics of Big Data

The underlying characteristics of big data include:

1.3.1   Volume

Big data is a form of data whose volume is so large that it would not fit on a single machine therefore specialized tools and frameworks are required to store process and analyze such data. For example, social media applications process billions of messages everyday, industrial and energy systems can generate terabytes of sensor data everyday, cab aggregation applications can process millions of transactions in a day, etc. The volumes of data generated by modern IT, industrial, healthcare, Internet of Things, and other systems is growing exponentially driven by the lowering costs of data storage and processing architectures and the need to extract valuable insights from the data to improve business processes, efficiency and service to consumers. Though there is no fixed threshold for the volume of data to be considered as big data, however, typically, the term big data is used for massive scale data that is difficult to store, manage and process using traditional databases and data processing architectures.

1.3.2   Velocity

Velocity of data refers to how fast the data is generated. Data generated by certain sources can arrive at very high velocities, for example, social media data or sensor data. Velocity is another important characteristic of big data and the primary reason for the exponential growth of data. High velocity of data results in the volume of data accumulated to become very large, in short span of time. Some applications can have strict deadlines for data analysis (such as trading or online fraud detection) and the data needs to be analyzed in real-time. Specialized tools are required to ingest such high velocity data into the big data infrastructure and analyze the data in real-time.

1.3.3   Variety

Variety refers to the forms of the data. Big data comes in different forms such as structured, unstructured or semi-structured, including text data, image, audio, video and sensor data. Big data systems need to be flexible enough to handle such variety of data.

1.3.4 Veracity

Veracity refers to how accurate is the data. To extract value from the data, the data needs to be cleaned to remove noise. Data-driven applications can reap the benefits of big data only when the data is meaningful and accurate. Therefore, cleansing of data is important so that incorrect and faulty data can be filtered out.

1.3.5 Value

Value of data refers to the usefulness of data for the intended purpose. The end goal of any big data analytics system is to extract value from the data. The value of the data is also related to the veracity or accuracy of the data. For some applications value also depends on how fast we are able to process the data.

1.4 Domain Specific Examples of Big Data

The applications of big data span a wide range of domains including (but not limited to) homes, cities, environment, energy systems, retail, logistics, industry, agriculture, Internet of Things, and healthcare. This section provides an overview of various applications of big data for each of these domains. In the later chapters, the reader is guided through reference implementations and examples that will help the readers in developing these applications.

1.4.1 Web

- **Web Analytics**: Web analytics deals with collection and analysis of data on the user visits on websites and cloud applications. Analysis of this data can give insights about the user engagement and tracking the performance of online advertisement campaigns. For collecting data on user visits, two approaches are used. In the first approach, user visits are logged on the web server which collects data such as the date and time of visit, resource requested, user's IP address, HTTP status code, for instance. The second approach, called page tagging, uses a JavaScript which is embedded in the web page. Whenever a user visits a web page, the JavaScript collects user data and sends it to a third party data collection server. A cookie is assigned to the user which identities the user during the visit and the subsequent visits. The benefit of the page tagging approach is that it facilitates real-time data collection and analysis. This approach allows third party services, which do not have access to the web server (serving the website) to collect and process the data. These specialized analytics service providers (such as Google Analytics) are offer advanced analytics and summarized reports. The key reporting metrics include user sessions, page visits, top entry and exit pages, bounce rate, most visited page, time spent on each page, number of unique visitors, number of repeat visitors, for instance.
- **Performance Monitoring**: Multi-tier web and cloud applications such as such as e-Commerce, Business-to-Business, Health care, Banking and Financial, Retail and Social Networking applications, can experience rapid changes in their workloads. To ensure market readiness of such applications, adequate resources need to be provisioned so that the applications can meet the demands of specified workload levels and at the same time ensure that the service level agreements are met.

Provisioning and capacity planning is a challenging task for complex multi-tier applications since each class of applications has different deployment configurations with web servers, application servers and database servers. Over-provisioning in advance for such systems is not economically feasible. Cloud computing provides a promising approach of dynamically scaling up or scaling down the capacity based on the application workload. For resource management and capacity planning decisions, it is important to understand the workload characteristics of such systems, measure the sensitivity of the application performance to the workload attributes and detect bottlenecks in the systems. Performance testing of cloud-based applications prior to deployment can reveal bottlenecks in the system and support provisioning and capacity planning decisions.

For performance monitoring, various types of tests can be performed such as load tests (which evaluate the performance of the system with multiple users and workload levels), stress tests (which load the application to a point where it breaks down) and soak tests (which subject the application to a fixed workload level for long periods of time). Big data systems can be used to analyze the data generated by such tests, to predict application performance under heavy workloads and identify bottlenecks in the system so that failures can be prevented. Bottlenecks, once detected, can be resolved by provisioning additional computing resources, by either scaling up systems (vertical scaling by using instances with more computing capacity) or scaling out systems (horizontal scaling by using more instances of the same kind).

- **Ad Targeting & Analytics**: Search and display advertisements are the two most widely used approaches for Internet advertising. In search advertising, users are displayed advertisements ("ads"), along with the search results, as they search for specific keywords on a search engine. Advertisers can create ads using the advertising networks provided by the search engines or social media networks. These ads are setup for specific keywords which are related to the product or service being advertised. Users searching for these keywords are shown ads along with the search results. Display advertising, is another form of Internet advertising, in which the ads are displayed within websites, videos and mobile applications who participate in the advertising network. Display ads can either be text-based or image ads. The ad-network matches these ads against the content on the website, video or mobile application and places the ads. The most commonly used compensation method for Internet ads is Pay-per-click (PPC), in which the advertisers pay each time a user clicks on an advertisement. Advertising networks use big data systems for matching and placing advertisements and generating advertisement statistics reports. Advertises can use big data tools for tracking the performance of advertisements, optimizing the bids for pay-per-click advertising, tracking which keywords link the most to the advertising landing pages and optimizing budget allocation to various advertisement campaigns.

- **Content Recommendation**: Content delivery applications that serve content (such as music and video streaming applications), collect various types of data such as user search patterns and browsing history, history of content consumed, and user ratings. Such applications can leverage big data systems for recommending new content to the users based on the user preferences and interests. Recommendation systems use two broad category approaches - user-based recommendation and item based recommendation. In user-based recommendation, new items are recommended to a user based on how similar users rate those items. Whereas in item-based recommendation, new items are recommended to a user based on how the user rated similar items. In Chapter-11, we describe a case study on building a movie recommendation system.

1.4.2 Financial

- **Credit Risk Modeling**: Banking and Financial institutions use credit risk modeling to score credit applications and predict if a borrower will default or not in the future. Credit risk models are created from the customer data that includes, credit scores obtained from credit bureaus, credit history, account balance data, account transactions data and spending patterns of the customer. Credit models generate numerical scores that summarize the creditworthiness of customers. Since the volume of customer data obtained from multiple sources can be massive, big data systems can be used for building credit models. Big data systems can help in computing credit risk scores of a large number of customers on a regular basis. In Chapter-11, we describe big data frameworks for building machine learning models. These frameworks can be used to build credit risk models by analysis of customer data.
- **Fraud Detection**: Banking and Financial institutions can leverage big data systems for detecting frauds such as credit card frauds, money laundering and insurance claim frauds. Real-time big data analytics frameworks can help in analyzing data from disparate sources and label transactions in real-time. Machine learning models can be built for detecting anomalies in transactions and detecting fraudulent activities. Batch analytics frameworks can be used for analyzing historical data on customer transactions to search for patterns that indicate fraud.

1.4.3 Healthcare

The healthcare ecosystem consists of numerous entities including healthcare providers (primary care physicians, specialists, or hospitals), payers (government, private health insurance companies, employers), pharmaceutical, device and medical service companies, IT solutions and services firms, and patients. The process of provisioning healthcare involves massive healthcare data that exists in different forms (structured or unstructured), is stored in disparate data sources (such as relational databases, or file servers) and in many different formats. To promote more coordination of care across the multiple providers involved with patients, their clinical information is increasingly aggregated from diverse sources into Electronic Health Record (EHR) systems. EHRs capture and store information on patient health and provider actions including individual-level laboratory results, diagnostic, treatment, and demographic data. Though the primary use of EHRs is to maintain all medical data for an individual patient and to provide efficient access to the stored data at the point of care, EHRs can be the source for valuable aggregated information about overall patient populations [5, 6].

With the current explosion of clinical data the problems of how to collect data from distributed and heterogeneous health IT systems and how to analyze the massive scale clinical data have become critical. Big data systems can be used for data collection from different stakeholders (patients, doctors, payers, physicians, specialists, etc) and disparate data sources (databases, structured and unstructured formats, etc). Big data analytics systems allow massive scale clinical data analytics and facilitate development of more efficient healthcare applications, improve the accuracy of predictions and help in timely decision making.

Let us look at some healthcare applications that can benefit from big data systems:

- **Epidemiological Surveillance**: Epidemiological Surveillance systems study the distribution and determinants of health-related states or events in specified populations and apply these studies for diagnosis of diseases under surveillance at national level to control health problems. EHR systems include individual-level laboratory results, diagnostic, treatment, and demographic data. Big data frameworks can be used for integrating data from multiple EHR systems and timely analysis of data for effectively and accurately predicting outbreaks, population-level health surveillance efforts, disease detection and public health mapping.

- **Patient Similarity-based Decision Intelligence Application**: Big data frameworks can be used for analyzing EHR data to extract a cluster of patient records most similar to a particular target patient. Clustering patient records can also help in developing medical prognosis applications that predicts the likely outcome of an illness for a patient based on the outcomes for similar patients.

- **Adverse Drug Events Prediction**: Big data frameworks can be used for analyzing EHR data and predict which patients are most at risk for having an adverse response to a certain drug based on adverse drug reactions of other patients.

- **Detecting Claim Anomalies**: Heath insurance companies can leverage big data systems for analyzing health insurance claims to detect fraud, abuse, waste, and errors.

- **Evidence-based Medicine**: Big data systems can combine and analyze data from a variety of sources, including individual-level laboratory results, diagnostic, treatment and demographic data, to match treatments with outcomes, predict patients at risk for a disease. Systems for evidence-based medicine enable providers to make decisions not only based on their own perceptions but also from the available evidence.

- **Real-time health monitoring**: Wearable electronic devices allow non-invasive and continuous monitoring of physiological parameters. These wearable devices may be in various forms such as belts and wrist-bands. Healthcare providers can analyze the collected healthcare data to determine any health conditions or anomalies. Big data systems for real-time data analysis can be used for analysis of large volumes of fast-moving data from wearable devices and other in-hospital or in-home devices, for real-time patient health monitoring and adverse event prediction.

1.4.4 Internet of Things

Internet of Things (IoT) refers to things that have unique identities and are connected to the Internet. The "Things" in IoT are the devices which can perform remote sensing, actuating and monitoring. IoT devices can exchange data with other connected devices and applications (directly or indirectly), or collect data from other devices and process the data either locally or send the data to centralized servers or cloud-based application back-ends for processing the data, or perform some tasks locally and other tasks within the IoT infrastructure, based on temporal and space constraints (i.e., memory, processing capabilities, communication latencies and speeds, and deadlines).

IoT systems can leverage big data technologies for storage and analysis of data. Let us look at some IoT applications that can benefit from big data systems:

- **Intrusion Detection**: Intrusion detection systems use security cameras and sensors (such as PIR sensors and door sensors) to detect intrusions and raise alerts. Alerts can be in the form of an SMS or an email sent to the user. Advanced systems can even send detailed alerts such as an image grab or a short video clip sent as an email attachment.
- **Smart Parkings**: Smart parkings make the search for parking space easier and convenient for drivers. Smart parkings are powered by IoT systems that detect the number of empty parking slots and send the information over the Internet to smart parking application back-ends. These applications can be accessed by the drivers from smart-phones, tablets and in-car navigation systems. In a smart parking, sensors are used for each parking slot, to detect whether the slot is empty or occupied. This information is aggregated by an on-site smart parking controller and then sent over the Internet to cloud-based big data analytics backend.
- **Smart Roads**: Smart roads equipped with sensors can provide information on driving conditions, travel time estimates and alerts in case of poor driving conditions, traffic congestions and accidents. Such information can help in making the roads safer and help in reducing traffic jams. Information sensed from the roads can be communicated via Internet to cloud-based big data analytics applications. The analysis results can be disseminated to the drivers who subscribe to such applications or through social media.
- **Structural Health Monitoring**: Structural Health Monitoring systems use a network of sensors to monitor the vibration levels in the structures such as bridges and buildings. The data collected from these sensors is analyzed to assess the health of the structures. By analyzing the data it is possible to detect cracks and mechanical breakdowns, locate the damages to a structure and also calculate the remaining life of the structure. Using such systems, advance warnings can be given in the case of imminent failures of the structures.
- **Smart Irrigation**: Smart irrigation systems can improve crop yields while saving water. Smart irrigation systems use IoT devices with soil moisture sensors to determine the amount of moisture in the soil and release the flow of water through the irrigation pipes only when the moisture levels go below a predefined threshold. Smart irrigation systems also collect moisture level measurements in the cloud where the big data systems can be used to analyze the data to plan watering schedules.

1.4.5 Environment

Environment monitoring systems generate high velocity and high volume data. Accurate and timely analysis of such data can help in understanding the current status of the environment and also predicting environmental trends. Let us look at some environment monitoring applications that can benefit from big data systems:

- **Weather Monitoring** : Weather monitoring systems can collect data from a number of sensor attached (such as temperature, humidity, or pressure) and send the data to cloud-based applications and big data analytics backends. This data can then be analyzed and visualized for monitoring weather and generating weather alerts.
- **Air Pollution Monitoring**: Air pollution monitoring systems can monitor emission of harmful gases (CO_2, CO, NO, or NO_2) by factories and automobiles using gaseous

and meteorological sensors. The collected data can be analyzed to make informed decisions on pollution control approaches.

- **Noise Pollution Monitoring**: Due to growing urban development, noise levels in cities have increased and even become alarmingly high in some cities. Noise pollution can cause health hazards for humans due to sleep disruption and stress. Noise pollution monitoring can help in generating noise maps for cities. Urban noise maps can help the policy makers in urban planning and making policies to control noise levels near residential areas, schools and parks. Noise pollution monitoring systems use a number of noise monitoring stations that are deployed at different places in a city. The data on noise levels from the stations is sent to cloud-based applications and big data analytics backends. The collected data is then aggregated to generate noise maps.

- **Forest Fire Detection**: Forest fires can cause damage to natural resources, property and human life. There can be different causes of forest fires including lightening, human negligence, volcanic eruptions and sparks from rock falls. Early detection of forest fires can help in minimizing the damage. Forest fire detection systems use a number of monitoring nodes deployed at different locations in a forest. Each monitoring node collects measurements on ambient conditions including temperature, humidity, light levels, for instance.

- **River Floods Detection**: River floods can cause extensive damage to the natural and human resources and human life. River floods occur due to continuous rainfall which causes the river levels to rise and flow rates to increase rapidly. Early warnings of floods can be given by monitoring the water level and flow rate. River flood monitoring system use a number of sensor nodes that monitor the water level (using ultrasonic sensors) and flow rate (using the flow velocity sensors). Big data systems can be used to collect and analyze data from a number of such sensor nodes and raise alerts when a rapid increase in water level and flow rate is detected.

- **Water Quality Monitoring**: Water quality monitoring can be helpful for identifying and controlling water pollution and contamination due to urbanization and industrialization. Maintaining good water quality is important to maintain good health of plant and animal life. Water quality monitoring systems use sensors to autonomously and continuously monitor different types contaminations in water bodies (such as chemical, biological, and radioactive). The scale of data generated by such systems is massive. Big data systems can help in real-time analysis of data generated by such systems and generate alerts about any any degradation in water quality, so that corrective actions can be taken.

1.4.6 Logistics & Transportation

- **Real-time Fleet Tracking**: Vehicle fleet tracking systems use GPS technology to track the locations of the vehicles in real-time. Cloud-based fleet tracking systems can be scaled up on demand to handle large number of vehicles. Alerts can be generated in case of deviations in planned routes. Big data systems can be used to aggregate and analyze vehicle locations and routes data for detecting bottlenecks in the supply chain such as traffic congestions on routes, assignment and generation of alternative routes, and supply chain optimization.

- **Shipment Monitoring**: Shipment management solutions for transportation systems allow monitoring the conditions inside containers. For example, containers carrying fresh food produce can be monitored to detect spoilage of food. Shipment monitoring systems use sensors such as temperature, pressure, humidity, for instance, to monitor the conditions inside the containers and send the data to the cloud, where it can be analyzed to detect food spoilage. The analysis and interpretation of data on the environmental conditions in the container and food truck positioning can enable more effective routing decisions in real time. Therefore, it is possible to take remedial measures such as - the food that has a limited time budget before it gets rotten can be re-routed to a closer destinations, alerts can be raised to the driver and the distributor about the transit conditions, such as container temperature exceeding the allowed limit, humidity levels going out of the allowed limit, for instance, and corrective actions can be taken before the food gets damaged.

For fragile products, vibration levels during shipments can be tracked using accelerometer and gyroscope sensors. Big data systems can be used for analysis of the vibration patterns of the shipments to reveal information related to its operating environment and integrity during transport, handling and storage.

- **Remote Vehicle Diagnostics**: Remote vehicle diagnostic systems can detect faults in the vehicles or warn of impending faults. These diagnostic systems use on-board devices for collecting data on vehicle operation (such as speed, engine RPM, coolant temperature, or fault code number) and status of various vehicle sub-systems. Modern commercial vehicles support on-board diagnostic (OBD) standards such as OBD-II. OBD systems provide real-time data on the status of vehicle sub-systems and diagnostic trouble codes which allow rapidly identifying the faults in the vehicle. Vehicle diagnostic systems can send the vehicle data to cloud-based big data analytics backends where it can be analyzed to generate alerts and suggest remedial actions.

- **Route Generation & Scheduling**: Modern transportation systems are driven by data collected from multiple sources which is processed to provide new services to the stakeholders. By collecting large amount of data from various sources and processing the data into useful information, data-driven transportation systems can provide new services such as advanced route guidance, dynamic vehicle routing, anticipating customer demands for pickup and delivery problem, for instance. Route generation and scheduling systems can generate end-to-end routes using combination of route patterns and transportation modes and feasible schedules based on the availability of vehicles. As the transportation network grows in size and complexity, the number of possible route combinations increases exponentially. Big data systems can provide fast response to the route generation queries and can be scaled up to serve a large transportation network.

- **Hyper-local Delivery**: Hyper-local delivery platforms are being increasingly used by businesses such as restaurants and grocery stores to expand their reach. These platforms allow customers to order products (such as grocery and food items) using web and mobile applications and the products are sourced from local stores (or restaurants). As these platforms scale up to serve a large number of customer (with thousands of transactions every hour), they face various challenges in processing the orders in real-time. Big data systems for real-time analytics can be used by hyper-local delivery platforms for determining the nearest store from where to source the order and finding a delivery agent near to the store who can pickup the order and deliver to the customer.

- **Cab/Taxi Aggregators**: On-demand transport technology aggregators (or cab/taxi aggregators) allow customers to book cabs using web or mobile applications and the requests are routed to nearest available cabs (sometimes even private drivers who opt-in their own cars for hire). The cab aggregation platforms use big data systems for real-time processing of requests and dynamic pricing. These platforms maintain record of all cabs and match the trip requests from customers to the nearest and most suitable cabs. These platforms adopt dynamic pricing models where the pricing increases or decreases based on the demand and the traffic conditions.

1.4.7 Industry

- **Machine Diagnosis & Prognosis**: Machine prognosis refers to predicting the performance of a machine by analyzing the data on the current operating conditions and the deviations from the normal operating conditions. Machine diagnosis refers to determining the cause of a machine fault. Industrial machines have a large number of components that must function correctly for the machine to perform its operations. Sensors in machines can monitor the operating conditions such as (temperature and vibration levels). The sensor data measurements are done on timescales of few milliseconds to few seconds, which leads to generation of massive amount of data. Machine diagnostic systems can be integrated with cloud-based storage and big data analytics backends for storage, collection and analysis of such massive scale machine sensor data. A number of methods have been proposed for reliability analysis and fault prediction in machines. Case-based reasoning (CBR) is a commonly used method that finds solutions to new problems based on past experience. This past experience is organized and represented as cases in a case-base. CBR is an effective technique for problem solving in the fields in which it is hard to establish a quantitative mathematical model, such as machine diagnosis and prognosis. Since for each machine, data from a very large number of sensors is collected, using such high dimensional data for creation of a case library reduces the case retrieval efficiency. Therefore, data reduction and feature extraction methods are used to find the representative set of features which have the same classification ability as the complete set of features.

- **Risk Analysis of Industrial Operations**: In many industries, there are strict requirements on the environment conditions and equipment working conditions. Monitoring the working conditions of workers is important for ensuring their health and safety. Harmful and toxic gases such as carbon monoxide (CO), nitrogen monoxide (NO), Nitrogen Dioxide (NO_2), for instance, can cause serious health problems. Gas monitoring systems can help in monitoring the indoor air quality using various gas sensors. Big data systems can also be used to analyze risks in industrial operations and identify the hazardous zones, so that corrective measures can be taken and timely alerts can be raised in case of any abnormal conditions.

- **Production Planning and Control**: Production planning and control systems measure various parameters of production processes and control the entire production process in real time. These systems use various sensors to collect data on the production processes. Big data systems can be used to analyze this data for production planning and identifying potential problems.

1.4.8   Retail

Retailers can use big data systems for boosting sales, increasing profitability and improving customer satisfaction. Let us look at some applications of big data analytics for retail:

- **Inventory Management**: Inventory management for retail has become increasingly important in the recent years with the growing competition. While over-stocking of products can result in additional storage expenses and risk (in case of perishables), under-stocking can lead to loss of revenue. RFID tags attached to the products allow them to be tracked in real-time so that the inventory levels can be determined accurately and products which are low on stock can be replenished. Tracking can be done using RFID readers attached to the retail store shelves or in the warehouse. Big data systems can be used to analyze the data collected from RFID readers and raise alerts when inventory levels for certain products are low. Timely replenishment of inventory can help in minimizing the loss in revenue due to out-of-stock inventory. Analysis of inventory data can help in optimizing the re-stocking levels and frequencies based on demand.
- **Customer Recommendations**: Big data systems can be used to analyze the customer data (such as demographic data, shopping history, or customer feedback) and predict the customer preferences. New products can be recommended to customers based on the customer preferences and personalized offers and discounts can be given. Customers with similar preferences can be grouped and targeted campaigns can be created for customers. In Chapter-11, we describe a case study on building a recommendation system based on collaborative filtering. Collaborative filtering allows recommending items (or filtering items from a collection of items) based on the preferences of the user and the collective preferences of other users (i.e. making use of the collaborative information available on the user-item ratings).
- **Store Layout Optimization**: Big data systems can help in analyzing the data on customer shopping patterns and customer feedback to optimize the store layouts. Items which the customers are more likely to buy together can be placed in the same or nearby racks.
- **Forecasting Demand**: Due to a large number of products, seasonal variations in demands and changing trends and customer preferences, retailers find it difficult to forecast demand and sales volumes. Big data systems can be used to analyze the customer purchase patterns and predict demand and sale volumes.

1.5   Analytics Flow for Big Data

In this section we propose a novel data science and analytics application system design methodology that can be used for big data analytics. A generic flow for big data analytics, detailing the steps involved in the implementation of a typical analytics application and the options available at each step, is presented. Figure 1.2 shows the analytics flow with various steps. For an application, selecting the options for each step in the analytics flow can help in determining the right tools and frameworks to perform the analyses.

1.5.1 Data Collection

Data collection is the first step for any analytics application. Before the data can be analyzed, the data must be collected and ingested into a big data stack. The choice of tools and frameworks for data collection depends on the source of data and the type of data being ingested. For data collection, various types of connectors can be used such as publish-subscribe messaging frameworks, messaging queues, source-sink connectors, database connectors and custom connectors. Chapter-5 provides implementations of several of these connectors.

1.5.2 Data Preparation

Data can often be dirty and can have various issues that must be resolved before the data can be processed, such as corrupt records, missing values, duplicates, inconsistent abbreviations, inconsistent units, typos, incorrect spellings and incorrect formatting. Data preparation step involves various tasks such as data cleansing, data wrangling or munging, de-duplication, normalization, sampling and filtering. Data cleaning detects and resolves issues such as corrupt records, records with missing values, records with bad formatting, for instance. Data wrangling or munging deals with transforming the data from one raw format to another. For example, when we collect records as raw text files form different sources, we may come across inconsistencies in the field separators used in different files. Some file may be using comma as the field separator, others may be using tab as the field separator. Data wrangling resolves these inconsistencies by parsing the raw data from different sources and transforming it into one consistent format. Normalization is required when data from different sources uses different units or scales or have different abbreviations for the same thing. For example, weather data reported by some stations may contain temperature in Celsius scale while data from other stations may use the Fahrenheit scale. Filtering and sampling may be useful when we want to process only the data that meets certain rules. Filtering can also be useful to reject bad records with incorrect or out-of-range values.

1.5.3 Analysis Types

The next step in the analysis flow is to determine the analysis type for the application. In Figure 1.2 we have listed various options for analysis types and the popular algorithms for each analysis type. In Chapter-11, we have described several of these analysis types and the algorithms along with the implementations of the algorithms using various big data tools and frameworks.

1.5.4 Analysis Modes

With the analysis types selected for an application, the next step is to determine the analysis mode, which can be either batch, real-time or interactive. The choice of the mode depends on the requirements of the application. If your application demands results to be updated after short intervals of time (say every few seconds), then real-time analysis mode is chosen. However if your application only requires the results to be generated and updated on larger timescales (say daily or monthly), then batch mode can be used. If your application demands flexibility to query data on demand, then the interactive mode is useful. Once you make a choice of the analysis type and the analysis mode, you can determine the data processing

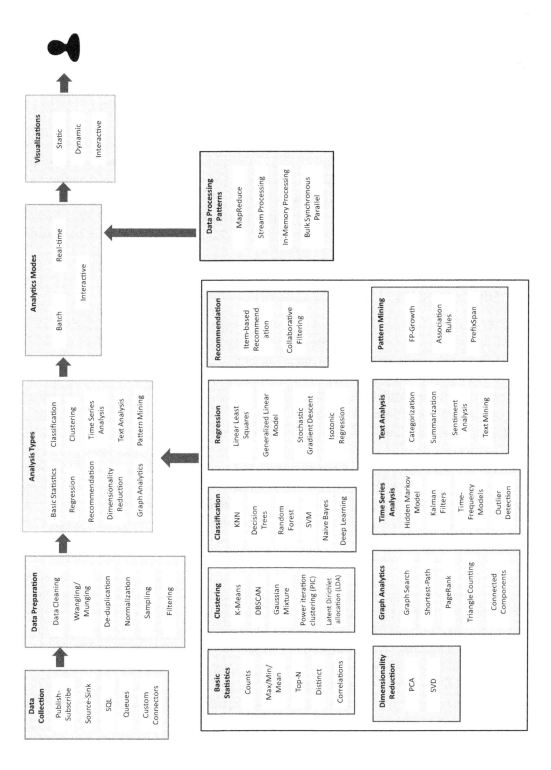

Figure 1.2: Big Data analytics flow

pattern that can be used. For example, for basic statistics as the analysis type and the batch analysis mode, MapReduce can be a good choice. Whereas for regression analysis as the analysis type and real-time analysis mode (predicting values in real-time), the Stream Processing pattern is a good choice. The choice of the analysis type, analysis mode, and the data processing pattern can help you in shortlisting the right tools and frameworks for data analysis.

1.5.5 Visualizations

The choice of the visualization tools, serving databases and web frameworks is driven by the requirements of the application. Visualizations can be static, dynamic or interactive. Static visualizations are used when you have the analysis results stored in a serving database and you simply want to display the results. However, if your application demands the results to updated regularly, then you would require dynamic visualizations (with live widgets, plots, or gauges). If you want your application to accept inputs from the user and display the results, then you would require interactive visualizations.

1.6 Big Data Stack

While the Hadoop framework has been one of the most popular frameworks for big data analytics, there are several types of computational tasks for which Hadoop does not work well. With the help of the mapping between the analytics types and the computational "giants" as shown in Figure 1.1, we will identify the cases where Hadoop works and where it does not, and describe the motivation for having a Big Data stack that can be used for various types of analytics and computational tasks.

Hadoop is an open source framework for distributed batch processing of massive scale data using the MapReduce programming model. The MapReduce programming model is useful for applications in which the data involved is so massive that it would not fit on a single machine. In such applications, the data is typically stored on a distributed file system (such as Hadoop Distributed File System - HDFS). MapReduce programs take advantage of locality of data and the data processing takes place on the nodes where the data resides. In other words, the computation is moved to where the data resides, as opposed the traditional way of moving the data from where it resides to where the computation is done. MapReduce is best suited for descriptive analytics and the basic statistics computational tasks because the operations involved can be done in parallel (for example, computing counts, mean, max/min, distinct, top-N, filtering and joins). Many of these operations are completed with a single MapReduce job. For more complex tasks, multiple MapReduce jobs can be chained together. However, when the computations are iterative in nature, where a MapReduce job has to be repeatedly run, MapReduce takes a performance hit because of the overhead involved in fetching the data from HDFS in each iteration.

For other types of analytics and computational tasks, there are other alternative frameworks which we will discuss as a part of the Big Data Stack. In this Chapter, we propose and describe a big data stack comprising of proven and open-source big data frameworks that form the foundation of this book. Figure 1.3 shows the big data stack with the Chapter numbers highlighted for the various blocks in the stack. The successive chapters in the book describe these blocks in detail along with hands-on examples and case studies. We have used

Python as the primary programming language for the examples and case studies throughout the book. Let us look at each block one-by-one:

1.6.1 Raw Data Sources

In any big data analytics application or platform, before the data is processed and analyzed, it must be captured from the raw data sources into the big data systems and frameworks. Some of the examples of raw big data sources include:

- **Logs**: Logs generated by web applications and servers which can be used for performance monitoring
- **Transactional Data**: Transactional data generated by applications such as eCommerce, Banking and Financial
- **Social Media**: Data generated by social media platforms
- **Databases**: Structured data residing in relational databases
- **Sensor Data**: Sensor data generated by Internet of Things (IoT) systems
- **Clickstream Data**: Clickstream data generated by web applications which can be used to analyze browsing patterns of the users
- **Surveillance Data**: Sensor, image and video data generated by surveillance systems
- **Healthcare Data**: Healthcare data generated by Electronic Health Record (EHR) and other healthcare applications
- **Network Data**: Network data generated by network devices such as routers and firewalls

1.6.2 Data Access Connectors

The Data Access Connectors includes tools and frameworks for collecting and ingesting data from various sources into the big data storage and analytics frameworks. The choice of the data connector is driven by the type of the data source. Let us look at some data connectors and frameworks which can be used for collecting and ingesting data. These data connectors and frameworks are described in detail in Chapter-5. These connectors can include both wired and wireless connections.

- **Publish-Subscribe Messaging**: Publish-Subscribe is a communication model that involves publishers, brokers and consumers. Publishers are the source of data. Publishers send the data to the topics which are managed by the broker. Publish-subscribe messaging frameworks such as Apache Kafka and Amazon Kinesis are described in Chapter-5.
- **Source-Sink Connectors**: Source-Sink connectors allow efficiently collecting, aggregating and moving data from various sources (such as server logs, databases, social media, streaming sensor data from Internet of Things devices and other sources) into a centralized data store (such as a distributed file system). In Chapter-5 we have described Apache Flume, which is a framework for aggregating data from different sources. Flume uses a data flow model that comprises sources, channels and sinks.
- **Database Connectors**: Database connectors can be used for importing data from relational database management systems into big data storage and analytics frameworks for analysis. In Chapter-5 we have described Apache Sqoop, which is a tool that allows importing data from relational databases.

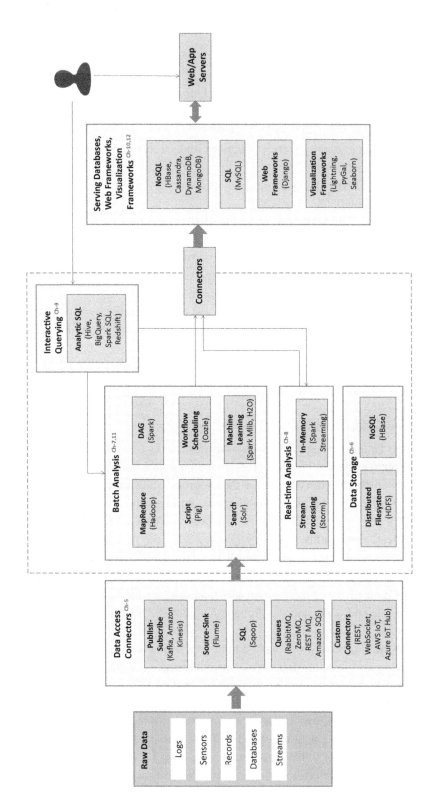

Figure 1.3: Big Data Stack

- **Messaging Queues**: Messaging queues are useful for push-pull messaging where the producers push data to the queues and the consumers pull the data from the queues. The producers and consumers do not need to be aware of each other. In Chapter-5 we have described messaging queues such as RabbitMQ, ZeroMQ, RestMQ and Amazon SQS.
- **Custom Connectors**: Custom connectors can be built based on the source of the data and the data collection requirements. Some examples of custom connectors include: custom connectors for collecting data from social networks, custom connectors for NoSQL databases and connectors for Internet of Things (IoT). In Chapter-5 we have described custom connectors based on REST, WebSocket and MQTT. IoT connectors such as AWS IoT and Azure IoT Hub are also described in Chapter-5.

1.6.3 Data Storage

The data storage block in the big data stack includes distributed filesystems and non-relational (NoSQL) databases, which store the data collected from the raw data sources using the data access connectors. In Chapter-6, we describe the Hadoop Distributed File System (HDFS), a distributed file system that runs on large clusters and provides high-throughput access to data. With the data stored in HDFS, it can be analyzed with various big data analytics frameworks built on top of HDFS. For certain analytics applications, it is preferable to store data in a NoSQL database such as HBase. HBase is a scalable, non-relational, distributed, column-oriented database that provides structured data storage for large tables. The architecture of HBase and its use cases are described in Chapter-4.

1.6.4 Batch Analytics

The batch analytics block in the big data stack includes various frameworks which allow analysis of data in batches. These include the following:

- **Hadoop-MapReduce**: Hadoop is a framework for distributed batch processing of big data. The MapReduce programming model is used to develop batch analysis jobs which are executed in Hadoop clusters. Examples of MapReduce jobs and case studies of using Hadoop-MapReduce for batch analysis are described in Chapter-7.
- **Pig**: Pig is a high-level data processing language which makes it easy for developers to write data analysis scripts which are translated into MapReduce programs by the Pig compiler. Examples of using Pig for batch data analysis are described in Chapter-7.
- **Oozie**: Oozie is a workflow scheduler system that allows managing Hadoop jobs. With Oozie, you can create workflows which are a collection of actions (such as MapReduce jobs) arranged as Direct Acyclic Graphs (DAG).
- **Spark**: Apache Spark is an open source cluster computing framework for data analytics. Spark includes various high-level tools for data analysis such as Spark Streaming for streaming jobs, Spark SQL for analysis of structured data, MLlib machine learning library for Spark, and GraphX for graph processing. In Chapter-7 we describe the Spark architecture, Spark operations and how to use Spark for batch data analysis.
- **Solr**: Apache Solr is a scalable and open-source framework for searching data. In Chapter-7 we describe the architecture of Solr and examples of indexing documents.
- **Machine Learning**: In Chapter-11 we describe various machine learning algorithms

with examples using the Spark MLib and H2O frameworks. Spark MLib is the Spark's machine learning library which provides implementations of various machine learning algorithms. H2O is an open source predictive analytics framework which provides implementations of various machine learning algorithms.

1.6.5   Real-time Analytics

The real-time analytics block includes the Apache Storm and Spark Streaming frameworks. These frameworks are described in detail in Chapter-8. Apache Storm is a framework for distributed and fault-tolerant real-time computation. Storm can be used for real-time processing of streams of data. Storm can consume data from a variety of sources such as publish-subscribe messaging frameworks (such as Kafka or Kinesis), messaging queues (such as RabbitMQ or ZeroMQ) and other custom connectors. Spark Streaming is a component of Spark which allows analysis of streaming data such as sensor data, click stream data, web server logs, for instance. The streaming data is ingested and analyzed in micro-batches. Spark Streaming enables scalable, high throughput and fault-tolerant stream processing.

1.6.6   Interactive Querying

Interactive querying systems allow users to query data by writing statements in SQL-like languages. We describe the following interactive querying systems, with examples, in Chapter-9:

- **Spark SQL**: Spark SQL is a component of Spark which enables interactive querying. Spark SQL is useful for querying structured and semi-structured data using SQL-like queries.
- **Hive**: Apache Hive is a data warehousing framework built on top of Hadoop. Hive provides an SQL-like query language called Hive Query Language, for querying data residing in HDFS.
- **Amazon Redshift**: Amazon Redshift is a fast, massive-scale managed data warehouse service. Redshift specializes in handling queries on datasets of sizes up to a petabyte or more parallelizing the SQL queries across all resources in the Redshift cluster.
- **Google BigQuery**: Google BigQuery is a service for querying massive datasets. BigQuery allows querying datasets using SQL-like queries.

1.6.7   Serving Databases, Web & Visualization Frameworks

While the various analytics blocks process and analyze the data, the results are stored in serving databases for subsequent tasks of presentation and visualization. These serving databases allow the analyzed data to be queried and presented in the web applications. In Chapter-10, we describe the following SQL and NoSQL databases which can be used as serving databases:

- **MySQL**: MySQL is one of the most widely used Relational Database Management System (RDBMS) and is a good choice to be used as a serving database for data analytics applications where the data is structured.
- **Amazon DynamoDB**: Amazon DynamoDB is a fully-managed, scalable, high-performance NoSQL database service from Amazon. DynamoDB is an excellent choice for a serving database for data analytics applications as it allows storing and

retrieving any amount of data and the ability to scale up or down the provisioned throughput.

- **Cassandra**: Cassandra is a scalable, highly available, fault tolerant open source non-relational database system.
- **MongoDB**: MongoDB is a document oriented non-relational database system. MongoDB is powerful, flexible and highly scalable database designed for web applications and is a good choice for a serving database for data analytics applications.

In Chapter-10, we also describe Django, which is an open source web application framework for developing web applications in Python. Django is based on the Model-Template-View architecture and provides a separation of the data model from the business rules and the user interface. While web applications can be useful for presenting the results, specialized visualizing tools and frameworks can help in understanding the data, and the analysis results quickly and easily. In Chapter-12, we describe the following visualization tools and frameworks:

- **Lightning**: Lightning is a framework for creating web-based interactive visualizations.
- **Pygal**: The Python Pygal library is an easy to use charting library which supports charts of various types.
- **Seaborn**: Seaborn is a Python visualization library for plotting attractive statistical plots.

1.7 Mapping Analytics Flow to Big Data Stack

For any big data application, once we come up with an analytics flow, the next step is to map the analytics flow to specific tools and frameworks in the big data stack. This section provides some guidelines in mapping the analytics flow to the big data stack.

For data collection tasks, the choice of a specific tool or framework depends on the type of the data source (such as log files, machines generating sensor data, social media feeds, records in a relational database, for instance) and the characteristics of the data. If the data is to ingested in bulk (such as log files), then a source-sink such as Apache Flume can be used. However, if high-velocity data is to be ingested at real-time, then a distributed publish-subscribe messaging framework such as Apache Kafka or Amazon Kinesis can be used. For ingesting data from relational databases, a framework such as Apache Sqoop can be used. Custom connectors can be built based on HTTP/REST, WebSocket or MQTT, if other solutions don't work well for an application or there are additional constraints. For example, IoT devices generating sensor data may be resource and power constrained, in which case a light-weight communication protocol such as MQTT may be chosen and a custom MQTT-based connector can be used.

For data cleaning and transformation, tools such as Open Refine [3] and Stanford DataWrangler [4] can be used. These tools support various file formats such as CSV, Excel, XML, JSON and line-based formats. With these tools you can remove duplicates, filter records with missing values, trim leading and trailing spaces, transpose rows to columns, transform the cell values, cluster similar cells and perform various other transformations. For filtering, joins, and other transformations, high-level scripting frameworks such as Pig can be very useful. The benefit of using Pig is that you can process large volumes of data in batch mode, which may be difficult with standalone tools. When you are not sure

Data Collection

Analysis Type	Framework (Mode)
Publish-Subscribe	Kafka, Kinesis
Source-Sink	Flume
SQL	Sqoop
Queues	SQS, RabbitMQ, ZeroMQ, RESTMQ
Custom Connectors	REST, WebSocket, MQTT

Data Preparation

Analysis Type	Framework
Data Cleaning	Open Refine
Data Wrangling	Open Refine, DataWrangler
De-Duplication	Open Refine, Pig, Hive, Spark SQL
Normalization, Sampling, Filtering	MapReduce, Pig, Hive, Spark SQL

Basic Statistics

Analysis Type	Framework (Mode)
Counts, Max, Min, Mean, Top-N, Distinct	Hadoop-MapReduce (Batch), Pig (Batch), Spark (Batch), Spark Streaming (Realtime), Spark SQL (Interactive), Hive (Integrative), Storm (Real-time)
Correlations	Hadoop-MapReduce (Batch), Spark Mlib (Batch)

Clustering

Analysis Type	Framework (Mode)
K-Means	Hadoop-MapReduce (Batch), Spark Mlib (Batch & Real-time) H2O (Batch)
DBSCAN	Spark (Batch)
Gaussian Mixture	Spark Mlib (Batch)
PIC	Spark Mlib (Batch)
LDA	Spark Mlib (Batch)

Classification

Analysis Type	Framework (Mode)
KNN	Spark Mlib (Batch, Realtime)
Decision Trees	Spark Mlib (Batch, Realtime)
Random Forest	Spark Mlib (Batch, Realtime), H2O (Batch)
SVM	Spark Mlib (Batch, Realtime)
Naïve Bayes	Spark Mlib (Batch, Realtime), H2O (Batch)
Deep Learning	H2O (Batch)

Regression

Analysis Type	Framework (Mode)
Linear Least Squares	Spark Mlib (Batch, Realtime)
Generalized Linear Model	H2O (Batch)
Stochastic Gradient Descent	Spark Mlib (Batch, Realtime)
Isotonic Regression	Spark Mlib (Batch, Realtime)

Figure 1.4: Mapping Analytics Flow to Big Data Stack - Part I

Graph Analytics

Analysis Type	Framework (Mode)
Graph Search	Spark GraphX (Batch)
Shortest-Path	Spark GraphX (Batch)
PageRank	Spark GraphX (Batch)
Triangle Counting	Spark GraphX (Batch)
Connected Components	Spark GraphX (Batch)

Time Series Analysis

Analysis Type	Framework (Mode)
Kalman Filter	Spark (Realtime)
Time Frequency Models	Spark (Realtime)
Outlier Detection	Storm (Realtime), Spark (Batch, Realtime)

Text Analysis

Analysis Type	Framework (Mode)
Categorization	Hadoop-MapReduce (Batch), Storm (Realtime), Spark (Batch, Realtime)
Summarization	Spark (Batch)
Sentiment Analysis	Storm (Realtime), Spark (Batch, Realtime)
Text Mining	Storm (Realtime), Spark (Batch, Realtime)

Pattern Mining

Analysis Type	Framework (Mode)
FP-Growth	Spark Mlib (Batch)
Association Rules	Spark Mlib (Batch)
PrefixSpan	Spark Mlib (Batch)

Dimensionality Reduction

Analysis Type	Framework (Mode)
SVD	Spark Mlib (Batch)
PCA	Spark Mlib (Batch), H2O (Batch)

Recommendation

Analysis Type	Framework (Mode)
Item-bases Recommendation	Spark Mlib (Batch)
Collaborative Filtering	Spark Mlib (Batch)

Visualization

Analysis Type	Framework (Mode)
Web Frameworks	Django, Flask
SQL Databases	MySQL
NoSQL Databases	Hbase, DynamoDB, Cassandra, MongoDB
Visualization Frameworks	Lightning, pyGal, Seaborn

Figure 1.5: Mapping Analytics Flow to Big Data Stack - Part II

about what transformation should be applied and want to explore the data and try different transformations, then interactive querying frameworks such as Hive, SparkSQL can be useful. With these tools, you can query data with queries written in an SQL-like language.

For the basic statistics analysis type (with analysis such as computing counts, max, min, mean, top-N, distinct, correlations, for instance), most of the analysis can be done using the Hadoop-MapReduce framework or with Pig scripts. Both MapReduce and Pig allow data analysis in batch mode. For basic statistics in batch mode, the Spark framework is also a good option. For basic statics in real-time mode, Spark Streaming and Storm frameworks can be used. For basic statistics in interactive mode, a framework such as Hive and SparkSQL can be used.

Like, basic statistics, we can similarly map other analysis types to one of the frameworks in the big data stack. Figures 1.4 and 1.5 show the mappings between the various analysis types and the big data frameworks.

1.8   Case Study: Genome Data Analysis

Let us look at a case study of using the Big Data stack for analysis of genome data. For this case study, we will use the synthetic data generator provided with the GenBase [2] genomics benchmark. This data generator generates four types of datasets: (1) Microarray data which includes the expression values for a large number of genes for different patients, (2) Patient meta-data which contains the demographic data (patient age, gender, zip code) and clinical information (disease and drug response) for each patient whose genomic data is available in the microarray dataset, (3) Gene meta-data which contains information such as target of the gene (i.e. ID of another gene that is targeted by the protein from the current gene), chromosome number, position (number of base pairs from the start of the chromosome to the start of the gene), length (in base pairs) and function (coded as an integer), (4) Gene Ontology (GO) data which specifies the GO categories for different genes. Figure 1.6 shows small samples for the four types of datasets.

To come up with a selection of the tools and frameworks from the Big Data stack that can be used for genome data analysis, let us come up with the analytics flow for the application as shown in Figure 1.7(a).

Data Collection

Let us assume that we have the raw datasets available either in an SQL database or as raw text files. To import datasets from the SQL database into the big data stack, we can use an SQL connector. Whereas for importing raw dataset files, a source-sink connector can be useful.

Data Preparation

In the data preparation step, we may have to perform data cleansing (to remove missing values and corrupt records) and data wrangling (to transform records in different formats to one consistent format).

Analysis Types

Let us say, for this application we want to perform two types of analysis as follows: (1) predict the drug response based on gene expressions, (2) find correlations between expression values of all pairs of genes to find genes which have similar expression patterns and genes which have opposing expression patterns. The first analysis comes under the regression analysis category, where a regression model can be built to predict the drug response. The target variable for the regression model is the patient drug response and the independent variables are the gene expression values. The second type of analysis comes under the basic statistics category, where we compute the correlations between expression values of all pairs of genes.

Analysis Modes

Based on the analysis types determined the previous step, we know that the analysis modes required for the application will be batch and interactive.

Visualizations

The front end application for visualizing the analysis results would be dynamic and interactive.

Mapping Analytics Flow to Big Data Stack

With the analytics flow for the application created, we can now map the selections at each step of the flow to the big data stack. Figure 1.7(b) shows a subset of the components of the big data stack based on the analytics flow. The implementation details of this application are provided in Chapter-11.

Figure 1.8 shows the steps involved in building a regression model for predicting drug response and the data at each step. Before we can build the regression model, we have to perform some transformations and joins to make the data suitable for building the model. We select genes with a particular set of functions and join the gene meta-data with patient meta-data and microarray data. Next, we pivot the results to get the expression values for each type of gene for each patient. Then we select the patient-ID, disease and drug response from the patient meta-data. Next, we join the tables obtained in previous two steps to generate a new table which has all the data in the right format to build a regression model.

Figure 1.9 shows the steps involved in computing correlation between the expression levels of all pairs of genes and the data at each step. We select patients with a specific disease and join the results with the microarray table. Next, we pivot the table in the previous step to get the expression values for all genes for each patient. We use this table to create the correlation matrix having correlations between the expression values of all pairs of genes.

Gene meta-data

geneid	target	position	length	function
0	-1	6.69E+08	175	633
1	-1	2.74E+09	974	7
2	-1	6.82E+08	260	909
3	-1	2.4E+09	930	28
4	1	2.01E+09	836	462
5	-1	1.64E+09	277	941
6	-1	2.6E+09	428	487
7	-1	1.02E+08	618	966
8	6	8.46E+08	635	328
9	3	2.77E+09	964	183

Gene Ontology data

geneid	goid	whether gene belongs to go
0	0	1
0	1	1
0	2	1
0	3	1
0	6	0
:	:	..
9	59993	1
9	59994	1
9	59995	1
9	59996	1

Patient meta-data

patientid	age	gender	zipcode	disease	drug response
0	41	0	7494	15	84.77
1	45	1	38617	6	62.4
2	51	1	62817	17	49.43
3	62	0	53316	18	25.88
4	23	1	49685	7	41.03
5	60	0	48726	8	23.35
6	77	0	99103	18	87.86
7	83	1	5210	18	55.05
8	56	1	7359	5	97.09
9	63	1	59483	17	15.05

Micro-array data

geneid	patientid	expression value
0	0	7.51
0	1	5.92
0	2	8.12
0	3	3.47
:	..	:
1	1	7.43
1	2	5.54
1	3	2.86
2	0	7.69
2	1	7.66
2	2	9.76
2	3	1.41

Figure 1.6: Genome datasets

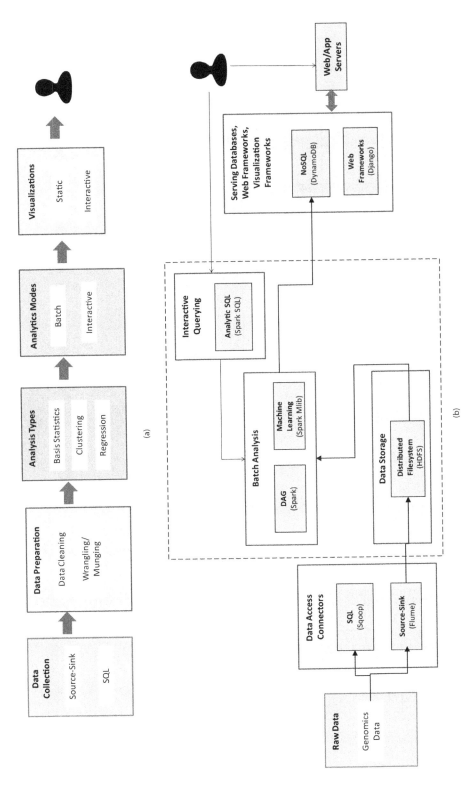

Figure 1.7: (a) Analytics flow for genome data analysis, (b) Using big data stack for analysis of genome data

Select genes with a particular set of functions and join gene meta-data with patient meta-data and microarray data

patientid	disease	geneid	exValue	drugResponse
0	14	0	701993.3	60.42
1	12	0	-16377.7	57.86
2	6	0	1296795	39.62
3	19	0	505206.7	24.83
4	10	0	732953.1	50.36
5	10	0	446293.6	12.63
6	8	0	-92641.8	12.24
7	14	0	-29881.8	73.71
8	7	0	115540.8	37.66
9	7	0	509479.7	62.43
0	14	9	1423755	60.42
1	12	9	1589411	57.86
2	6	9	7045.72	39.62
3	19	9	-65459.3	24.83
4	10	9	1373435	50.36
5	10	9	233481.5	12.63
6	8	9	832897.5	12.24
7	14	9	1258119	73.71
8	7	9	679142	37.66
9	7	9	1143324	62.43

Pivot

Pivot the table in previous step to get expression values for each type of gene for each patient

patientid	0	9
0	701993.3	1423755
1	-16377.7	1589411
2	1296795	7045.72
3	505206.7	-65459.3
4	732953.1	1373435
5	446293.6	233481.5
6	-92641.8	832897.5
7	-29881.8	1258119
8	115540.8	679142
9	509479.7	1143324

Select patient ID, disease and drugResponse from patient meta-data

patientid	disease	drugResponse
0	14	60.42
1	12	57.86
2	6	39.62
3	19	24.83
4	10	50.36
5	10	12.63
6	8	12.24
7	14	73.71
8	7	37.66
9	7	62.43

Join

patientid	disease	drugResponse	patientid	0	9
0	14	60.42	0	701993.3	1423755
1	12	57.86	1	-16377.7	1589411
2	6	39.62	2	1296795	7045.72
3	19	24.83	3	505206.7	-65459.3
4	10	50.36	4	732953.1	1373435
5	10	12.63	5	446293.6	233481.5
6	8	12.24	6	-92641.8	832897.5
7	14	73.71	7	-29881.8	1258119
8	7	37.66	8	115540.8	679142
9	7	62.43	9	509479.7	1143324

Use this table to train Linear Regression model to predict drug response (target variable is the patient drug response and the independent variables are gene expression values)

Figure 1.8: Steps involved in building a regression model for predicting drug response

Select patients with some disease and join results with the micro-array table

patientid	disease	geneid	exValue
3	18	0	3.47
3	18	1	2.86
3	18	2	1.41
3	18	3	5.3
3	18	4	7.73
3	18	5	1.51
3	18	6	4.92
3	18	7	1.97
3	18	8	8.02
3	18	9	8.32
6	18	0	1.42
6	18	1	9.17
6	18	2	1.37
6	18	3	9.2
6	18	4	1.4
6	18	5	8.86
6	18	6	7.88
6	18	7	9.52
6	18	8	3.24
6	18	9	3.54

Pivot

Pivot the table to get the expression values for all genes for each patients

patientid	0	1	2	3	4	5	6	7	8	9
3	3.47	2.86	1.41	5.3	7.73	1.51	4.92	1.97	8.02	8.32
6	1.42	9.17	1.37	9.2	1.4	8.86	7.88	9.52	3.24	3.54
7	1.48	2.58	7.52	1.66	4.55	8.55	5.45	4.35	2.81	3.7

Compute the correlation between the expression levels of all pairs of genes

Correlation Matrix

	Gene-0	Gene-1	Gene-2	Gene-3	Gene-4	Gene-5	Gene-6	Gene-7	Gene-8	Gene-9
Gene-0	1	-0.48969	-0.47259	-0.04561	0.8799	-0.99993	-0.65789	-0.75961	0.994991	0.999993
Gene-1	-0.48969	1	-0.53696	0.893321	-0.84517	0.499756	0.978801	0.939038	-0.40008	-0.49297
Gene-2	-0.47259	-0.53696	1	-0.85881	0.002915	0.462357	-0.35279	-0.21418	-0.55832	-0.46928
Gene-3	-0.04561	0.893321	-0.85881	1	-0.5148	0.057171	0.782337	0.684345	0.054482	-0.04936
Gene-4	0.8799	-0.84517	0.002915	-0.5148	1	-0.88534	-0.93673	-0.97741	0.827993	0.881678
Gene-5	-0.99993	0.499756	0.462357	0.057171	-0.88534	1	0.666563	0.76709	-0.99377	-0.99997
Gene-6	-0.65789	0.978801	-0.35279	0.782337	-0.93673	0.666563	1	0.989549	-0.57931	-0.66071
Gene-7	-0.75961	0.939038	-0.21418	0.684345	-0.97741	0.76709	0.989549	1	-0.69079	-0.76205
Gene-8	0.994991	-0.40008	-0.55832	0.054482	0.827993	-0.99377	-0.57931	-0.69079	1	0.994608
Gene-9	0.999993	-0.49297	-0.46928	-0.04936	0.881678	-0.99997	-0.66071	-0.76205	0.994608	1

Figure 1.9: Steps involved in computing correlation between the expression levels of all pairs of genes

1.9   Case Study: Weather Data Analysis

Let us look at a case study of using the big data stack for analysis of weather data. To come up with a selection of the tools and frameworks from the big data stack that can be used for weather data analysis, let us first come up with the analytics flow for the application as shown in Figure 1.10.

Data Collection

Let us assume, we have multiple weather monitoring stations or end-nodes equipped with temperature, humidity, wind, and pressure sensors. To collect and ingest streaming sensor data generated by the weather monitoring stations, we can use a publish-subscribe messaging framework to ingest data for real-time analysis within the Big Data stack and a Source-Sink connector to ingest data into a distributed filesystem for batch analysis.

Data Preparation

Since the weather data received from different monitoring stations can have missing values, use different units and have different formats, we may need to prepare data for analysis by cleaning, wrangling, normalizing and filtering the data.

Analysis Types

The choice of the analysis types is driven by the requirements of the application. Let us say, we want our weather analysis application to aggregate data on various timescales (minute, hourly, daily or monthly) to determine the mean, maximum and minimum readings for temperature, humidity, wind and pressure. We also want the application to support interactive querying for exploring the data, for example, queries such as: finding the day with the lowest temperature in each month of a year, finding the top-10 most wet days in the year, for instance. These type of analysis come under the basic statistics category. Next, we also want the application to make predictions of certain weather events, for example, predict the occurrence of fog or haze. For such an analysis, we would require a classification model. Additionally, if we want to predict values (such as the amount of rainfall), we would require a regression model.

Analysis Modes

Based on the analysis types determined the previous step, we know that the analysis modes required for the application will be batch, real-time and interactive.

Visualizations

The front end application for visualizing the analysis results would be dynamic and interactive.

Mapping Analysis Flow to Big Data Stack

Now that we have the analytics flow for the application, let us map the selections at each step of the flow to the big data stack. Figure 1.11 shows a subset of the components of the big data stack based on the analytics flow. To collect and ingest streaming sensor data generated by the weather monitoring stations, we can use a publish-subscribe messaging framework

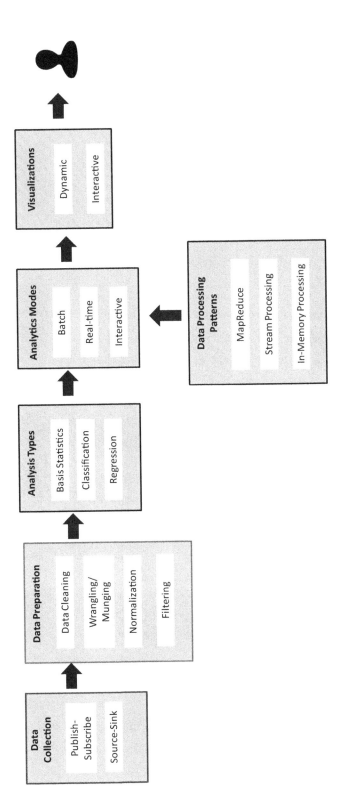

Figure 1.10: Analytics flow for weather data analysis application

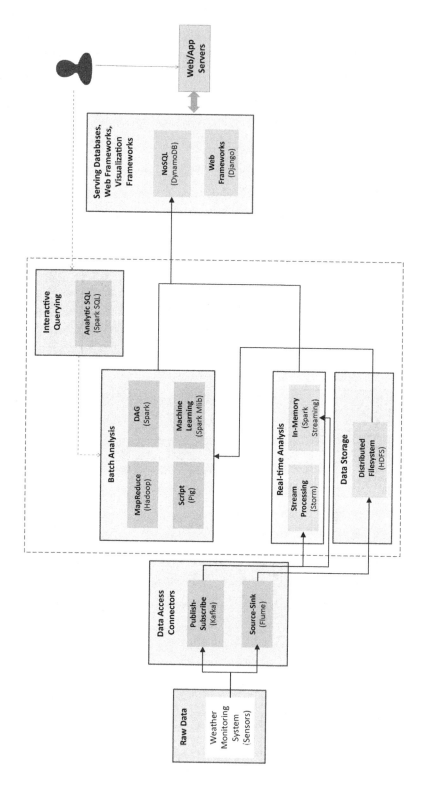

Figure 1.11: Using Big Data stack for weather data analysis

such as Apache Kafka (for real-time analysis within the Big Data stack). Each weather station publishes the sensor data to Kafka. Python examples of publishing data to Kafka are described in Chapter-5. Real-time analysis frameworks such as Storm and Spark Streaming can receive data from Kafka for processing. Python examples of real-time analysis with Kafka as data source are described in Chapter-8.

For batch analysis, we can use a source-sink connector such as Flume to move the data to HDFS. Once the data is in HDFS, we can use batch processing frameworks such as Hadoop-MapReduce. We can also use Spark for such Map and Reduce transformations. Python examples of batch processing using Hadoop- MapReduce and Spark are described in Chapter-7.

While the batch and real-time processing frameworks are useful when the analysis requirements and goals are known upfront, interactive querying tools can be useful for exploring the data. We can use interactive querying framework such as Spark SQL, which can query the data in HDFS for interactive queries. Examples of Spark SQL for interactive querying of weather data are described in Chapter-9.

For presenting the results of batch and real-time analysis, a NoSQL database such as DynamoDB can be used as a serving database. Python examples of writing data to DynamoDB tables and reading data from the tables are described in Chapter-10. For developing web applications and displaying the analysis results we can use a web framework such as Django. Examples of Django applications are described in Chapter-10.

1.10 Analytics Patterns

In the previous sections we proposed a novel data science and analytics application system design methodology and its realization through use of open-source big data frameworks. In this section we propose, four analytics patterns: Alpha, Beta, Gamma and Delta, that comprise tools and frameworks for collecting and ingesting data from various sources into the big data analytics infrastructure, distributed filesystems and non-relational (NoSQL) databases for data storage, processing frameworks for batch and real-time analytics, interactive querying frameworks, serving databases, and web and visualization frameworks. These patterns and the data science and analytics application system design methodology, forms the pedagogical foundation of this book.

- **Alpha Pattern**: Figures 1.12(a) shows the Alpha pattern for batch data analysis. This pattern can be used for ingesting large volumes of data into a distributed filesystem (such as HDFS) or a NoSQL database (such as HBase) using source-sink connectors (such as Flume) and SQL connectors (such as Sqoop). After the data is moved to the stack, the data can be analyzed in batch mode with batch analysis frameworks including MapReduce (using Hadoop), scripting frameworks (such as Pig), distributed acyclic graph frameworks (such as Spark), machine learning frameworks (such as Spark MLlib). The analysis results are stored either in relational or non-relational databases. Some of the domain specific applications described in section 1.4 that can use the Alpha pattern include: web analytics, weather monitoring, epidemiological surveillance, and machine diagnosis.
- **Beta Pattern**: Figures 1.12(b) shows the Beta pattern for real-time analysis. This pattern can be used for ingesting streaming data using publish-subscribe messaging

frameworks, queues and custom connectors. For real-time analysis, we can use stream processing frameworks (such as Storm) or in-memory processing frameworks (such as Spark). The Beta pattern can be used by various Internet of Things applications and real-time monitoring applications described in section 1.4.

- **Gamma Pattern**: Figures 1.13(a) shows the Gamma pattern which combines batch and real-time analysis patterns. This pattern is meant for ingesting streaming data into a big data stack and analyzing the data both in real-time and in batch modes. For batch analysis, the data is collected and analyzed over certain intervals. For example, let us see how this pattern can be used for a system that detects forest fires based on sensor data collected from a large number of IoT devices deployed in a forest. The real-time analysis blocks in this pattern can filter and analyze the data in real-time and make predictions using pre-trained machine learning models. Whereas the batch analysis blocks can analyze data aggregated over certain intervals (such as hourly, daily monthly or yearly).

- **Delta Pattern**: Figures 1.13(b) shows the Delta pattern for interactive querying. This pattern uses, source-sink connectors (such as Flume) or SQL connectors (such as Sqoop) to ingest bulk data into the big data stack. After the data is moved to a distributed filesystem, you can use interactive querying frameworks (such as Hive or Spark SQL) for querying data with SQL-like queries in an interactive mode. The Delta pattern can be used by applications such as web analytics, advertisement targeting, inventory management, production planning and control, and various types of enterprise applications.

The proposed patterns are generic in nature and specific realizations of these patterns can be created by mapping them to the specific frameworks or cloud and analytics services from different cloud vendors. For example, in Figure 1.14 we provide the mappings of the various blocks used in the analytics patterns to specific services from Amazon AWS and Microsoft Azure. The patterns enable reuse of code, thus making the design process quicker. Code templates for specific realizations of the patterns can be used to automate the generation or construction of the code for various components which can then be customized for specific applications.

For each of these patterns, there can be multiple levels of complexity and configuration options based on features such as performance, scalability, fault tolerance and security. Figure 1.15 describes the various levels for these patterns. For example, the Alpha pattern can be scaled up to thousands of nodes to store and process several petabytes of data. Similarly, the Beta pattern can be scaled to hundreds of nodes to process very high throughout streaming data. Most of the frameworks used for these patterns have distributed and fault tolerant architectures. Security is another important aspect for big data applications which store and process sensitive data. For securing the big data frameworks, specialized security frameworks such as Apache Ranger [16] and Apache Knox [17] can be used. Apache Ranger, for example, brings security features such as authorization, authentication, auditing, data encryption and centralized security administration to most of the frameworks that can used for realizing these patterns. Apache Knox is a REST API Gateway for Hadoop clusters, that provides security features such as authentication, authorization identity federation, and auditing.

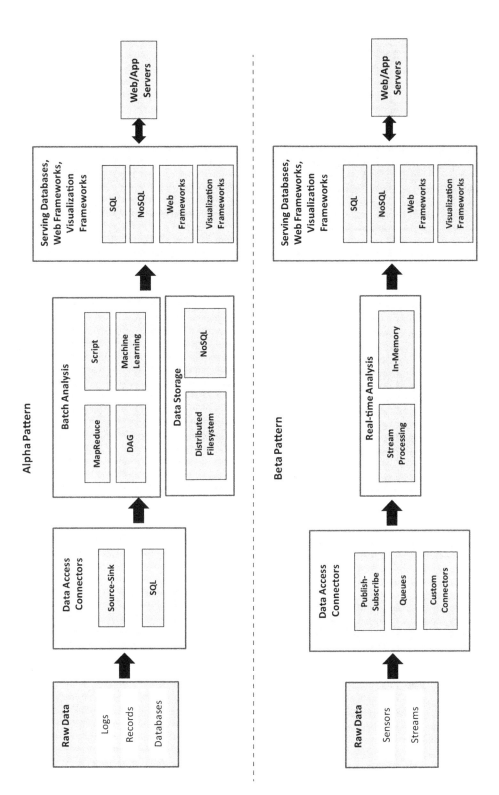

Figure 1.12: (a) Alpha Pattern: Batch analysis, (b) Beta Pattern: Real-time analysis

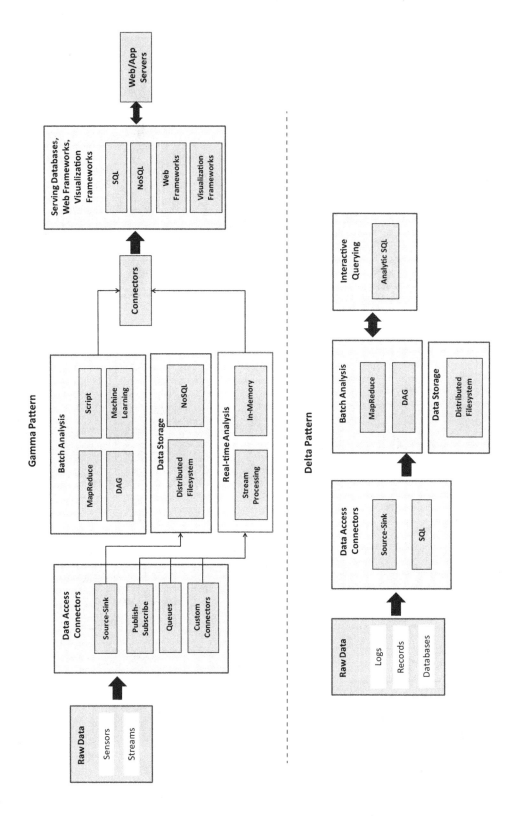

Figure 1.13: (a) Gamma Pattern: Batch & Real-time analysis, (b) Delta Pattern: Interactive querying

Data Access Connector	AWS Service	Azure Service
Publish-Subscribe	AWS Kinesis	Azure Event Hubs
Source-Sink	Flume on EMR	Flume on HDInsight
SQL	Sqoop on EMR	Sqoop on HDInsight
Queues	AWS SQS	Azure Queue Service
Custom Connectors	AWS IoT	Azure IoT Hub

Real-time Analysis	AWS Service	Azure Service
Stream Processing	Storm cluster on AWS EC2	Storm on Azure HDInsight, Azure Stream Analytics
In-Memory Processing	Spark on AWS EMR	Spark on Azure HDInsight

Data Storage	AWS Service	Azure Service
Distributed Filesystem	HDFS on AWS EMR	HDFS on Azure HDInsight
NoSQL	AWS DynamoDB	Azure DocumentDB

Serving Databases, Web & Visualization Frameworks	AWS Service	Azure Service
SQL	AWS RDS	Azure SQL DB
NoSQL	AWS DynamoDB	Azure DocumentDB
Web Framework	Django on AWS EC2 instance	Django on Azure Virtual Machines instance
Visualization Framework	Lightning, Pygal, Seaborn, on AWS Virtual Machines instance	Lightning, Pygal, Seaborn, on Azure Virtual Machines instance, Azure Power BI

Batch Analysis	AWS Service	Azure Service
MapReduce	Hadoop on AWS EMR	Hadoop on Azure HDInsight
Script	Pig on AWS EMR	Pig on Azure HDInsight
DAG	Spark on AWS EMR	Spark on Azure HDInsight
Machine Learning	Spark MLlib on AWS EMR, AWS Machine Learning	Spark MLlib on Azure HDInsight, Azure Machine Learning

Figure 1.14: Mapping of blocks in analytics patterns to AWS and Azure services

Levels	Alpha	Beta	Gamma	Delta
Security	**Apache Ranger**: Authorization, authentication, auditing, data encryption, security administration **Apache Knox Gateway**: REST API gateway, LDAP and Active Directory Authentication, Federation/SSO, Authorization, Auditing			
Fault Tolerance	Distributed, fault tolerant and highly available architectures Data replication, automatic failovers			
Scalability	Scalable to thousands of nodes that can store and process several Petabytes of data	Scalable to thousands of nodes that can process very high throughput streaming data	Scalable to thousands of nodes that can process very high throughput streaming data	Scalable to thousands of nodes that can store and process several Petabytes of data
Performance	Process large volumes of data with within timescales of few minutes	Process streaming data on the timescales of few milliseconds to seconds	Combines batch and real-time processing for streaming data, with timescales of milliseconds to seconds for real-time, and few minutes for batch	Interactively query large volumes of data with within timescales of few milliseconds to seconds
Functionality	Batch Processing	Real time processing	Batch & Real-time processing	Interactive querying

Analytics Patterns

Figure 1.15: Complexity levels for analytics patterns

Summary

In this chapter, we described what is analytics and the various types of analytics applications. Analytics is the process of extracting and creating information from raw data by filtering, processing, categorizing, condensing and contextualizing the data. Descriptive analytics deals with analyzing past data to present it in a summarized form which can be easily interpreted. Diagnostic analytics deals with the analysis of past data to diagnose the reason for happening of certain events. Predictive analytics involves predicting the occurrence of an event or the likely outcome of an event or forecasting the future values using prediction models. Prescriptive analytics uses multiple prediction models to predict various outcomes and the best course of action for each outcome. Big data analytics deals with collection, storage, processing and analysis of massive-scale data. Big data analytics involves several steps starting from data cleansing, data munging (or wrangling), data processing and visualization. We described the characteristics of big data including volume, velocity, variety, veracity and value. Domain specific examples and applications of big data were described. Next, we proposed a generic flow for big data analytics, detailing the steps involved in a typical analytics task and the options available at each step. Data preparation step involves various tasks such as data cleansing, data wrangling or munging, de-duplication, normalization, sampling and filtering. We described the various analysis types and the computational 'giants'. We proposed and described a big data stack comprising of proven and open-source big data frameworks that form the foundation of this book. An approach for mapping the analytics flow to specific tools and frameworks in the big data stack was described. Finally, we propose four analytics patterns that include different categories of big data frameworks such as data acquisition, data storage, batch analysis, real-time analysis, interactive querying, serving databases, and web and visualization frameworks. The proposed patterns are generic in nature and specific realizations of these patterns can be created by mapping them to the specific frameworks or cloud and analytics services from different cloud vendors.

2 - Setting up Big Data Stack

This chapter covers

- Setting up Big Data Stack
  - Hortonworks Data Platform
  - Cloudera CDH Stack
  - Amazon EMR cluster
  - Azure HDInsight cluster

This chapter provides various options for setting up big data stacks and the big data frameworks used for the examples in this book. The trademarks belong to their respective owners.

2.1 Hortonworks Data Platform (HDP)

The Hortonworks Data Platform (HDP) [7] is an open source platform distribution comprising of various big data frameworks for data access and integration, batch processing, real-time processing, interactive querying, security and operations tools. The key frameworks in the HDP stack which are used for the examples in this book include:

- Hadoop
- YARN
- HDFS
- HBase
- Hive
- Pig
- Sqoop
- Flume
- Oozie
- Storm
- Zookeeper
- Kafka
- Spark

For setting up these frameworks, we recommend using Apache Ambari [15]. Ambari is a tool for provisioning, managing and monitoring clusters that run these frameworks. This section provides the instructions for setting up a Big Data stack comprising of the frameworks listed above using Apache Ambari.

Ambari cluster can be setup on any machine(s) running the following supported operating systems:

- Ubuntu Precise 12.04 or 14.04
- Red Hat Enterprise Linux (RHEL) v6.x
- CentOS v6.x
- Oracle Linux v6.x
- SUSE Linux Enterprise Server (SLES) v11, SP1 and SP3

Launching an AWS EC2 instance

In this section, we describe how to launch an Amazon EC2 instance running Ubuntu 14.04, on which we will later setup an Apache Ambari cluster. Sign into your Amazon AWS account and open the EC2 console. To launch a new instance click on the launch instance button from the Amazon EC2 console. Select Ubuntu 14.04 Amazon Machine Image (AMI) as shown in Figure 2.1.

Next, choose the instance type as shown in Figure 2.2. We recommend an m4.2xlarge instance type if you want to setup an Ambari cluster on a single instance.

In the next step, configure the instance details as shown in Figure 2.3.

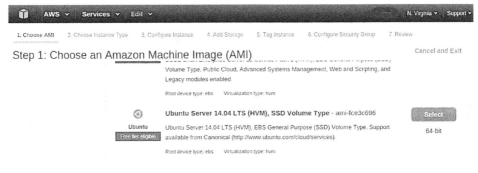

Figure 2.1: Select Ubuntu 14.04 AMI

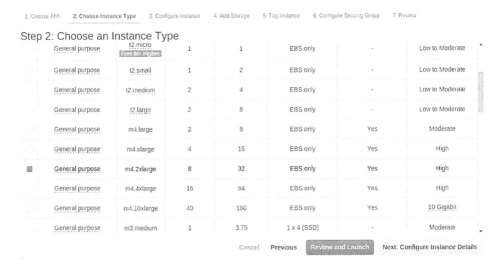

Figure 2.2: Select instance type

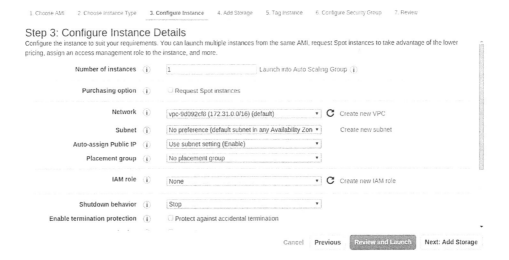

Figure 2.3: Amazon EC2 instance launch wizard showing instance details

Add storage in the next step as shown in Figure 2.4. We recommend at least 20GB storage.

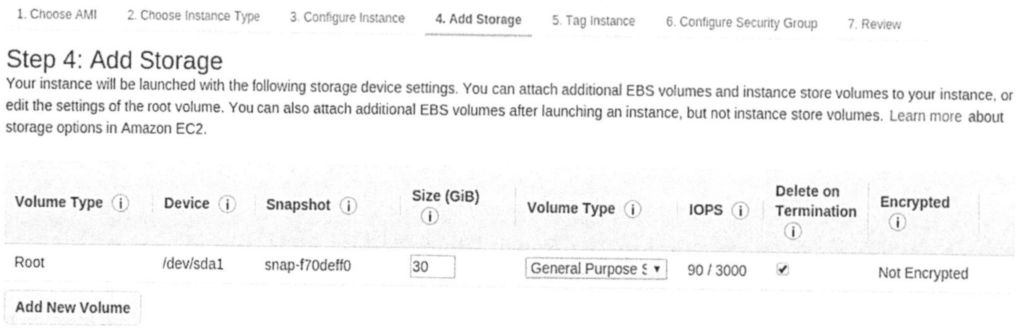

1. Choose AMI   2. Choose Instance Type   3. Configure Instance   **4. Add Storage**   5. Tag Instance   6. Configure Security Group   7. Review

Step 4: Add Storage

Your instance will be launched with the following storage device settings. You can attach additional EBS volumes and instance store volumes to your instance, or edit the settings of the root volume. You can also attach additional EBS volumes after launching an instance, but not instance store volumes. Learn more about storage options in Amazon EC2.

Volume Type (i)	Device (i)	Snapshot (i)	Size (GiB) (i)	Volume Type (i)	IOPS (i)	Delete on Termination (i)	Encrypted (i)
Root	/dev/sda1	snap-f70deff0	30	General Purpose S ▾	90 / 3000	☑	Not Encrypted

Add New Volume

Figure 2.4: Amazon EC2 instance launch wizard showing storage details

Specify instance tags that can be used to identify the instance as shown in Figure 2.5.

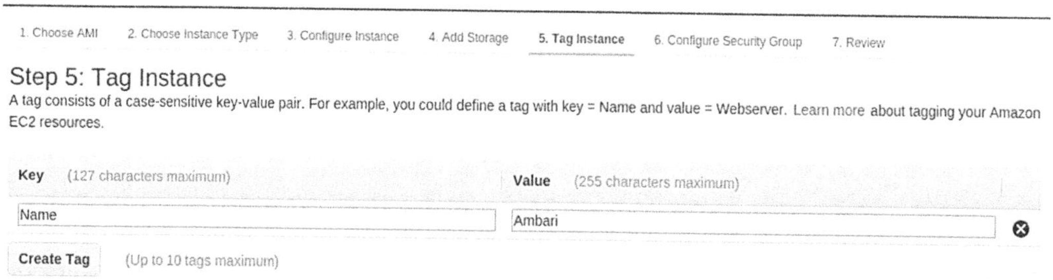

1. Choose AMI   2. Choose Instance Type   3. Configure Instance   4. Add Storage   **5. Tag Instance**   6. Configure Security Group   7. Review

Step 5: Tag Instance

A tag consists of a case-sensitive key-value pair. For example, you could define a tag with key = Name and value = Webserver. Learn more about tagging your Amazon EC2 resources.

Key (127 characters maximum)	Value (255 characters maximum)
Name	Ambari

Create Tag   (Up to 10 tags maximum)

Figure 2.5: Amazon EC2 instance launch wizard showing instance tags

Figure 2.6 shows the security groups page of the instance launch wizard. This page allows you to choose an existing security group or create a new security group. Security groups are used to open or block a specific network port for the launched instances. Create a new security group and open all TCP traffic. The frameworks we will setup with Apache Ambari use different ports for their web interfaces. So it is easier (though not recommended in a production environment) to open all TCP traffic without having to identify the individual ports for the various frameworks.

In the final step, review the instance details and create a new key-pair (or select an existing key-pair) for the instance and launch the instance as shown in Figure 2.7.

The status of the launched instance can be viewed in the EC2 console. When an instance is launched, its state is pending. It takes a couple of minutes for the instance to come into the running state. When the instance comes into the running state, it is assigned a public DNS, private DNS, public IP and private IP. We will use the public DNS to connect securely to the instance using SSH.

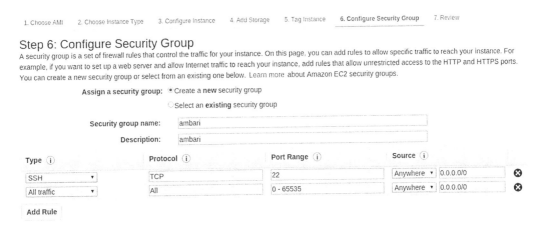

Figure 2.6: Amazon EC2 instance launch wizard showing security groups

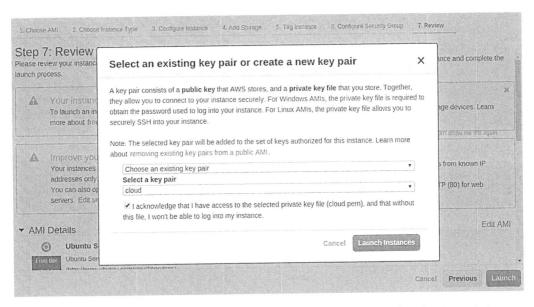

Figure 2.7: Amazon EC2 instance launch wizard showing key-pair selection window

Apache Ambari Setup

Connect to the EC2 instance launched in the previous section from your local machine using:

- `ssh -i myKeyPair.pem ubuntu@publicDNS`

where publicDNS is the Public DNS of the instance you created.

Box 2.1 shows the commands for installing Apache Ambari, the dependencies and some other packages that are used for the examples in this book.

■ Box 2.1: Commands for setting up Ambari

```
sudo apt-get -q -y update
sudo ufw disable
sudo apt-get -q -y install ntp
sudo service ntp start
sudo wget http://public-repo-1.hortonworks.com/ambari/
ubuntu12/1.x/updates/1.7.0/ambari.list

sudo cp ambari.list /etc/apt/sources.list.d/
sudo apt-key adv -recv-keys -keyserver
keyserver.ubuntu.com B9733A7A07513CAD
sudo apt-get -q -y update

sudo apt-get -q -y install ambari-server

sudo apt-get -q -y install ant gcc g++ libkrb5-dev libmysqlclient-dev
libssl-dev libsasl2-dev libsasl2-modules-gssapi-mit libsqlite3-dev
libtidy-0.99-0 libxml2-dev libxslt-dev python-dev python-simplejson
python-setuptools maven libldap2-dev python2.7-dev make python-pip
```

On your local machine run the following command to copy the keypair to the EC2 instance (change publicDNS to the public DNS of your instance):

- `scp -i myKeyPair myKeyPair.pem ubuntu@publicDNS:/home/ubuntu/.ssh/`

On your EC2 instance change the name of the keypair you just copied from your local machine to id_rsa:

- `cd /home/ubuntu/.ssh/`
`mv myKeyPair.pem id_rsa`

Run the following command to setup Apache Ambari:

- `sudo ambari-server setup`

Start Apache Ambari:

- `sudo ambari-server start`

Setting up HDP Stack with Ambari

Open the URL http://<publicDNS>:8080 in a browser. Login into Ambari Server with username *admin* and password *admin* as shown in Figure 2.8.

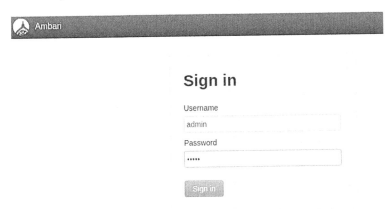

Figure 2.8: Apache Ambari login page

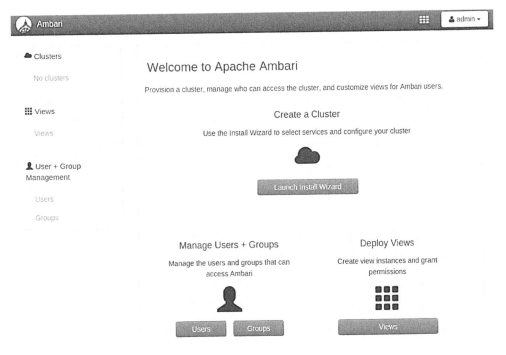

Figure 2.9: Apache Ambari setup wizard

Next, launch the install wizard as shown in Figure 2.9. Provide a name for the cluster as shown in Figure 2.10 and then select the HDP stack to install as shown in Figure 2.11. Enter the private DNS of the instance in the Target Hosts section. Select the EC2 key-pair

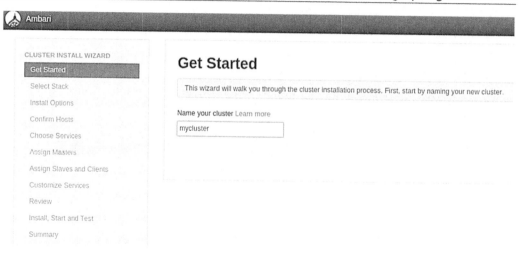

Figure 2.10: Apache Ambari setup wizard - provide cluster name

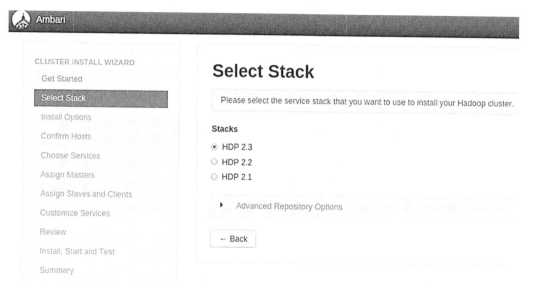

Figure 2.11: Apache Ambari setup wizard - select stack

file associated with the instance and change SSH user to ubuntu as shown in Figure 2.11. Follow the wizard to create the cluster as shown in the Figures 2.12 - 2.18.

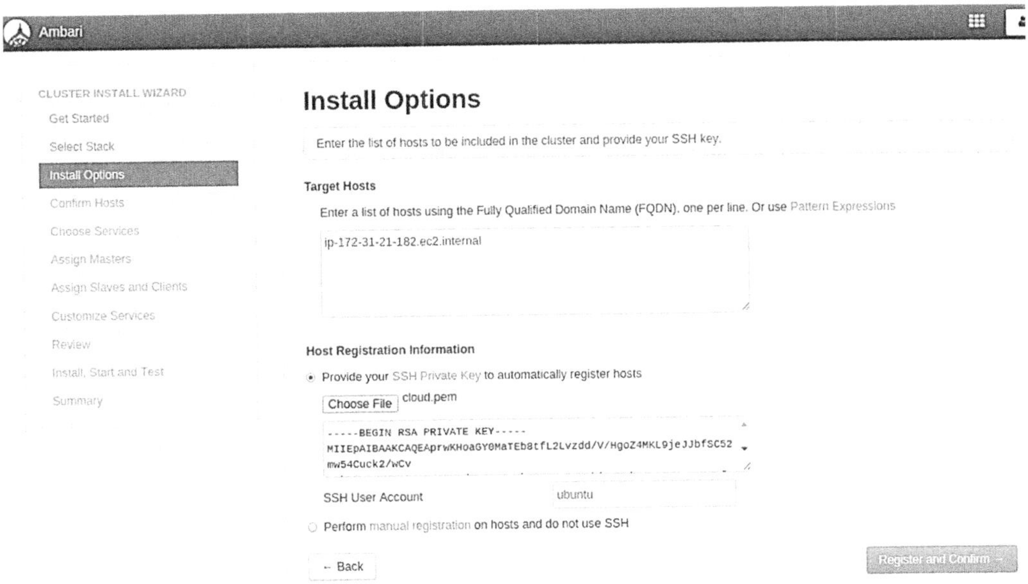

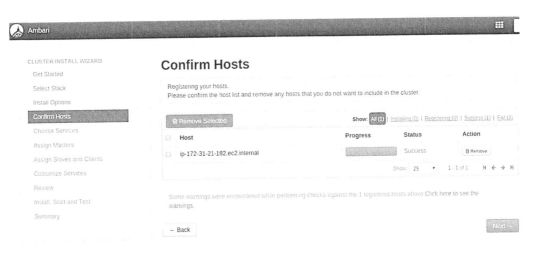

Figure 2.12: Apache Ambari setup wizard - install options

Figure 2.13: Apache Ambari setup wizard - confirm hosts

Choose Services

Choose which services you want to install on your cluster.

Service	Version	Description
☑ HDFS	2.7.1.2.3	Apache Hadoop Distributed File System
☑ YARN + MapReduce2	2.7.1.2.3	Apache Hadoop NextGen MapReduce (YARN)
☑ Tez	0.7.0.2.3	Tez is the next generation Hadoop Query Processing framework written on top of YARN.
☑ Hive	1.2.1.2.3	Data warehouse system for ad-hoc queries & analysis of large datasets and table & storage management service
☑ HBase	1.1.1.2.3	A Non-relational distributed database, plus Phoenix, a high performance SQL layer for low latency applications.
☑ Pig	0.15.0.2.3	Scripting platform for analyzing large datasets
☑ Sqoop	1.4.6.2.3	Tool for transferring bulk data between Apache Hadoop and structured data stores such as relational databases
☑ Oozie	4.2.0.2.3	System for workflow coordination and execution of Apache Hadoop jobs. This also includes the installation of the optional Oozie Web Console which relies on and will install the ExtJS Library.
☑ ZooKeeper	3.4.6.2.3	Centralized service which provides highly reliable distributed coordination
☑ Falcon	0.6.1.2.3	Data management and processing platform
☑ Storm	0.10.0	Apache Hadoop Stream processing framework
☑ Flume	1.5.2.2.3	A distributed service for collecting, aggregating, and moving large amounts of streaming data into HDFS
☑ Accumulo	1.7.0.2.3	Robust, scalable, high performance distributed key/value store.
☑ Ambari Metrics	0.1.0	A system for metrics collection that provides storage and retrieval capability for metrics collected from the cluster
☑ Atlas	0.5.0.2.3	Atlas Metadata and Governance platform
☑ Kafka	0.9.0.2.3	A high-throughput distributed messaging system
☑ Knox	0.6.0.2.3	Provides a single point of authentication and access for Apache Hadoop services in a cluster
☑ Mahout	0.9.0.2.3	Project of the Apache Software Foundation to produce free implementations of distributed or otherwise scalable machine learning algorithms focused primarily in the areas of collaborative filtering, clustering and classification
☑ Slider	0.80.0.2.3	A framework for deploying, managing and monitoring existing distributed applications on YARN.
☑ SmartSense	1.2.0.0-1310	SmartSense - Hortonworks SmartSense Tool (HST) helps quickly gather configuration, metrics, logs from common HDP services that aids to quickly troubleshoot support cases and receive cluster-specific recommendations.
☑ Spark	1.5.2.2.3	Apache Spark is a fast and general engine for large-scale data processing.

← Back   Next →

Figure 2.14: Apache Ambari setup wizard - choose services

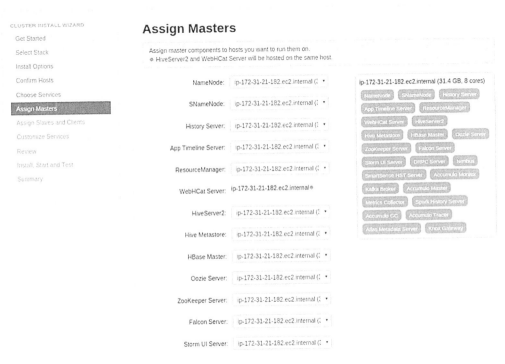

Figure 2.15: Apache Ambari setup wizard - assign masters

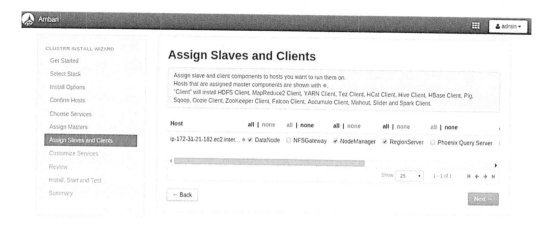

Customize Services

We have come up with recommended configurations for the services you selected. Customize them as you see fit.

HDFS   MapReduce2   YARN   Tez   Hive   HBase   Pig   Sqoop   Oozie   ZooKeeper   Falcon   Storm   Flume

Accumulo   Ambari Metrics   Atlas   Kafka   Knox   Mahout   Slider   SmartSense   Spark   Misc

Group   Default (1)   ▾   Manage Config Groups   Filter...   ▾

Settings   Advanced

NameNode

NameNode directories

/hadoop/hdfs/namenode

NameNode Java heap size

1GB

0 GB   15.75 GB   31.421 GB

NameNode Server threads

200

1   101   200

DataNode

DataNode directories

/hadoop/hdfs/data

DataNode failed disk tolerance

0

0   1

DataNode maximum Java heap size

1GB

0 GB   15.75 GB   31.421 GB

Figure 2.16: Apache Ambari setup wizard - assign slaves and clients

Ambari   ▦   👤 admin ▾

CLUSTER INSTALL WIZARD
Get Started
Select Stack
Install Options
Confirm Hosts
Choose Services
Assign Masters
Assign Slaves and Clients
Customize Services
Review
Install, Start and Test
Summary

Assign Slaves and Clients

Assign slave and client components to hosts you want to run them on.
Hosts that are assigned master components are shown with ⊕.
"Client" will install HDFS Client, MapReduce2 Client, YARN Client, Tez Client, HCat Client, Hive Client, HBase Client, Pig, Sqoop, Oozie Client, ZooKeeper Client, Falcon Client, Accumulo Client, Mahout, Slider and Spark Client.

Host	all | none	all | none	all | none	all | none	all | none
ip-172-31-21-182.ec2.inter... ⊕	☑ DataNode	☐ NFSGateway	☑ NodeManager	☑ RegionServer	☐ Phoenix Query Server

Show: 25 ▾   1 - 1 of 1   ⬅ ← → ⮕

← Back   Next →

Figure 2.17: Apache Ambari setup wizard - customize services

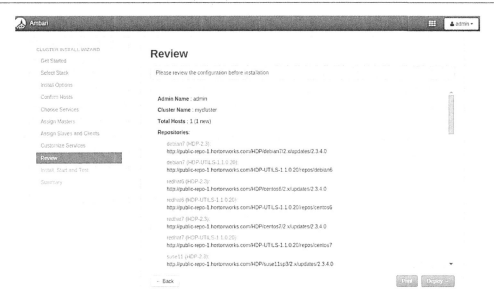

Figure 2.18: Apache Ambari setup wizard - review and deploy

After the wizard is complete, you will have a working HDP cluster as shown in Figure 2.19. You can monitor the services and frameworks installed from the Ambari dashboard. Make sure all services are running. For each of these services, you can edit the configurations, monitor and restart the services from the Ambari dashboard.

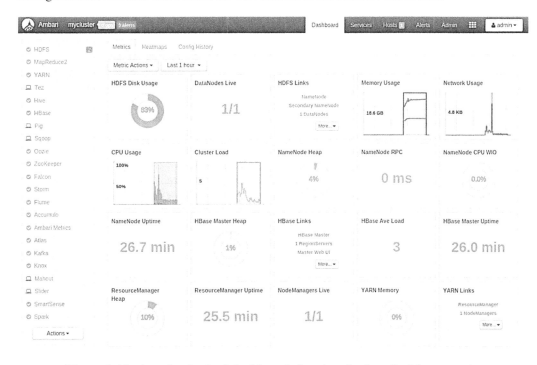

Figure 2.19: Apache Ambari dashboard showing the installed frameworks

2.2   Cloudera CDH Stack

Cloudera CDH [8] is an open source platform distribution that includes various big data tools and frameworks. The key frameworks in the CDH stack which are used for the examples in this book include:

- Hadoop
- YARN
- HDFS
- HBase
- Hive
- Pig
- Sqoop
- Flume
- Zookeeper
- Kafka
- Spark

There are various methods to setup a CDH stack, the easiest one being the automated method using Cloudera Manager. Cloudera Manager installer can be downloaded and run from the command line as shown in the box below:

```
■ wget http://archive.cloudera.com/cm5/installer/
        latest/cloudera-manager-installer.bin

chmod a+x cloudera-manager-installer.bin
sudo ./cloudera-manager-installer.bin
```

Follow the steps shown in Figures 2.20-2.22 to install Cloudera Manager Server.

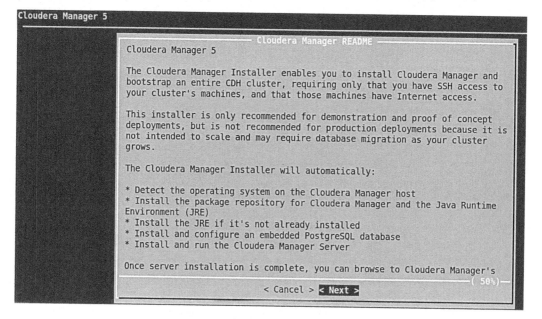

Figure 2.20: Cloudera Manager install wizard

Figure 2.21: Cloudera Manager installation in progress

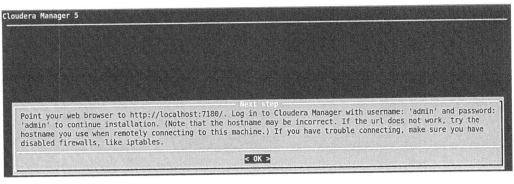

Figure 2.22: Cloudera Manager installation confirmation

Once the Cloudera Manager Server is installed, you can open the URL: http://<hostname>:7180 in a browser to access the Cloudera Manager. Follow the steps as shown in Figures 2.23-2.33 to complete the installation of CDH stack.

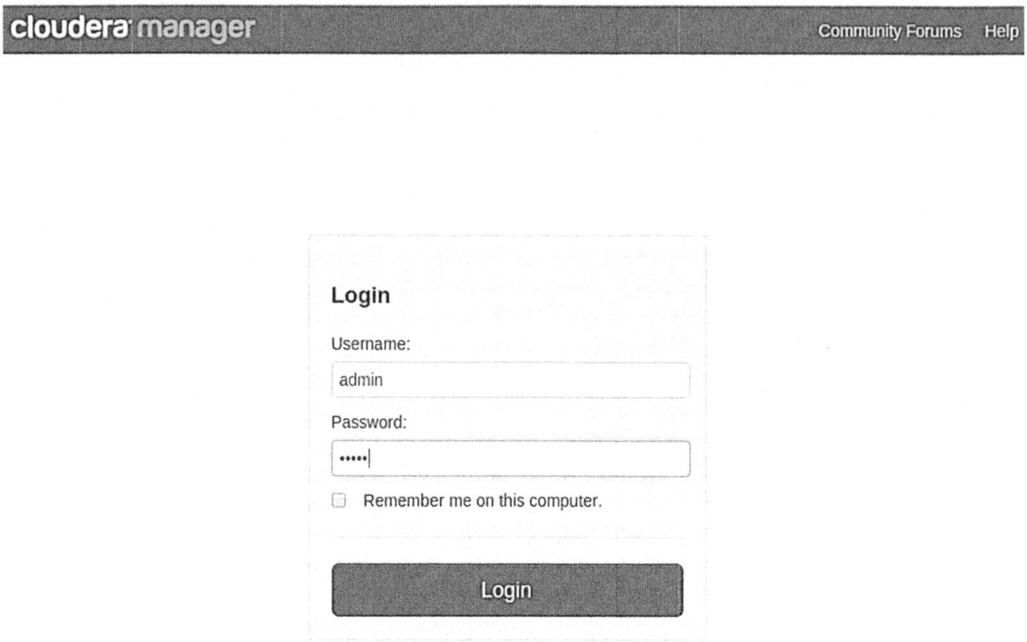

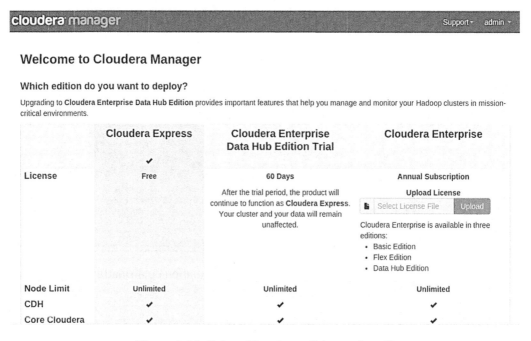

Figure 2.23: Cloudera Manager login page

Figure 2.24: Select Cloudera edition to install

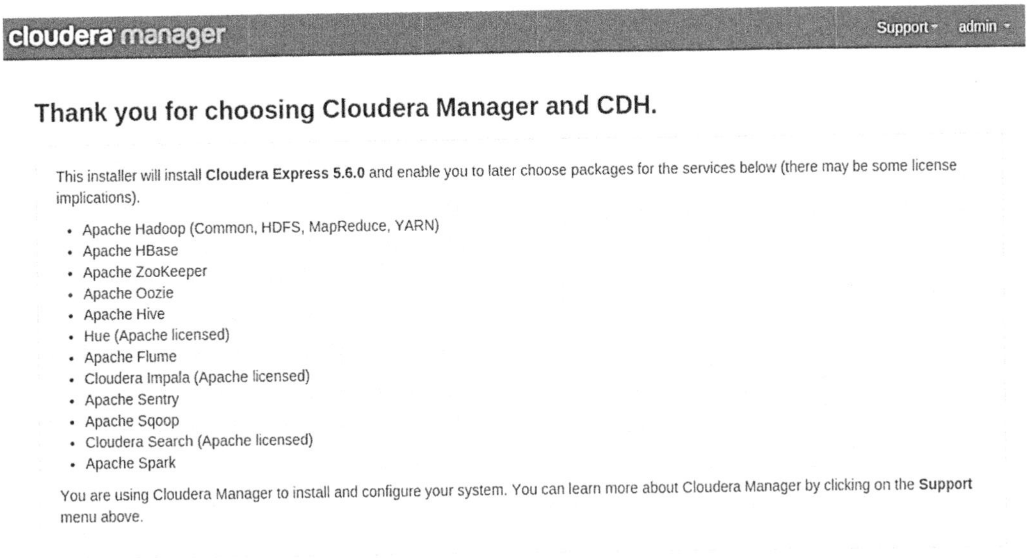

cloudera manager

Support ▾   admin ▾

Thank you for choosing Cloudera Manager and CDH.

This installer will install **Cloudera Express 5.6.0** and enable you to later choose packages for the services below (there may be some license implications).

- Apache Hadoop (Common, HDFS, MapReduce, YARN)
- Apache HBase
- Apache ZooKeeper
- Apache Oozie
- Apache Hive
- Hue (Apache licensed)
- Apache Flume
- Cloudera Impala (Apache licensed)
- Apache Sentry
- Apache Sqoop
- Cloudera Search (Apache licensed)
- Apache Spark

You are using Cloudera Manager to install and configure your system. You can learn more about Cloudera Manager by clicking on the **Support** menu above.

Figure 2.25: Cloudera Express edition services

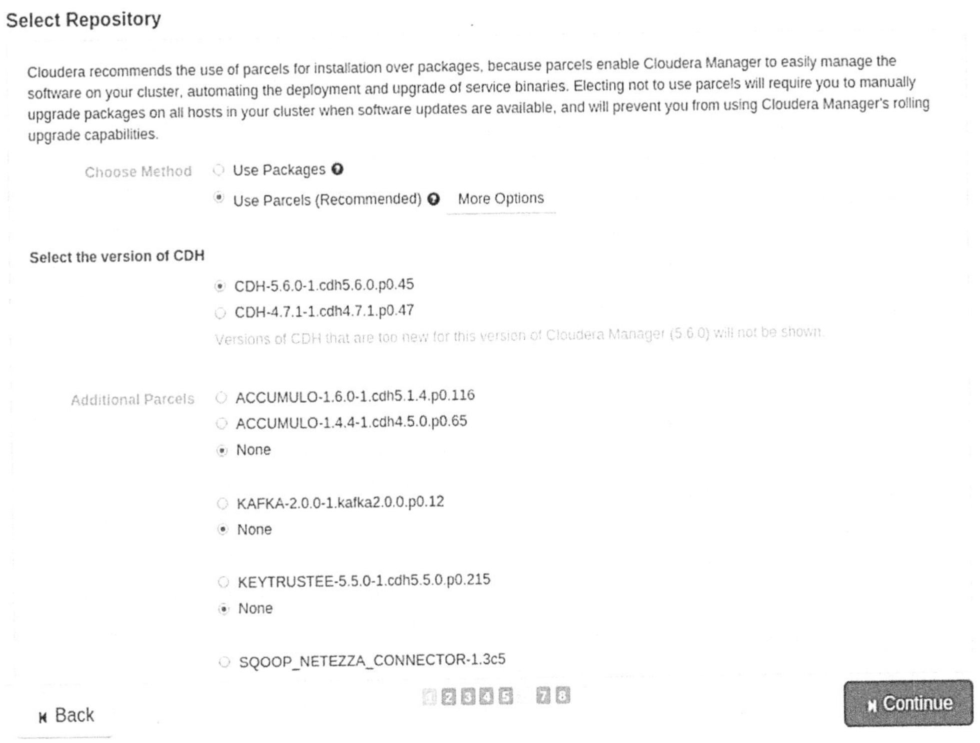

Select Repository

Cloudera recommends the use of parcels for installation over packages, because parcels enable Cloudera Manager to easily manage the software on your cluster, automating the deployment and upgrade of service binaries. Electing not to use parcels will require you to manually upgrade packages on all hosts in your cluster when software updates are available, and will prevent you from using Cloudera Manager's rolling upgrade capabilities.

Choose Method ○ Use Packages ❷

⦿ Use Parcels (Recommended) ❷   More Options

Select the version of CDH

⦿ CDH-5.6.0-1.cdh5.6.0.p0.45

○ CDH-4.7.1-1.cdh4.7.1.p0.47

Versions of CDH that are too new for this version of Cloudera Manager (5.6.0) will not be shown.

Additional Parcels ○ ACCUMULO-1.6.0-1.cdh5.1.4.p0.116

○ ACCUMULO-1.4.4-1.cdh4.5.0.p0.65

⦿ None

○ KAFKA-2.0.0-1.kafka2.0.0.p0.12

⦿ None

○ KEYTRUSTEE-5.5.0-1.cdh5.5.0.p0.215

⦿ None

○ SQOOP_NETEZZA_CONNECTOR-1.3c5

1 2 3 4 5   7 8

◄ Back

◄ Continue

Figure 2.26: Select repository for CDH installation

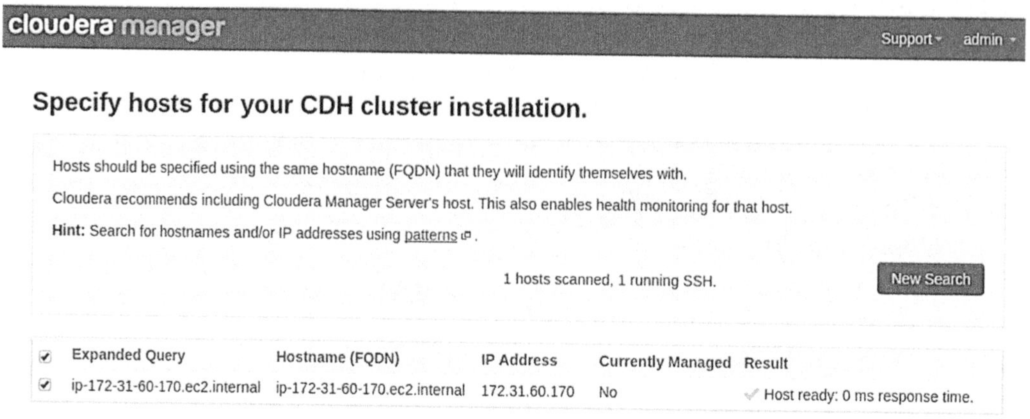

cloudera manager   Support ▾   admin ▾

Specify hosts for your CDH cluster installation.

Hosts should be specified using the same hostname (FQDN) that they will identify themselves with.

Cloudera recommends including Cloudera Manager Server's host. This also enables health monitoring for that host.

Hint: Search for hostnames and/or IP addresses using patterns ⌗ .

1 hosts scanned, 1 running SSH.   New Search

☑	Expanded Query	Hostname (FQDN)	IP Address	Currently Managed	Result
☑	ip-172-31-60-170.ec2.internal	ip-172-31-60-170.ec2.internal	172.31.60.170	No	✓ Host ready: 0 ms response time.

Figure 2.27: Specify hosts for CDH installation

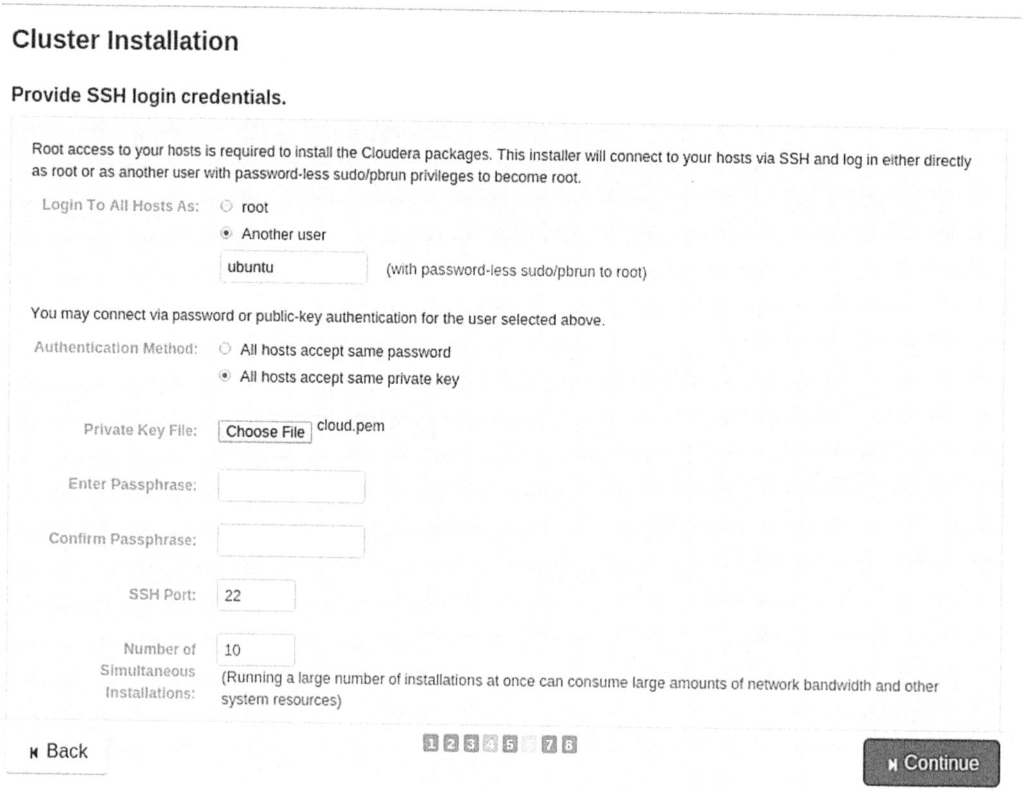

Cluster Installation

Provide SSH login credentials.

Root access to your hosts is required to install the Cloudera packages. This installer will connect to your hosts via SSH and log in either directly as root or as another user with password-less sudo/pbrun privileges to become root.

Login To All Hosts As: ○ root
                          ◉ Another user

                          [ubuntu]   (with password-less sudo/pbrun to root)

You may connect via password or public-key authentication for the user selected above.

Authentication Method: ○ All hosts accept same password
                          ◉ All hosts accept same private key

Private Key File: [Choose File] cloud.pem

Enter Passphrase: [   ]

Confirm Passphrase: [   ]

SSH Port: [22   ]

Number of   [10   ]
Simultaneous   (Running a large number of installations at once can consume large amounts of network bandwidth and other
Installations: system resources)

ĸ Back   1 2 3 4 5 6 7 8   ĸ Continue

Figure 2.28: Provide SSH login credentials for hosts

cloudera manager
Support ▾   admin ▾

Cluster Installation

Installation in progress.

0 of 1 host(s) completed successfully.   Abort Installation

Hostname	IP Address	Progress	Status	
ip-172-31-60-170.ec2.internal	172.31.60.170		⟳ Installing cloudera-manager-agent package...	Details ⧉

Figure 2.29: Cloudera Manager showing cluster installation in progress

cloudera manager
Support ▾   admin ▾

Cluster Installation

Installing Selected Parcels

The selected parcels are being downloaded and installed on all the hosts in the cluster.

✔ CDH 5.6.0-1.cdh5.6.0.p0.45   Downloaded: 100%   Distributed: 1/1 (51.8 MiB/s)   Unpacked: 1/1   Activated: 0/1

Figure 2.30: Cloudera Manager showing installation of selected parcels in progress

cloudera manager
Support ▾   admin ▾

Cluster Installation

Inspect hosts for correctness   ↻ Run Again

Validations

- ✓ Inspector ran on all 1 hosts.
- ✓ The following failures were observed in checking hostnames...
- ✓ No errors were found while looking for conflicting init scripts.
- ✓ No errors were found while checking /etc/hosts.
- ✓ All hosts resolved localhost to 127.0.0.1.
- ✓ All hosts checked resolved each other's hostnames correctly and in a timely manner.
- ✓ Host clocks are approximately in sync (within ten minutes).
- ✓ Host time zones are consistent across the cluster.
- ✓ No users or groups are missing.
- ✓ No conflicts detected between packages and parcels.
- ✓ No kernel versions that are known to be bad are running.
- ⚠ Cloudera recommends setting /proc/sys/vm/swappiness to a maximum of 10. Current setting is 60. Use the `sysctl` command to change this

◄ Back   1 2 3 4 5 7 8   ► Finish

Figure 2.31: Cloudera Manager showing cluster installation summary

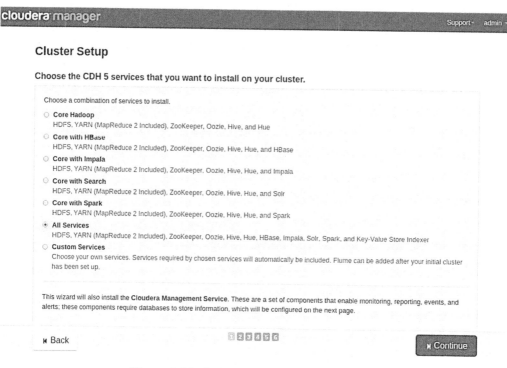

Figure 2.32: Select CDH services to install

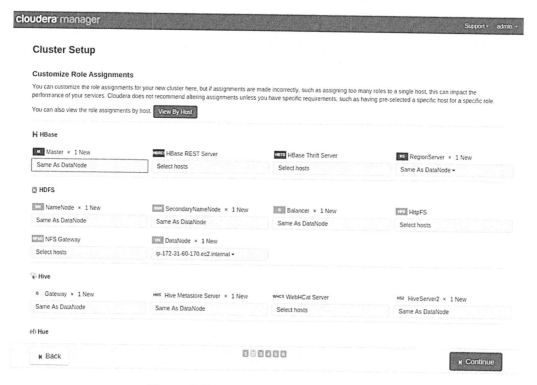

Figure 2.33: Customize role assignments

After the installation wizard is complete, you will have a working CDH cluster as shown in Figure 2.34. You can monitor the services installed, edit the service configurations and restart the services from the dashboard.

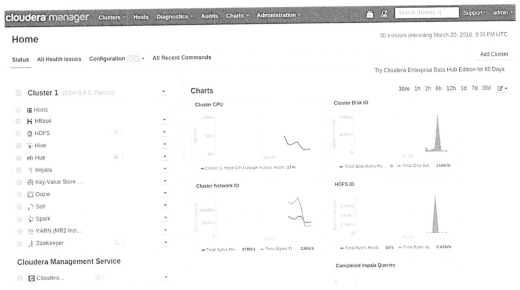

Figure 2.34: Cloudera Manager dashboard showing installed services

2.3 Amazon Elastic MapReduce (EMR)

Amazon Elastic MapReduce is a managed big data cluster platform that supports the following frameworks:

- Hadoop
- Hive
- Hue
- Mahout
- Pig
- Spark

EMR supports two launch modes - Cluster and Step execution. With the cluster launch mode, you can create clusters running the big data frameworks. You can choose the type of stack to use for the cluster (or the vendor type - EMR stack or MapR big data stack).

With the Step execution option, you add steps (which is a unit or work) to run after the cluster launches. The EMR service automatically determines the applications/frameworks that are required to complete the steps. When you create the cluster, the steps are completed, and the cluster is terminated automatically. EMR supports the following types of steps:

- Custom JAR: Custom JAR job flow runs a Java program that you have uploaded to Amazon S3.
- Hive program: You can create a Hive job flow with EMR which can either be an interactive Hive job or a Hive script.
- Streaming job: Streaming job flow runs a single Hadoop job consisting of the map and reduce functions implemented in a script or binary that you have uploaded to Amazon

S3. You can write map and reduce scripts in Ruby, Perl, Python, PHP, R, Bash, or C++.

- Pig programs: You can create a Pig job flow with EMR which can either be an interactive Pig job or a Pig script.
- Spark application: You can run a Spark application by providing the Spark application JAR and the Spark-submit options.

An EMR cluster can be created from the EMR dashboard as shown in Figure 2.35. Provide a cluster name, select an EMR release and the applications to install. Next, select the instance type to use for the cluster and the number of instances in the cluster. Next, select the EC2 key-pair that you will use to connect securely to the cluster.

Figure 2.35: Creating an Amazon EMR cluster

Once the cluster is setup, you can obtain the cluster connection details and the links to the web interfaces of the individual applications from the cluster details page as shown in Figure 2.36.

Figure 2.36: Amazon EMR cluster details

Figures 2.37-2.39 show the web interfaces of some of the applications installed on the EMR cluster.

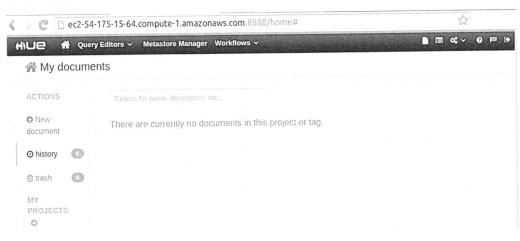

Figure 2.37: Apache Hue interface

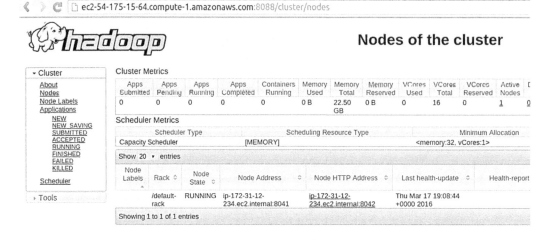

Figure 2.38: Hadoop ResourceManager interface

Overview 'ip-172-31-12-234.ec2.internal:8020' (active)

Started:	Thu Mar 17 18:56:22 UTC 2016
Version:	2.7.1-amzn-1, r72c57a1c06c471da40827b432ecff0de6a5c6dcc
Compiled:	2016-02-25T00:23Z by ec2-user from (detached from 72c57a1)
Cluster ID:	CID-5452118c-eb49-4b96-9847-3b370bf40e2c
Block Pool ID:	BP-490440241-172.31.12.234-1458240978432

Figure 2.39: Hadoop HDFS NameNode interface

2.4   Azure HDInsight

Azure HDInsight service allows you to setup managed clusters running the Hadoop ecosystem of components. HDInsight cluster can be created from the Azure portal as shown in Figure 2.40. The supported cluster types include Hadoop, HBase, Spark, and Storm.

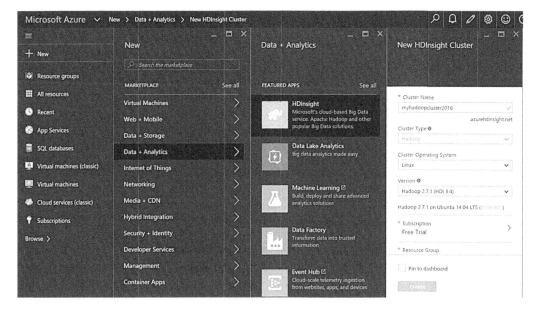

Figure 2.40: Creating Azure HDInsight cluster

Summary

In this chapter we provided four options of setting up the big data stacks and the frameworks for batch, real-time and interactive processing that are used for the examples in this book. The readers can choose any stack that suits their requirements. While the Amazon EMR and Azure HDInsight services require you to setup accounts on the respective cloud service platforms, the HDP and CDH stacks can be setup on local machines as well.

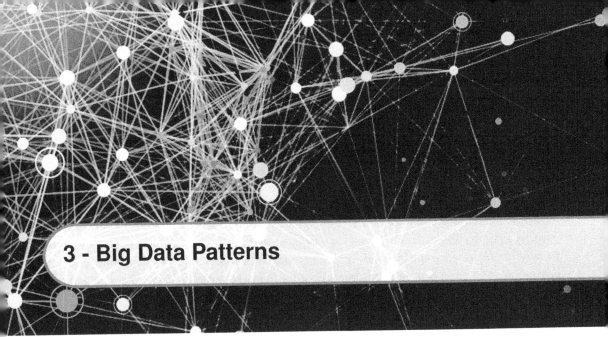

3 - Big Data Patterns

This chapter covers
- Analytics Architectural Components & Styles
  - Load Leveling with Queues
  - Load Balancing with Multiple Consumers
  - Leader Election
  - Sharding
  - Consistency, Availability & Partition Tolerance (CAP)
  - Bloom Filter
  - Materialized Views
  - Lambda Architecture
  - Scheduler-Agent-Supervisor
  - Pipes & Filters
  - Web Service
  - Consensus in Distributed Systems
- MapReduce Patterns
  - Numerical Summarization
  - Top-N
  - Filter
  - Distinct
  - Binning
  - Inverted Index
  - Sorting
  - Joins

In this chapter, we will describe various architectural components and design styles for big data systems and applications.

3.1   Analytics Architecture Components & Design Styles

3.1.1   Load Leveling with Queues

Messaging queues can be used between the data producers and data consumers in a big data system, for load leveling. Queues are are useful for push-pull messaging where the producers push data to the queues and the consumers pull the data from the queues. Since big data applications can experience high velocity of data being ingested for processing, queues can be used as buffers between the producers and consumers to prevent the consumers from being overloaded during peak loads. Queues allow decoupling of the producers and consumers. The producers and consumers do not need to be aware of each other and can run asynchronously.

When queues are used, the consumers can be scaled-up or down based on the load levels. Queues help in improving the system reliability and availability. In case the consumer becomes unavailable temporarily, the producer can still continue pushing messages to the queue.

In Chapter-5, we describe messaging queues such as RabbitMQ, ZeroMQ, RESTMQ and Amazon SQS.

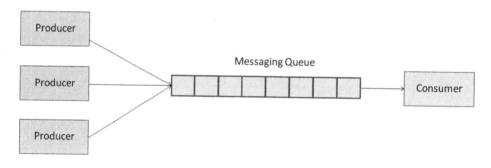

Figure 3.1: Load Leveling with Queues

3.1.2   Load Balancing with Multiple Consumers

While messaging queues can be used between data producer and consumer for load leveling, having multiple consumers can help in load balancing and making the system more scalable, reliable and available. Data producer(s) push messages to the queue and the consumers retrieve and process the messages. Multiple consumers can make the system more robust as there is no single point of failure. More consumers can be added on-demand if the workload is high. Load balancing between consumers improves the system performance as multiple consumers can process messages in parallel. This patterns is useful when the messages can be processed independently without any dependencies. When multiple consumers are used, the messaging queue is configured to deliver each message at-least once. When a consumer retrieves a message, it is not deleted from the queue, but hidden from other consumers (with a visibility timeout) to prevent duplicate processing. After the message is processed, the consumer deletes it from the queue. In case the consumer fails while processing a message, the message become available to other consumers after the visibility timeout period. This ensures that the message is not lost and is processed by one of the consumers before being deleted.

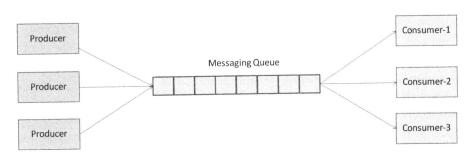

Figure 3.2: Load Balancing with Multiple Consumers

3.1.3 Leader Election

Big data systems include multiple nodes or instances which store, process and analyze data. In such systems, there is a need for coordinating the actions performed by the instances, as the instances may be accessing shared resources. Coordination becomes important when the instances are running in parallel and each instance is computing a small portion of a complex computation. In such distributed systems, a leader is assigned the role of managing the instances and coordinating their state and actions.

Leader election is a mechanism by which the instances in a distributed system can elect one of the instances as their leader. In the simplest leader election mechanism the instance with the highest ID is elected as the leader. This mechanism works when the instances have unique IDs assigned to them. When the leader election process is run, the instances communicate amongst themselves and elect the instance with highest ID as their leader. Each instance is aware of the leader when the election process is completed. An important requirement for any leader election mechanism is that the mechanism should be able to elect exactly one instance as the leader and all the instances should know who the leader is when the election process completes.

Another leader election algorithm is the Bully algorithm. This algorithm assumes that the instances are able to communicate with each other and each instance knows the ID of every other instance. The Bully algorithm works as follows. An instance A initiates the leader election if it notices that the leader has failed. The instance A sends the election message to other instances with higher IDs and awaits for their response. If no response is received, A declares itself as the leader and notifies all other instances. If the instance A receives a response from some other instance, it drops out of the election and waits for another instance to declare itself as the leader. If the instance does not receive any response from another instance declaring itself as the leader, it resends the election message to instances with higher IDs. If the instance A receives a message from an instance with lower ID declaring itself as the leader, the instance A initiates a new election.

3.1.4   Sharding

Sharding involves horizontally partitioning the data across multiple storage nodes in a data storage system. In big data applications, the volume of data involved is so large that is not possible to store the data on a single machine. While vertical scaling (by addition of more compute, storage and memory resources) can be a temporary solution to handle larger volumes of data, however, the data will ultimately become too large to be stored on a single storage node. Moreover, a single machine can only serve a limited number of concurrent user queries. When applications have large number of concurrent users, sharding can help in improving the system performance and response times for the users as the queries are served by multiple nodes. Many data storage systems provide auto-sharding, where the data is automatically partitioned and distributed among the storage nodes. Sharding enables the storage system to be scaled out by addition of new nodes. The data shards (partitions) can be replicated across the storage nodes to make the system more reliable. When the shards are replicated, load balancing of queries can be done to improve the response times.

Sharding can be accomplished by various sharding strategies, that can either be managed by the application or the data storage system. Sharding strategies determine which data should be sent to which shard. Most sharding strategies use one or more fields in the data as the shard key (or partition key). The shard key used must be unique (can be either the primary key or a composite key). The most common approach is to use a hash function that evenly partitions the data across the storage nodes. The hash function is applied to the shard key to determine the shard in which the data should be stored. By evenly spreading the data across the storage nodes, the hashing approach prevents a single storage node becoming a hotspot. Another approach is to store data within a range of shard keys in one shard. The system maintains a map of the range keys and the corresponding shards. This strategy is useful when you want to keep data which is retrieved and updated together in one shard to avoid repeated lookups. For example, the most recent orders (with order IDs within a particular range) in an eCommerce application can be stored in one shard.

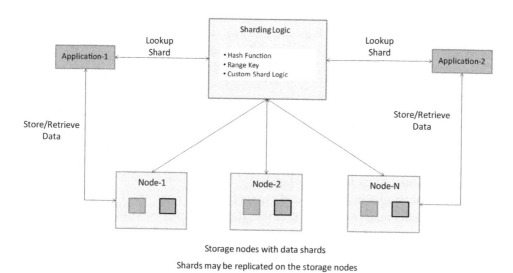

Figure 3.3: Sharding

3.1.5 Consistency, Availability & Partition Tolerance (CAP)

For distributed data systems, a trade-off exists between consistency and availability. These trade-offs are explained with the CAP Theorem, which states that under partitioning, a distributed data system can either be consistent or available but not both at the same time.

A consistent system is one in which all reads are guaranteed to incorporate the previous writes. In a consistent system, after an update operation is performed by a writer, it is seen by all the readers. Availability refers to the ability of the system to respond to all the queries without being unavailable. A distributed data system is called available when it can continue to perform its operations even in the event of failure of some of the nodes. Partition tolerance refers to the ability of the system to continue performing its operations in the event of network partitions. Network paritions can occur when two (or more) sets of nodes are unable to connect to each other.

The CAP theorem states that the system can either favor consistency and partition tolerance over availability, or favor availability and partition tolerance over consistency. Let us take the example of NoSQL databases such as Amazon DynamoDB and Cassandra. These databases prefer consistency and partition tolerance over availability. Such systems are said to be "eventually consistent" as all the writes are eventually (not immediately) seen by all the nodes. In an eventually consistent system, clients can experience an inconsistent state of the system while the updates are being propagated to all the nodes and the system has not yet reached a steady state. In the event of network partitions, all the nodes may not have the most recent updates and may return inconsistent or out-dated information. When the network partitions are resolved all the nodes eventually see the updates.

HBase, in contrast to DynamoDB and Cassandra, prefers consistency and partition tolerance over availability. By adopting strong consistency, HBase ensures that updates are immediately available to all clients. In the event of network partitions, the system can become unavailable to ensure consistency.

3.1.6 Bloom Filter

In many big data systems and applications, the
element is a member of a set. For example, te
of values. In distributed data systems, where th
there may be a requirement to check whether a
particular partition. For such systems, Bloom fil

Bloom filter is a probabilistic data structure
initially set to 0. To add an element to the set
map the element to one of the positions in the
set membership of an element, the same hash f
bit array. If the bit in that position is 0, the elen
bit is 1, the element may or may not be preser
mapped to the same position could have set the
that it can give a definitive answer whether an
false positives, claiming that an element is in the set while it is not. The number of false positives can be tuned to less 1%. False positives are not a problem for systems using Bloom filters because the systems are designed to further check for set membership after checking with Bloom filter.

The benefit of using Bloom filter is that it is a space-efficient structure and stores only a small number of bits instead of storing the elements themselves. The time required for adding a new element to the set or testing for set membership is a fixed constant ($O(k)$) and independent of the number of elements already in set.

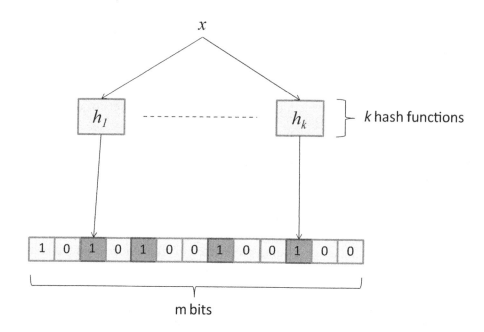

Figure 3.4: Bloom Filter

3.1.7   Materialized Views

For big data applications that involve certain queries that are frequently performed, it is beneficial to pre-compute such queries to improve the response times. Such pre-computed views are called Materialized Views. Materialized views are suitable for queries that are either too complex to compute in real-time (such as complex joins) or involve large volumes of data to be aggregated. Such queries can be precomputed and stored on the disk or a cache. Materialized views are also beneficial for applications which use distributed data storage systems such as distributed NoSQL databases. In such data storage systems, the data stored may not be in a format to enable fast computation of complex queries (as the data may be in a normalized form or unstructured). For example, let us consider an eCommerce application that allows various sellers to list and sell their products online. In such an application, each seller can view the total orders in last 30 days or total sale volume in last 30 days. For such queries, materialized views can be used to improve the application performance as computing these at runtime may involve retrieving a large number of orders. Materialized views can either be updated on a regular basis (hourly or daily basis) or every time there is an update to the data involved (for example, every time a new order comes in). Materialized views are suitable for queries where even approximate or slightly inconsistent results would suffice.

3.1.8 Lambda Architecture

Lambda Architecture is a scalable and fault-tolerant data processing architecture suitable for applications involving fast streams of incoming data (which is immutable and timestamped). Lambda architecture enables both querying real-time and historical data, by pre-computing the queries. Lambda architecture comprises of the following layers:

- **Batch Layer**: Batch layer is responsible for storing the master dataset (which is immutable and append-only set of raw data), and pre-computing the batch views.
- **Serving Layer**: The Serving layer indexes the batch views to enable fast querying of the data.
- **Speed Layer**: The Speed layer fills in the gap created due to the high latency of updates of the batch layer, by processing the recent data in real time. Speed layer uses incremental algorithms to process the recent data and generate real-time views.

To batch views and real-time views are merged to respond to the incoming queries. In Chapter-7 we describe the Hadoop framework that can be used for the batch layer. In Chapter-8, we describe the Storm and Spark frameworks that can be used for the speed layer. In Chapter-10, we describe various NoSQL databases which can be used for the serving layer.

Lambda architecture can be used to respond to queries in an ad-hoc manner by pre-computing the views. While the batch layer processes all the data, the speed layer only processes the most recent data. The speed layer processes the recent data which is not represented in the batch view, i.e. the data which comes in after the batch view is updated (and while the batch layer is processing the next batch). The speed layer does not process all the recent data at one time. Instead, speed layer uses incremental algorithms which enable the speed layer to update the real-time views as the new data comes in. If new queries are to be served which are not precomputed, the batch and speed layers can be updated with the logic to pre-compute the new queries and batch analytics tasks can be run on the entire dataset to pre-compute views. The serving layer supports batch updates, so that whenever new views are generated they can be updated and indexed. By indexing the views, serving layers enables fast random reads to serve the queries.

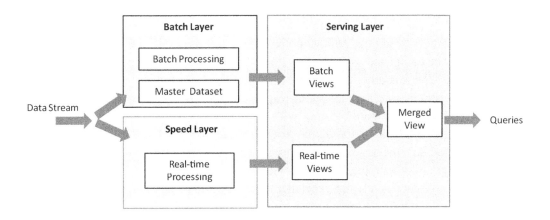

Figure 3.5: Lambda Architecture

3.1.9   Scheduler-Agent-Supervisor

Big data systems comprising of distributed set of worker nodes that executes the tasks submitted by the applications, require some mechanism to ensure that the task executions can be coordinated and the tasks that fail can be retried. The Scheduler-Agent-Supervisor pattern can be used to make the system more resilient and fault tolerant.

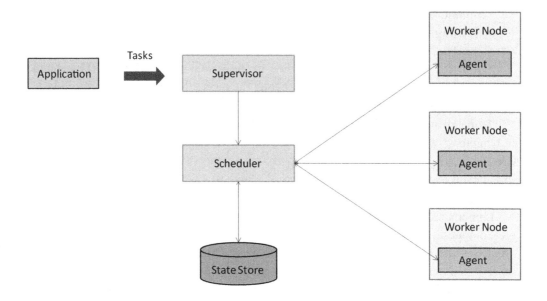

Figure 3.6: Scheduler-Agent-Supervisor

This pattern defines three types of components:

- **Scheduler**: The Scheduler component is responsible for assigning the tasks to the worker nodes and tracking the progress of each task. Applications submit new tasks to the Scheduler, which assigns them to the available worker nodes. The Scheduler maintains a state store (which can be maintained in a NoSQL database or an in-memory key-value store), in which the status of each task is stored and updated as the tasks progress. The state information for each task may include the status of the task (such as scheduled, running, completed or failed) and the desired time by which the task should be completed (*complete-by* time).
- **Agent**: The scheduler assigns the tasks to the worker nodes by notifying the agent. Each worker node has an agent (typically running on the node itself). Agent is responsible for communicating with the scheduler for new tasks and notifying the worker node for provisioning the resources required for execution of the tasks. Agent sends the information on the task progress to the scheduler. In some implementations, the agent may send heart-beast messages to the scheduler to notify it about the task progress. Alternatively, the scheduler while assigning a task can notify the agent of the *complete-by* time. When the task completes, the agent notifies the scheduler. If the scheduler does not receive the task completion notification, it can assume that the task failed.
- **Supervisor**: The Supervisor is responsible for monitoring the status of each task (for

which the task status is tracked by the Scheduler). The Supervisor, checks for tasks which have failed or tasks which have timed out, and notifies the Scheduler to retry the tasks. In some implementations, the Supervisor can keep track of the *retry-counts* for each task to prevent the tasks which continually fail from being retried. The Supervisor can also increase the *retry-interval* after each unsuccessful attempt to complete a task.

3.1.10   Pipes & Filters

In many big data applications, a complex data processing task can be split into a series of distinct tasks to improve the system performance, scalability, and reliability. This pattern of splitting a complex task into a series of distinct tasks is called the Pipes and Filters pattern, where pipes are the connections between the filters (processing components).

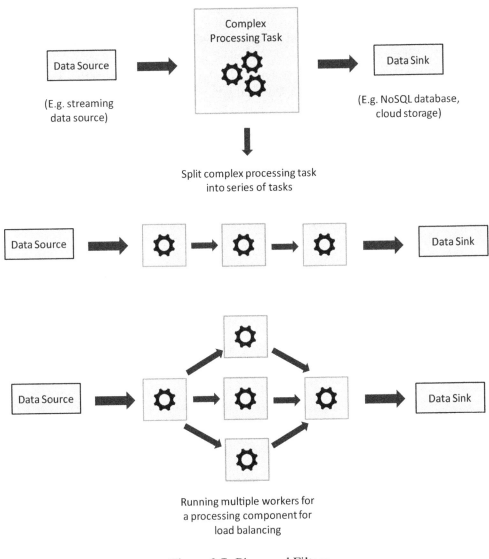

Figure 3.7: Pipes and Filters

The benefit of this pattern is that each task performs a portion of the work and can be scaled independently. By running multiple workers for each task, processing can be done in parallel. Running multiple workers also makes the system more reliable, because even if some workers fail, the entire pipeline does not fail as other workers can continue processing. This pattern is particularly useful for real-time analytics applications that involve processing of streams of data. In Chapter-8, we describe how the Storm framework makes use of a similar pattern for reliable processing of streams of data.

3.1.11   Web Service

Big data systems can use different data storage systems and databases. A client application that accesses the big data systems for querying and retrieving the data can be decoupled from the big data system by using a web service. The web service can provide an interface that exposes the functionality of the system to the clients in the form of various endpoints. When a web service is used, the client does not need to be aware of how the data is stored by the system. The client can send a request to the web service in a standard format (such as REST) and receive the response in a standard format (such as JSON or XML). The web service allows the client and the system to be developed independently. The system can switch to a different database (while keeping the web service interface the same) and the client is unaffected by the change.

To make the system more secure, a Gatekeeper component can be used, which is typically deployed on a separate node. The gatekeeper performs authentication, authorization, and validation of the requests. Authentication involves verifying the identity of a client whereas authentication involves verifying if the client has sufficient permissions for the requested operation. The use of a Gatekeeper makes the system more secure and minimizes the risk of a client gaining access to the system (or the servers) which processes the request and has access to the data.

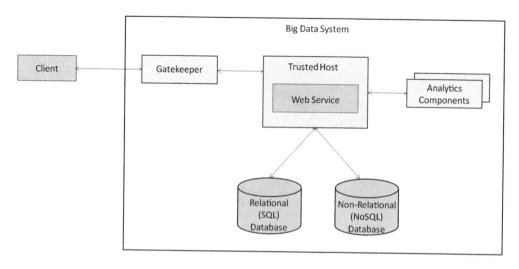

Figure 3.8: Web service to decouple client from big data system

3.1.12 Consensus in Distributed Systems

In distributed systems, the consensus is the problem of getting all the nodes to agree on something. Consensus may be required for various purposes such as agreeing on a data value to commit, deciding if a transaction should be committed, agreeing on a node to act as the leader or synchronization of clocks. The consensus problem becomes more complicated for distributed systems in which the nodes can be unreliable and can fail. Consensus protocols for such systems must be fault tolerant. A consensus protocol for a distributed system is correct if it satisfies the following properties:

- Agreement: The nodes in the distributed system must agree on some value.
- Validity: Only a value that has been proposed by some node must be chosen.
- Termination: All nodes must eventually agree on some value.

The most famous protocol for consensus in distributed systems is the Paxos protocol that was proposed by Leslie Lamport [19]. In this section, we will briefly describe the Paxos protocol. (For a more detailed description on Paxos, refer to the 'Paxos Made Simple' paper from Leslie Lamport [20]). Paxos defines the following actors:

- Proposer: Proposer is the node which initiates the protocol and acts as the coordinator.
- Acceptor: Acceptors are the nodes which try to agree on some value which is proposed by a proposer.
- Learners: Learners are the nodes which learn the value which is agreed on by the acceptors.

The protocol proceeds with the following steps:

- Prepare: A Proposer sends a proposal identified by a sequence number N to a majority of the Acceptors (called the Quorum) and waits for their response.
- Promise: Each Acceptor on receiving a proposal compares it with the highest numbered proposal which it has already received. If the new proposal has a higher sequence number, the acceptor agrees to accept the proposal with the *Promise* that all future proposals with a sequence number lower than N will be rejected. When the Acceptors agree on a proposal, they also send back to the proposer, the value of any proposal already accepted.

  If the new proposal has a sequence number lower than some earlier proposal, the Acceptors reject the new proposal.
- Accept Request: When the Proposer receives responses from a majority of the Acceptors (i.e. the Quorum), accepting the proposal, it knows the value accepted by the Acceptors and any value previously accepted. The Proposer then picks the value with the highest sequence number and sends an *Accept Request* to the Acceptors. If the Acceptors have not agreed on any previous value, the Proposer selects its value and send the Accept Request.

  If the majority of the Acceptors reject the proposal, the proposal is abandoned and the process is initiated again.
- Accepted: When the Acceptors receive the Accept Request, they accept the value, if it is the same as any previously accepted value and its sequence number is the highest number they have agreed to. Otherwise, the request is rejected. When the Accept Request is accepted, the accepted value is committed by the acceptors and also communicated to all the Learners.

Since the process of agreeing on a value proposed by a proposer also identifies the proposer whose value is accepted, the same process can also be used for leader election. The protocol discussed above is the basic form of Paxos protocol. However, in practice, a more optimized version of the protocol called Multi-Paxos is used which does away with the Prepare and Promise steps assuming that in a steady state, one of the proposers has already been chosen as the distinguished proposer (or the leader) and leadership change is going to be rare.

The use of sequence numbers for proposal allows the acceptors to order the proposals and accept the proposal with the highest sequence number. Since in a distributed system where messages are delivered asynchronously, the messages can take arbitrarily long time to get delivered, the acceptors can decide on which value to agree by ordering the proposals by the sequence numbers.

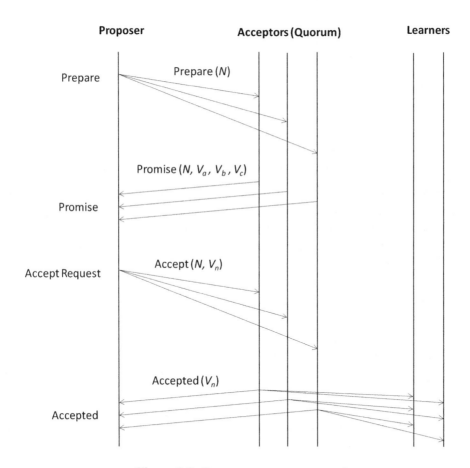

Figure 3.9: Paxos consensus protocol

3.2 MapReduce Patterns

MapReduce is a popular programming model for data intensive applications. MapReduce has been used for batch analysis of data in a wide range of applications (such as social networking, e-Commerce, finance, entertainment, government, healthcare, telecom, etc.). MapReduce allows the developers to focus on developing data-intensive applications without having to worry about issues such as input splitting, scheduling, load balancing and failover.

MapReduce programming model for processing data on large clusters was originally proposed by Dean and Ghemawat [22]. Hadoop, which is an open source large-scale distributed batch processing framework, provides an implementation of the MapReduce model. Hadoop and MapReduce have made it easier for developing scalable and data intensive applications for cloud computing environments.

MapReduce model has two phases: Map and Reduce. MapReduce programs are written in a functional programming style to create Map and Reduce functions. The input data to the map and reduce phases is in the form of key-value pairs. Run-time systems for MapReduce are typically large clusters built of commodity hardware. The MapReduce run-time systems take care of tasks such partitioning the data, scheduling of jobs and communication between nodes in the cluster. This makes it easier for programmers to analyze massive scale data without worrying about tasks such as data partitioning and scheduling.

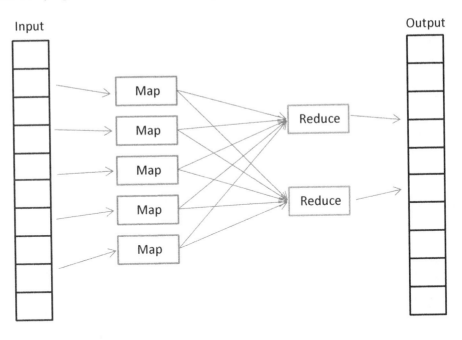

Figure 3.10: Data flow in MapReduce

Figure 3.10 shows the flow of data for a MapReduce job. MapReduce programs take a set of input key-value pairs and produce a set of output key-value pairs. In the Map phase, data is read from a distributed file system, partitioned among a set of computing nodes in the cluster, and sent to the nodes as a set of key-value pairs. The Map tasks process the input records independently of each other and produce intermediate results as key-value pairs. The intermediate results are stored on the local disk of the node running the Map task. The choice of the key and value pairs at this step depends on the data analysis task to be accomplished.

When all the Map tasks are completed, the Reduce phase begins with the shuffle and sort step, in which the intermediate data is sorted by the key and the key-value pairs are grouped and shuffled to the reduce tasks. The reduce tasks then take the key-value pairs grouped by the key and run the reduce function for each group of key-value pairs. The data processing logic in reduce function depends on the analysis task to be accomplished.

An optional Combine task can be used to perform data aggregation on the intermediate data of the same key for the output of the mapper before transferring the output to the Reduce task.

In this section, we will describe various MapReduce patterns for data analysis, along with the implementations in Python. The Python implementations use the MRJob Python library which lets you write MapReduce jobs in Python and run them on several platforms including local machine, Hadoop cluster and Amazon Elastic MapReduce (EMR). The Hadoop framework is covered in detail in Chapter-7, where more detailed case studies for batch analysis of data using MapReduce are described. MapReduce schedulers are also described in Chapter-7.

3.2.1   Numerical Summarization

Numerical summarization patterns are used to compute various statistics such as counts, maximum, minimum, mean, etc. These statistics help in presenting the data in a summarized form. For example, computing the total number of likes for a particular post, computing the average monthly rainfall or finding the average number of visitors per month on a website.

For the examples in this section, we will use synthetic data similar to the data collected by a web analytics service that shows various statistics for page visits for a website. Each page has some tracking code which sends the visitor's IP address along with a timestamp to the web analytics service. The web analytics service keeps a record of all page visits and the visitor IP addresses and uses MapReduce programs for computing various statistics. Each visit to a page is logged as one row in the log. The log file contains the following columns: Date (YYYY-MM-DD), Time (HH:MM:SS), URL, IP, Visit-Length.

Count

To compute count, the mapper function emits key-value pairs where the key is the field to group-by and value is either '1' or any related items required to compute count. The reducer function receives the key-value pairs grouped by the same key and adds up the values for each group to compute count. Let us look at an example of computing the total number of times each page is visited in the year 2014, from the web analytics service logs. Box 3.1 shows the Python program for counting the page visits using MapReduce. Figure 3.11 shows the data and the key-value pairs at each step of the MapReduce job for computing count. The mapper function in this example parses each line of the input and emits key-value pairs where the key is the URL and value is '1'. The reducer receives the list of values grouped by the key and sums up the values to compute count.

■ Box 3.1: Python program for computing count with MapReduce

```python
#Total number of times each page is visited in the year 2014

from mrjob.job import MRJob

class MRmyjob(MRJob):
  def mapper(self, _, line):
    #Split the line with tab separated fields
    data=line.split('')

    #Parse line
    date = data[0].strip()
    time = data[1].strip()
    url = data[2].strip()
    ip = data[3].strip()

    #Extract year from date
    year=date[0:4]

    #Emit URL and 1 if year is 2014
    if year=='2014':
      yield url, 1


  def reducer(self, key, list_of_values):
    yield key,sum(list_of_values)


if __name__ == '__main__':
  MRmyjob.run()
```

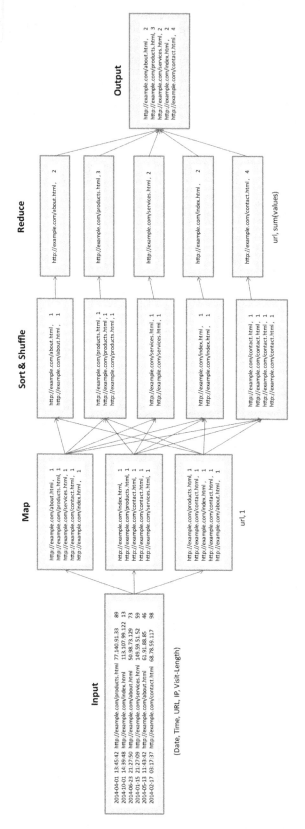

Figure 3.11: Computing count with MapReduce

Max/Min

To compute maximum or minimum, the mapper function emits key-value pairs where the key is the field to group-by and value contains related items required to compute maximum or minimum. The reducer function receives the list of values grouped by the same key and finds the minimum or maximum value. Let us look at an example of computing the most visited page in each month of the year 2014, from the web analytics service logs. Box 3.2 shows the Python program for computing the most visited page using MapReduce. Figure 3.12 shows the data and the key-value pairs at each step of the MapReduce job for finding most visited page. This example uses the multi-step feature of the mrJob Python library which allows you to have multiple reduce phases within a job. The MapReduce execution framework may consider it as multiple MapReduce jobs chained together. The mapper function in this example parses each line of the input and emits key-value pairs where the key is a tuple comprising of month and URL, and the value is '1'. The reducer receives the list of values grouped by the key and sums up the values to count the visits for each page in each month. The reducer emits month as the key and a tuple comprising of page visit count and page URL as the value. The second reducer receives a list of (visit count, URL) pairs grouped by the same month, and computes the maximum visit count from the list of values. The second reducer emits month as the key and a tuple comprising of maximum page visit count and page URL and the value. In this example, a two-step job was required because we need to compute the page visit counts first before finding the maximum count.

■ **Box 3.2: Python program for computing maximum with MapReduce**

```
# Most visited page in each month of year 2014

from mrjob.job import MRJob

class MRmyjob(MRJob):
  def mapper1(self, _, line):
    #Split the line with tab separated fields
    data=line.split('')

    #Parse line
    date = data[0].strip()
    time = data[1].strip()
    url = data[2].strip()
    ip = data[3].strip()

    #Extract year from date
    year=date[0:4]
    month=date[5:7]

    #Emit (month,url) pair and 1 if year is 2014
    if year=='2014':
      yield (month,url), 1


  def reducer1(self, key, list_of_values):
    yield key[0], (sum(list_of_values), key[1])
```

```
def reducer2(self, key, list_of_values):
  yield key, max(list_of_values)


def steps(self):
  return [self.mr(mapper=self.mapper1,
    reducer=self.reducer1), self.mr(reducer=self.reducer2)]


if __name__ == '__main__':
  MRmyjob.run()
```

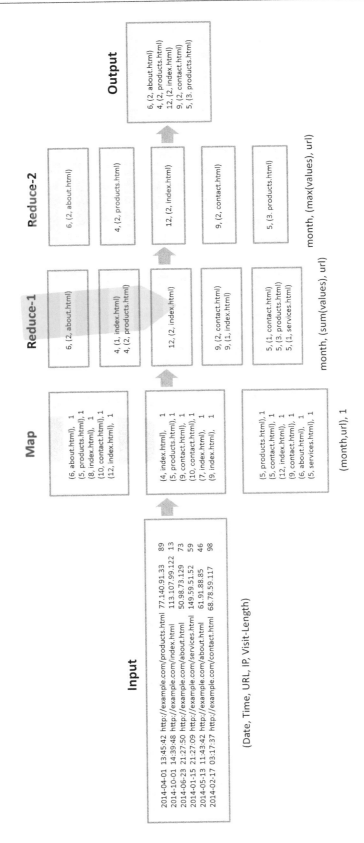

Figure 3.12: Computing maximum with MapReduce

Average

To compute the average, the mapper function emits key-value pairs where the key is the field to group-by and value contains related items required to compute the average. The reducer function receives the list of values grouped by the same key and finds the average value. Let us look at an example of computing the average visit length for each page. Box 3.3 shows the Python program for computing the average visit length using MapReduce. Figure 3.13 shows the data and the key-value pairs at each step of the MapReduce job. The mapper function in this example parses each line of the input and emits key-value pairs where the key is the URL and value is the visit length. The reducer receives the list of values grouped by the key (which is the URL) and finds the average of these values.

■ **Box 3.3: Python program for computing average with MapReduce**

```
#Average visit length for each page

from mrjob.job import MRJob

class MRmyjob(MRJob):
  def mapper(self, _, line):
    #Split the line with tab separated fields
    data=line.split('\t')

    #Parse line
    date = data[0].strip()
    time = data[1].strip()
    url = data[2].strip()
    ip = data[3].strip()
    visit_len = int(data[4].strip())

    year=date[0:4]
    month=date[5:7]

    yield url, visit_len


  def reducer(self, key, list_of_values):
    count = 0
    total = 0.0
    for x in list_of_values:
      total = total+x
      count=count+1

    avgLen = ("%.2f" % (total/count))
    yield key, avgLen


if __name__ == '__main__':
  MRmyjob.run()
```

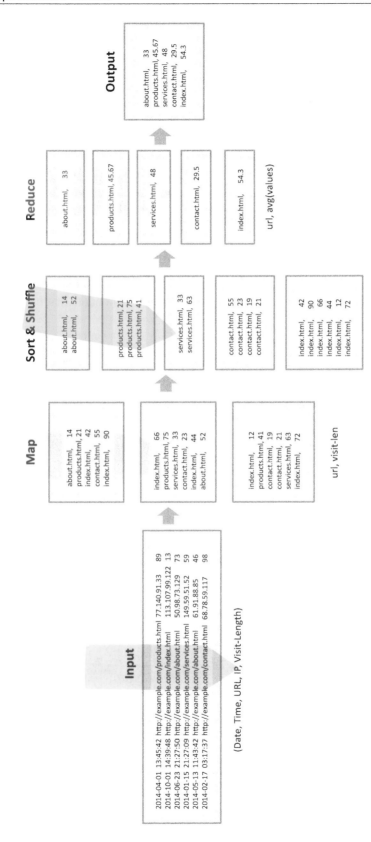

Figure 3.13: Computing average with MapReduce

3.2.2 Top-N

To find the top-N records, the mapper function emits key-value pairs where the key is the field to group by and value contains related items required to compute top-N. The reducer function receives the list of values grouped by the same key, sorts the values and emits the top-N values for each key. In an alternative approach, each mapper emits its local top-N records and the reducer then finds the global top-N. Let us look at an example of computing the top 3 visited page in each month of the year 2014. Box 3.4 shows the Python program for computing the top visited pages using MapReduce. Figure 3.14 shows the data and the key-value pairs at each step of the MapReduce job. The mapper function in this example parses each line of the input and emits key-value pairs where the key is the URL and value is '1'. The reducer receives the list of values grouped by the key and sums up the values to count the visits for each page. The reducer emits None as the key and a tuple comprising of page visit count and page URL and the value. The second reducer receives a list of (visit count, URL) pairs all grouped together (as the key is None). The reducer sorts the visit counts and emits top 3 visit counts along with the page URLs. In this example, a two-step job was required because we need to compute the page visit counts first before finding the top 3 visited pages.

■ **Box 3.4: Python program for computing Top-N with MapReduce**

```
# Top 3 visited page in each month of year 2014

from mrjob.job import MRJob

class MRmyjob(MRJob):
  def mapper(self, _, line):
    #Split the line with tab separated fields
    data=line.split('')

    #Parse line
    date = data[0].strip()
    time = data[1].strip()
    url = data[2].strip()
    ip = data[3].strip()
    visit_len=int(data[4].strip())
    #Extract year from date
    year=date[0:4]
    month=date[5:7]

    #Emit url and 1 if year is 2014
    if year=='2014':
      yield url, 1


  def reducer(self, key, list_of_values):
    total_count = sum(list_of_values)
    yield None, (total_count, key)


  def reducer2(self, _, list_of_values):
```

```
    N = 3
    list_of_values = sorted(list(list_of_values), reverse=True)
    return list_of_values[:N]


  def steps(self):
    return [self.mr(mapper=self.mapper1,
      reducer=self.reducer1), self.mr(reducer=self.reducer2)]


if __name__ == '__main__':
  MRmyjob.run()
```

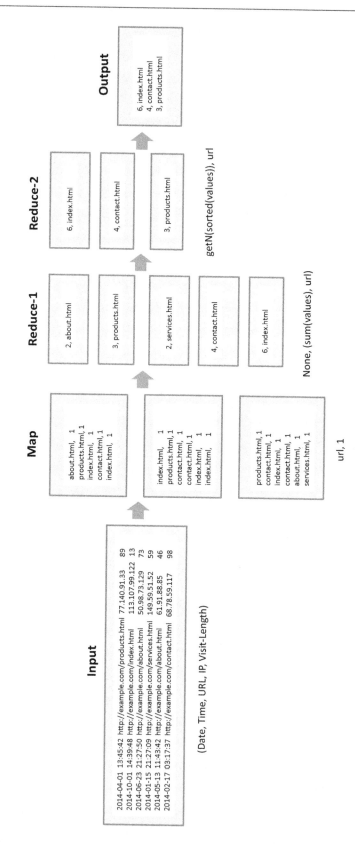

Figure 3.14: Computing Top-N with MapReduce

3.2.3 Filter

The filtering pattern is used to filter out a subset of the records based on a filtering criteria. The records themselves are not changed or processed. Filtering is useful when you want to get a subset of the data for further processing. Filtering requires only a Map task. Each mapper filters out its local records based on the filtering criteria in the map function. Let us look at an example of filtering all page visits for the page 'contact.html' in the month of Dec 2014, in the web analytics service log. Box 3.5 shows the Python program for filtering records using MapReduce. Figure 3.15 shows the data and the key-value pairs at each step of the MapReduce job. The mapper function in this example parses each line of the input, extracts the month, year and page URL and emits key-value pairs if the month and year are Dec 2014 and the page URL is 'http://example.com/contact.html'. The key is the URL, and the value is a tuple containing the rest of the parsed fields.

■ **Box 3.5: Python program for filtering data with MapReduce**

```
# Filter all page visits for the page 'contact.html' in the month of Dec
2014.

from mrjob.job import MRJob

class MRmyjob(MRJob):
  def mapper(self, _, line):
    #Split the line with tab separated fields
    data=line.split('⌒')

    #Parse line
    date = data[0].strip()
    time = data[1].strip()
    url = data[2].strip()
    ip = data[3].strip()
    visit_len=int(data[4].strip())
    #Extract year from date
    year=date[0:4]
    month=date[5:7]

    #Emit (month,url) pair and 1 if year is 2014
    if year=='2014' and month=='12' and
      url=='http://example.com/contact.html':
      yield url, (date,time,ip,visit_len)


if __name__ == '__main__':
  MRmyjob.run()
```

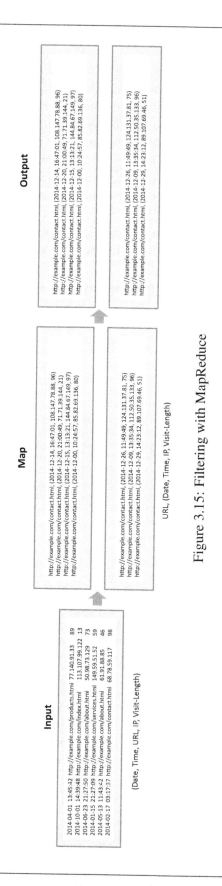

Figure 3.15: Filtering with MapReduce

3.2.4 Distinct

Distinct pattern is used to filter out duplicate records or emit distinct values of sub-fields in the dataset. Finding distinct records is simple with MapReduce as the records with the same key are grouped together in the reduce phase. The mapper function emits key-value pairs where key is the field for which we want to find distinct (maybe a sub-field in a record or the entire record) and value is None. The reducer function receives key-value pairs grouped by the same key and emits the key and value as None. Let us look at an example of distinct IP addresses in the web analytics service log. Box 3.6 shows the Python program for finding distinct values using MapReduce. Figure 3.16 shows the data and the key-value pairs at each step of the MapReduce job. The mapper function in this example parses each line of the input and emits key-value pairs where the key is the IP address and value is None. The reducer receives the list of values (all None) grouped by the key (unique IP addresses) and emits the key and value as None.

■ **Box 3.6: Python program for computing distinct with MapReduce**

```
# Distint IP addresses

from mrjob.job import MRJob

class MRmyjob(MRJob):
  def mapper(self, _, line):
    #Split the line with tab separated fields
    data=line.split('')

    #Parse line
    date = data[0].strip()
    time = data[1].strip()
    url = data[2].strip()
    ip = data[3].strip()
    visit_printlen=int(data[4].strip())
    yield ip, None


  def reducer(self, key, list_of_values):
    yield key, None


if __name__ == '__main__':
  MRmyjob.run()
```

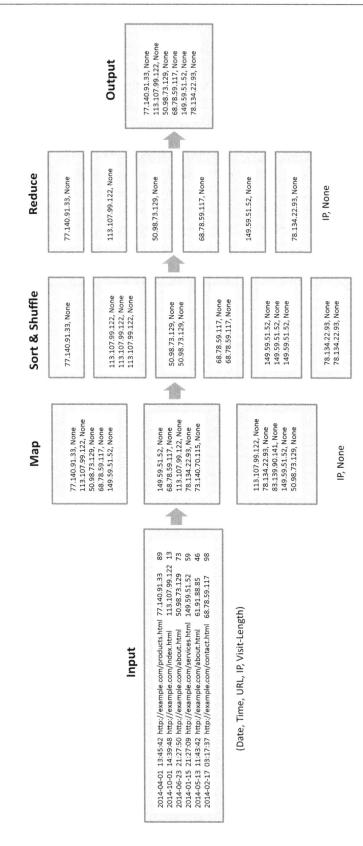

Figure 3.16: Finding distinct with MapReduce

3.2.5 Binning

The Binning pattern is used to partition records into bins or categories. Binning is useful when you want to partition your dataset into different bins (based on a partitioning criteria) and further process records in each bin separately or process records in certain bins. Binning requires a Map task only. In the mapper function, each record is checked using a list of criteria and assigned to a particular bin. The mapper function emits key-value pairs where the key is the bin and value is the record. No processing is done for the record in this pattern. Let us look at an example of partitioning records by the quarter (Q1-Q4) in the web analytics service log. Box 3.7 shows the Python program for partitioning records using MapReduce. Figure 3.17 shows the data and the key-value pairs at each step of the MapReduce job.

■ **Box 3.7: Python program for binning data with MapReduce**

```python
# Parition records by Quarter

from mrjob.job import MRJob

class MRmyjob(MRJob):
  def mapper(self, _, line):
    #Split the line with tab separated fields
    data=line.split('')

    #Parse line
    date = data[0].strip()
    time = data[1].strip()
    url = data[2].strip()
    ip = data[3].strip()
    visit_len=int(data[4].strip())

    #Extract year from date
    year=date[0:4]
    month=int(date[5:7])

    #Emit url and 1 if year is 2014
    if year=='2014':
      if month<=3:
        yield "Q1", (date, time, url, ip, visit_len)
      elif month<=6:
        yield "Q2", (date, time, url, ip, visit_len)
      elif month<=9:
        yield "Q3", (date, time, url, ip, visit_len)
      else:
        yield "Q4", (date, time, url, ip, visit_len)


if __name__ == '__main__':
  MRmyjob.run()
```

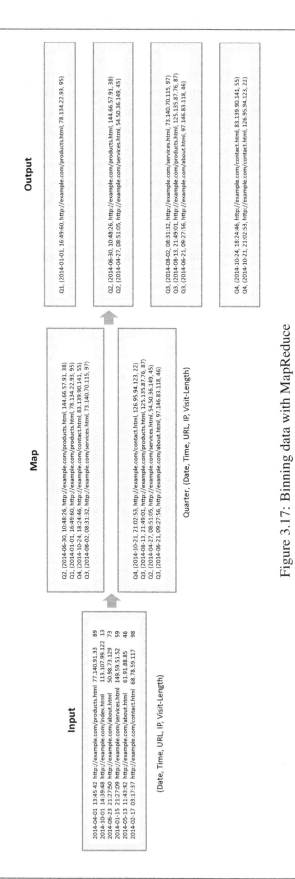

Figure 3.17: Binning data with MapReduce

3.2.6 Inverted Index

An inverted index is an index data structure which stores the mapping from the content (such as words in a document or on a webpage) to the location of the content (such as document filename or a page URL). Search engines use inverted indexes to enable faster searching of documents or pages containing some specific content.

To generate an inverted index, the mapper function emits key-value pairs where key contains the fields for the index (such as each word in the document), and the value is a unique identifier of the document. The reducer function receives the list of values (such as document IDs) grouped by the same key (word) and emits a key and the list of values. Let us look at an example of an inverted index for multiple books. Let us assume we have all the content from all the books combined into one large file with two fields separated by a pipe symbol ('|'). The first field is the filename and the second field contains all the content in the file. Box 3.8 shows the Python program for generating an inverted index using MapReduce. Figure 3.18 shows the data and the key-value pairs at each step of the MapReduce job. The mapper function in this example parses each line of the input and emits key-value pairs where the key is each word in the line and value is the filename. The reducer receives the list of values (filenames) grouped by the key (word) and emits the word and the list of filenames in which the word occurs.

■ **Box 3.8: Python program for computing inverted index with MapReduce**

```
#Inverted index

from mrjob.job import MRJob

class MRmyjob(MRJob):
  def mapper(self, _, line):
    doc_id, content = line.split('|')
    words = content.split()
    for word in words:
      yield word, doc_id

  def reducer(self, key, list_of_values):
    docs=[]
    for x in list_of_values:
      docs.append(x)

    yield key, docs


if __name__ == '__main__':
  MRmyjob.run()
```

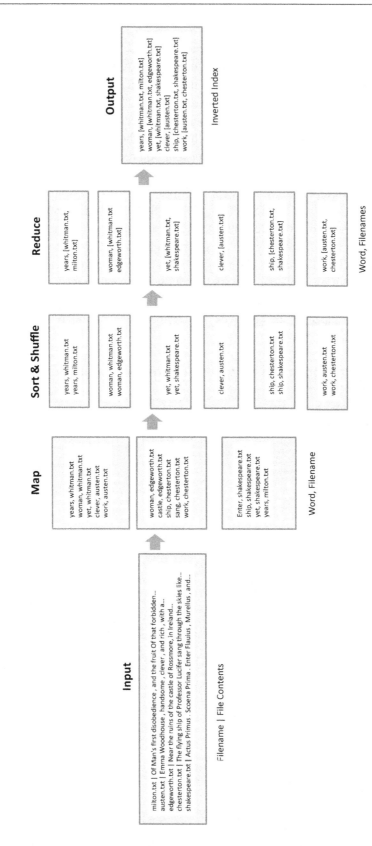

Figure 3.18: Computing inverted index with MapReduce

3.2.7 Sorting

The sorting pattern is used to sort the records based on a particular field. Let us look at
an example of sorting records in the web analytics service log by the visit length. Box 3.9
shows the Python program for sorting using MapReduce. Figure 3.19 shows the data and the
key-value pairs at each step of the MapReduce job. The mapper function in this example
parses each line of the input and emits key-value pairs where the key is None and value is
a tuple comprising of visit length and the rest of the fields in the record (as a nested tuple).
The reducer receives the list of values all grouped together (as the key is None). The reducer
uses the sorted function of Python, which sorts the list of tuples by the first elements in the
tuples (which is the visit length).

■ **Box 3.9: Python program for sorting with MapReduce**

```
# Sort by visit length

from mrjob.job import MRJob

class MRmyjob(MRJob):
  def mapper(self, _, line):
    #Split the line with tab separated fields
    data=line.split('')

    #Parse line
    date = data[0].strip()
    time = data[1].strip()
    url = data[2].strip()
    ip = data[3].strip()
    visit_len=int(data[4].strip())
    #Extract year from date
    year=date[0:4]
    month=date[5:7]

    #Emit url and 1 if year is 2014
    if year=='2014':
      yield None, (visit_len, (date, time, url, ip))


  def reducer(self, key, list_of_values):
    list_of_values = sorted(list(list_of_values), reverse=True)
    return list_of_values


if __name__ == '__main__':
  MRmyjob.run()
```

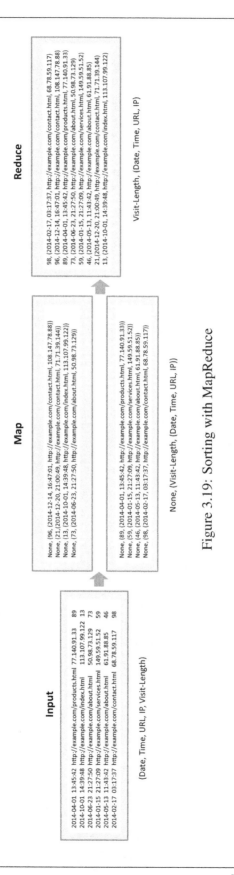

Figure 3.19: Sorting with MapReduce

3.2.8 Joins

When datasets contain multiple files, joins are used to combine the records in the files for further processing. Joins combine two or more datasets or records in multiple files, based on a field (called the join attribute or foreign key). Let take the example of joining two tables A and B. Figure 3.20 shows various types of joins. An Inner Join returns rows from both the tables which have the same value of the matching columns or the foreign key. The output contains columns of both tables with the matching foreign keys. Any unmatched records from both tables are not included in the output. A Full Outer Join is another type of join which includes all the matched and unmatched records from both the tables. Full Outer Join returns all the rows from both tables and returns NULL values in columns of each table where no row matches. In Left Outer Join, the unmatched columns in the table of the left side of the join are included and along with all the matched records from both tables. Left Outer Join returns all rows from the table of the left side of the join and returns NULL in columns of the table on the right where no row matches. In Right Outer Join, the unmatched columns in the table of the right side of the join are included and along with all the matched records from both tables. Right Outer Join returns all rows from the table of the right side of the join and returns NULL in columns of the table on the right where no row matches.

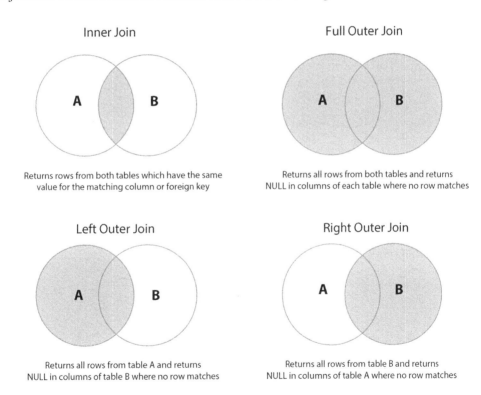

Figure 3.20: Types of Joins

Let us look at examples of joins using MapReduce. For these examples, we will use two datasets containing records of employees and departments in an organization. The employees dataset contains fields such as Employee ID, Employee Name, Department ID, Joining Data and Salary. The departments dataset contains fields such as Department ID, Department

Name and Number of Employees. The first field in the employees dataset contains the word 'Employee' followed by the rest of the fields containing employee details. Similarly, the first field in the departments dataset contains the word 'Department', followed by the rest of the fields containing department details. Let us look at examples of joining the employee and department datasets by the Department ID field. Box 3.10 shows the Python program for inner join using MapReduce. Figure 3.21 shows the data and the key-value pairs at each step of the MapReduce job. The mapper function in this example parses each line of the input and emits key-value pairs where the key is the Department ID and value is the complete record. The reducer receives the list of values all grouped by the Department ID. In the reducer, we check the first field of each value and if the field is 'Employee', we add the value to an employees list and if the first field is 'Department', we add the value to the departments list. Next, we iterate over both the lists and perform the join.

Boxes 3.11, 3.12 and 3.13 show the Python programs for left outer join, right outer join, and full outer join respectively. The only difference in these programs is in the reducer where we iterate over the employees and departments lists to perform the join.

■ **Box 3.10: Python program for computing inner join with MapReduce**

```
from mrjob.job import MRJob

class MyMRJob(MRJob):
  def mapper(self, _, line):
    data=line.split(' ')
    if data[0]=='Employee':
      deptID = data[3]
    elif data[0]=='Department':
      deptID = data[1]
    yield deptID, data

  def reducer(self, key, list_of_values):
    values = list(list_of_values)
    employees = [ ]
    departments=[ ]
    for v in values:
      if v[0]=='Employee':
        employees.append(v)
      elif v[0]=='Department':
        departments.append(v)

    #Inner Join
    for e in employees:
      for d in departments:
        yield None, (e+d)

if __name__ == '__main__':
  MyMRJob.run()
```

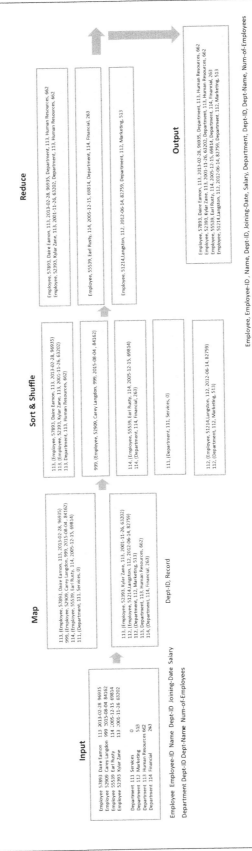

Figure 3.21: Computing join with MapReduce

■ Box 3.11: Python program for computing left outer join with MapReduce

```python
from mrjob.job import MRJob

class MyMRJob(MRJob):
  def mapper(self, _, line):
    data=line.split(' ')
    if data[0]=='Employee':
      deptID = data[3]
    elif data[0]=='Department':
      deptID = data[1]
    yield deptID, data

  def reducer(self, key, list_of_values):
    values = list(list_of_values)
    employees = []
    departments=[]
    for v in values:
      if v[0]=='Employee':
        employees.append(v)
      elif v[0]=='Department':
        departments.append(v)

    #Left Outer Join
    for e in employees:
      if len(departments)>0:
        for d in departments:
          yield None, (e+d)
      else:
        yield None, (e)

if __name__ == '__main__':
  MyMRJob.run()
```

■ Box 3.12: Python program for computing right outer join with MapReduce

```python
from mrjob.job import MRJob

class MyMRJob(MRJob):
  def mapper(self, _, line):
    data=line.split(' ')
    if data[0]=='Employee':
      deptID = data[3]
    elif data[0]=='Department':
      deptID = data[1]
    yield deptID, data

  def reducer(self, key, list_of_values):
    values = list(list_of_values)
    employees = []
    departments=[]
    for v in values:
```

```
      if v[0]=='Employee':
         employees.append(v)
      elif v[0]=='Department':
         departments.append(v)

    #Right Outer Join
    for d in departments:
     if len(employees)>0:
       for e in employees:
         yield None, (e+d)
     else:
       yield None, (d)

if __name__ == '__main__':
  MyMRJob.run()
```

■ **Box 3.13: Python program for computing full outer join with MapReduce**

```
from mrjob.job import MRJob

class MyMRJob(MRJob):
  def mapper(self, _, line):
    data=line.split(' ')
    if data[0]=='Employee':
      deptID = data[3]
    elif data[0]=='Department':
      deptID = data[1]
    yield deptID, data

  def reducer(self, key, list_of_values):
    values = list(list_of_values)
    employees = []
    departments=[]
    for v in values:
      if v[0]=='Employee':
         employees.append(v)
      elif v[0]=='Department':
         departments.append(v)

    #Full Outer Join
    if len(employees)>0:
      for e in employees:
        if len(departments)>0:
          for d in departments:
            yield None, (e+d)
        else:
          yield None, (e)
    else:
      for d in departments:
        yield None, (d)

if __name__ == '__main__':
  MyMRJob.run()
```

Summary

In this chapter we described various architectural component patterns and design styles for
big data systems and applications. Messaging queues can be used between the data producers
and data consumers in a big data system, for load leveling. Queues allow decoupling of the
producers of data from the consumers. Having multiple consumers can help in load balancing
and making the system more scalable, reliable and available. We described approaches for
leader election, by which the instances in a distributed system can elect one of the instances
as their leader. Next, we described sharding which involves horizontally partitioning the
data across multiple storage nodes in a data storage system. For distributed data systems, a
trade-off exists between consistency and availability. These trade-offs are explained with
the CAP Theorem, which states that under partitioning, a distributed data system can either
be consistent or available but not both at the same time. Next, we described Bloom filter,
a probabilistic data structure for testing set membership. For big data applications that
involve certain queries that are frequently performed, it is beneficial to pre-compute such
queries. These pre-computed queries are called materialized views. We described the Lambda
architecture which comprises of batch, speed and serving layers. Lambda architecture enables
both querying real-time and historical data, by pre-computing the queries. Next, we described
the Scheduler-Agent-Supervisor pattern, which can be used to make big data systems more
resilient and fault tolerant. The pipes and filter pattern involves splitting a complex task
into a series of distinct tasks. We described the benefits of using a web service, which
provides an interface that exposes the functionality of the system to the clients in the form
of various endpoints. Next, we described the Paxos consensus protocol. In the second part
of the chapter, we described various MapReduce patterns for data analysis, along with the
implementations in Python.

4 - NoSQL

This chapter covers

- Key-value databases
- Document databases
- Column family databases
- Graph databases

Non-relational databases ("NoSQL databases") are becoming popular with the increasing use of cloud computing services. Non-relational databases have better horizontal scaling capability and improved performance for big data at the cost of having less rigorous consistency models.

NoSQL databases are popular for applications in which the scale of data involved is massive and the data may not be structured. Furthermore, real-time performance is more important than consistency. These systems are optimized for fast retrieval and appending operations on records. Unlike relational databases, the NoSQL databases do not have a strict schema. The records can be in the form of key-value pairs or documents. Most NoSQL databases are classified in terms of the data storage model or type of records that can be stored.

In this chapter, we describe some frequently used NoSQL databases, the characteristics of each database type, an example of each type of database and implementations with complete source code for reading and writing data.

4.1   Key-Value Databases

Key-value databases are the simplest form of NoSQL databases. These databases store data in the form of key-value pairs. The keys are used to identify uniquely the values stored in the database. Applications that want to store data generate unique keys and submit the key-value pairs to the database. The database uses the key to determine where the value should be stored. Most key-value databases have distributed architectures comprising of multiple storage nodes. The data is partitioned across the storage nodes by the keys. For determining the partitions for the keys, hash functions are used. The partition number for a key is obtained by applying a hash function to the key. The hash functions are chosen such that the keys are evenly distributed across the partitions.

Key-value databases provide a lot of flexibility in terms of the type of values that can be stored. The values can be virtually of any type (such as strings, integers, floats, binary large object (BLOB), etc.). Most key-value stores have support for native programming language data types. There are limits on the size of the values that can be stored.

Unlike relational databases in which the tables have fixed schemas and there are constraints on the columns, in key-value databases, there are no such constraints. Key-value databases do not have tables like in relational databases. However, some key-value databases support tables, buckets or collections to create separate namespaces for the keys. Keys within a table, bucket or collection are unique.

Key-value databases are suited for applications that require storing unstructured data without a fixed schema. These databases can be scaled up horizontally and can store a very large number of key-value pairs. Unlike relational databases which provide specialized query languages (such as SQL), the key-value databases only provide basic querying and searching capabilities. Key-value databases are suitable for applications for which the ability to store and retrieve data in a fast and efficient manner is more important than imposing structure or constraints on the data. For example, key-value databases can be used to store configuration data, user data, transient or intermediate data (such as shopping cart data), item-attributes and BLOBs (such as audio and images).

4.1.1 Amazon DynamoDB

Amazon DynamoDB is a fully-managed, scalable, high-performance NoSQL database service from Amazon. DynamoDB provides fast and predictable performance and seamless scalability without any operational overhead. DynamoDB is an excellent choice for a serving database for data analytics applications as it allows storing and retrieving any amount of data and the ability to scale up or down the provisioned throughput depending on the application's performance requirements. DynamoDB is a highly available and reliable service. The data stored in DynamoDB is replicated across multiple availability zones.

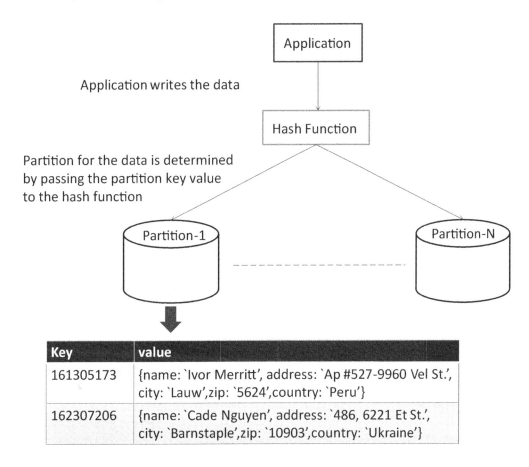

Figure 4.1: Using key-value database for storing customer records

DynamoDB's data model includes Tables, Items, and Attributes. A table is a collection of items and each item is a collection of attributes. Tables in DynamoDB do not have a fixed schema. While creating a table, only the primary key needs to be specified. The primary key uniquely identifies the items in a table. The primary key is a combination of a partition key and an optional sort key. The partition key is hashed using a hash function to determine the partition where the item should be stored. The partition key value must be unique across all items if no sort is specified. An optional sort key can be specified which is used to sort items within a partition. If the primary key used is a combination of the hash key and sort key then it is possible for two items to have the same value of the partition key, but the sort key must have different values. Items are composed of attributes. The attributes can be added at runtime. Different items in a table can have different attributes. Each attribute is a key-value pair.

For reading items, DynamoDB provides scan and query operations. The scan operation is used to retrieve all items in the table. You can specify optional filtering criteria. The filtering criteria can look for specific values of attributes or range of values. The query operation is used to query for items with the primary key (either only the partition key or the partition key and the sort key). To query the table using attributes other than the primary key, secondary indexes can be added.

Let us look at an example of using DynamoDB to store customer information for an eCommerce application. The first step is to create a DynamoDB table. You can either create a table from the DynamoDB dashboard or using the DynamoDB APIs. Figure 4.2 shows an example of creating a DynamoDB table. In this example, the customerID is specified as the partition key and the customer name as the sort key. We use rest of the default settings for secondary indexes, provisioned capacity and alarms.

Create DynamoDB table

Tutorial

DynamoDB is a schema-less database that only requires a table name and primary key. The table's primary key is made up of one or two attributes that uniquely identify items, partition the data, and sort data within each partition.

Table name* `customers`

Primary key* Partition key

`customerID`   String

☑ Add sort key

`name|`   String

Table settings

Default settings provide the fastest way to get started with your table. You can modify these default settings now or after your table has been created.

☑ Use default settings

- No secondary indexes.
- Provisioned capacity set to 5 reads and 5 writes.
- Basic alarms with 80% upper threshold using SNS topic "dynamodb".

Additional charges may apply if you exceed the AWS Free Tier levels for CloudWatch or Simple Notification Service. Advanced alarm settings are available in the CloudWatch management console.

Cancel   **Create**

Figure 4.2: Creating a DynamoDB table

Box 4.1 shows a Python example of writing data to a DynamoDB table. For this example, we created synthetic customer data from www.generatedata.com and saved the data in a CSV file. In the Python example, each row of the CSV file is read one by one in a loop and the customer data is written to the DynamoDB table.

■ Box 4.1: Writing data to DynamoDB table

```python
import boto.dynamodb2
from boto.dynamodb2.table import Table
from awscredentials import ACCESS_KEY,SECRET_KEY
import csv

REGION="us-east-1"

conn = boto.dynamodb2.connect_to_region(REGION,
aws_access_key_id=ACCESS_KEY,
aws_secret_access_key=SECRET_KEY)


table=Table('customers',connection=conn)
desc = table.describe()
print desc

reader = csv.reader(open('customers.csv','r'))
header=reader.next()
for row in reader:
 item = table.put_item(data={
   'customerID':row[0],
   'name':row[1],
   'address':  row[2],
   'city':   row[3],
   'zip':   row[4],
   'country':   row[5],
   'createdAt':   row[6]
 },overwrite=True)
```

Figure 4.3 shows an example of using a scan operation from the DynamoDB dashboard for retrieving data. Box 4.2 shows a Python example of reading data from DynamoDB using scan and query operations.

■ Box 4.2: Reading data from DynamoDB table with query and scan operations

```python
import boto.dynamodb2
from boto.dynamodb2.table import Table
from awscredentials import ACCESS_KEY,SECRET_KEY,EC2_KEY_HANDLE

REGION="us-east-1"

conn = boto.dynamodb2.connect_to_region(REGION,
aws_access_key_id=ACCESS_KEY,
aws_secret_access_key=SECRET_KEY)
```

```
table=Table('customers',connection=conn)
desc = table.describe()
print desc

#Scan table
result=table.scan()

for item in result:
 print item.items()

#Scan table with filter
result = table.scan(country__eq='India')

for item in result:
 print item.items()

#Scan table with filters
result = table.scan(name__beginswith='A',
 createdAt__between=['2012-03-26T00:00:00-00:00',
 '2016-03-26T00:00:00-00:00'])

for item in result:
 print item.items()

#Query table with partition key
result = table.query_2(customerID__eq='1623072020799')

for item in result:
 print item.items()
```

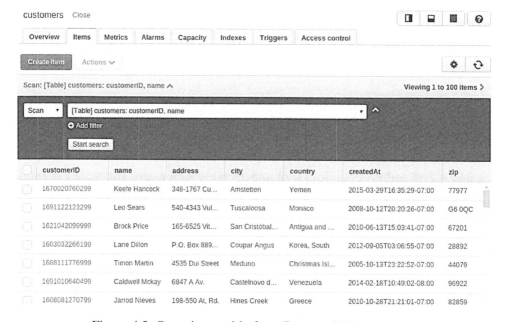

Figure 4.3: Scanning a table from DynamoDB Dashboard

4.2 Document Databases

Document store databases store semi-structured data in the form of documents which are encoded in different standards such as JSON, XML, BSON or YAML. By semi-structured data we mean that the documents stored are similar to each other (similar fields, keys or attributes) but there are no strict requirements for a schema. Documents are organized in different ways in different document database such in the form of collections, buckets or tags.

Each document stored in a document database has a collection of named fields and their values. Each document is identified by a unique key or ID. There is no need to define any schema for the documents before storing them in the database. While it is possible to store JSON or XML-like documents as values in a key-value database, the benefit of using document databases over key-value databases is that these databases allow efficiently querying the documents based on the attribute values in the documents. Document databases are useful for applications that want to store semi-structured data with a varying number of fields.

While in relational databases the data is stored in a normalized form to eliminate duplicates, in document databases data is stored in denormalized form. Document databases do not provide the join functionality provided by relational databases. Therefore, all data that needs to be retrieved together is stored in a document. For example, in an eCommerce application all data related to a particular product is usually retrieved together. In this case, a document can be created for each product. Each document comprises of the data on the product features and attributes.

4.2.1 MongoDB

MongoDB is a document-oriented non-relational database system. MongoDB is powerful, flexible and highly scalable database designed for web applications and is a good choice for a serving database for data analytics applications. The basic unit of data stored by MongoDB is a document. A document includes a JSON-like set of key-value pairs.

■ **Box 4.3: Commands for setting up and running MongoDB**

```
#Import the public key used by the package management system
sudo apt-key adv -keyserver hkp://keyserver.ubuntu.com:80 -recv 7F0CEB10

#Create a list file for MongoDB
echo "deb http://repo.mongodb.org/apt/ubuntu trusty/mongodb-org/3.0
multiverse" | sudo tee /etc/apt/sources.list.d/mongodb-org-3.0.list

#Reload local package database
sudo apt-get update

#Install MongoDB
sudo apt-get install -y mongodb-org

#Start MongoDB service
sudo service mongod start
```

Documents are grouped together to form collections. Collections do not have a fixed schema and different documents in a collection can have different sets of key-value pairs. Collections are organized into databases, and there can be multiple databases running on a single MongoDB instance. Box 4.3 shows the commands for setting up and running MongoDB.

ID	Document

56fd4f59849f6367af489537	{
	    "title" : "Motorola Moto G (3rd Generation)",
	    "features" : [
	        "Advanced water resistance",
	        "13 MP camera",
	        "5in HD display",
	        "Quad core processing power",
	        "5MP rear camera",
	        "Great 24hr battery",
	        "4G LTE Speed"
	    ],
	    "specifications" : {
	        "Color" : "Black",
	        "Size" : "16 GB",
	        "Dimensions" : "0.2 x 2.9 x 5.6 inches",
	        "Weight" : "5.4 ounces"
	    },
	    "price" : 219.99
	}

56fd504d849f6367af489538	{
	    "title" : "Canon EOS Rebel T5",
	    "features" : [
	        "18 megapixel CMOS (APS-C) sensor",
	        "EF-S 18-55mm IS II standard zoom lens",
	        "3-inch LCD TFT color, liquid-crystal monitor",
	        "EOS 1080p full HD movie mode"
	    ],
	    "specifications" : {
	        "Color" : "Black",
	        "MaximumAperture" : "f/3.5",
	        "Dimensions" : "3.94 x 3.07 x 5.12 inches",
	        "Weight" : "1.06 pounds"
	    },
	    "price" : 399
	}

Figure 4.4: Using document database for storing product records

Box 4.4 shows examples of using the MongoDB shell commands for writing data to a MongoDB database and querying the data. The data used in this example is the products data for an eCommerce application. Data for each product is stored as a single document.

■ Box 4.4: Using MongoDB shell commands

```
#Launch MongoDB shell
mongo localhost:27017

#Switch to new database named storedb
> use storedb
switched to db storedb

post = {
 "title" :  "Motorola Moto G (3rd Generation)",
 "features" :  [
 "Advanced water resistance",
 "13 MP camera which includes a color-balancing dual LED Flash",
 "5in HD display",
 "Quad core processing power",
 "5MP rear camera",
 "Great 24hr battery performance with a 2470mAh battery",
 "4G LTE Speed"
 ],
 "specifications" :  {
 "Color" :  "Black",
 "Size" :  "16 GB",
 "Dimensions" :  "0.2 x 2.9 x 5.6 inches",
 "Weight" :  "5.4 ounces"
 },
 "price" :  219.99
}

> db.collection.insert(post)
WriteResult({ "Inserted" :  1 })

#Get all documents
> db.collection.find()
{ "_id" :  ObjectId("56fd4f59849f6367af489537"),
 "title" :  "Motorola Moto G (3rd Generation)",
 "features" :  [ "Advanced water resistance",
 "13 MP camera which includes a color-balancing dual LED Flash",
 "5in HD display", "Quad core processing power", "5MP rear camera",
 "Great 24hr battery performance with a 2470mAh battery", "4G LTE Speed" ],
 "specifications" :  { "Color" :  "Black", "Size" :  "16 GB",
 "Dimensions" :  "0.2 x 2.9 x 5.6 inches", "Weight" :  "5.4 ounces" },
 "price" :  219.99 }

{ "_id" :  ObjectId("56fd504d849f6367af489538"),
 "title" :  "Canon EOS Rebel T5",
 "features" :  [ "18 megapixel CMOS (APS-C) sensor",
 "EF-S 18-55mm IS II standard zoom lens",
 "3-inch LCD TFT color, liquid-crystal monitor",
 "EOS 1080p full HD movie mode" ],
 "specifications" :  { "Color" :  "Black",
 "MaximumAperture" :  "f3.5", "Dimensions" :  "3.94 x 3.07 x 5.12 inches",
 "Weight" :  "1.06 pounds" }, "price" :  399 }
```

```
#Get documents with specific attribute values
> db.collection.find({"title" :   "Canon EOS Rebel T5"})
{ "_id" :   ObjectId("56fd504d849f6367af489538"),
"title" :   "Canon EOS Rebel T5",
"features" :   [ "18 megapixel CMOS (APS-C) sensor",
"EF-S 18-55mm IS II standard zoom lens",
"3-inch LCD TFT color, liquid-crystal monitor",
"EOS 1080p full HD movie mode" ],
"specifications" :   { "Color" :   "Black",
"MaximumAperture" :   "f3.5", "Dimensions" :   "3.94 x 3.07 x 5.12 inches",
"Weight" :   "1.06 pounds" }, "price" :   399 }
```

Box 4.5 shows a Python program for writing data to MongoDB and reading the data. For this example, we use the pyMongo python library.

■ **Box 4.5: Python program for writing data to MongoDB and reading the data**

```
import time
from datetime import date
import datetime
import cPickle
from pymongo import MongoClient

client = MongoClient()
db = client['storedb']
collection = db['current']

item = {
 "title" :   "Motorola Moto G (3rd Generation)",
 "features" :   [
  "Advanced water resistance",
  "13 MP camera which includes a color-balancing dual LED Flash",
  "5in HD display",
  "Quad core processing power",
  "5MP rear camera",
  "Great 24hr battery performance with a 2470mAh battery",
  "4G LTE Speed"
 ],
 "specifications" :   {
  "Color" :   "Black",
  "Size" :   "16 GB",
  "Dimensions" :   "0.2 x 2.9 x 5.6 inches",
  "Weight" :   "5.4 ounces"
 },
 "price" :   219.99
}

#Insert an item
collection.insert_one(item)

#Retrieve all items
results=db.collection.find()
for item in results:
 print item
```

```
#Find an item
results = collection.find({"title" :  "Motorola Moto G"})

for item in results:
 print item
```

4.3 Column Family Databases

In column family databases the basic unit of data storage is a column, which has a name and a value. A collection of columns make up a row which is identified by a row-key. Columns are grouped together into columns families. Unlike, relational databases, the column family databases do not need to have fixed schemas and a fixed number of columns in each row. The number of columns in a column family database can vary across different rows. A column family can be considered as a map having key-value pairs and this map can vary across different rows. Column family databases store data in a denormalized form so that all relevant information related to an entity required by the applications can be retrieved by reading a single row. Column family databases support high-throughput reads and writes and have distributed and highly available architectures.

4.3.1 HBase

HBase is a scalable, non-relational, distributed, column-family database that provides structured data storage for large tables. HBase can store both structured and unstructured data. The data storage in HBase can scale linearly and automatically by the addition of new nodes. HBase has been designed to work with commodity hardware and is a highly reliable and fault tolerant system. HBase allows fast random reads and writes.

Data Model

Figure 4.5 shows the structure of an HBase table. A table is consists of rows, which are indexed by the row key. Each row includes multiple column families. Each column family includes multiple columns. Each column includes multiple cells or entries which are timestamped. HBase tables are indexed by the row key, column key and timestamp. Unlike relational database tables, HBase tables do not have a fixed schema. HBase columns families are declared at the time of creation of the table and cannot be changed later. Columns can be added dynamically, and HBase can have millions of columns.

HBase is often described as a sparse, distributed, persistent, multi-dimensional sorted map. Let us look at these features in detail:
- **Sparse**: In traditional relational databases, tables have fixed schemas. Each row in a table has the same number of columns. Each row has all the columns even if all of them are not populated. HBase, in contrast, has sparse tables as each row doesn't need to have all the columns. Only the columns which are populated in a row are stored.
- **Distributed**: HBase is a distributed database. HBase tables are partitioned based on row keys into regions. Each region contains a range of row keys. A typical HBase deployment contains multiple Region Servers. Each Region Server contains several regions from different tables.

- **Persistent**: HBase works on top of HDFS and all data stored in HBase tables is persisted on HDFS.
- **Multi-dimensional** : HBase stores data as key-value pairs where the keys are multi-dimensional. A key includes: (Table, RowKey, ColumnFamily, Column, TimeStamp) as shown in Figure 4.6. For each entry/cell, multiple versions are stored, which are timestamped.
- **Sorted Map**: HBase rows are sorted by the row key in lexicographic order. Columns in a column family are sorted by the column key.

HBase cells cannot be over-written. Since the cells are versioned with timestamps, when newer values are added, the older values are also retained. Data is stored in cells as byte arrays. The applications are responsible for correctly interpreting the data type.

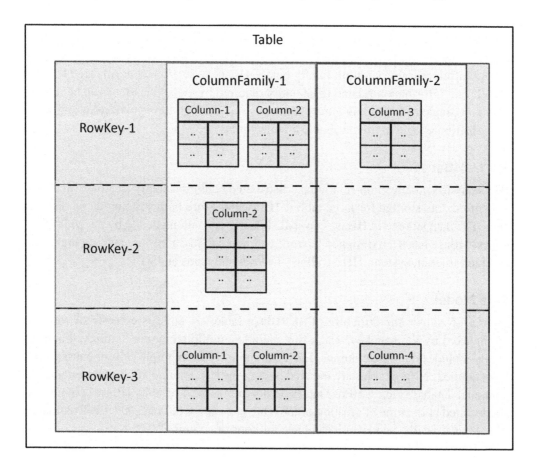

Figure 4.5: HBase table structure

Key Length	Value Length	Row Length	Row Key	Column Family Length	Column Family	Column Qualifier	Time Stamp	Key Type	Value

Figure 4.6: HBase key-value format

Architecture

HBase has a distributed architecture as shown in Figure 4.7. An HBase deployment comprises multiple region servers which usually run on the same machines as the Hadoop data nodes. HBase tables are partitioned by the row key into multiple regions (HRegions). Each region server has multiple regions. HBase has a master-slave architecture with one of the nodes acting as the master node (HMaster) and other nodes are slave nodes. The HMaster is responsible for maintaining the HBase meta-data and assignment of regions to region servers.

HBase uses Zookeeper for distributed state coordination. HBase has two special tables - ROOT and META, for identifying which region server is responsible for serving a read/write request for a specific row key.

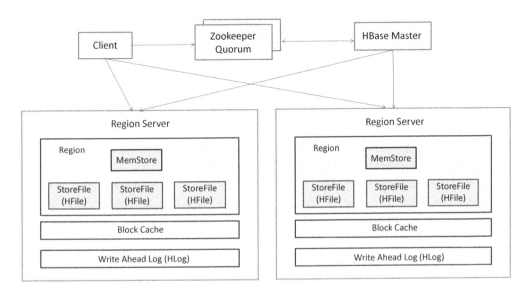

Figure 4.7: HBase architecture

Data Storage & Operations

Each Region Server stores two types of files - a store file (HFile) and a write-ahead log (HLog).

The HFile contains a variable number of data blocks and the fixed blocks for file information and trailer. Each data block contains a magic number and multiple key-value pairs. The default size of a data block is 64 KB. The index block stores the offset for the data and the meta-blocks. The trailer stores pointers to other blocks. HFiles are persisted on HDFS.

Each Region Server has a Memstore and a Block Cache. The Mcmstore stores the recent edits to the data in memory and the Block Cache caches the data blocks.

Each Region Server also maintains a write-ahead log (WAL) known as the Hlog which logs the writes (that are also written to Memstore). Since HLog is stored on HDFS, it ensures that even in the event of loss of Memstore (which is an in-memory buffer), the writes are never lost.

Each Region Server has a Block cache, which is an in-memory store that caches the most recently used blocks for fast lookup.

HBase supports the following operations:

- **Get**: Get operation is used to return values for a given row key.
- **Scan**: Scan operation returns values for a range of row keys.
- **Put**: Put operation is used to add a new entry.
- **Delete**: Delete operation adds a special marker called Tombstone to an entry. Entries marked with Tombstones are removed during the compaction process (discussed later in this chapter).

The storage structure used by HBase is a Log Structured Merge (LSM) Tree. LSM Tree uses two trees, one which is a smaller in-memory tree (in Memstore) and the other is a larger tree that is persisted on the disk (as store files). When the size of the in-memory tree exceeds a certain limit, it is merged with the larger tree on the disk using merge sort algorithm and a new in-memory tree is created. LSM Tree enables HBase to handle fast random reads and writes for large amounts of data. LSM Tree achieves this by transforming random data access to sequential data access.

Read Path

For read operations (get or scan) the client first contacts Zookeeper to get the location of the ROOT table. The client then checks the ROOT table for correct META table containing the row key and obtains the Region Server name that is responsible for serving requests for that row-key. The client then contacts the Region Server directly to complete the read operation. The ROOT and META table lookups are cached by the client so that in subsequent read operations the client can directly contact the correct Region Server for a given row-key.

Write Path

All write requests are first logged into the WAL (HLog) sequentially. Once data is logged, it is also written to the Memstore. The Memstore stores the most recent updates to enable fast lookups. Over time, the Memstore starts filling up as new updates are stored. When the Memstore is filled up, it is flushed to the disk creating a new store file (HFile).

Compactions

Every time the Memstore is flushed to the disk, a new store file is created. Over time, many small store files are created on HDFS. Since HDFS is designed to work better with a smaller number of large files (as opposed to a large number of small files), a process called compaction is performed to merge the small files into a single file. The compaction process improves the read efficiency as a large number of small files don't need to be looked up. HBase compactions are of two types - minor and major. Minor compaction merges the small files into a single file when the number exceeds a threshold. Minor compactions are done on a regular basis (typically multiple times in a day). Major compactions merge all store files into a single large store file. In the major compaction process, the outdated and deleted values (cells which have expired versions or cells marked with Tombstones) are removed. Compaction process improves the performance of HBase as looking up a single large store file for a get or scan operation is more efficient than looking up multiple small store files.

Bloom Filters

HBase uses Bloom Filters for the exclusion of store files that need to be looked up while serving read requests for a particular row key. Bloom filter is a probabilistic data structure which is used to test whether an element is a member of a set. Bloom filter can give a definitive answer if the element is in the set, however, it can also say that an element is in the set while it is not. In other words, false positives are possible, but false negatives are not possible. The number of false positives can be tuned to less than 1%.

HBase Usage Examples

Command Line

HBase comes with an interactive shell from where the users can perform various HBase operations. The HBase shell can be launched as follows:

```
■ # Launch HBase Shell
$ hbase shell
hbase(main):001:0>
```

To create a table, the *create* command is used as shown below. The table name and column families are specified while creating a table.

```
■ # Create HBase table
> create 'products', 'details', 'sale'

=> Hbase::Table - products
```

In this example, we created a table named *products* having two column families named *details* and *sale*. The *list* command can be used to list all the tables in HBase, as shown below:

```
■ #List HBase tables
> list
TABLE
products
1 row(s) in 1.7470 seconds
=> ["products"]
```

To write data to HBase, the *put* command can be used. The box below shows an example of writing to the *products* table. For row with row keys *row-1* and *row-2* data is written to the column family *details* and column (*name*).

```
■ > put 'products', 'row-1', 'details:name', 'Cloud Book'
> put 'products', 'row-2', 'details:name', 'IoT Book'
```

Columns can be added dynamically. The box below shows examples of adding new columns to the rows previously created.

```
■ > put 'products', 'row-1', 'details:ISBN', '9781494435141'
> put 'products', 'row-2', 'sale:Price', '50'
```

For reading data, HBase provides *get* and *scan* operations. The box below shows an example of reading the row with row-key *row-1*.

```
■ hbase(main):027:0> get 'products', 'row-1'
COLUMN CELL
details:name timestamp=1434772884378, value=Cloud Book
details:ISBN timestamp=1434772890556, value=9781494435141
```

The results of the *get* operation show two cells in *row-1*. The values are timestamped, and multiple versions can be stored for a cell. The box below shows an example of a scan operation which returns all rows in a table.

```
■ > scan 'products'
ROW COLUMN+CELL
row-1 column=details:name, timestamp=1434772884378, value=Cloud Book
row-2 column=details:name, timestamp=1434772923678, value=IoT Book
2 row(s) in 0.0210 seconds
```

HBase - Python Examples

Let us look at some examples of HBase operations using Python. We will use *happybase* Python library for these examples.

■ Box 4.6: HBase operations using Python

```
# Start thrift server first:
# hbase thrift start

import happybase

connection = happybase.Connection(host='localhost')
table = connection.table('products')

# Put
table.put('row-1', 'details:name':  'Cloud Book')

# Get
row = table.row('row-1')
print row['details:name']

# Scan
for key, data in table.scan():
print key, data

# Delete row
row = table.delete('row-1')

# Batch put
b = table.batch()
```

```
b.put('row-key-1', 'details:name':  'Cloud Book',
'details:ISBN': '9781494435141',
'sale:StartSale':  '01-01-2014', 'sale:Price':'50')


b.put('row-key-2', 'details:name':  'IoT Book',
'details:ISBN': '9780996025515',
'sale:StartSale':  '01-01-2015', 'sale:Price':'55')
b.send()
```

HBase Web Interface

Figures 4.8 - 4.10 show the HBase web interface.

Master ip-172-31-63-53.ec2.internal

Region Servers

ServerName	Start time	Requests Per Second	Num. Regions
ip-172-31-63-53.ec2.internal,60020,1434768371938	Sat Jun 20 02:46:11 UTC 2015	0	4
Total:1		0	4

Backup Masters

ServerName	Port	Start Time
Total:0		

Tables

User Tables   Catalog Tables   Snapshots
2 table(s) in set. [Details]

Table Name	Online Regions	Description
ambarismoketest	1	'ambarismoketest', {NAME => 'family'}
products	1	'products', {NAME => 'details'}, {NAME => 'sale'}

Figure 4.8: HBase web interface showing details of HBase Master and list of tables

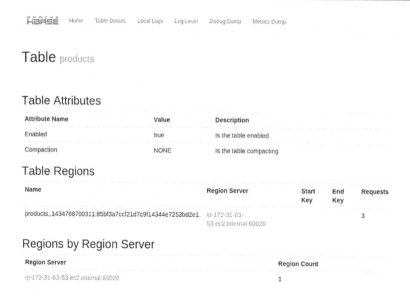

Figure 4.9: HBase web interface showing table details

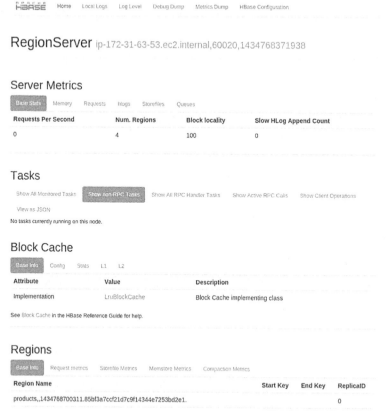

Figure 4.10: HBase web interface showing region server details

4.4   Graph Databases

Graph stores are NoSQL databases designed for storing data that has graph structure with nodes and edges. While relational databases model data in the form of rows and columns, the graph databases model data in the form of nodes and relationships. Nodes represent the entities in the data model. Nodes have a set of attributes. A node can represent different types of entities, for example, a person, place (such as a city, restaurant or a building) or an object (such as a car). The relationships between the entities are represented in the form of links between the nodes. Links also have a set of attributes. Links can be directed or undirected. Directed links denote that the relationship is unidirectional. For example, for two entities author and book, a unidirectional relationship called 'writes' exists between them, such that an author writes a book. Whereas for two friends, say A and B, the friendship relationship between A and B is bidirectional. In the graph theory terminology, the vertices in a graph are the nodes representing the entities and the edges between the vertices are the links between the nodes representing the relationships between the entities. A set of nodes along with the links between them form a path.

Graph databases are useful for a wide range of applications, where you may need to model entities and the relationships between them, such as social media, financial, networking or various types of enterprise applications. In relational databases, the relationships between entities are modeled in the form on different tables with primary keys and foreign keys. The steps involved in mapping an entity-relationship diagram into relational tables are described in Chapter-10. Computing relationships and querying related entities in relational databases require complex join operations between the database tables. Graph databases, in contrast to relational databases, model relationships in the form of links between the nodes. Since the relationships between the entities are explicitly stored in the form of links, querying for related entities in graph databases is much simpler and faster than relational databases as the complex join operations are avoided. Graph databases are suitable for applications in which the primary focus is on querying for relationships between entities and analyzing the relationships.

4.4.1   Neo4j

In this section, we will describe the Neo4j graph database with the help of some examples. Neo4j is one the popular graph databases which provides support for Atomicity, Consistency, Isolation, Durability (ACID). Neo4j adopts a graph model that consists of nodes and relationships. Both nodes and relationships have properties which are captured in the form of multiple attributes (key-value pairs). Nodes are tagged with labels which are used to represent different roles in the domain being modeled. Box 4.7 shows the commands for setting up Neo4j.

> ■ **Box 4.7: Setting up Neo4j graph database**

```
#Download the stable release of Neo4j for Linux
#from http://neo4j.com/download/

#Extract the archive
tar -xf neo4j-*.tar.gz
```

```
#Run neo4j
NEO4J_HOME/bin/neo4j start

#Visit http://localhost:7474 in your web browser.
```

Let us look at an example of using a Graph database for an eCommerce application. Figure 4.11 shows a labeled property graph model for an eCommerce application. In this graph, we have two types of nodes: *Customer* and *Product*. The *Customer* nodes have attributes such as customer name, address, city, country and zip code. The *Product* nodes have attributes such as product title, price and various other product-specific properties (such as color, size, weight, etc.). There are two types of relationships between the customer and product nodes: *Orders* or *Rates*. The *Order* relationship between a customer and product has properties such as the order date and quantity. The *Rates* relationship between a customer and product has a single property to capture the customer rating.

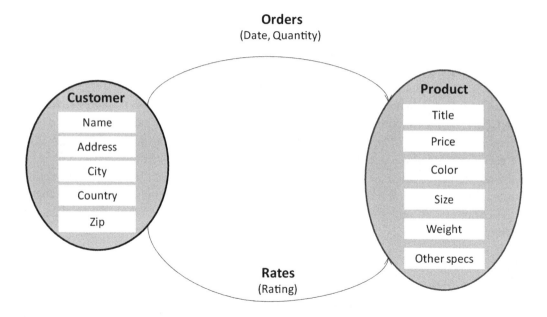

Figure 4.11: Labeled property graph example

For create, read, update and delete (CRUD) operations, Neo4j provides a query language called Cypher. Cypher has some similarities with the SQL query language used for relational databases. Figure 4.12 describes the usage of some of the commonly used Cypher constructs.

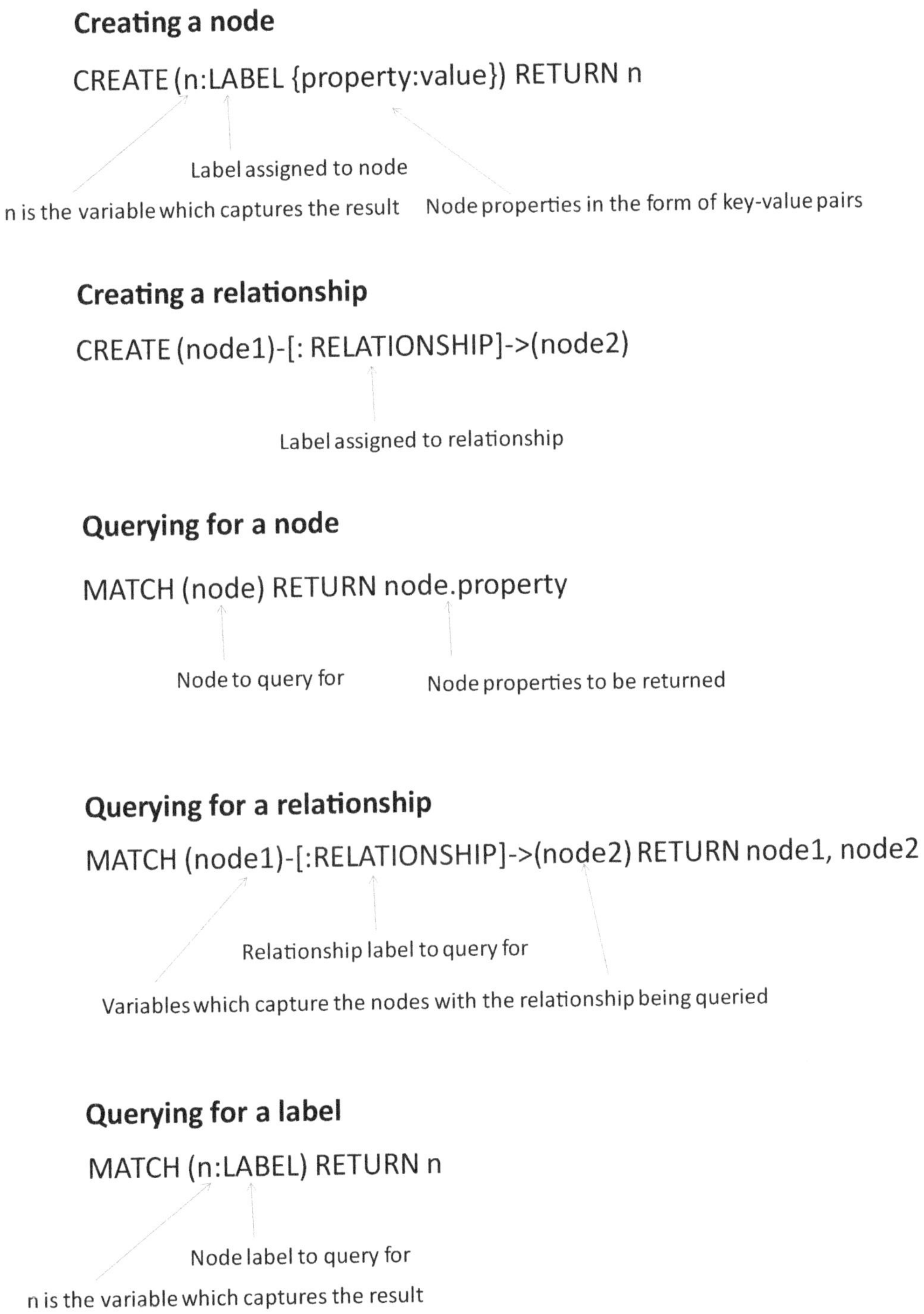

Creating a node

CREATE (n:LABEL {property:value}) RETURN n

Label assigned to node

n is the variable which captures the result   Node properties in the form of key-value pairs

Creating a relationship

CREATE (node1)-[: RELATIONSHIP]->(node2)

Label assigned to relationship

Querying for a node

MATCH (node) RETURN node.property

Node to query for   Node properties to be returned

Querying for a relationship

MATCH (node1)-[:RELATIONSHIP]->(node2) RETURN node1, node2

Relationship label to query for

Variables which capture the nodes with the relationship being queried

Querying for a label

MATCH (n:LABEL) RETURN n

Node label to query for

n is the variable which captures the result

Figure 4.12: Commonly used Cypher constructs

Box 4.8 shows examples of using Cypher for creating customer and product nodes and the relationships between the nodes.

■ Box 4.8: Examples of Neo4j Cypher statements

```
#Create customer
CREATE (c:CUSTOMER {name:  "Bradley Russo",
  address:"P.O. Box 486, 6221 Et St.,Barnstaple",
  country:"Ukraine", zipcode:"10903"});

#Create product
CREATE (p:PRODUCT {title :  "Motorola Moto G",
  Color :  "Black", Size :  "16 GB",
  Weight :  "5.4 ounces", price :  219.99 });

#Create relationship between customer and product
MATCH(c:CUSTOMER{name:"Bradley Russo"}),
  (p:PRODUCT{title:"Motorola Moto G"}) WITH c, p
  CREATE  (c)-[:RATES]->(p);

#Return all data
MATCH (n) RETURN n;

#Query for a customer
MATCH (n:CUSTOMER {name:  "Bradley Russo"}) RETURN n;

#Query for a product
MATCH (n:PRODUCT) WHERE n.price>200 RETURN n;
```

Neo4j also exposes a variety of REST APIs for performing the CRUD operations. These REST APIs enabled the development of language-specific client libraries for Neo4j. Let us look at some examples of using the Python Py2neo client library for Neo4j. Box 4.9 shows an example of using the Py2neo client library. In this example, we first authenticate with a Neo4j server by providing the server hostname, username and password. Next, we create an instance of the *Graph* class which provides methods for creating nodes and relationships, searching nodes, executing Cypher queries and various other methods. To define a node, we create an instance of the *Node* class by providing the node label, name and properties. In this example, we define three nodes (c1,c2,c3) to represent three customers and two nodes (p1,p2) to represent two products. Next, we define the relationships between the nodes by creating instances of the *Relationship* class. For each relationship, we provide the related nodes, a label for the relationship and relationship properties. Finally, we use the *create* method of the *Graph* class to create the nodes and relationships.

■ Box 4.9: Using Python Py2neo client library for Neo4j

```
import py2neo
from py2neo import Graph, Node, Relationship

# Authenticate the user using py2neo.authentication
py2neo.authenticate("localhost:7474", "neo4j", "password")
```

```
# Connect to Graph and get the instance of Graph
graph = Graph("http://localhost:7474/db/data/")

#Define nodes
c1 = Node("CUSTOMER", name="Bradley Russo",
 address="486, 6221 Et St.,Barnstaple",
 country="Ukraine", zipcode="10903")

c2 = Node("CUSTOMER", name="Jarrod Nieves",
 address="198-550 At, Rd.,Hines Creek",
 country="Greece", zipcode="10903")

c3 = Node("CUSTOMER", name="Ivor Merritt",
 address="527-9960 Vel Street,Lauw",
 country="Peru", zipcode="5624")

p1 = Node("PRODUCT",title = "Motorola Moto G (3rd Generation)",
 features = ["Advanced water resistance", "13 MP camera",
 "5in HD display", "Quad core processing power",
 "5MP rear camera", "4G LTE Speed"],
 Color ="Black", Size = "16GB",
 Dimensions = "0.2 x 2.9 x 5.6 inches",
  Weight = "5.4 ounces",price = 219.99)

p2=Node("PRODUCT",title = "Canon EOS Rebel T5",
 features = ["18 megapixel CMOS (APS-C) sensor",
 "EF-S 18-55mm IS II standard zoom lens", "3-inch LCD TFT color,
 liquid-crystal monitor", "EOS 1080p full HD movie mode"],
 Color = "Black", MaximumAperture = "f3.5",
 Dimensions = "3.94 x 3.07 x 5.12 inches",
 Weight = "1.06 pounds", price = 399)

#Define relationships
r1 = Relationship(c1,"ORDERS",p1,date="2015-11-03", quantity="2")
r2 = Relationship(c2,"ORDERS",p1,date="2015-11-03", quantity="1")
r3 = Relationship(c1,"ORDERS",p2,date="2015-11-03", quantity="1")
r4 = Relationship(c2,"ORDERS",p2,date="2015-11-03", quantity="1")

r5 = Relationship(c1,"RATES",p1,rating="4.8")
r6 = Relationship(c2,"RATES",p2,quantity="4.5")

#Create nodes
result = graph.create(c1, c2, p1, p2)

#Create relationships
result = graph.create(r1, r2, r3, r4, r5, r6)

#Print the results
print result
```

Neo4j provides a web interface from where you can execute Cypher statements and view the graphs in the database. Figure 4.13 shows the graph created using the Python program in Box 4.9.

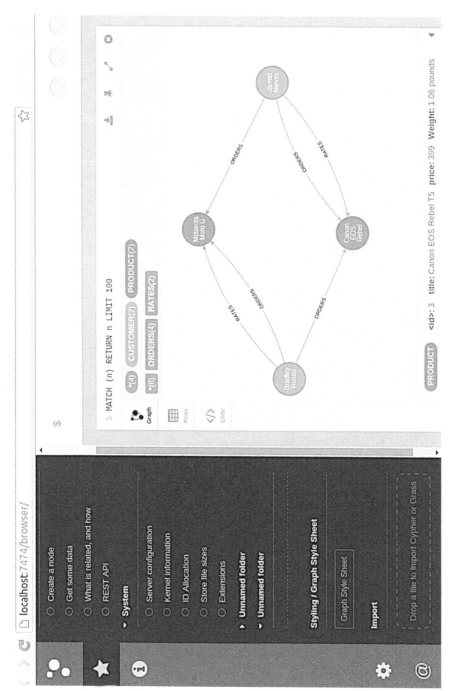

Figure 4.13: Neo4j web interface showing the created nodes and relationships

	Key-Value DB	Document DB	Column Family DB	Graph DB
Data model	Key-value pairs uniquely identified by keys	Documents (having key-value pairs) uniquely identified by document IDs	Columns having names and values, grouped into column families	Graphs comprising of nodes and relationships
Querying	Query items by key, Database specific APIs	Query documents by document-ID, Database specific APIs	Query rows by key, Database specific APIs	Graph query language such as Cypher, Database specific APIs
Use	Applications involving frequent small reads and writes with simple data models	Applications involving data in the form of documents encoded in formats such as JSON or XML, documents can have varying number of attributes	Applications involving large volumes of data, high throughput reads and writes, high availability requirements	Applications involving data on entities and relationships between the entities, spatial data
Examples	DynamoDB, Cassandra	MongoDB, CouchDB	HBase, Google BigTable	Neo4j, AllegroGraph

Figure 4.14: Comparison of NoSQL databases

Summary

Non-relational databases or NoSQL databases are popular for applications in which the scale of data involved is massive and the data may not be structured. Furthermore, real-time performance is considered more important than consistency. In this chapter we described four types of NoSQL databases. Figure 4.14 provides a comparison of these four types of NoSQL databases. The key-value databases store data in the form of key-value pairs where the keys are used to identify uniquely the values stored. Hash functions are applied to the key to determine where the value should be stored. Document store databases store semi-structured data in the form of documents which are encoded in different standards such as JSON, XML, BSON or YAML. The benefit of using document databases over key-value databases is that these databases allow efficiently querying the documents based on the attribute values in the documents. Column family databases store data as columns where a column has a name and a value. Columns are grouped into column families and a collection of columns make up a row which is identified by a row-key. Column family databases support high-throughput reads and writes and have distributed and highly available architectures. Graph databases model data in the form of nodes and relationships. Nodes represent the entities in the data model and have a set of attributes. The relationships between the entities are represented in the form of links between the nodes.

Part II

BIG DATA ANALYTICS IMPLEMENTATIONS

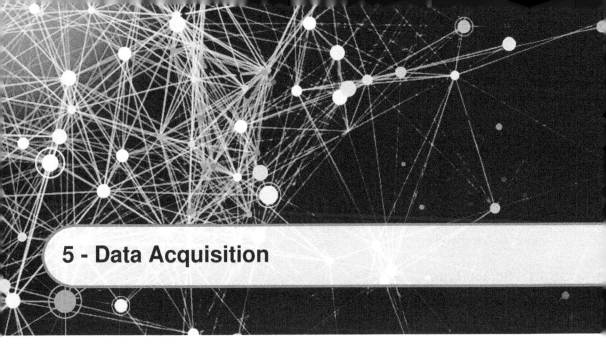

5 - Data Acquisition

This chapter covers

- Data Acquisition Considerations
- Publish - Subscribe Messaging Frameworks
- Big Data Collection Systems
- Messaging Queues
- Custom Connectors

In Chapter-1, we proposed a big data stack and various analytics patterns. An important component of the analytics stack and the patterns is the data connectors which allow collecting data from various data sources into a distributed file system or a NoSQL database for batch analysis of data, or which connect the data sources to stream or in-memory processing frameworks for real-time analysis of data.

5.1 Data Acquisition Considerations

Before we look at specific tools and frameworks for data acquisition and data connectors, let us first look at the various considerations for data acquisition, which will drive the choice of the tools or frameworks.

5.1.1 Source Type

The type of the data source has to be kept into consideration while making a choice for a data connector. Data sources can either publish bulk data in batches or data in small batches (micro-batches) or streaming real-time data.

Some examples of batch data sources are:
- Files
- Logs
- Relational databases

Some examples of real-time data sources are:
- Machines generating sensor data
- Internet of Things (IoT) systems sending real-time data
- Social media feeds
- Stock market feeds

5.1.2 Velocity

The velocity of data refers to how fast the data is generated and how frequently it varies. For data with a high velocity (real-time or streaming data), communication mechanisms which have low overhead and low latency are required. Later in this Chapter, we describe how WebSocket and MQTT based connectors can be used for ingesting real-time and streaming data. For such applications, distributed publish-subscribe messaging frameworks such as Apache Kafka are also good choices as they support high throughput and low latency communication. With such frameworks the downstream data consumers can subscribe to the data feeds and receive data in near real-time.

5.1.3 Ingestion Mechanism

The data ingestion mechanism can either be a push or pull mechanism. The choice of the specific tool or framework for data ingestion will be driven by the data consumer. If the consumer has the capability (or requirement) to pull data, publish-subscribe messaging frameworks which allow the consumers to pull the data (such as Apache Kafka) or messaging queues can be used. The data producers push data to the a messaging framework or a queue from which the consumers can pull the data. An alternative design approach that is adopted in systems such as Apache Flume is the push approach, where the data sources first push data to the framework and the framework then pushes the data to the data sinks. Figures 5.1 and 5.2 show the data flow in push-pull and publish-subscribe messaging.

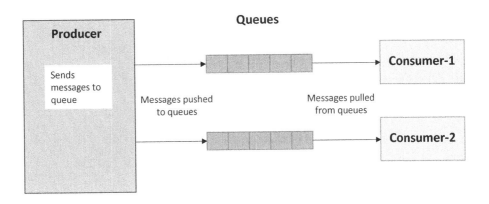

Figure 5.1: Push-Pull messaging

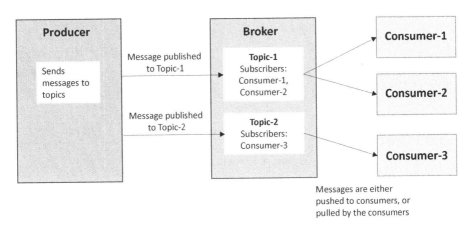

Figure 5.2: Publish - Subscribe Messaging

5.2 Publish - Subscribe Messaging Frameworks

Publish-Subscribe is a communication model that comprises publishers, brokers and consumers. Publishers are the sources of data. Publishers send data to topics which are managed by the broker. Publishers are not aware of the consumers. Consumers subscribe to the topics which are managed by the broker. When the broker receives data for a topic from a publisher, it sends the data to all the subscribed consumers. Alternatively, the consumers can pull data for specific topics from the broker.

In this section, we will describe two publish-subscribe messaging frameworks - Apache Kafka and Amazon Kinesis.

5.2.1   Apache Kafka

Apache Kafka is a high throughput distributed messaging system. Kafka can also be considered as a distributed, partitioned, replicated commit log service. Kafka can be used for applications such as stream processing, messaging, website activity tracking, metrics collection and monitoring, log aggregation, etc.

Architecture

Figure 5.3 shows the architecture and components of Kafka.

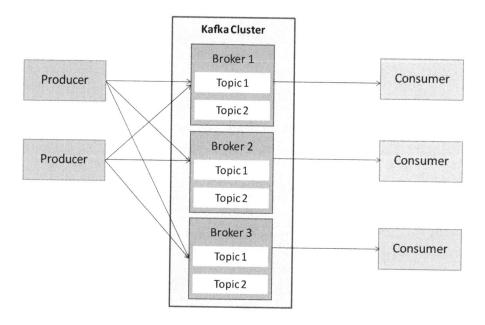

Figure 5.3: Kafka Architecture

A Kafka system includes the following components:
- **Topic:** A topic is a user-defined category to which messages are published.
- **Producer:** Producer is a component that publishes messages to one or more topics.
- **Consumer:** Consumer is a component that subscribes to one or more topics and processes the messages.
- **Broker:** Broker is a component that manages the topics and handles the persistence, partitioning, and replication of the data. A Kafka cluster can have multiple Kafka Brokers (or servers), with each Broker managing multiple topics.

Partitions

Kafka topics are subdivided into multiple partitions as shown in Figure 5.4. Each partition is an ordered and immutable sequence of messages. Topics are stored on the disk in the form of partitioned logs (commit logs). The benefit of using partitions is that the log can scale to massive sizes, which will not fit onto the disk of a single server. Partitions also allow multiple consumers to consume messages in parallel.

Partitions are distributed among the brokers, where each broker is typically a separate physical server. Partitions are also replicated across multiple brokers for fault tolerance

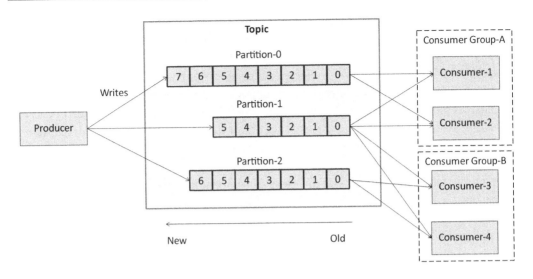

Figure 5.4: Kafka topic partitions

purposes. For each partition, one of the servers acts as the 'leader' for the partition and handles all the writes and reads for the partition. Other servers which hold the partition replicas are called the 'followers'. Partitions and replicas can be reassigned between the brokers as more brokers become available.

Publishing Messages

Producers publish messages to topics. A producer decides which message should be published to which partition of a topic. Producers can either publish messages to different partitions of a topic in a round-robin fashion (for load balancing purposes) or publish messages with specific keys to specific partitions.

Consuming Messages

Consumers consume (and later process) messages from topics. Each message in a partition is assigned a sequence ID called the offset. Offsets are used by the consumers to track which messages have been consumed. Kafka Brokers are not responsible for keeping a track of the messages consumed by the consumers. The published messages are retained on the disk for a configurable duration of time. Since the topics are retained on the disk, the consumers can replay the messages using the offset. The consumers increment the offset as they consume the messages in a sequence.

Consumers can be grouped together into consumer groups. Each message which is published to a topic by a producer is delivered to one consumer within a consumer group. The consumers within a consumer group can either be separate processes or separate instances. Having multiple consumers within a consumer group makes the system scalable and fault tolerant. The partitions in a topic are assigned to consumers such that each partition is consumed by exactly one consumer in a consumer group. The individual consumer processes can process different partitions in parallel. Since only one consumer process consumes from a given partition, messages are delivered in order. Kafka provides ordering of messages within a partition, but not between partitions.

Log Storage & Compaction

Kafka is structured to store messages in the form of append-only logs. For each partition of each topic, a log file is maintained which contains an ordered and immutable sequence of messages. Messages are made available to consumers only after they have been committed to the log. This ensure that all the messages which are consumed by the consumers also persist in the logs so that they can be consumed by other consumers if need be. Unlike, queuing systems which delete the messages after they have been consumed, Kafka retains the messages in the log files, which are retained for a certain amount of time (that can be configured). Kafka provides two options for log cleanup policy - *delete* or *compact*. Log for a topic partition is stored as a directory of segment files. The maximum size to which a segment file can grow before a new segment is rolled over in the log can be configured. If the log cleanup policy is set to *delete*, the log segments are deleted when they reach the size or time limits set. If the log cleanup policy is set to *compact*, then log compaction is used to clean out obsolete records. While for temporal data the *delete* retention policy works well, the *compact* policy is useful when you have keyed and mutable data. For example, if each message which is published to a topic is uniquely identified by a primary key (like a row in a database table), and the message values are going to change over time, then it is preferable to use log compaction which removes old and obsolete values for a key. Log compaction ensures that at least the last known value for each message key for each topic partition is retained.

Using Kafka

In this section, we will describe some examples of Kafka producers and consumers. We will the use the Kafka python library called *kafka-python* for the examples. The *kafka-python* library can be installed using *pip* as follows:

```
sudo pip install kafka-python
```

Kafka uses Zookeeper for state coordination. A Kafka topic can be created as follows:

```
bin/kafka-topics.sh --create --zookeeper localhost:2181
--replication-factor 1 --partitions 1 --topic test
```

If Zookeeper is running on a separate machine than Kafka, then change the Zookeeper hostname from localhost to the correct hostname.

To make sure that the topic has been created, you can use the following command to list all topics:

```
bin/kafka-topics.sh --list --zookeeper localhost:2181
```

Box 5.1 shows an example of a Kafka producer that sends messages synchronously.

■ **Box 5.1: Kafka Producer for sending messages synchronously**

```
import time
from datetime import datetime
```

```
from kafka.client import KafkaClient
from kafka.producer import SimpleProducer

client = KafkaClient("localhost:6667")
producer = SimpleProducer(client)

while True:
   ts=time.time()
   timestamp = datetime.fromtimestamp(ts).strftime('%Y-%m-%d %H:%M:%S')
   data = "This is a test string generated at:  " + str(timestamp)

   producer.send_messages('test', data)

   time.sleep(1)
```

Box 5.2 shows an example of a Kafka producer that sends messages asynchronously.

■ **Box 5.2: Kafka Producer for sending messages asynchronously**

```
import time
from datetime import datetime
from kafka.client import KafkaClient
from kafka.producer import SimpleProducer

client = KafkaClient("localhost:6667")
producer = SimpleProducer(client, async=True)

while True:
   ts=time.time()
   timestamp = datetime.fromtimestamp(ts).strftime('%Y-%m-%d %H:%M:%S')
   data = "Test message sent asynchronously at:  " + str(timestamp)

   producer.send_messages('test', data)

   time.sleep(1)
```

Box 5.3 shows an example of a Kafka producer that sends messages in batch. The producer collects the messages and sends the messages after 20 messages are collected or after every 60 seconds.

■ **Box 5.3: Kafka Producer for sending messages in batch**

```
import time
from datetime import datetime
from kafka.client import KafkaClient
from kafka.producer import SimpleProducer

client = KafkaClient("localhost:6667")

#The following producer will collect messages in batch
#and send them to Kafka after 20 messages are
```

```
# collected or every 60 seconds

producer = SimpleProducer(client,batch_send=True,
        batch_send_every_n=20,
        batch_send_every_t=60)

while True:
   ts=time.time()
   timestamp = datetime.fromtimestamp(ts).strftime('%Y-%m-%d %H:%M:%S')
   data = "This is a test string generated at:   " + str(timestamp)

   producer.send_messages('test', data)

   time.sleep(1)
```

Box 5.4 shows an example of a Kafka producer that sends keyed messages. The default partitioner class for partitioning messages is the *HashedPartitioner* that partitions based on the hash of the key. Another option is to use the *RoundRobinPartitioner* that sends messages to different partitions in a round-robin fashion.

■ Box 5.4: Kafka Producer for sending keyed messages

```
import time
import datetime
from kafka import KafkaClient, KeyedProducer,
from kafka import HashedPartitioner, RoundRobinPartitioner

kafka = KafkaClient("localhost:6667")

#Default partitioner is HashedPartitioner
producer = KeyedProducer(kafka)
producer.send("test", "key1", "Test message with key1")
producer.send("test", "key2", "Test message with key2")

#Using RoundRobinPartitioner
producer = KeyedProducer(kafka, partitioner=RoundRobinPartitioner)
producer.send("test", "key3", "Test message with key3")
producer.send("test", "key4", "Test message with key4")
```

Box 5.5 shows an example of a Kafka consumer that consumes messages from a topic.

■ Box 5.5: Kafka Consumer

```
from kafka.client import KafkaClient
from kafka.consumer import SimpleConsumer

client = KafkaClient("localhost:6667")
consumer = SimpleConsumer(client, "test-group", "test")

for message in consumer:
   #Print message object
```

```
print message

#Print only message value
print message.message.value
```

Box 5.6 shows an alternative implementation of a Kafka consumer.

■ Box 5.6: Kafka Consumer - alternative implementation

```
from kafka.client import KafkaClient
from kafka.consumer import KafkaConsumer

client = KafkaClient("localhost:6667")
consumer = KafkaConsumer("test", metadata_broker_list=['localhost:6667'])

while True:
   data = consumer.next().value
   print data
```

5.2.2 Amazon Kinesis

Amazon Kinesis is a fully managed commercial service for ingesting real-time streaming data. Kinesis scales automatically to handle high volume streaming data coming from a large number of sources. The streaming data collected by Kinesis can be processed by applications running on Amazon EC2 instances or any other compute instance that can connect to Kinesis.

Kinesis allows rapid and continuous data intake and support data blobs of size upto 50Kb. The data producers write data records to Kinesis streams. A data record comprises a sequence number, a partition key, and the data blob. Data records in a Kinesis stream are distributed in shards. Each shard provides a fixed unit of capacity, and a stream can have multiple shards. A single shard of throughput allows capturing 1MB per second of data, at up to 1,000 PUT transactions per second and allows applications to read data at up to 2 MB per second.

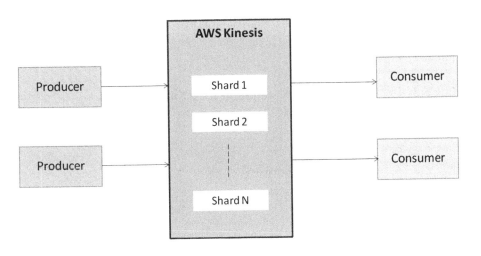

Figure 5.5: Amazon Kinesis architecture

Box 5.7 shows a Python program for writing to a Kinesis stream. In this example, a connection to the Kinesis service is first established and then a new Kinesis stream is either created (if not existing) or described. The data is written to the Kinesis stream using the *kinesis.put_record* function.

■ Box 5.7: Python program for writing to a Kinesis stream

```
from random import randrange
import time
import datetime
import boto
import json
from boto.kinesis.exceptions import ResourceNotFoundException

ACCESS_KEY = "<enter>"
SECRET_KEY = "<enter>"

kinesis = boto.connect_kinesis(aws_access_key_id=ACCESS_KEY,
    aws_secret_access_key=SECRET_KEY)

#Send some synthetic data to AWS Kinesis
while True:
 ts=time.time()

 data = str(ts) + ',' + str(randrange(0,60)) + ',' +
    str(randrange(0,100)) + ',' + str(randrange(5000,12000)) +
     ',' + str(randrange(0,100))

 print data
 response = kinesis.put_record('forestfire', data, data)
 print response
 time.sleep(1)
```

Box 5.8 shows a Python program for reading from a Kinesis stream. In this example, a shard iterator is obtained using the *kinesis.get_shard_iterator* function. The shard iterator specifies the position in the shard from which you want to start reading data records sequentially. The data is read using the *kinesis.get_records* function which returns one or more data records from a shard.

■ Box 5.8: Python program for reading from a Kinesis stream

```
from random import randrange
import time
import datetime
import boto
import json
from boto.kinesis.exceptions import ResourceNotFoundException

ACCESS_KEY = "<enter>"
SECRET_KEY = "<enter>"
```

```
kinesis = boto.connect_kinesis(aws_access_key_id=ACCESS_KEY,
    aws_secret_access_key=SECRET_KEY)

response = kinesis.describe_stream('forestfire')

if response['StreamDescription']['StreamStatus'] == 'ACTIVE':
  shard_id = response['StreamDescription']['Shards'][0]['ShardId']

response = kinesis.get_shard_iterator('forestfire', shard_id,
'TRIM_HORIZON')
shard_iterator = response['ShardIterator']

response = kinesis.get_records(shard_iterator)
shard_iterator = response['NextShardIterator']

for record in response['Records']:
  print record
```

5.3 Big Data Collection Systems

Data collection systems allow collecting, aggregating and moving data from various sources (such as server logs, databases, social media, streaming sensor data from Internet of Things devices and other sources) into a centralized data store (such as a distributed file system or a NoSQL database).

5.3.1 Apache Flume

Apache Flume is a distributed, reliable, and available system for collecting, aggregating, and moving large amounts of data from different data sources into a centralized data store.

Flume Architecture

Flume's architecture is based on data flows and includes the following components:
- **Source**: Source is the component which receives or polls for data from external sources. A Flume data flow starts from a source. For example, Flume source can receive data from a social media network (using streaming APIs).
- **Channel**: After the data is received by a Flume source, the data is transmitted to a channel. Each channel in a data flow is connected to one sink to which the data is drained. A data flow can comprise of multiple channels, where a source writes the data to multiple channels.
- **Sink**: Sink is the component which drains data from a channel to a data store (such as a distributed file system or to another agent). Each sink in a data flow is connected to a channel. Sinks either deliver data to its final destination or are chained to other agents.
- **Agent**: A Flume agent is a collection of sources, channels and sinks. Agent is a process that hosts the sources, channels and sinks from which the data moves from an external source to its final destination.
- **Event**: An event is a unit of data flow having a payload and an optional set of attributes. Flume sources consume events generated by external sources.

Flume uses a data flow model which includes sources, channels and sinks, encapsulated into agents. Figure 5.7 shows some examples of Flume data flows. The simplest data flow has one source, one channel and one sink. Sources can multiplex data to multiple channels for either load balancing purposes, or, for parallel processing. More complex data flows can be created by chaining multiple agents where the sink of one agent delivers data to a source of another agent.

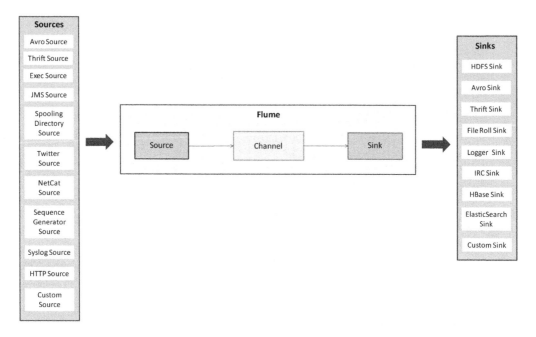

Figure 5.6: Apache Flume architecture

Flume agents are defined in the configuration files. Box 5.9 shows a generic definition of a Flume agent. In the configuration file, first the sources, channels and sinks for the agent are listed and then each source, channel and sink is defined. Finally the bindings between the sources, channels and sinks are defined.

■ Box 5.9: Generic definition of a Flume agent

```
<agent name>.sources = <source-1> <source-2> ...  <source-N>
<agent name>.channels = <channel-1> <channel-2> ...  <channel-N>
<agent name>.sinks = <sink-1> <sink-2> ...  <sink-N>

# Define sources
<agent name>.sources.<source-1>.type = <source type>
:
<agent name>.sources.<source-N>.type = <source type>

# Define sinks
<agent name>.sinks.<sink-1>.type = <sink type>
:
<agent name>.sinks.<sink-1>.type = <sink type>


# Define channels
```

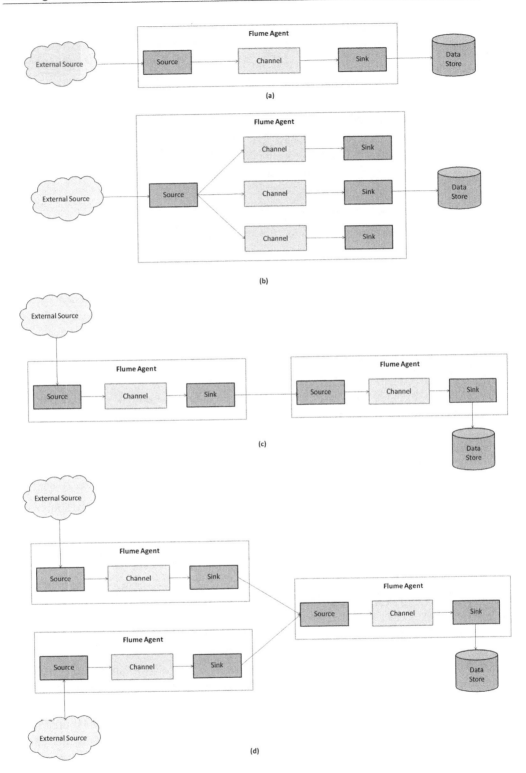

Figure 5.7: Flume data flow examples

```
myagent.channels.<channel-1>.type = <channel type>
:
myagent.channels.<channel-N>.type = <channel type>

# Bind the sources and sinks to the channels
myagent.sources.<source-1>.channels = <channel-1>
myagent.sinks.<sink-1>.channel = <channel-1
:
myagent.sources.<source-N>.channels = <channel-1> ...  <channel-N>
myagent.sinks.<sink-N>.channel = <channel-N
```

```
■ #Format of command to run a Flume agent
#sudo flume-ng agent -c <conf file path> -f <conf file> -n <agent name>

#Example
sudo flume-ng agent -c /etc/flume/conf -f
    /etc/flume/conf/flume.conf -n myagent
```

Flume Sources

Flume comes with multiple built-in sources that allow collecting and aggregating data from a wide range of external systems. Flume also provides the flexibility to add custom sources.

- **Avro Source**: Apache Avro is a data serialization system that provides a compact and fast binary data format. Avro uses an Interface Definition Language (IDL) to define the structure of data in the form of schemas. Avro is defined with JSON, and the schema is always stored with the data, which allows the programs reading the data to interpret the data. Avro can also be used with Remote Procedure Calls (RPC) where the client and server exchange the schemas in the handshake process. Avro provides serialization functionality similar to other systems such as Thrift and Protocol Buffers. The Flume Avro source receives events from external Avro client streams. An Avro source can be setup using the following properties in the Flume configuration file for the agent:

  ```
  ■ myagent.sources = source1
  myagent.sources.source1.type = avro
  myagent.sources.source1.bind = 0.0.0.0
  myagent.sources.source1.port = 4141
  ```

  The *bind* and *port* properties specify the hostname of the external Avro client and the Avro port.

- **Thrift Source**: Apache Thrift is a serialization framework similar to Avro. Thrift provides a software stack and a code generation engine to build services that transparently and efficiently work with multiple programming languages. Like Avro, Thrift also provides a stack for Remote Procedure Calls (RPC). The Flume Thrift source receives events from external Thrift client streams. A Thrift source can be setup using the following properties in the Flume configuration file for the agent:

  ```
  ■ myagent.sources = source1
  myagent.sources.source1.type = thrift
  ```

```
myagent.sources.source1.bind = 0.0.0.0
myagent.sources.source1.port = 4141
```

- **Exec Source**: Exec source can be used to ingest data from the standard output. When an agent with an Exec source is started, it runs the Unix command (specified in the Exec source definition) and continues to receive data from the standard output as long as the process runs. The typical use case for the Exec source is the *tail* command which emits few lines of any text file given to it as an input and writes them to standard output. The *tail* when used with the -F options outputs the appended data as the file grows. The box below shows an example of setting up an Exec source with the *tail* command.

```
■ myagent.sources = source1
myagent.sources.source1.type = exec
myagent.sources.source1.command = tail -F /var/log/eventlog.log
```

- **JMS Source**: Java Message Service (JMS) is a messaging service that can be used by Java applications to create, send, receive, and read messages. The JMS source receives messages from a JMS queue or topic. The box below shows an example of setting up a JMS source:

```
■ myagent.sources = s1
myagent.sources.s1.type = jms
myagent.sources.s1.initialContextFactory =
      org.apache.activemq.jndi.ActiveMQInitialContextFactory
myagent.sources.s1.connectionFactory = GenericConnectionFactory
myagent.sources.s1.providerURL = tcp://mqserver:61616
myagent.sources.s1.destinationName = DATA
myagent.sources.s1.destinationType = QUEUE
```

To connect with a JMS destination an initial context factory name, a connection factory and a provider URL are required. The destination type can either be a queue or a topic.

- **Spooling Directory Source**: Spooling Directory source is useful for ingesting log files. A spool directory is setup on the disk from where the Spooling Directory source ingests the files. To use the source for ingesting logs, the log generation system is setup such that when the log files are rolled over they are moved to the spool directory. The Spooling Directory source parses the files and creates events. The parsing logic can be configured for the source. The default logic is to parse each line as an event. Though an alternative approach to Spooling Directory source is to use Exec source with *tail* command, however, it is not as reliable. The box below shows an example of setting up a Spooling Directory source:

```
■ myagent.sources = source1
myagent.sources.source1.type = spooldir
myagent.sources.source1.spoolDir = /var/log/apache/flumeSpool
myagent.sources.source1.fileHeader = true
```

- **Twitter Source**: The Flume Twitter source connects to the Twitter streaming API and receives tweets in real-time. The Twitter source converts the tweet objects to Avro format before sending them to the downstream channel. The box below shows an example of setting up a Twitter source:

```
■ myagent.sources = source1
myagent.sources.source1.type =
        org.apache.flume.source.twitter.TwitterSource
myagent.sources.source1.consumerKey = CONSUMER_KEY
myagent.sources.source1.consumerSecret = CONSUMER_SECRET
myagent.sources.source1.accessToken = ACCESS_TOKEN
myagent.sources.source1.accessTokenSecret = ACCESS_TOKEN_SECRET
myagent.sources.source1.maxBatchSize = 10
myagent.sources.source1.maxBatchDurationMillis = 200
```

Before setting up the Twitter source, you will need to create a Twitter application from the Twitter developer account and obtain the consumer and access tokens and secrets for the application.

- **NetCat Source**: NetCat is a simple Unix utility which reads and writes data across network connections, using TCP or UDP protocol. The NetCat source listens to a specific port to which the data is written by a NetCat client and turns each line of text received into a Flume event. The box below shows an example of setting up a NetCat source:

```
■ myagent.sources = source1
myagent.sources.source1.type = netcat
myagent.sources.source1.bind = 0.0.0.0
myagent.sources.source1.port = 6666
```

- **Sequence Generator Source**: Sequence Generator source generates events with a sequence of numbers starting from 0 and incremented by 1. This source is mainly used for testing purposes. The box below shows an example of setting up a Sequence Generator source:

```
■ myagent.sources = source1
myagent.sources.source1.type = seq
```

- **Syslog Source**: Syslog source is used for ingesting syslog data. The box below shows an example of setting up a Syslog TCP source.

```
■ myagent.sources = source1
myagent.sources.source1.type = syslogtcp
myagent.sources.source1.host = localhost
myagent.sources.source1.port = 5140
```

- **HTTP Source**: HTTP source receives HTTP events (POST or GET requests) and converts them into Flume events. While the source can receive events in the form of HTTP POST and GET requests, GET command is used for experimentation only. To convert the HTTP requests into events, a pluggable handler is used. The default handler is JSONHandler, which expects an array of JSON objects. The box below shows an example of setting up a HTTP source:

```
■ myagent.sources = source1
myagent.sources.source1.type = http
myagent.sources.source1.bind = localhost
myagent.sources.source1.port = 81
myagent.sources.source1.handler =
        org.apache.flume.source.http.JSONHandler
```

The *bind* and *port* properties specify the hostname and port on which the source should listen to.

- **Custom Source**: Flume allows customs sources to be integrated into the system. Custom sources are implemented in Java. The Java class files of the custom source along with the dependencies are included in the classpath of the Flume agent and also specified in the agent configuration file shown below:

```
■ myagent.sources = source1
myagent.sources.source1.type = org.example.MySource
```

Flume Sinks

Flume comes with multiple built-in sinks. Each sink in a Flume agent connects to a channel and drains the data from the channel to a data store.

- **HDFS Sink**: The Hadoop Distributed File System (HDFS) Sink drains events from a channel to HDFS. The data is written to HDFS in the form of a configurable file type. HDFS sink supports SequenceFile, DataStream and CompressedStream file types. HDFS sink allows the files to be rolled either when the size of the file exceeds a certain limit, or after a specified interval, or after a certain number of events have been written to a file. The box below shows an example of setting up an HDFS sink:

```
■ myagent.sinks = sink1
myagent.sinks.sink1.type = hdfs
myagent.sinks.sink1.hdfs.fileType = DataStream
myagent.sinks.sink1.hdfs.path = /flume/events
myagent.sinks.sink1.hdfs.filePrefix = eventlog
myagent.sinks.sink1.hdfs.fileSuffix = .log
myagent.sinks.sink1.hdfs.batchSize = 1000
```

- **Avro Sink**: An Avro sink retrieves events from a channel and drains the events to a downstream host. The box below shows an example of setting up an Avro sink:

```
■ myagent.sinks = sink1
myagent.sinks.sink1.type = avro
myagent.sinks.sink1.hostname = 10.10.10.10
myagent.sinks.sink1.port = 4545
```

- **Thrift Sink**: A Thrift sink retrieves events from a channel and drains the events to a downstream host. The box below shows an example of setting up an Thrift sink:

```
■ myagent.sinks = sink1
myagent.sinks.sink1.type = thrift
myagent.sinks.sink1.hostname = 10.10.10.10
myagent.sinks.sink1.port = 4545
```

- **File Roll Sink**: A File Roll sink drains the events to a file on the local filesystem. The box below shows an example of setting up an File Roll sink:

```
■ myagent.sinks = sink1
myagent.sinks.sink1.type = file_roll
myagent.sinks.sink1.sink.directory = /var/log/flume
```

- **Logger Sink**: A Logger sink retrieves events from a channel and logs the events. The box below shows an example of setting up an Logger sink:

```
■ myagent.sinks = sink1
myagent.sinks.sink1.type = logger
```

- **IRC Sink**: An IRC sink retrieves events from a channel and drains the events to an IRC host. The box below shows an example of setting up an IRC sink:

```
■ myagent.sinks = sink1
myagent.sinks.sink1.type = irc
myagent.sinks.sink1.hostname = irc.example.com
myagent.sinks.sink1.nick = flume
myagent.sinks.sink1.chan = #flume
```

- **HBaseSink**: An HBase sink retrieves events from a channel and drains the events to an HBase table. The box below shows an example of setting up an HBase sink:

```
■ myagent.sinks = sink1
myagent.sinks.sink1.type = hbase
myagent.sinks.sink1.table = mytable
myagent.sinks.sink1.columnFamily = myfam
myagent.sinks.sink1.serializer =
    org.apache.flume.sink.hbase.RegexHbaseEventSerializer
```

- **Custom Sink**: Flume allows customs sinks to be integrated into the system. Custom sinks are implemented in Java. The Java class files of the custom sink along with the dependencies are included in the classpath of the Flume agent and also specified in the agent configuration file shown below:

```
■ myagent.sinks = sink1
myagent.sinks.sink1.type = org.example.MySink
```

Flume Channels

Channels store the events while they are being moved from a source to sink.

- **Memory Channel**: Memory channel stores the events in the memory and provides high throughput. However, in the event of an agent failure, the events can be lost. The box below shows an example of setting up a memory channel.

```
■ myagent.channels = channel1
myagent.channels.channel1.type = memory
myagent.channels.channel1.capacity = 10000
myagent.channels.channel1.transactionCapacity = 10000
myagent.channels.channel1.byteCapacityBufferPercentage = 20
myagent.channels.channel1.byteCapacity = 800000
```

- **File Channel**: File channel stores the events in files on the local filesystem. Events are stored in a checkpoint file in the data directory specified in the channel configuration. The a maximum file size for the checkpoint file can be specified. The box below shows an example of setting up a file channel.

```
■ myagent.channels = channel1
myagent.channels.channel1.type = file
myagent.channels.channel1.checkpointDir = /mnt/flume/checkpoint
myagent.channels.channel1.dataDirs = /mnt/flume/data
```

- **JDBC Channel**: JDBC channel stores the events in an embedded Derby database. This channel provides a durable storage for events, and the events can be recovered easily in case of agent failures. The box below shows an example of setting up a JDBC channel.

```
■ myagent.channels = channel1
myagent.channels.channel1.type = jdbc
```

- **Spillable Memory Channel**: Spillable Memory channel stores events in an in-memory queue and when the queue fills up, the events are spilled onto the disk. This channel provides high throughput and fault tolerance. The box below shows an example of setting up a Spillable Memory channel.

```
■ myagent.channels = channel1
myagent.channels.channel1.type = SPILLABLEMEMORY
myagent.channels.channel1.memoryCapacity = 10000
myagent.channels.channel1.overflowCapacity = 1000000
myagent.channels.channel1.byteCapacity = 800000
myagent.channels.channel1.checkpointDir = /mnt/flume/checkpoint
myagent.channels.channel1.dataDirs = /mnt/flume/data
```

Maximum number of events stored in a memory queue are specified using the *memoryCapacity* property and the maximum size of the memory queue is specified using the *byteCapacity* property. The in-memory queue is considered full, and the events are spilled to the disk when either the *memoryCapacity* or *byteCapacity* limit is reached.

- **Custom Channel**: Flume allows customs channels to be integrated into the system. Custom channels are implemented in Java. The Java class files of the custom channel along with the dependencies are included in the classpath of the Flume agent and also specified in the agent configuration file shown below:

```
■ myagent.channels = channel1
myagent.channels.channel1.type = org.example.MyChannel
```

Channel Selectors

Flume agents can have a single source connected to multiple channels. In such cases, the channel selector defines policy about distributing the events among the channels connected to a single source.

- **Replicating Channel Selector**: The default channel selected is the replicating selector, which replicates events received from the source to all the connected channels. The box below shows an example of the configuration of an agent which has a single source connected to three channels and uses a replicating channel selector.

```
■ myagent.sources = source1
myagent.channels = channel1 channel2 channel3
myagent.source.source1.selector.type = replicating
myagent.source.source1.channels = channel1 channel2 channel3
myagent.source.source1.selector.optional = channel3
```

- **Multiplexing Channel Selector**: Multiplexing channel selector distributes events from a source to all the connected channels. The box below shows an example of the configuration of an agent which has a single source connected to three channels and uses a multiplexing channel selector.

```
■ myagent.sources = source1
myagent.channels = channel1 channel2 channel3
myagent.sources.source1.selector.type = multiplexing
myagent.sources.source1.selector.header = country
myagent.sources.source1.selector.mapping.IN = channel1
myagent.sources.source1.selector.mapping.US = channel2
myagent.sources.source1.selector.default = channel3
```

  The *header* property specifies the attribute name to check for distributing the events among the channels and the *mapping* properties specify the mappings between the attribute values and the channels. For example, in the above configuration the *header* property is set to the country attribute. All the events which have the country attribute value as IN are sent to channel1 while all the events with country attribute value as the US are sent to channel2. The default channel is set as channel3.

- **Custom Channel Selector**: Flume allows customs channel selectors to be integrated into the system. Custom channel selectors are implemented in Java. The Java class files of the custom channel selector along with the dependencies are included in the classpath of the Flume agent and also specified in the agent configuration file shown below:

```
■ myagent.sources = source1
myagent.channels = channel1
myagent.sources.source1.selector.type =
```

```
      org.example.MyChannelSelector
```

Sink Processors

Flume allows creating sink groups where a channel can be attached to a sink group to which the events are drained. A sink processor defines how the events are drained from a channel to a sink. Sink processors enable parallelism, priorities, and automatic failover.

- **Load balancing Sink Processor**: The load balancing sink processor allows load balancing of events drained from a channel between the sinks in the attached sink group. The load is distributed among the list of sinks specified using a round robin or random selection mechanism. The box below shows an example of an agent with a sink group and a load balancing sink processor.

```
■ myagent.sinkgroups = group1
myagent.sinkgroups.group1.sinks = sink1 sink2
myagent.sinkgroups.group1.processor.type = load_balance
myagent.sinkgroups.group1.processor.backoff = true
myagent.sinkgroups.group1.processor.selector = random
```

- **Failover Sink Processor**: With Failover Sink processor, priorities can be assigned to sinks between in a sink group. The attached channel then drains the events to the highest priority sink. When the highest priority sink fails, the events are drained to the sink with one lower priority, providing automatic failover. The box below shows an example of an agent with a sink group and a failover sink processor.

```
■ myagent.sinkgroups = group1
myagent.sinkgroups.group1.sinks = sink1 sink2
myagent.sinkgroups.group1.processor.type = failover
myagent.sinkgroups.group1.processor.priority.sink1 = 2
myagent.sinkgroups.group1.processor.priority.sink2 = 4
myagent.sinkgroups.group1.processor.maxpenalty = 10000
```

Flume Interceptors

Flume interceptors allow events to be modified, filtered or dropped as they flow from the source to a channel. Interceptors are connected to the source. Interceptors can also be chained to each other.

- **Timestamp Interceptor**: The Timestamp interceptor adds the current timestamp to the headers of the events processed. Timestamp interceptor can be configured as follows:

```
■ myagent.sources = source1
myagent.sources.source1.interceptors = i1
myagent.sources.source1.interceptors.i1.type = timestamp
```

- **Host Interceptor**: The Host interceptor adds the hostname of the Flume agent to the headers of the events processed. Host interceptor can be configured as follows:

```
■ myagent.sources = source1
myagent.sources.source1.interceptors = i1
```

```
myagent.sources.source1.interceptors.i1.type = host
myagent.sources.source1.interceptors.i1.hostHeader = hostname
myagent.sources.source1.interceptors.i1.useIP = false
```

- **Static Interceptor**: Static interceptor adds a static header to the events processed. The box below shows an example of adding a static header, country, with the value set to US.

```
■ myagent.sources = source1
myagent.sources.source1.interceptors = i1
myagent.sources.source1.interceptors.i1.type = static
myagent.sources.source1.interceptors.i1.key = country
myagent.sources.source1.interceptors.i1.value = US
```

- **UUID Interceptor**: The UUID adds a universally unique identifier to the headers of the events processed. UUID interceptor can be configured as follows:

```
■ myagent.sources = source1
myagent.sources.source1.interceptors = i1
myagent.sources.source1.interceptors.i1.type = uuid
myagent.sources.source1.interceptors.i1.headerName=id
```

- **Regex Filtering Interceptor**: Regex Filtering interceptor applies a regular expression to the event body and filters the matching events. The events matching the regular expression can either be included or excluded. Regex Filtering interceptor can be configured as follows:

```
■ myagent.sources = source1
myagent.sources.source1.interceptors = i1
myagent.sources.source1.interceptors.i1.type = regex_filter
myagent.sources.source1.interceptors.i1.regex = .*
myagent.sources.source1.interceptors.i1.excludeEvents = false
```

Flume Examples

Box 5.10 shows an example of setting up a Flume agent with NetCat Source & File Roll Sink.

■ Box 5.10: Flume agent with NetCat Source & File Roll Sink

```
myagent.sources = r1
myagent.channels = c1
myagent.sinks = k1

# Define source
myagent.sources.r1.type = netcat
myagent.sources.r1.bind = 0.0.0.0
myagent.sources.r1.port = 6666

#Define Sink
myagent.sinks.k1.type = file_roll
myagent.sinks.k1.sink.directory = /var/log/flume
```

```
#Define Channel
myagent.channels.c1.type = file
myagent.channels.c1.checkpointDir = /var/flume/checkpoint
myagent.channels.c1.dataDirs = /var/flume/data

# Bind the source and sink to the channel
myagent.sources.r1.channels = c1
myagent.sinks.k1.channel = c1
```

To test the agent, run the Flume agent and then open a new terminal and run the following command:

```
■ nc localhost 6666
```

Type some text. The same text will be sent to sink file.

```
■ sudo flume-ng agent -c /etc/flume/conf -f /etc/flume/conf/flume.conf -n
myagent
```

Box 5.11 shows an example of setting up a Flume agent with Twitter Source & HDFS Sink.

■ Box 5.11: Flume agent with Twitter Source & HDFS Sink

```
myagent.sources = r1
myagent.channels = c1
myagent.sinks = k1

# Define source
myagent.sources.r1.type = org.apache.flume.source.twitter.TwitterSource
myagent.sources.r1.consumerKey = <enter key here>
myagent.sources.r1.consumerSecret = <enter secret here>
myagent.sources.r1.accessToken = <enter token here>
myagent.sources.r1.accessTokenSecret = <enter token secret here>
myagent.sources.r1.maxBatchSize = 10
myagent.sources.r1.maxBatchDurationMillis = 200

#Define sink
myagent.sinks.k1.type = hdfs
myagent.sinks.k1.hdfs.fileType = DataStream
myagent.sinks.k1.hdfs.path = /flume/events
myagent.sinks.k1.hdfs.filePrefix = eventlog
myagent.sinks.k1.hdfs.fileSuffix = .log
myagent.sinks.k1.hdfs.batchSize = 1000

#Define Channel
myagent.channels.c1.type = file
myagent.channels.c1.checkpointDir = /var/flume/checkpoint
myagent.channels.c1.dataDirs = /var/flume/data

# Bind the source and sink to the channel
myagent.sources.r1.channels = c1
myagent.sinks.k1.channel = c1
```

Box 5.12 shows an example of setting up a Flume agent with HTTP Source & File Roll Sink.

■ **Box 5.12: Flume agent with HTTP Source & File Roll Sink**

```
myagent.sources = r1
myagent.channels = c1
myagent.sinks = k1

# Define source
myagent.sources.r1.type = http
myagent.sources.r1.bind = 0.0.0.0
myagent.sources.r1.port = 8000
myagent.sources.r1.handler = org.apache.flume.source.http.JSONHandler
myagent.sources.r1.handler.nickname = randomprops

#Define sink
myagent.sinks.k1.type = file_roll
myagent.sinks.k1.sink.directory = /var/log/flume

#Define Channel
myagent.channels.c1.type = file
myagent.channels.c1.checkpointDir = /var/flume/checkpoint
myagent.channels.c1.dataDirs = /var/flume/data

# Bind the source and sink to the channel
myagent.sources.r1.channels = c1
myagent.sinks.k1.channel = c1
```

5.3.2 Apache Sqoop

Apache Sqoop is a tool that allows importing data from relational database management systems (RDBMS) into the Hadoop Distributed File System (HDFS), Hive or HBase tables. Sqoop also allows exporting data from HDFS to RDBMS. Table 5.1 lists the various Sqoop commands.

Tool	Function
import	Import a table from a database to HDFS
import-all-tables	Import tables from a database to HDFS
export	Export an HDFS directory to a database table
codegen	Generate code to interact with database records
create-hive-table	Import a table definition into Hive
eval	Evaluate a SQL statement and display the results
list-databases	List available databases on a server
list-tables	List available tables in a database

Table 5.1: Sqoop Tools

5.3.3 Importing Data with Sqoop

Figure 5.8 shows the process of importing data from RDBMS using Sqoop. The import process begins with the user submitting a Sqoop import command. The format of an import command is shown below:

```
sqoop import --connect jdbc:mysql://<IP Address>/<Database Name>
--username <Username> --password <Password> --table <Table Name>
```

The import command includes a connection string which specifies the database type, database server hostname (or IP address) and database name. Sqoop can connect to any JDBC compliant database.

An example of an import command for importing data from a table named *Courses* from MySQL database named *Department* is shown below:

```
sqoop import --connect jdbc:mysql://localhost/Department
--username admin --password admin123 --table Courses
```

Sqoop import command launches multiple Map tasks (default is four tasks) which connect to the database and import the rows in the table in parallel to HDFS as delimited text files, binary Avro files or Hadoop SequenceFiles. The number of Map tasks used for importing data (and hence the parallelism) can be controlled using the —*m* option as shown in example below:

```
#Use 8 map tasks to import sqoop import --connect
jdbc:mysql://localhost/Department
--username admin --password admin123 --table Courses --m 8
```

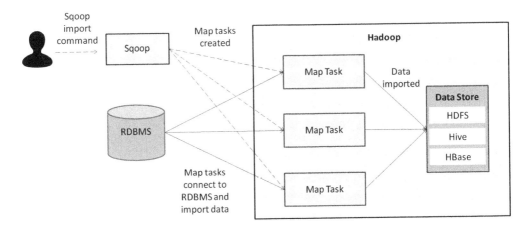

Figure 5.8: Importing data using Apache Sqoop

5.3.4   Selecting Data to Import

While in the previous example, we imported all the data from a table, Sqoop also allows importing selected data. With Sqoop import, it is possible to select a subset of columns (using the *columns* option) to import from a table as shown in the example below:

```
■ sqoop import --connect jdbc:mysql://localhost/Department
--username admin --password admin123 --table Courses
--columns "name,semester,year"
```

You can also use an SQL query with Sqoop import to select the data to import as shown in the example below:

```
■ sqoop import --connect jdbc:mysql://localhost/myDB --username admin
--password admin123 --query 'SELECT a.*, b.* FROM a JOIN b on
(a.id == b.id) WHERE $CONDITIONS'
--split-by a.id --target-dir /user/admin/joinresults
```

In the above example, Sqoop will import the results of the query in parallel. Since each Map task will execute the same query, certain conditions are required to split the data that each Map task imports. The $CONDITIONS token is replaced with the conditions by the Sqoop import tool at the run time. The *split-by* option specifies, on which column the data split should be performed to import data in parallel. When using an SQL query to specify what data to import, the *target-dir* option is required to provide the target location for the data to be imported.

5.3.5   Custom Connectors

While Sqoop ships with a generic JDBC connector, it may be preferable to use a vendor-specific JDBC connector as they can provide higher performance. Moreover, some databases provide data movement tools which can move data with higher performance. For example, MySQL provides *mysqldump* tool which can be used to export data from MySQL databases. Sqoop allows such database-specific tools to be used with the Sqoop import command using the *direct* option. The box below shows an example of importing data from MySQL with Sqoop using the *mysqldump* tool:

```
■ sqoop import --connect jdbc:mysql://localhost/Department
--username admin --password admin123 --table Courses --direct

#Passing additional arguments to database-specific tool
sqoop import --connect jdbc:mysql://localhost/Department
--username admin --password admin123
--table Courses --direct -- --default-character-set=latin1
```

5.3.6   Importing Data to Hive

Sqoop allows importing data into Hive using the *hive-import* option as shown in the example below. When this option is set, Sqoop will automatically create a Hive table and import data into the table.

```
■ sqoop import --connect jdbc:mysql://localhost/Department
--username admin --password admin123 --table Courses --hive-import
```

5.3.7   Importing Data to HBase

Sqoop allows importing data into HBase using the *hbase-table* option along with a target HBase table name, as shown in the example below. Sqoop also supports bulk loading of data into HBase using the *hbase-bulkload* option.

```
■ sqoop import --connect jdbc:mysql://localhost/Department
--username admin --password admin123 --table Courses
--hbase-table Courses
```

5.3.8   Incremental Imports

Incremental imports are useful when you have previously imported some rows from a table, and you want to import the newer rows. Sqoop provides an *incremental* option for incremental imports. When this option is used, a mode is also required, which can either be *append* or *lastmodified*. The *append* mode is used when a table is updated with new rows with increasing row ID values. The column to check for the row IDs is specified using the *check-column* option.

The *lastmodified* mode is used when the rows of a table are updated and the timestamp when a row was last modified is set in a last-modified column. The column to check for the last modified timestamp is specified using the *check-column* option. The *last-value* option is used in the *lastmodified* mode to specify the timestamp. When Sqoop import process completes it prints the *last-value*. In the next import, this *last-value* is specified, so that Sqoop can import only rows which have a last-modified timestamp greater than the *last-value*.

The box below shows examples of incremental imports:

```
■ sqoop import --connect jdbc:mysql://localhost/Department
--username admin --password admin123 --table Students
--check-column id --incremental append

#Import last modified rows
sqoop import --connect jdbc:mysql://localhost/Department
--username admin --password admin123 --table Students
--check-column last-modified --incremental
lastmodified --last-value "2015-04-03 15:08:45.66"
```

5.3.9   Importing All Tables

The Sqoop *import-all-tables* command can be used to import all tables from a database to HDFS, as shown the following example:

```
■ sqoop import-all-tables --connect jdbc:mysql://localhost/Department
```

5.3.10   Exporting Data with Sqoop

The Sqoop *export* command can be used to export files from HDFS to RDBMS, as shown in the following example:

```
■ sqoop export --connect jdbc:mysql://localhost/Department -table Courses
-export-dir /user/admin/courses
```

The target table must exist in the database. Sqoop translates the export command into a set of INSERT statements to append new rows to the table. The data from the input files is parsed and inserted into the target table. Instead of the default "insert" mode, you can also specify an "update" mode, in which Sqoop will use UPDATE statements to replace existing records in the target table. The *update-mode* option can be used to specify the "update" mode. With *update-mode* option, a mode needs to be specified which can either be *updateonly* or *allowinsert*. When *updateonly* mode is specified, the rows in the table are updated in the export process only if they exist. With *allowinsert* mode, the rows are updated if they exist in the table already or inserted if they do not exist.

5.4 Messaging Queues

Messaging queues are useful for push-pull messaging where the producers push data to the queues, and the consumers pull the data from the queues. The producers and consumers do not need to be aware of each other. Messaging queues allow decoupling of producers of data from the consumers. In this section, we will describe some message queuing systems based on protocols such as Advanced Message Queuing Protocol (AMQP) and ZeroMQ Message Transfer Protocol (ZMTP).

5.4.1 RabbitMQ

RabbitMQ implements the Advanced Message Queuing Protocol (AMQP), which is an open standard that defines the protocol for exchanges of messages between systems. AMQP clients can either be producers or consumers. The clients conforming with the standard can communicate with each other through brokers. Broker is a middleware application that receives messages from producers and routes them to consumers. The producers publish messages to the exchanges, which then distribute the messages to queues based on the defined routing rules (or bindings). AMQP brokers provide four types of exchanges: direct exchange (for point-to-point messaging), fanout exchange (for multicast messaging), topic exchange (for publish-subscribe messaging) and header exchange (that uses header attributes for making routing decisions). Exchanges use bindings which are the rules to route messages to the queues. The consumers consume the messages from the queues. AMQP is an application level protocol that uses TCP for reliable delivery. A logical connection between a producer or consumer and a broker is called a Channel. For applications which need to establish multiple connections with a broker, it is undesirable to have multiple TCP connections. For such applications, multiple Channels can be setup over a single connection.

RabbitMQ is an AMQP Broker implemented in Erlang and is designed to be highly scalable and reliable. The commands for setting up RabbitMQ are given in Box 5.13.

■ Box 5.13: Setting up RabbitMQ

```
echo 'deb http://www.rabbitmq.com/debian/ testing main' |
sudo tee /etc/apt/sources.list
```

```
wget https://www.rabbitmq.com/rabbitmq-signing-key-public.asc
sudo apt-key add rabbitmq-signing-key-public.asc
sudo apt-get install rabbitmq-server
sudo pip install pika
```

Box 5.14 shows an example of a producer that sends data to a RabbitMQ queue. This example uses the *pika* library which is a pure-Python implementation of AMQP. The producer sends synthetic data along with the timestamp to a RabbitMQ queue.

■ **Box 5.14: Example of a Producer that sends data to RabbitMQ**

```
import pika
from time import time
import json
import pickle, re, os, urllib, urllib2
from datetime import datetime
from random import randrange
import time
import datetime

connection = pika.BlockingConnection(pika.ConnectionParameters(
host='localhost'))
channel = connection.channel()

channel.queue_declare(queue='test')

while True:
    data = str(randrange(0,60)) + ',' +
        str(randrange(0,100)) + ',' + str(randrange(5000,12000)) +
        ',' + str(randrange(50,350))

    ts=time.time()
    timestamp =
    datetime.datetime.fromtimestamp(ts).strftime('%Y-%m-%d %H:%M:%S')

    msg='timestamp': timestamp, 'data': data
    print msg

    channel.basic_publish(exchange='',
 routing_key='test',
 body=json.dumps(msg))

    print data
    time.sleep(1)
```

Box 5.15 shows an example of a consumer that consumes data from RabbitMQ queue.

■ **Box 5.15: Example of a Consumer that consumes data from RabbitMQ**

```
import pika

connection = pika.BlockingConnection(pika.ConnectionParameters(
host='localhost'))
```

```
channel = connection.channel()

channel.queue_declare(queue='hello')

def callback(ch, method, properties, body):
print "Received %r" % (body,)

channel.basic_consume(callback,
queue='hello',
no_ack=True)

channel.start_consuming()
```

5.4.2   ZeroMQ

ZeroMQ is a high-performance messaging library which provides tools to build a messaging system. Unlike other message queuing systems, ZeroMQ can work without a message broker. ZeroMQ provides various messaging patterns such as Request-Reply, Publish-Subscribe, Push-Pull and Exclusive Pair.

The commands for setting up ZeroMQ are given in Box 5.16.

■ Box 5.16: Setting up ZeroMQ

```
sudo apt-get install libtool
autoconf automake uuid-dev build-essential
wget http://download.zeromq.org/zeromq-4.0.4.tar.gz
tar zxvf zeromq-4.0.4.tar.gz && cd zeromq-4.0.4
./configure
make
sudo make install
sudo apt-get install python-zmq
```

Box 5.17 shows an example of a producer that sends data to a ZeroMQ queue.

■ Box 5.17: Example of Producer that sends data to ZeroMQ

```
import zmq
from time import time
import json
from random import randrange
import time
import datetime

context = zmq.Context()

socket = context.socket(zmq.PUSH)
socket.bind('tcp://127.0.0.1:5555')

while True:
#Generate some synthetic data
   data = str(randrange(0,60)) + ',' +
      str(randrange(0,100)) + ',' + str(randrange(5000,12000)) +
```

```
           ',' + str(randrange(50,350))

    ts=time.time()
    timestamp =
    datetime.datetime.fromtimestamp(ts).strftime('%Y-%m-%d %H:%M:%S')

    msg='timestamp': timestamp, 'data':  data
    print msg
    data = zmq.Message(json.dumps(msg))
    socket.send(data)

    print data
    time.sleep(1)
```

Box 5.18 shows an example of a consumer that consumes data from ZeroMQ queue.

■ **Box 5.18: Example of a Consumer that consumes data from ZeroMQ**

```
import zmq
context = zmq.Context()

socket = context.socket(zmq.PULL)
socket.connect('tcp://127.0.0.1:5555')

while True:
   data = socket.recv()
   print data
```

5.4.3   RestMQ

RESTMQ is a message queue which is based on a simple JSON-based protocol and uses HTTP as transport. The queue is organized as REST resources. RESTMQ can be used by any client which can make HTTP calls. The commands for setting up RestMQ are given in Box 5.19.

■ **Box 5.19: Setting up RESTMQ**

```
#Install RESTMQ
sudo apt-get install build-essential curl python-pip redis-server
    libffi-dev python-dev -y libssl-dev python-setuptools
git clone https://github.com/gleicon/restmq.git
cd restmq
sudo pip install -r requirements.txt
sudo python setup.py install

# Start RESTMQ
cd restmq/start_scripts
touch acl.conf
bash restmq_server -acl=acl.conf -listen=0.0.0.0 &
```

Box 5.20 shows an example of a producer that sends data to a RESTMQ queue.

■ **Box 5.20: Example of a Producer that sends data to RESTMQ**

```python
import requests
import json
import urllib2
from random import randrange
import time
import datetime

while True:
#Generate some synthetic data
   data = str(randrange(0,60)) + ',' +
       str(randrange(0,100)) + ',' + str(randrange(5000,12000)) +
          ',' + str(randrange(50,350))

   ts=time.time()
   timestamp =
      datetime.datetime.fromtimestamp(ts).strftime('%Y-%m-%d %H:%M:%S')

   msg='timestamp': timestamp, 'data': data

   data = urllib.urlencode('queue':'test', 'value':json.dumps(msg))
   r = urllib2.Request('http://localhost:8888/', data)
   f = urllib2.urlopen(r)
   data = f.read()
   f.close()
```

Box 5.21 shows an example of a consumer that consumes data from RESTMQ queue.

■ **Box 5.21: Example of a Consumer that consumes data from RESTMQ**

```python
import json
from twisted.web import client
from twisted.python import log
from twisted.internet import reactor

class CometClient(object):
   def write(self, content):
      try:
         data = json.loads(content)
      except Exception, e:
         log.err("cannot decode json: %s" % str(e))
         log.err("json is: %s" % content)
      else:
         log.msg("got data: %s" % repr(data))

   def close(self):
      pass

if __name__ == "__main__":
   log.startLogging(sys.stdout)
   client.downloadPage("http://localhost:8888/c/test", CometClient())
   reactor.run()
```

```
#Post data to RESTMQ
curl -X POST -d "value=data" http://localhost:8888/q/test

#Get data from RESTMQ
curl http://localhost:8888/c/test
```

5.4.4 Amazon SQS

Amazon SQS offers a highly scalable and reliable hosted queue for storing messages as they travel between distinct components of applications. SQS only guarantees that the messages will arrive, not that they will arrive in the same order in which they were put in the queue. Though, at first look, Amazon SQS may seem to be similar to Amazon Kinesis, however, both are intended for very different types of applications. While Kinesis is meant for real-time applications that involve high data ingress and egress rates, SQS is simply a queue system that stores and releases messages in a scalable manner.

SQS can be used in distributed applications in which various application components need to exchange messages. Let us look at some examples of using SQS. Box 5.22 shows the Python code for creating an SQS queue. In this example, a connection to SQS service is first established by calling *boto.sqs.connect_to_region*. The AWS region, access key and secret key are passed to this function. After connecting to SQS service, *conn.create_queue* is called to create a new queue with queue name as an input parameter. The function *conn.get_all_queues* is used to retrieve all SQS queues.

■ **Box 5.22: Python program for creating an SQS queue**

```
import boto.sqs

ACCESS_KEY="<enter access key>"
SECRET_KEY="<enter secret key>"
REGION="us-east-1"

print "Connecting to SQS"

conn = boto.sqs.connect_to_region(
      REGION,
      aws_access_key_id=ACCESS_KEY,
      aws_secret_access_key=SECRET_KEY)

queue_name = 'mytestqueue'

print "Creating queue with name:  " + queue_name
q = conn.create_queue(queue_name)

print "Created queue with name:  " + queue_name

print " \n Getting all queues"

rs = conn.get_all_queues()
```

```
for item in rs:
   print item
```

Box 5.23 shows the Python code for writing to an SQS queue. After connecting to an SQS queue, the *queue.write* method is called with the message as an input parameter.

■ Box 5.23: Python program for writing to an SQS queue

```
import boto.sqs
from boto.sqs.message import Message
import time

ACCESS_KEY="<enter access key>"
SECRET_KEY="<enter secret key>"

REGION="us-east-1"

print "Connecting to SQS"

conn = boto.sqs.connect_to_region(
     REGION,
     aws_access_key_id=ACCESS_KEY,
     aws_secret_access_key=SECRET_KEY)

queue_name = 'mytestqueue'

print "Connecting to queue:  " + queue_name
q = conn.get_all_queues(prefix=queue_name)

msg_datetime = time.asctime(time.localtime(time.time()))

msg = "Test message generated on:  " + msg_datetime
print "Writing to queue:  " + msg

m = Message()
m.set_body(msg)
status = q[0].write(m)

print "Message written to queue"

count = q[0].count()

print "Total messages in queue:  " + str(count)
```

Box 5.24 shows the Python code for reading from an SQS queue. After connecting to an SQS queue, the *queue.read* method is called to read a message from a queue.

■ Box 5.24: Python program for reading from an SQS queue

```
import boto.sqs
from boto.sqs.message import Message

ACCESS_KEY="<enter access key>"
```

```
SECRET_KEY="<enter secret key>"

REGION="us-east-1"

print "Connecting to SQS"

conn = boto.sqs.connect_to_region(
      REGION,
      aws_access_key_id=ACCESS_KEY,
      aws_secret_access_key=SECRET_KEY)

queue_name = 'mytestqueue'

print "Connecting to queue:  " + queue_name
q = conn.get_all_queues(prefix=queue_name)

count = q[0].count()

print "Total messages in queue:  " + str(count)

print "Reading message from queue"

for i in range(count):
   m = q[0].read()
   print "Message %d:  %s" % (i+1,str(m.get_body()))
   q[0].delete_message(m)

print "Read %d messages from queue" % (count)
```

5.5 Custom Connectors

Custom connectors and web services for acquiring data from data producers can be developed to meet the application requirements.

5.5.1 REST-based Connectors

Figure 5.9 shows the architecture of a REST-based custom connector. The connector exposes a REST web service. Data producers can publish data to the connector using HTTP POST requests which contain the data payload. The request data received by the connector is stored to the sink (such as local filesystem, distributed filesystem or cloud storage). The data sinks in the connector provide the functionality for processing the HTTP request and storing the data to the sink. The benefit of using a REST-based connector is that any client that can make HTTP requests can send data to the connector. Requests are stateless in nature, and each request carries all the information that is required to process the request. The HTTP headers add to the request overhead making this method unsuitable for high-throughput and real-time applications.

Implementing a REST-based Custom Connector

Let us look at an example of implementing a custom REST-based connector as shown in Figure 5.9. Box 5.25 shows the Python implementation of the REST-based connector. In this example, we use the Flask Python web framework to implement the web service. This connector publishes a single end point (such as 'http://public-ip/api/data'), to which the

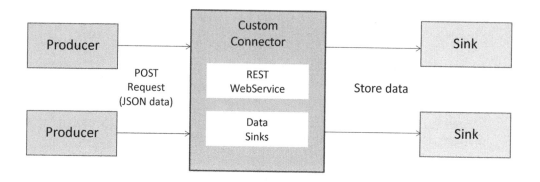

Figure 5.9: REST-based custom connector

client applications can send an HTTP POST request along with the data payload. Box 5.26 shows an example of a client which sends some synthetic sensor data to the web service. The web service receives the data from the POST request payload and then publishes the data to an Amazon SQS queue and also writes the data to an Amazon DynamoDB table.

The benefit of having such a custom connector is that the client and the server become independent of each other. The web service decouples the client from the server. The server can add or change the actions (such as publishing data to a queue or storing data in a database) without the client having to be aware of the changes. The client can use any tool or programming language from which it can make an HTTP POST request. (Note: Though we call this as a REST-connector, it is not fully REST compliant as we have only implemented the POST functionality. Other methods such as GET, PUT, DELETE may not be required if the connector only allows data to be ingested.)

■ **Box 5.25: Python implementation of a REST-based custom connector**

```
import boto.sqs
from boto.sqs.message import Message
import boto.dynamodb2
from boto.dynamodb2.table import Table
import cPickle as pickle
import time
import datetime
import json
from flask import Flask, jsonify, abort,
from flask import request, make_response, url_for

app = Flask(__name__, static_url_path="")


ACCESS_KEY = <Enter AWS Access Key>
SECRET_KEY = <Enter Secret Key>
REGION="us-east-1"
queue_name = 'sensordata'
table_name = 'sensordata'
```

```python
#Connect to AWS SQS
conn = boto.sqs.connect_to_region(REGION,aws_access_key_id=ACCESS_KEY,
aws_secret_access_key=SECRET_KEY)

q = conn.get_all_queues(prefix=queue_name)

#Connect to AWS DynamoDB
conn_dynamo = boto.dynamodb2.connect_to_region(REGION,
 aws_access_key_id=ACCESS_KEY,
 aws_secret_access_key=SECRET_KEY)

table=Table(table_name,connection=conn_dynamo)

#Publishes data to SQS
def publish_to_sqs(data):
   m = Message()
   m.set_body(data)
   status = q[0].write(m)
   return status

#Writes data to DynamoDB table
def publish_to_dynamo(datadir):
   item = table.put_item(data=datadir)

@app.errorhandler(400)
def bad_request(error):
   return make_response(jsonify({'error':  'Bad request'}), 400)

@app.errorhandler(404)
def not_found(error):
   return make_response(jsonify({'error':  'Not found'}), 404)


@app.route('/api/data', methods=['POST'])
def post_data():
   data = json.loads(request.data)

   publish_to_sqs(pickle.dumps(data))

   publish_to_dynamo(data)

   return jsonify({'result':  'true'}), 201


if __name__ == '__main__':
   app.run(debug=True)
```

■ **Box 5.26: Python implementation of client program that publishes data to a custom connector**

```python
from random import randint
import time
import datetime
import requests
import json

def getData():
   ts=time.time()
   timestamp = datetime.datetime.fromtimestamp(ts).strftime('%Y-%m-%d %H:%M:%S')
   temp = str(randint(0,100))
   humidity = str(randint(0,100))
   co2 = str(randint(50,500))
   light = str(randint(0,10000))
   data = {"timestamp": timestamp, "temperature": temp,
        "humidity": humidity , "co2": co2, "light": light}
   return data

def publish(datadir):
   r = requests.post("http://localhost:5000/api/data",
        data = json.dumps(datadir),
        headers={"Content-Type": "application/json"})

while True:
   data = getData()
   print data
   publish(data)
   time.sleep(1)
```

5.5.2 WebSocket-based Connectors

Figure 5.10 shows the architecture of a WebSocket-based custom connector. The connector exposes a WebSocket web service. The Web Application Messaging Protocol (WAMP) which is a sub-protocol of WebSocket can be used for creating a WebSocket-based connector. WAMP provides publish-subscribe and remote procedure call (RPC) messaging patterns. Clients (or data producers) establish a TCP connection with the connector and send data frames. WebSocket connection is stateful in nature and allows full duplex communication over a single TCP connection. Data producers publish data to the WebSocket endpoints which are published by the connector. The subscribers subscribe to the WebSocket endpoints and receive data from the WebSocket web service.

Unlike request-response communication with REST, WebSockets allow full duplex communication and do not require a new connection to be setup for each message to be sent. WebSocket communication begins with a connection setup request sent by the client to the server. This request (called a WebSocket handshake) is sent over HTTP and the server interprets it as an upgrade request. If the server supports WebSocket protocol, the server responds to the WebSocket handshake response. After the connection is setup, the client and server can send data/messages to each other in full-duplex mode. There is no overhead for connection setup and termination requests for each message. WebSocket communication is

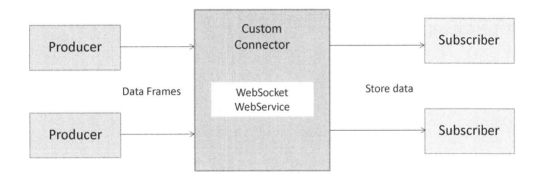

Figure 5.10: WebSocket-based custom connector

suitable for applications that have low latency or high throughput requirements.

5.5.3 MQTT-based Connectors

MQTT (MQ Telemetry Transport) is a lightweight publish-subscribe messaging protocol designed for constrained devices. MQTT is suitable for Internet of Things (IoT) applications that involve devices sending sensor data to a server or cloud-based analytics backends to be processed and analyzed. The entities involved in MQTT include:

- Publisher: Publisher is the component which publishes data to the topics managed by the Broker.
- Broker/Server: Broker manages the topics and forwards the data received on a topic to all the subscriber which are subscribed to the topic.
- Subscriber: Subscriber is the component which subscribes to the topics and receives data published on the topics by the publishers.

Implementing a MQTT-based Custom Connector

Let us look at an example of implementing a custom MQTT-based connector. Boxes 5.27 and 5.28 show the Python implementation of the MQTT subscriber and publisher components. The subscriber component in this example runs on the server, which also has an MQTT Broker running. The publisher component runs on the devices which need to publish data to the server. The devices publish data to an MQTT topic (e.g. $iot/test). The subscriber which is subscribed to the topic receives the data and processes or forwards the data. The forwarding actions may include forwarding the data to a messaging queue, writing the data to a NoSQL database or storing the data to a distributed file system.

The benefit of using the MQTT-based custom connector is that it decouples the client and the server (in space, time and synchronization dimensions). By space decoupling, we mean that the client and server do not need to know about each other. Time decoupling means that the client and server do not need to be running simultaneously. Synchronization decoupling means that the communication between client and server can happen asynchronously. The client and server do not have to wait while the messages are being processed.

■ Box 5.27: Python implementation of a MQTT-based custom connector (subscriber)

```python
import paho.mqtt.client as mqtt
import json
import boto.sqs
from boto.sqs.message import Message

REGION="us-east-1"
queue_name = 'sensordata'
ACCESS_KEY = <Enter AWS Access Key>
SECRET_KEY = <Enter Secret Key>

conn = boto.sqs.connect_to_region(REGION,aws_access_key_id=ACCESS_KEY,
                  aws_secret_access_key=SECRET_KEY)

q = conn.get_all_queues(prefix=queue_name)


def publish_to_sqs(data):
   m = Message()
   m.set_body(data)
   status = q[0].write(m)
   return status


def on_connect(client, userdata, flags, rc):
   print("Connected with result code "+str(rc))
   client.subscribe("$iot/test")

def on_message(client, userdata, msg):
   data = json.loads(msg.payload)
   publish_to_sqs(data)


client = mqtt.Client()
client.on_connect = on_connect
client.on_message = on_message

client.connect("localhost", 1883, 60)

client.loop_forever()
```

■ Box 5.28: Python implementation of a MQTT-based custom connector (publisher)

```python
import paho.mqtt.client as mqtt
import paho.mqtt.publish as publish
import time
from random import randint
import datetime
import requests
```

```
import json

def getData():
    ts=time.time()
    timestamp = datetime.datetime.fromtimestamp(ts).strftime('%Y-%m-%d %H:%M:%S')
    temp = str(randint(0,100))
    humidity = str(randint(0,100))
    co2 = str(randint(50,500))
    light = str(randint(0,10000))

    data = {"timestamp": timestamp,
        "temperature": temp, "humidity": humidity ,
        "co2": co2, "light": light}

    return data

def publish_to_topic(data):
    publish.single("$iot/test", payload=json.dumps(data),
            hostname="localhost")

while True:
    data = getData()
    print data
    publish_to_topic(data)
    time.sleep(1)
```

5.5.4   Amazon IoT

Amazon IoT is a service for collecting data from Internet of Things (IoT) devices (such as sensors and smart appliances) into the AWS cloud. The data collected can be sent to various AWS services, e.g. stored in Amazon DynamoDB database, stored in a file on S3, sent to an Amazon Kinesis data stream, sent to Amazon SNS as a push notification and inserted into a code for executing it with Amazon Lambda service.

Figure 5.11 shows the various components of the AWS IoT service.

- **Device Gateway**: Device Gateway enables devices to communicate with AWS IoT using MQTT or HTTP protocols. Devices can publish or subscribe to topics.
- **Device Registry**: Device registry (also called things registry) maintains the resources associated with each device including attributes, certificates and meta-data.
- **Device Shadow**: Device shadow maintains the state of a device as a JSON document. Applications can retrieve or update the device state using the AWS IoT REST APIs. Device shadow persists the state of the device even when the device is offline. When a device becomes online, the state is synchronized with the device shadow.
- **Rules Engine**: Rules engine allows you to define rules for processing messages received from devices. Using an SQL-like language, you can define rules to select data, process data and send the data to other AWS services such as DynamoDB, S3, Kinesis, SNS and Lambda.
- **Security and Identity Service**: This service allows devices to securely exchange data with the AWS IoT service. For devices communicating via MQTT, certificate-based authentication is used. Certificates have policies associated with them which authorize devices to access specific resources.

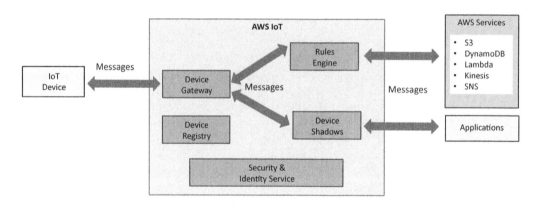

Figure 5.11: Amazon IoT components

Let us look at some examples of using AWS IoT service. The first step is to create a thing from the AWS IoT dashboard as shown in Figure 5.12. Thing represents a device in the AWS IoT service. When a thing is created, an entry is created in the device registry for the device and a device shadow is also created. At this step, you can also add the optional attributes to describe the device capabilities.

Create a thing

Create a thing to represent your device in the cloud. This step creates an entry in the Registry and also a Device Shadow for your device.

Name   thermostat

Attributes

Next (optional), you can use thing attributes to describe the identity and capabilities of your device. Each attribute is a key-value pair.

Add Attribute

Create

Figure 5.12: Creating a Thing from Amazon IoT dashboard

In the next step, we create a certificate which is used by the device for connecting to AWS IoT. The certificate is attached to a thing. Three files are created in this step - a certificate file, a public key file, and a private key file. Next, we create a policy and attach the policy to the certificate to assign permissions.

Box 5.29 shows a Python example for publishing messages to AWS IoT. This example uses the Paho Python MQTT client. For connecting to AWS IoT a Root Certificate Authority (CA) certificate, a client certificate and private key file is required. This example simulates a thermostat device sending the current state (temperature) to AWS IoT, which stores the state in the device shadow. To report the state over MQTT, a message is published on the topic

$aws/things/thingName/shadow/update.

> ■ **Box 5.29: Python code for publishing messages to AWS IoT**

```
import paho.mqtt.client as mqtt
import ssl
import paho.mqtt.publish as publish

connection={
"host":  "A26VGTA50P1HNL.iot.us-east-1.amazonaws.com",
"port":  8883,
"clientId":  "thermostat",
"thingName":  "thermostat",
"caCert":  "root-CA.crt",
"clientCert":  "9795072c41-certificate.pem.crt",
"privateKey":  "9795072c41-private.pem.key"
}

tlsdict= {'ca_certs':connection['caCert'],
   'certfile':connection['clientCert'],
   'keyfile':connection['privateKey'],
   'tls_version':ssl.PROTOCOL_SSLv23, 'ciphers':None}

state="{ \"state\":  {\"reported\":  { \"temperature\":  \"70\" } } }"

publish.single("$aws/things/thermostat/shadow/update", payload=str(state),
  qos=1, retain=False, hostname=connection['host'],
  port=8883, client_id=connection['clientId'], keepalive=60,
  will=None, auth=None, tls=tlsdict,
  protocol=mqtt.MQTTv311)
```

The current state for a device can be seen from the AWS IoT dashboard as shown in Figure 5.13. Box 5.30 shows a Python example for subscribing to the state updates for a device. To receive updates from the device shadow over MQTT, the device/application can subscribe to topic the $aws/things/thingName/shadow/update/accepted.

Applications can also use the AWS IoT REST API to query for the last reported state for a device or update the device state. For example, a mobile application that controls the temperature setting for a smart thermostat can be built. The thermostat reports its current state (temperature) to AWS IoT, and the state is stored in the device shadow. The mobile application can update the desired state in the device shadow instead of directly communicating with the thermostat. The desired state is synchronized with the device, the next time it is connected to the AWS IoT service. The device state can also be updated from the AWS IoT dashboard as shown in Figure 5.14.

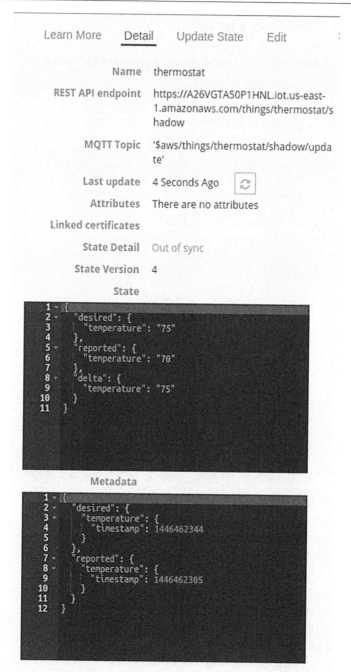

Figure 5.13: Viewing the state of a thing from Amazon IoT dashboard

■ **Box 5.30: Python code for subscribing to a topic in AWS IoT**

```
import paho.mqtt.client as mqtt
import ssl
```

```
connection={
"host": "A26VGTA50P1HNL.iot.us-east-1.amazonaws.com",
"port": 8883,
"clientId": "thermostat",
"thingName": "thermostat",
"caCert": "root-CA.crt",
"clientCert": "9795072c41-certificate.pem.crt",
"privateKey": "9795072c41-private.pem.key"
}

def on_connect(client, userdata, flags, rc):
 print("Connected with result code "+str(rc))
 client.subscribe("$aws/things/rpi/shadow/update/accepted")

def on_message(client, userdata, msg):
 print(msg.topic+" "+str(msg.payload))

client = mqtt.Client()
client.on_connect = on_connect
client.on_message = on_message

client.tls_set(ca_certs=connection['caCert'],
     certfile=connection['clientCert'],
     keyfile=connection['privateKey'], cert_reqs=ssl.CERT_REQUIRED,
     tls_version=ssl.PROTOCOL_SSLv23, ciphers=None)

client.connect(connection['host'], connection['port'])

client.loop_forever()
```

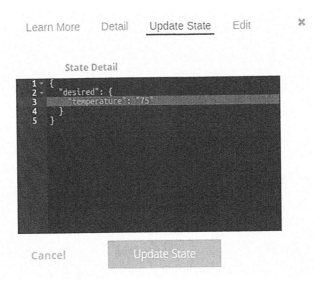

Figure 5.14: Updating the state of a thing from Amazon IoT dashboard

Let us now look at a more advanced example where we use the rule engine to send data collected from a device to different AWS services. For this example, we will create a new thing called 'forest' which represents a device deployed in a forest for reporting data collected from various sensors (temperature, humidity, light, CO_2). Data collected from multiple such devices deployed in a forest can be analyzed to detect forest fires. While you can use the AWS IoT Starter Kits to build physical devices with real sensors connected to them, for simplicity we will use a program which generates and sends synthetic data to AWS IoT. Box 5.31 shows a Python program for sending synthetic sensor data to AWS IoT.

■ **Box 5.31: Python program for sending synthetic sensor data to AWS IoT**

```
from random import randrange
import time
import datetime
import paho.mqtt.client as mqtt
import ssl
import paho.mqtt.publish as publish

connection={
"host":  "A26VGTA50P1HNL.iot.us-east-1.amazonaws.com",
"port":  8883,
"clientId":  "forest",
"thingName":  "forest",
"caCert":  "root-CA.crt",
"clientCert":  "9795072c41-certificate.pem.crt",
"privateKey":  "9795072c41-private.pem.key"
}

tlsdict= {'ca_certs':connection['caCert'],
   'certfile':connection['clientCert'],
   'keyfile':connection['privateKey'],
   'tls_version':ssl.PROTOCOL_SSLv23, 'ciphers':None}

#Send some synthetic data to AWS IoT
while True:
 ts=time.time()

 data = "{ \"state\":  { \"location\":  \"123\",
  \"timestamp\":  \""+str(ts)+"\",
  \"temperature\":  "+str(randrange(0,60))+",
 \"humidity\":  "+str(randrange(0,60))+",
  \"light\":  "+str(randrange(0,60))+", \"co2\":  "+str(randrange(0,60))+"
}}"

 print data

 publish.single("$aws/things/forest/test", payload=str(data),
  qos=1, retain=False, hostname=connection['host'],
  port=8883, client_id=connection['clientId'],
  keepalive=60, will=None, auth=None, tls=tlsdict,
  protocol=mqtt.MQTTv311)

 time.sleep(1)
```

Next, we create two different rules in AWS IoT for analyzing this data further. The first rule as shown in Figure 5.15 sends data to an Amazon Kinesis data stream. The second rule as shown in Figure 5.16 writes the data to an Amazon DynamoDB table.

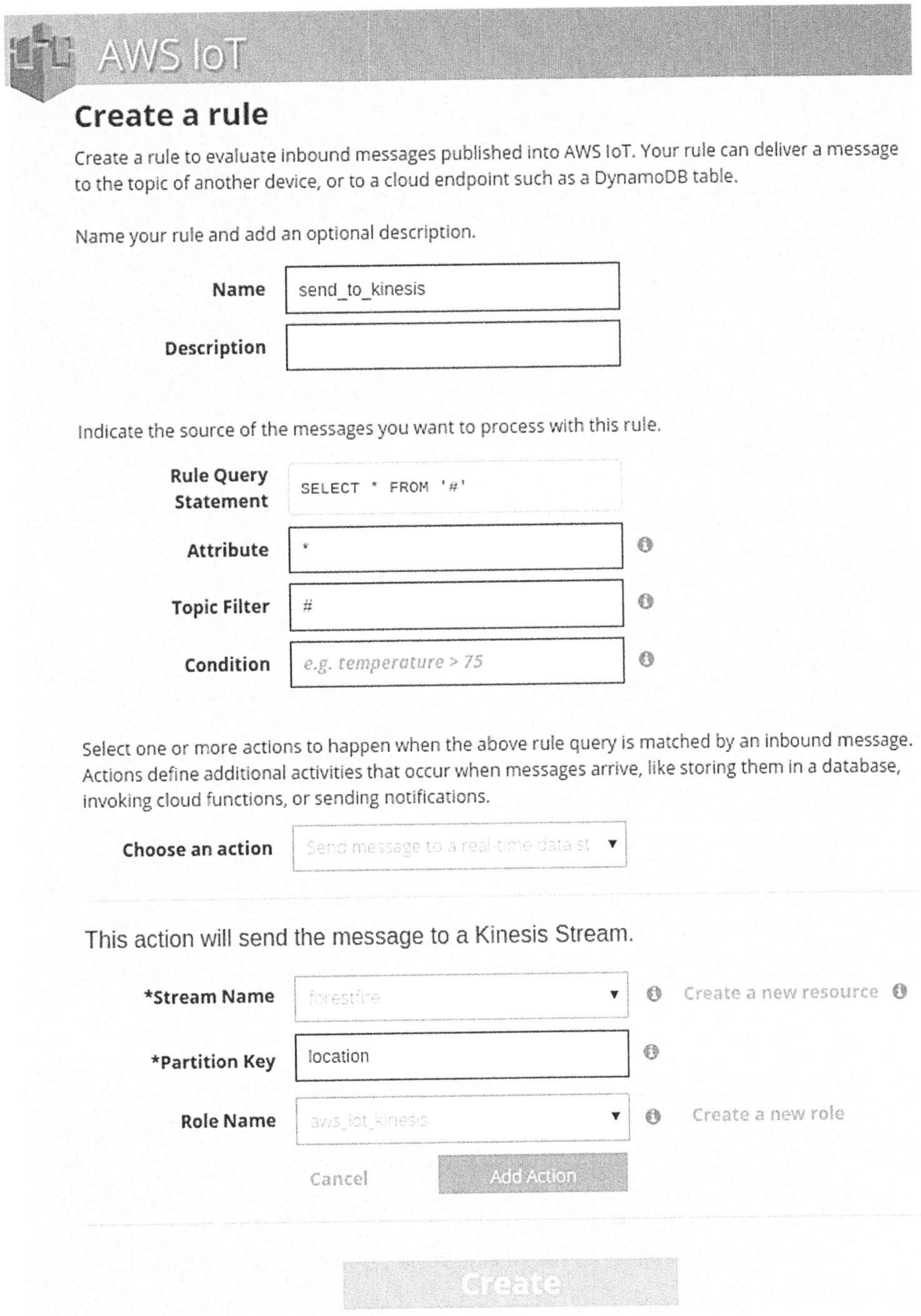

Create a rule

Create a rule to evaluate inbound messages published into AWS IoT. Your rule can deliver a message to the topic of another device, or to a cloud endpoint such as a DynamoDB table.

Name your rule and add an optional description.

Name send_to_kinesis

Description

Indicate the source of the messages you want to process with this rule.

Rule Query Statement SELECT * FROM '#'

Attribute *

Topic Filter #

Condition e.g. temperature > 75

Select one or more actions to happen when the above rule query is matched by an inbound message. Actions define additional activities that occur when messages arrive, like storing them in a database, invoking cloud functions, or sending notifications.

Choose an action Send message to a real-time data st ▾

This action will send the message to a Kinesis Stream.

*Stream Name forestfire ▾   Create a new resource

*Partition Key location

Role Name aws_iot_kinesis ▾   Create a new role

Cancel   Add Action

Create

Figure 5.15: Creating a rule from Amazon IoT dashboard

With the rules defined, run the Python program in Box 5.31. The synthetic data generated by this program will be published to the topic $aws/things/forest/test in AWS IoT. The rules will send the data to Amazon Kinesis and Amazon DynamoDB. Figure 5.17 shows a screenshot of the Amazon DynamoDB table with the data published by the device. To read

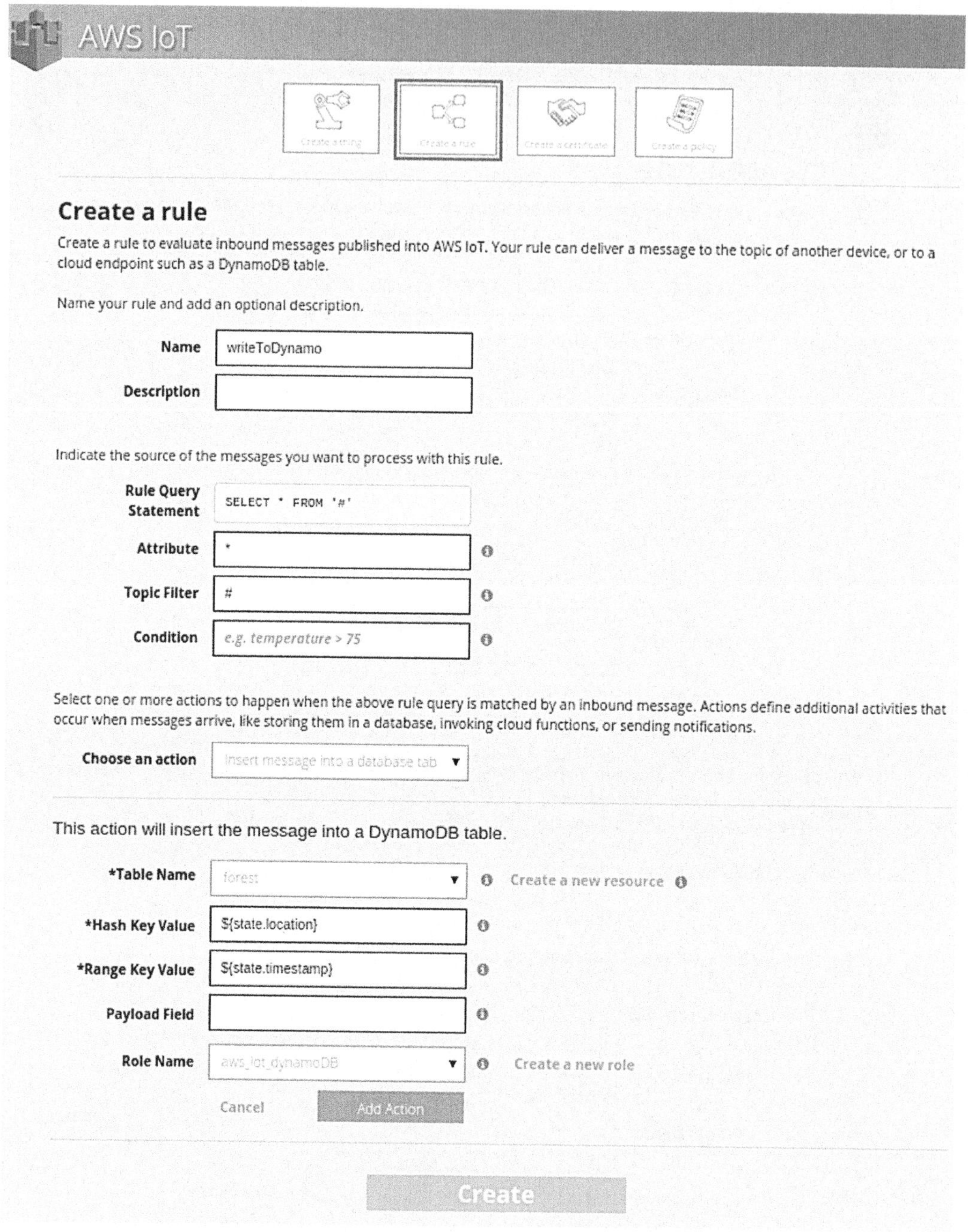

Figure 5.16: Creating a rule from Amazon IoT dashboard

data from the Kinesis data stream, you can use the program shown in Box 5.8.

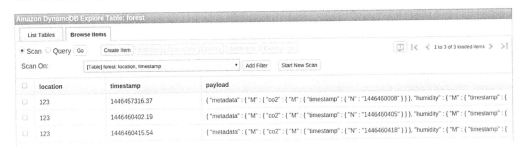

Figure 5.17: Viewing the data stored by an AWS IoT rule into a DynamoDB table

5.5.5 Azure IoT Hub

Azure IoT Hub is a fully managed service for bi-directional communication between IoT devices and the Azure cloud. Azure IoT Hub receives messages from IoT devices and sends them to various Azure services (such as Azure Stream Analytics) for further processing of messages. IoT Hub can store up to 7 days of data. Applications can use IoT Hub to send messages to the devices. Azure provides device libraries for connecting various devices to the IoT Hub. Supported protocols include HTTP 1.1 and AMQP 1.0. Support for MQTT can be added by running Azure IoT Protocol Gateway, an open source component, which can be run either locally or in the cloud. IoT Hub includes a device identity registry which is used to provision devices with their own security keys for securely connecting to the IoT Hub. Figure 5.18 shows the various components of Azure IoT Hub.

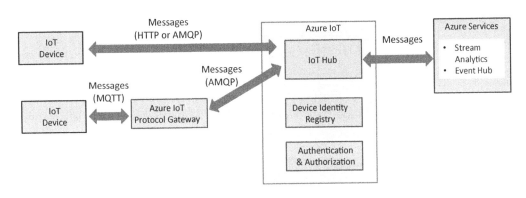

Figure 5.18: Azure IoT components

In the previous section, we described the example of IoT devices deployed in a forest for reporting data collected from various sensors (temperature, humidity, light, CO_2) for detecting forest fires. Let us repeat the same example using Azure IoT Hub. The first step is to create an IoT Hub that will receive data from devices. Log into the Azure Preview Portal and create a new IoT Hub as shown in Figure 5.19. Once the IoT Hub has been created, open the IoT hub tile in the Preview Portal, and note down the IoT Hub Hostname. Next, select the Key icon in the IoT Hub and click on the *iothubowner* shared access policy as shown in Figure 5.20. Note down the connection string and primary key.

Now that the IoT Hub is operational, let us register a device with the Hub. To create a

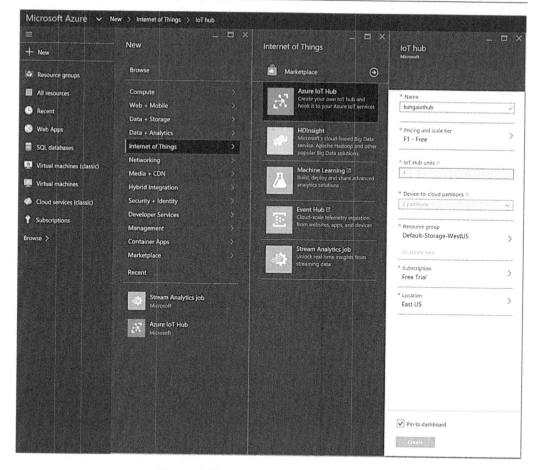

Figure 5.19: Creating an Azure IoT hub

new device identity, you can either use a standalone tool called Device Explorer (which runs on Windows) or a NodeJS tool called *iothub-explorer*. NodeJS can be installed as follows:

```
#Installing NodeJS
curl -sL https://deb.nodesource.com/setup_4.x | sudo -E bash -
sudo apt-get install -y nodejs
```

Next, install the *iothub-explorer* tool and then generate a unique identity and connection string as follows:

```
#Create a new device identity in the IoT Hub
npm install -g iothub-explorer
node iothub-explorer "<enter iothubowner connection string>"
create mydevice -connection-string
```

Note down the device connection string generated by *iothub-explorer*. As of writing this book, Python support libraries for IoT Hub have not been released. Therefore, we will provide an example using NodeJS. Box 5.32 shows a simple example of sending data to IoT Hub using NodeJS. In this example, use the device connection string generated by the

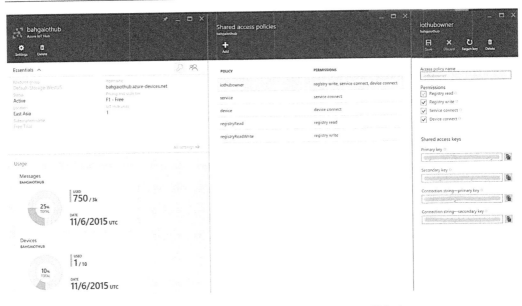

Figure 5.20: Viewing details of an Azure IoT hub

iothub-explorer tool. This program generates some random synthetic data and sends it to the IoT Hub every second.

■ **Box 5.32: NodeJS code for sending data to Azure IoT Hub**

```
var device = require('azure-iot-device');
var connectionString = '<enter>';
var client = new device.Client(connectionString, new device.Https());

// Send some synthetic data to IoT Hub every second
setInterval(function(){
  var temperature = Math.random() * 100 ;
  var humidity = Math.random() * 100 ;
  var light = Math.random() * 10000 ;
  var co2 = Math.random() * 300 ;

  var data = "{deviceid:" + "mydevice" + ",temperature:" +
    String(temperature) + ", humidity:" + String(humidity) +
    ", light:" + String(light) + ", co2:" + String(co2) + " }";

  var message = new device.Message(data);
  console.log("Sending message:   " + message.getData());
  client.sendEvent(message);
}, 1000);
```

To run the program use the commands show in box below:

```
■ #Running NodeJS program shown in Box 5.32
npm install node .
```

You will be able to see the count of messages received and the devices connected in the IoT Hub dashboard as seen in Figure 5.20. Now that we can send messages to IoT Hub, let us define some rules for further processing of messages. In the case of AWS IoT, we used the Rule Engine to define the rules using an SQL-like language. Azure provides a real-time event processing engine called Azure Stream Analytics. Azure Stream Analytics allows defining real-time analytic computations on streaming data using an SQL-like language (called Stream Analytics query language). Let us create a Stream Analytics job as shown in Figure 5.21 from the Azure dashboard. A Stream Analytics job includes an input source of streaming data, a query expressed in SQL-like language and an output sink to which the results are sent. Figures 5.22, 5.23 and 5.24 show the settings for the input, query and output of the Stream Analytics job. The input source, in this case, is the IoT Hub we created previously and the output sink is an Azure Event Hub. Event Hub is a managed service for reliably collecting and processing massive amounts of data with low latency. Event Hub provides similar functionality as Amazon Kinesis.

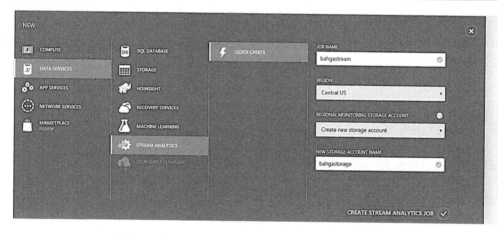

Figure 5.21: Creating an Azure stream analytics job

Figure 5.25 shows how to create a new Event Hub from the Azure dashboard. Once the Event Hub is created, go to the configure tab and add a new shared access policy (with Name = "read-write" and Permissions = Send, Listen). Copy the Primary Key for the read-write policy. This policy name and the primary key are used while creating the output sink for the Stream Analytics job as shown in Figure 5.24.

Next, run the program show in Box 5.32 and monitor the Stream Analytics job and Events Hub from the Azure dashboard. You will be able to see messages being processed by the Stream Analytics job and the output being posted to the Events Hub as seen in Figures 5.26 and 5.27.

```
■ #Running the Javascript code in Box 5.32
npm install node .
```

bahgastreamin

general

SUBSCRIPTION	
IOT HUB	bahgaiothub.azure-devices.net
IOT HUB SHARED ACCESS POLICY NAME	iothubowner
IOT HUB POLICY KEY	••••••••••••••••••••••
IOT HUB CONSUMER GROUP	

serialization

EVENT SERIALIZATION FORMAT	
ENCODING	

Figure 5.22: Input settings for stream analytics job

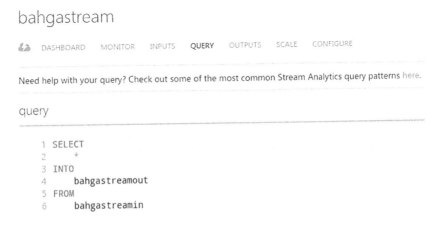

bahgastream

DASHBOARD   MONITOR   INPUTS   **QUERY**   OUTPUTS   SCALE   CONFIGURE

Need help with your query? Check out some of the most common Stream Analytics query patterns here.

query

```
1 SELECT
2     *
3 INTO
4     bahgastreamout
5 FROM
6     bahgastreamin
```

Figure 5.23: Query settings for stream analytics job

bahgastreamout

general

SUBSCRIPTION   Use Event Hub from Another Subscription ▾

SERVICE BUS NAMESPACE   bahgaeventhub-ns

EVENT HUB NAME   bahgaeventhub

EVENT HUB POLICY NAME   readwrite

EVENT HUB POLICY KEY   ••••••••••••••••••••••

serialization

EVENT SERIALIZATION FORMAT   JSON ▾

ENCODING   UTF8 ▾

FORMAT   Line separated ▾

advanced

PARTITION KEY COLUMN   1

Figure 5.24: Output settings for stream analytics job

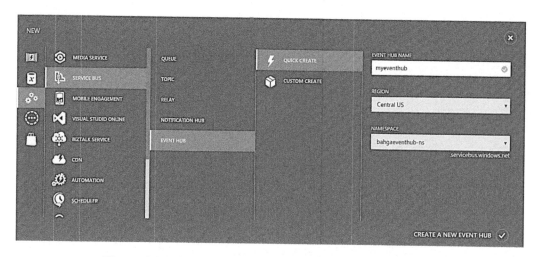

Figure 5.25: Creating an Event Hub from Azure dashboard

Figure 5.26: Azure Events Hub output

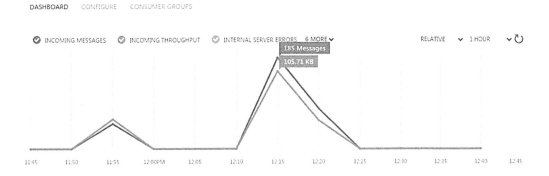

Figure 5.27: Azure Events Hub output

Summary

In this chapter, we described various data connectors which allow collecting data from raw data sources for ingesting into a distributed file system or a NoSQL database, for batch analysis of data, or which connect the data sources to stream or in-memory processing frameworks for real-time analysis of data. We described the publish-subscribe and push-pull messaging models. Publish-Subscribe is a communication model that involves publishers, brokers and consumers. Publishers send the data to the topics which are managed by the broker. When the broker receives data for a topic from the publisher, it sends the data to all the subscribed consumers. We described the Apache Kafka and Amazon Kinesis publish-subscribe messaging frameworks. Next, we described a source-sink data collection framework called Apache Flume. Apache Flume is a distributed, reliable, and available system for collecting, aggregating, and moving large amounts of data from different data sources into a centralized data store. Next, we described Apache Sqoop, which is a tool that allows importing data from relational database management systems (RDBMS) into the HDFS, Hive or HBase tables. We described various messaging queues such as RabbitMQ, ZeroMQ, RestMQ and Amazon SQS. Examples of building REST-based and MQTT-based custom connectors were provided. Finally, we described IoT services from Amazon and Azure which allow collecting data from Internet of Things (IoT) devices into the cloud, where the data can be processed further.

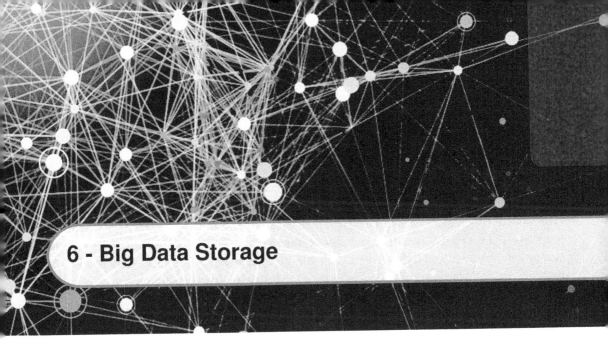

6 - Big Data Storage

This chapter covers

- Hadoop Distributed File System (HDFS)

In the previous chapter we described tools and frameworks for the acquisition of data from various types of sources and ingesting the data into a big data stack. The options for data storage within a big data stack include a distributed filesystem or a NoSQL database. In this chapter, we will describe the Hadoop Distributed File System (HDFS) for big data storage. Once the data is moved from the data source to HDFS, we can use specialized frameworks for batch analysis or interactive querying for analyzing the data.

6.1   HDFS

HDFS is a distributed file system (DFS) that runs on large clusters and provides high-throughput access to data. HDFS is a highly fault-tolerant system and is designed to work with commodity hardware. HDFS stores each file as a sequence of blocks. The blocks of each file are replicated on multiple machines in a cluster to provide fault tolerance.

Let us look at the characteristics of HDFS:

- **Scalable Storage for Large Files**: HDFS has been designed to store large files (typically from gigabytes to terabytes in size). Large files are broken into chunks or blocks and each block is replicated across multiple machines in the cluster. HDFS has been designed to scale to clusters comprising of thousands of nodes.
- **Replication**: HDFS replicates data blocks to multiple machines in a cluster which makes the system reliable and fault-tolerant. The default block size used is 64MB and the default replication factor is 3.
- **Streaming Data Access**: HDFS has been designed for streaming data access patterns and provides high throughput streaming reads and writes. The HDFS design relaxes some of the POSIX requirements to enable streaming data access and make it suitable for batch operations thus trading off interactive access capability. This design choice has been made to meet the requirements of applications that involve write-once, read many times data access patterns. HDFS is not suited for applications that require low-latency access to data. Instead, HDFS provides high throughput data access.
- **File Appends**: HDFS was originally designed to have immutable files. Files once written to HDFS could not be modified by writing at arbitrary locations in the file or appending to the file. Recent versions of HDFS have introduced the append capability. The file append process is discussed later in the chapter.

6.1.1   HDFS Architecture

Figure 6.1 shows the architecture of HDFS. HDFS has two types of nodes: Namenode and Datanode.

Namenode

Namenode manages the filesystem namespace. All the filesystem meta-data is stored on the Namenode. While Namenode is responsible for executing operations such as opening and closing of files, no data actually flows through the Namenode. Namenode executes the read and write operations while the data is transferred directly to/from the Datanodes. HDFS splits files into blocks, and the blocks are stored on the Datanodes. For each block, multiple replicas are kept. Namenode persistently stores the filesystem meta-data and the mappings of the blocks to the datanodes, on the disk as two files: *fsimage* and *edits* files. The *fsimage* contains a complete snapshot of the filesystem meta-data. The *edits* file stores the incremental updates to the meta-data.

When the Namenode starts, it loads the *fsimage* file into the memory and applies the *edits* file to bring the in-memory view of the filesystem up-to-date. Namenode then writes a new *fsimage* file to the disk.

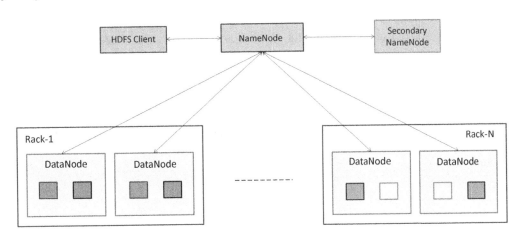

Figure 6.1: HDFS architecture

Secondary Namenode

The *edits* file keeps growing in size, over time, as the incremental updates are stored. The responsibility of applying the updates to the *fsimage* file is delegated to the Secondary Namenode, as the Namenode may not have enough resources available, as it is performing other operations. This process is called checkpointing. The checkpointing process is done either periodically (default 1 hour) or after a certain number of uncheckpointed transactions have been reached on the Namenode.

When the checkpointing process begins, the Secondary Namenode downloads the *fsimage* and *edits* files from the Namenode to the checkpoint directory on the Secondary Namenode. The Secondary Namenode then applies the *edits* on the *fsimage* file and creates a new *fsimage* file. The new *fsimage* is uploaded by the Secondary Namenode to the Namenode.

Datanode

While the Namenode stores the filesystem meta-data, the Datanodes store the data blocks and serve the read and write requests. Datanodes periodically send heartbeat messages and block reports to the Namenode. While the heartbeat messages tell the Namenode that a Datanode is alive, the block reports contain information on the blocks on a Datanode.

Data Blocks & Replication

Blocks are replicated on the Datanodes and by default three replicas are created. The placement of replicas on the Datanodes is determined by a rack-aware placement policy. This placement policy ensures reliability and availability of the blocks. For a replication factor of three, one replica is placed on a node on a local rack, the second replica is placed on a different node on a remote rack and the third replica is placed on a different node on the same remote rack. This ensures that even if the rack becomes unavailable, at least one replica will remain available. Placement of replicas on different nodes in the same rack minimizes the network traffic between the racks.

HDFS Read Path

Figure 6.2 shows the HDFS read path. The read process begins with the client sending a request to the Namenode to obtain the locations of the data blocks for a file. The Namenode checks if the file exists and whether the client has sufficient permissions to read the file. The Namenode responds with the data block locations sorted by the distance to the client. This helps in minimizing the traffic between the nodes as the client can read the blocks from the nearest node. For example, if the client is on the same node as a data block, it can read the data block locally. The client reads the data blocks directly from the Datanodes in order, till all the blocks have been read. The Datanodes stream the data to the client. During the read process, if a replica becomes unavailable, the client can read another replica on a different Datanode.

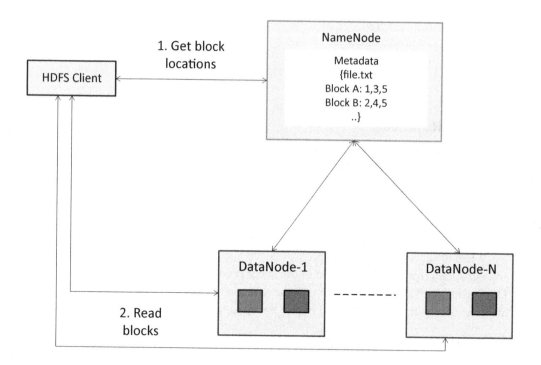

Figure 6.2: HDFS read path

HDFS Write Path

Figure 6.3 shows the HDFS write path. The write process begins with the client sending a request to the Namenode to create a new file in the filesystem namespace. The Namenode checks if the user has sufficient permissions to create the file and whether the file doesn't already exist in the filesystem. The Namenode responds to the client with an output stream object. The client writes data to the output stream object which splits the data into packets and enqueues them into a data queue. The packets are consumed from the data queue in a separate thread, which requests the Namenode to allocate new blocks on the Datanodes to which the data should be written. Namenode responds with the locations of the blocks on the Datanodes. The client then establishes direct connections to the Datanodes on which the blocks are to be replicated forming a replication pipeline. The data packets consumed from the data queue are written to the first Datanode on the replication pipeline, which writes data to the second Datanode in the pipeline and so on. Once the packets are successfully written, each Datanode in the pipeline sends an acknowledgment. The client keeps a track of which all packets are acknowledged by the Datanodes. The process of writing data packets to the Datanodes proceeds till the block size is reached. Upon reaching the block size, the client again requests the Namenode to return a set of new blocks on the Datanodes. The client then streams the packets to the Datanodes. This process repeats till all the data packets are written and acknowledged. Finally, the client closes the output stream and sends a request to the Namenode to close the file.

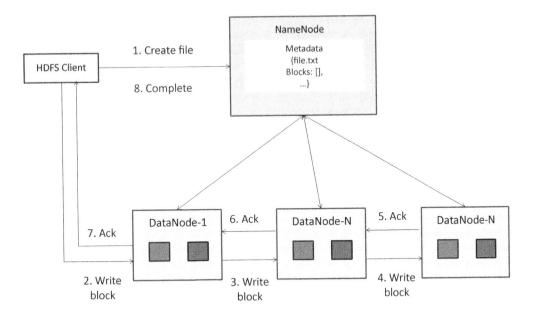

Figure 6.3: HDFS write path

6.1.2   HDFS Usage Examples

HDFS Command Line Tools

```
■ #Copy file to HDFS
#Format of command:
hdfs dfs -put <local source> <destination on HDFS>

#Example:
hdfs dfs -put file /user/hadoop/file


■ #Get file from HDFS
#Format of command:
hdfs dfs -get <source on hdfs> <local destination>

#Example:
hdfs dfs -get /user/hadoop/file file


■ #List files on HDFS
#Format of command:
hdfs dfs -ls <args>

#Example:
hdfs dfs -ls /user/hadoop/


■ #Show contents of a file on HDFS
#Format of command:
hdfs dfs -cat <HDFS Path>

#Example:
hdfs dfs -cat /user/hadoop/file


■ #Remove a file on HDFS
#Format of command:
hdfs dfs -rm <HDFS Path>

#Example:
hdfs dfs -rm /user/hadoop/file


■ #Create a directory on HDFS
#Format of command:
hdfs dfs -mkdir <paths>

#Example:
hdfs dfs -mkdir /user/hadoop/dir
```

Accessing HDFS with Python

In this section we provide Python examples of accessing HDFS using the Snakebite python package.

```
■ #Listing files on HDFS with Python
from snakebite.client import Client
client = Client("localhost", 8020, use_trash=False)
list(client.ls(["/"]))
```

```
■ #Reading a file from HDFS with Python
from snakebite.client import Client
client = Client("localhost", 8020, use_trash=False)
list(client.text(["/user/input.txt"]))
```

```
■ #Copying a file from HDFS with Python
from snakebite.client import Client
client = Client("localhost", 8020, use_trash=False)
list(client.copyToLocal(["/user/input.txt"], '/home/ubuntu/'))
```

HDFS Web Interface

HDFS provides a web interface from where you can browse the filesystem and also also download specific files as shown in Figures 6.4 and 6.5.

Hadoop	Overview	Datanodes	Snapshot	Startup Progress	Utilities

Browse Directory

/   Go!

Permission	Owner	Group	Size	Replication	Block Size	Name
drwxrwxrwx	yarn	hadoop	0 B	0	0 B	app-logs
drwxr-xr-x	mapred	hdfs	0 B	0	0 B	mapred
drwxr-xr-x	hdfs	hdfs	0 B	0	0 B	mr-history
drwxr-xr-x	hdfs	hdfs	0 B	0	0 B	system
drwxrwxrwx	hdfs	hdfs	0 B	0	0 B	tmp
drwxr-xr-x	hdfs	hdfs	0 B	0	0 B	user

Figure 6.4: Browsing files on HDFS using web interface

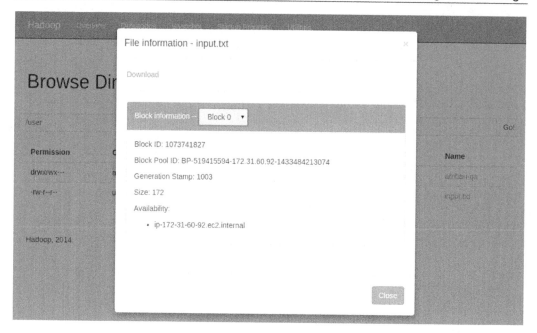

Figure 6.5: Download a file from HDFS using web interface

Summary

HDFS is a distributed file system that runs on large clusters and provides high-throughput access to data. HDFS provides scalable storage for large files which are broken into blocks. The blocks are replicated to make the system reliable and fault-tolerant. The HDFS Namenode stores the filesystem meta-data and is responsible for executing operations such as opening and closing of files. The Secondary Namenode helps in the checkpointing process by applying the updates in the *edits* file to the *fsimage* file which contains a complete snapshot of the filesystem meta-data. Datanodes store the data blocks which are replicated. The placement of replicas on the Datanodes is determined by a rack-aware placement policy. We described examples of accessing HDFS using the command line tools, a Python library for HDFS and the HDFS web interface.

7 - Batch Analysis

This chapter covers

- Batch Analysis frameworks
- Hadoop and MapReduce
- Pig
- Apache Oozie
- Apache Spark
- Apache Solr

In this chapter we describe tools and frameworks for "batch processing" of data including: Hadoop-MapReduce, Pig, Oozie, Spark, and Solr.

7.1 Hadoop and MapReduce

Apache Hadoop [64] is an open source framework for distributed batch processing of big data. Similarly, MapReduce is a parallel programming model [22] suitable analysis of big data. MapReduce algorithms allow large-scale computations to be automatically parallelized across a large cluster of servers.

7.1.1 MapReduce Programming Model

MapReduce is a parallel data processing model for processing and analysis of massive scale data [22]. MapReduce model has two phases: Map and Reduce. MapReduce programs are written in a functional programming style to create Map and Reduce functions. The input data to the map and reduce phases is in the form of key-value pairs. Run-time systems for MapReduce are typically large clusters built of commodity hardware. The MapReduce run-time systems take care of tasks such partitioning the data, scheduling of jobs and communication between nodes in the cluster. This makes it easier for programmers to analyze massive scale data without worrying about tasks such as data partitioning and scheduling.

In the Map phase, data is read from a distributed file system, partitioned among a set of computing nodes in the cluster, and sent to the nodes as a set of key-value pairs. The Map tasks process the input records independently of each other and produce intermediate results as key-value pairs. The intermediate results are stored on the local disk of the node running the Map task. When all the Map tasks are completed, the Reduce phase begins in which the intermediate data with the same key is aggregated. An optional Combine task can be used to perform data aggregation on the intermediate data of the same key for the output of the mapper before transferring the output to the Reduce task.

MapReduce programs take advantage of locality of data and the data processing takes place on the nodes where the data resides. In traditional approaches for data analysis, data is moved to the compute nodes which results in the delay in data transmission between the nodes in a cluster. However, the MapReduce programming model moves the computation to where the data resides thus decreasing the transmission of data and improving efficiency. The MapReduce programming model is well suited for parallel processing of massive scale data in which the data analysis tasks can be accomplished by independent map and reduce operations.

Figures 7.1 and 7.2 show the execution flow of word count and inverted index MapReduce jobs. As seen from these figures, the sort and shuffle phase begins as soon as a map task completes and the reduce phase begins after the intermediate key-value pairs from all the map tasks are shuffled to the reducer.

7.1.2 Hadoop YARN

Hadoop YARN is the next generation architecture of Hadoop (version 2.x). In the YARN architecture, the original processing engine of Hadoop (MapReduce) has been separated from the resource management component (which is now part of YARN) as shown in

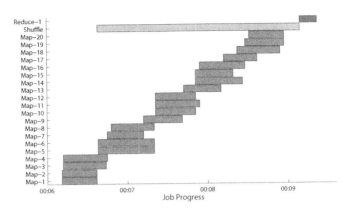

Figure 7.1: Map/Reduce slot assignments for a word count MapReduce job

Figure 7.2: Map/Reduce slot assignments for an inverted index MapReduce job

Figure 7.3. This makes YARN effectively an operating system for Hadoop that supports different processing engines on a Hadoop cluster such as MapReduce for batch processing, Apache Tez [60] for interactive queries, Apache Storm [65] for stream processing, for instance.

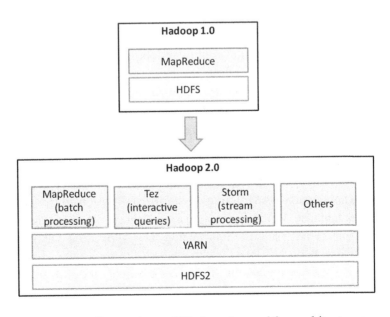

Figure 7.3: Comparison of Hadoop 1.x and 2.x architectures

Figure 7.4 shows the MapReduce job execution workflow for the next generation Hadoop MapReduce framework (MR2). The next-generation MapReduce architecture divides the two major functions of the JobTracker in Hadoop 1.x - resource management and job life-cycle management - into separate components - ResourceManager and ApplicationMaster. The key components of YARN are described as follows:

- **Resource Manager (RM):** RM manages the global assignment of compute resources to applications. RM consists of two main services:
  - Scheduler: Scheduler is a pluggable service that manages and enforces the resource scheduling policy in the cluster.
  - Applications Manager (AsM): AsM manages the running Application Masters in the cluster. AsM is responsible for starting application masters and for monitoring and restarting them on different nodes in case of failures.
- **Application Master (AM):** A per-application AM manages the application's life cycle. AM is responsible for negotiating resources from the RM and working with the NMs to execute and monitor the tasks.
- **Node Manager (NM):** A per-machine NM manages the user processes on that machine.
- **Containers:** Container is a bundle of resources allocated by RM (memory, CPU and network). A container is a conceptual entity that grants an application the privilege to use a certain amount of resources on a given machine to run a task. Each node has an NM that spawns multiple containers based on the resource allocations made by the RM.

Figure 7.4 shows a YARN cluster with a Resource Manager node and three Node Manager nodes. There are as many Application Masters running as there are applications (jobs). Each application's AM manages the application tasks such as starting, monitoring and restarting tasks in case of failures. Each application has multiple tasks. Each task runs in a separate container. Containers in YARN architecture are similar to task slots in Hadoop MapReduce 1.x (MR1). However, unlike MR1 which differentiates between map and reduce slots, each container in YARN can be used for both map and reduce tasks. The resource allocation model in MR1 consists of a predefined number of map slots and reduce slots. This static allocation of slots results in low cluster utilization. The resource allocation model of YARN is more flexible with the introduction of resource containers which improve cluster utilization.

To better understand the YARN job execution workflow let us analyze the interactions between the main components on YARN. Figure 7.5 shows the interactions between a Client and Resource Manager. Job execution begins with the submission of a new application request by the client to the RM. The RM then responds with a unique application ID and information about cluster resource capabilities that the client will need in requesting resources for running the application's AM. Using the information received from the RM, the client constructs and submits an Application Submission Context which contains information such as scheduler queue, priority and user information. The Application Submission Context also contains a Container Launch Context which contains the application's jar, job files, security tokens and any resource requirements. The client can query the RM for application reports. The client can also "force kill" an application by sending a request to the RM.

Figure 7.6 shows the interactions between Resource Manager and Application Master. Upon receiving an application submission context from a client, the RM finds an available

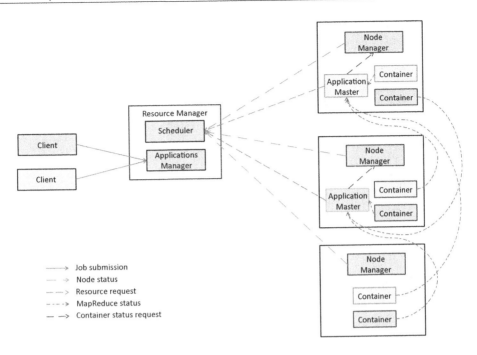

Figure 7.4: Hadoop MapReduce Next Generation (YARN) job execution

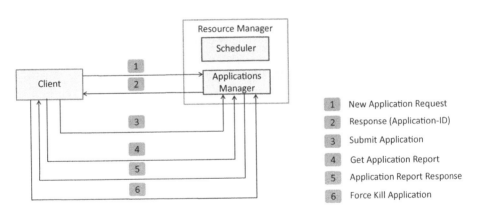

Figure 7.5: Client - Resource Manager interaction

container meeting the resource requirements for running the AM for the application. On finding a suitable container, the RM contacts the NM for the container to start the AM process on its node. When the AM is launched it registers itself with the RM. The registration process consists of handshaking that conveys information such as the RPC port that the AM will be listening on, the tracking URL for monitoring the application's status and progress, etc. The registration response from the RM contains information for the AM that is used in calculating and requesting any resource requests for the application's individual tasks (such as minimum and maximum resource capabilities for the cluster). The AM relays heartbeat and progress information to the RM. The AM sends resource allocation requests to the RM that contains a

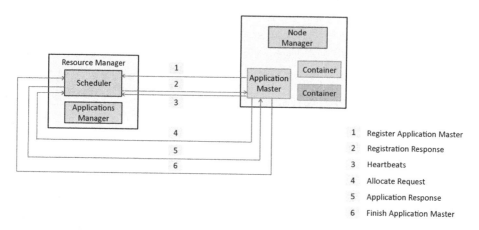

Figure 7.6: Resource Manager - Application Master interaction

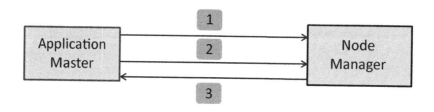

Figure 7.7: Application Master - Node Manager interaction

list of requested containers, and may also contain a list of released containers by the AM. Upon receiving the allocation request, the scheduler component of the RM computes a list of containers that satisfy the request and sends back an allocation response. Upon receiving the resource list, the AM contacts the associated NMs for starting the containers. When the job finishes, the AM sends a Finish Application message to the RM.

Figure 7.7 shows the interactions between the an Application Master and the Node Manager. Based on the resource list received from the RM, the AM requests the hosting NM for each container to start the container. The AM can request and receive a container status report from the Node Manager. Figure 7.8 shows the MapReduce job execution within a YARN cluster.

7.1.3 Hadoop Schedulers

The scheduler is a pluggable component in Hadoop that allows it to support different scheduling algorithms. The pluggable scheduler framework provides the flexibility to support

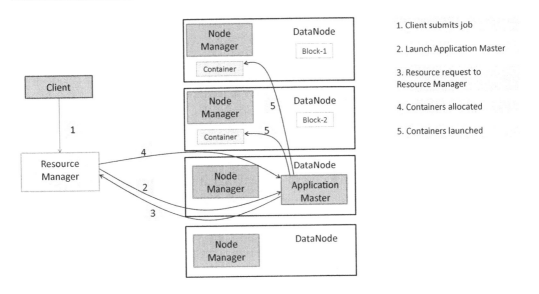

Figure 7.8: MapReduce job execution within a YARN cluster

a variety of workloads with varying priority and performance constraints. The Hadoop scheduling algorithms are described as follows:

FIFO

FIFO scheduler maintains a work queue in which the jobs are queued. The scheduler pulls jobs in first-in first-out manner (oldest job first) for scheduling. There is no concept of priority or size of the job in FIFO scheduler.

Fair Scheduler

The Fair Scheduler [50] was originally developed by Facebook. Facebook uses Hadoop to manage the massive content and log data it accumulates every day. It is our understanding that the need for Fair Scheduler arose when Facebook wanted to share the data warehousing infrastructure between multiple users. The Fair Scheduler allocates resources evenly between multiple jobs and also provides capacity guarantees. Fair Scheduler assigns resources to jobs such that each job gets an equal share of the available resources on average over time. Unlike the FIFO scheduler, which forms a queue of jobs, the Fair Scheduler lets short jobs finish in reasonable time while not starving long jobs. Tasks slots that are free are assigned to the new jobs, so that each job gets roughly the same amount of CPU time. The Fair Scheduler maintains a set of pools into which jobs are placed. Each pool has a guaranteed capacity. When there is a single job running, all the resources are assigned to that job. When there are multiple jobs in the pools, each pool gets at least as many task slots as guaranteed. Each pool receives at least the minimum share. When a pool does not require the guaranteed share the excess capacity is split between other jobs. This lets the scheduler guarantee capacity for pools while utilizing resources efficiently when these pools don't contain jobs. The Fair Scheduler keeps track of the compute time received by each job. The scheduler computes periodically the difference between the computing time received by each job and the time it should have received in ideal scheduling. The job which has the highest deficit of the compute time received is scheduled next. This ensures that over time, each job gets its fair share of compute time.

Fair scheduler is useful when a small or large Hadoop cluster is shared between multiple groups of users in an organization. Though the fair scheduler ensures fairness by maintaining a set of pools and providing guaranteed capacity to each pool, it does not provide any timing guarantees and hence it is ill-equipped for real-time jobs.

Capacity Scheduler

The Capacity Scheduler [51] was developed by Yahoo. Capacity scheduler has similar functionality as the Fair Scheduler but adopts a different scheduling philosophy. In Capacity Scheduler, multiple named queues are defined, each with a configurable number of map and reduce slots. Each queue is also assigned a guaranteed capacity. The Capacity Scheduler gives each queue its capacity when it contains jobs, and shares any unused capacity between the queues. Within each queue FIFO scheduling with priority is used. For fairness, it is possible to place a limit on the percentage of running tasks per user, so that users share a cluster equally. A wait time for each queue can be configured. When a queue is not scheduled for more than the wait time, it can preempt tasks of other queues to get its fair share. When a TaskTracker has free slots, the Capacity Scheduler picks a queue for which the ratio of number of running slots to capacity is the lowest. The scheduler then picks a job from the selected queue to run. Jobs are sorted based on when they're submitted and their priorities. Jobs are considered in order, and a job is selected if its user is within the user-quota for the queue, i.e., the user is not already using queue resources above the defined limit.

The capacity scheduler is useful when a large Hadoop cluster is shared between with multiple clients and different types and priorities of jobs. Though the capacity scheduler ensures fairness by maintaining a set of queues and providing guaranteed capacity to each queue, it does not provide any timing guarantees and, therefore, it may be ill-equipped for real-time jobs.

7.2 Hadoop - MapReduce Examples

7.2.1 Batch Analysis of Sensor Data

Figure 7.9 shows a Hadoop MapReduce workflow for batch analysis of weather data. Batch analysis is done to aggregate data (such as computing mean, maximum, and minimum) on various timescales. For this example, we will assume that we have a data collector which retrieves the sensor data collected in the cloud database and creates a raw data file in a form suitable for processing by Hadoop. The raw data file consists of the raw sensor readings along with the timestamps as shown below:
"2015-04-29 10:15:32",38,42,34,5
:

"2015-04-30 10:15:32",87,48,21,4

Box 7.1 shows the map program for the batch analysis of sensor data. The map program reads the data from standard input (*stdin*) and splits the data into the timestamp and individual sensor readings. The map program emits key-value pairs where the key is a portion of the timestamp (that depends on the timescale on which the data is to be aggregated), and the

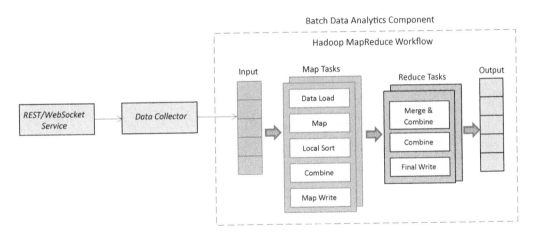

Figure 7.9: Using Hadoop MapReduce for batch analysis of sensor data

value is a comma separated string of sensor readings.

■ **Box 7.1: Map program - mapper.py**

```python
#!/usr/bin/env python
import sys

#Calculates mean temperature, humidity, light and CO2
# Input data format:
#"2014-04-29 10:15:32",37,44,31,6
#Output:
#"2014-04-29 10:15 [48.75, 31.25, 29.0, 16.5]"

#Input comes from STDIN (standard input)
for line in sys.stdin:
    # remove leading and trailing whitespace
    line = line.strip()
    data = line.split(',')
    l=len(data)

    #For aggregation by minute
    key=str(data[0][0:17])

    value=data[1]+','+data[2]+','+data[3]+','+data[4]
    print '%s \t%s' % (key, value)
```

Box 7.2 shows the reduce program for the batch analysis of sensor data. The key-value pairs emitted by the map program are shuffled to the reducer and grouped by the key. The reducer reads the key-value pairs grouped by the same key from standard input and computes the means of temperature, humidity, light and CO readings. Box 7.3 shows the commands for submitting the MapReduce job on a Hadoop cluster and viewing the output files on HDFS.

■ **Box 7.2: Reduce program - reducer.py**

```python
#!/usr/bin/env python
from operator import itemgetter
import sys
import numpy as np

current_key = None
current_vals_list = []
word = None

#Input comes from STDIN
for line in sys.stdin:
  # remove leading and trailing whitespace
  line = line.strip()

#Parse the input from mapper
  key, values = line.split('\t', 1)
  list_of_values = values.split(',')

#Convert to list of strings to list of int
  list_of_values = [int(i) for i in list_of_values]

  if current_key == key:
    current_vals_list.append(list_of_values)
  else:
    if current_key:
      l = len(current_vals_list)+ 1
      b = np.array(current_vals_list)
      meanval = [np.mean(b[0:l,0]),np.mean(b[0:l,1]),
      np.mean(b[0:l,2]), np.mean(b[0:l,3])]
      print '%s\t%s' % (current_key, str(meanval))

    current_vals_list = []
    current_vals_list.append(list_of_values)
    current_key = key

#Output the last key if needed
if current_key == key:
  l = len(current_vals_list)+ 1
  b = np.array(current_vals_list)
  meanval = [np.mean(b[0:l,0]),np.mean(b[0:l,1]),
    np.mean(b[0:l,2]), np.mean(b[0:l,3])]
  print '%s\t%s' % (current_key, str(meanval))
```

■ **Box 7.3: Running MapReduce program on Hadoop cluster**

```
#Testing locally
$cat data.txt | python mapper.py | python reducer.py

#Running on Hadoop cluster
#Copy data file to HDFS sudo -u user1 bin/hadoop dfs -copyFromLocal
```

```
data.txt input

#Run MapReduce job bin/hadoop jar
contrib/streaming/hadoop-*streaming*.jar
-mapper mapper.py -reducer reducer.py
-file /home/ubuntu/hadoop/mapper.py
-file /home/ubuntu/hadoop/reducer.py
-input input/* -output output

#View output bin/hadoop dfs -ls output
bin/hadoop dfs -cat output/part-00000
```

7.2.2   Batch Analysis of N-Gram Dataset

Let us look at another example of MapReduce to analyze Google N-Gram dataset [29], which is a freely-available collection of n-grams (fixed size tuples of words) extracted from the Google Books corpus. The *n* specifies the number of elements in the tuple, so for example, a 5-gram contains five words.

The n-grams in this dataset were produced by passing a sliding window over the text of books and outputting a record for each new token. For example, for the line – 'Python is a high level language', The 2-grams (or bigrams) will be:
(Python, is)
(is, a)
(a, high)
(high, level)
(level, language)

Each row of data contains:
1) n-gram itself
2) year in which the n-gram appeared
3) number of times the n-gram appeared in the books from the corresponding year (count)
4) number of pages on which the n-gram appeared in this year (page-count)
5) number of distinct books in which the n-gram appeared in this year (book count)

Example (5-gram): analysis is often described as 1991 1 1 1
Interpretation of the 5-gram: In 1991, the phrase "analysis is often described as" occurred one time (that's the first 1), and on one page (the second 1), and in one book (the third 1).

Box 7.4 shows MapReduce program that calculates the most popular bigram (2-gram) of all time in the dataset. This example uses the MRJob Python library which lets you write MapReduce jobs in Python and run them on several platforms including local machine, Hadoop cluster and Amazon Elastic MapReduce (EMR). MRJob can be installed as follows:

```
■ #Installing MRJob
sudo apt-get install git
git clone https://github.com/Yelp/mrjob.git
cd mrjob
python setup.py install
```

The example in Box 7.4 implements a class MyMRJob that defines mapper and reducer functions. In this example, we have one map-reduce pair and another reduce function which is chained to the output of the first reducer. When the program is run, the mapper function is invoked for each line of the input file.

■ **Box 7.4: MapReduce program that calculates the most popular bigram of all time - mr.py**

```
from mrjob.job import MRJob

class MyMRJob(MRJob):
   def mapper(self, _, line):
      data=line.split('\t')
      ngram = data[0].strip()
      year = data[1].strip()
      count = data[2].strip()
      pages = data[3].strip()
      books = data[4].strip()

      #Emit key-value pairs where key is ngram+year and value is count
      yield ngram+year, int(count)

   def reducer(self, key, list_of_values):
      # Send all (count, ngram+year) pairs to the same reducer.
      # So we can easily use Python's max() function.
      yield None, (sum(list_of_values),key)

   def reducer2(self, _, list_of_values):
      # Reducer-2 get input tuples as follows:
      # None, [(212, cloud computing 2006), (156, mobile phones 2003)]
      # max function will yield tuple with max value of the count
      yield max(list_of_values)

   def steps(self):
      return [self.mr(mapper=self.mapper,
         reducer=self.reducer), self.mr(reducer=self.reducer2)]

if __name__ == '__main__':
   MyMRJob.run()
```

The MapReduce program is run as follows:

```
■ #Running MapReduce program
python mr.py googlebooks-eng-us-all-2gram-20090715-50-subset.csv
```

7.2.3 Find top-N words with MapReduce

Let us look at another MapReduce example that finds the top-N words in a text file, where N is a configurable number. Box 7.5 shows a Python MapReduce program for finding top-3 words in a file. When this program is executed, the lines in the input text file are passed to the mapper. The mapper function splits the lines and emits key-value pairs where key is each word in the line and value is 1. The first reducer function sums up the list of values for each key, thus computing the word counts. The reducer function emits key-value pairs where key is None and value is a tuple containing the count and the word. Setting the key as None ensures that all (count, word) tuples are sent to the same reducer. The second reducer function sorts the list of values (where each value is a (count, word) tuple) and emits the top-N values.

■ **Box 7.5: MapReduce program that finds the top-N words in a file- topNwords.py**

```
from mrjob.job import MRJob

class MyMRJob(MRJob):
  def mapper(self, _, line):
    line = line.strip()
    words = line.split()
    for word in words:
       yield (word, 1)

  def reducer(self, key, list_of_values):
    word = key
    total_count = sum(list_of_values)
    yield None, (total_count, word)

  def reducer2(self, _, list_of_values):
    N = 3
    list_of_values = sorted(list(list_of_values), reverse=True)
    return list_of_values[:N]

  def steps(self):
    return [self.mr(mapper=self.mapper,
    reducer=self.reducer), self.mr(reducer=self.reducer2)]

if __name__ == '__main__':
  MyMRJob.run()
```

7.3 Pig

While MapReduce is a powerful programming model for big data analysis, for certain complex analysis jobs developers may find it difficult to identify the key-value pairs involved at each step and then implement the map and reduce functions. Moreover, complex analysis jobs may require multiple MapReduce jobs to be chained.

Pig is a high-level data processing language which makes it easy for developers to write data analysis scripts, which are translated into MapReduce programs by the Pig compiler. Pig includes: (1) a high-level language (called Pig Latin) for expressing data analysis programs and (2) a complier which produces sequences of MapReduce programs from the pig scripts.

Pig can be executed either in local mode or MapReduce mode. In local mode, Pig runs inside a single JVM process on a local machine. Local mode is useful for development purpose and testing the scripts with small data files on a single machine. MapReduce mode requires a Hadoop cluster. In MapReduce mode, Pig can analyze data stored in HDFS. Pig compiler translates the pig scripts into MapReduce programs which are executed in a Hadoop cluster. Pig provides an interactive shell called grunt, for developing pig scripts. Grunt can be launched as follows:

```
■ # Launching Pig Grunt Shell
# Pig local mode
>pig -x local

#Pig MapReduce mode
>pig
```

Let us look at some commonly used Pig operators with examples. We will use the NCDC weather dataset [52] for the examples. NCDC provides access to daily data from the U.S. Climate Reference Network / U.S. Regional Climate Reference Network (USCRN/USRCRN) via FTP.

7.3.1 Loading Data

Pig provides the LOAD operator for loading data. LOAD operator loads data from a file into a relation. A Pig relation is a collection of tuples where each tuple has multiple fields. An example of LOAD operator is shown below:

```
■ # LOAD example
data = LOAD 'data.txt' as (text:chararray);
```

7.3.2 Data Types in Pig

Pig support simple data types such as int, long, float, double, chararray, bytearray, boolean, datetime, and complex data types such as tuple, bag and map. The simple data types work the same way as in other programming languages. Let is look at the complex data types in detail.

Tuple

A tuple is an ordered set of fields.

```
■ # Tuple example
(1,10)
```

Bag

A bag is an unordered collection of tuples. A bag is represented with curly braces.

```
■ # Bag example
{(1,10.4),(1,4.9),(1,5.0)})
```

Map

A Map is a set of key-value pairs. Map is represented with square brackets and a # is used to separate the key and value.

```
■ # Map example
[temp#20.0, humidity#70]
```

7.3.3   Data Filtering & Analysis

The FOREACH operator is used to process each row in a relation and the GENERATE operator is used to define the fields and generate a new row from the original. For example, with the weather dataset loaded previously, to generate a relation with only the month and the temperature, FOREACH and GENERATE can be used as follows:

```
■ # FOREACH example
monthTemp = FOREACH data GENERATE SUBSTRING(text, 10,12) as month,
(double)SUBSTRING(text, 38,45) as temp;
DUMP monthTemp;
(01,22.9)
:
(12,5.6)
```

The FILTER operator is used to filter out tuples from a relation based on the condition specified. For example, to filter out all rows with temperature less than 20, the FILTER operator can be used as follows:

```
■ # FILTER example
low = FILTER monthTemp by temp<20.0;
DUMP low;
(01,10.4)
:
(12,4.8)
```

The GROUP operator can be used to group data in one or more relations. For example, to group monthTemp relation by the month field, the GROUP operator can be used as follows:

```
■ #GROUP example
monthTempGroup = GROUP monthTemp by month;
DESCRIBE monthTempGroup;
monthTempGroup: {group: chararray,monthTemp: {(month: chararray,temp:
double)}}
DUMP monthTempGroup;
(1,{(1,11.7),...,(1,9.7)})
(12,{(12,20.3),...,(12,4.8)})
```

The UNION operator can be used to merge the contents of two or more relations. The example below shows how to obtain union of two relations:

```
■ #UNION example
low = FILTER monthTemp by temp<10.0;
high = FILTER monthTemp by temp>20.0;
lowHigh = UNION low,high;
```

The JOIN operator is used to join two relations. For example to join two relations (one which holds the maximum temperature in each month and the other which holds the minimum temperature in each month), JOIN can be used as follows:

```
■ # JOIN example
maxTemp = FOREACH monthTempGroup GENERATE group, MAX(monthTemp.temp);
minTemp = FOREACH monthTempGroup GENERATE group, MIN(monthTemp.temp);
maxMinTemp = JOIN maxTemp BY $0, minTemp BY $0;
```

Pig provides various built-in functions such as AVG, MIN, MAX, SUM, and COUNT. In the above example, MAX and MIN were used to obtain the maximum and minimum temperature in each month. The $N expression in the join statement is used to specify the column by which the join should be performed. Alternatively, the column name can also be provided.

7.3.4 Storing Results

To save the results on the filesystem the STORE operator is used. Pig uses a lazy evaluation strategy and delays the evaluation of expressions till a STORE or DUMP operator triggers the results to be stored or displayed.

```
■ # STORE example
low = FILTER monthTemp by temp<20.0;
STORE low;
```

7.3.5 Debugging Operators

The DUMP operator is used to dump the results on the console. DUMP is used in interactive mode for debugging purposes.

The DESCRIBE operator is used to view the schema of a relation.

```
■ # DESCRIBE example
monthTempGroup = GROUP monthTemp by month;
DESCRIBE monthTempGroup;
monthTempGroup: {group: chararray, monthTemp:
{(month: chararray,temp: double)}}
```

The EXPLAIN operator is used to view the logical, physical, and MapReduce execution plans for computing a relation. The following example shows the execution plan for computing monthTemp relation.

```
■ # EXPLAIN example
EXPLAIN monthTemp;
#----------------------------------
# Map Reduce Plan
#----------------------------------
MapReduce node scope-308
Map Plan
monthTemp:   Store(fakefile:org.apache.pig.builtin.PigStorage) - scope-307
|
|--monthTemp:  New For Each(false,false)[bag] - scope-306
  | |
```

```
| POUserFunc(org.apache.pig.builtin.SUBSTRING)[chararray] - scope-298
| |
| |--Project[chararray][0] - scope-295
| |
| |--Constant(10) - scope-296
| |
| |--Constant(12) - scope-297
| |
| Cast[double] - scope-304
| |
| |--POUserFunc(org.apache.pig.builtin.SUBSTRING)[chararray] - scope-303
| |
| |--Project[chararray][0] - scope-300
| |
| |--Constant(38) - scope-301
| |
| |--Constant(45) - scope-302
|
|--data:  New For Each(false)[bag] - scope-294
 | |
 | Cast[chararray] - scope-292
 | |
 | |--Project[bytearray][0] - scope-291
 |
 |--data:
Load(file:///home/ubuntu/pig-0.15.0/data.txt:org.apache.pig.builtin.PigStorage) -
scope-290-----
Global sort:  false
-----------
```

The ILLUSTRATE operator is used to display the step by step execution of statements to compute a relation with a small sample of data. The example below shows the ILLUSTRATE statement for monthTemp relation.

```
■ # ILLUSTRATE example
ILLUSTRATE monthTemp;
-----------------------
| data | text:chararray
|
-----------------------
| | 03739 20140207 2.422 -75.93 37.29 3.7 -2.8 0.5 0.8 0.0 12.02 C
15.1 -5.0 1.9 89.5 41.2 67.1 0.231 0.214 0.214
0.215 0.214 2.9 3.2 3.4 4.0 5.2 |
-----------------------------
| monthTemp | month:chararray | temp:double |
-----------------------------------------
| | 02 | 3.7 |
-----------------------------------------
```

7.3.6 Pig Examples

Let us look at some examples of batch data analysis with Pig. Box 7.6 shows an example
of computing word count with Pig. In this example, the data is first loaded from a text file.
The lines are tokenized using the TOKENIZE function which creates a bag of tuples (from
the words in a line) for each line in the text file. The FLATTEN function is used to flatten
the bag so that the tuples can be grouped. The GROUP operator is used to group the words.
Finally, the COUNT function is used to count the occurrences for each word. The best way to
understand the relations involved at each step is to use the debugging operators like DUMP,
DESCRIBE and ILLUSTRATE.

■ **Box 7.6: Pig script for computing word count**

```
data = LOAD 'input.txt' as (lines:chararray);
words = FOREACH data GENERATE FLATTEN(TOKENIZE(lines)) AS word;
wordGroup = GROUP words BY word;
counts = FOREACH wordGroup GENERATE group, COUNT(words);
store counts into 'counts';
```

Earlier in this chapter, we described an example of a MapReduce program that calculates
the most popular bigram of all time from the Google N-Gram dataset. Let us look at an
example of using Pig for computing the most common bigram in each year in the dataset.
Box 7.7 shows a Pig script for computing the most common bigram in each year.

■ **Box 7.7: Pig script for computing the most common bigram in each year in the
dataset**

```
#Expted output:  (year, bigram, count)
data = LOAD 'hdfs:///ngraminput' using
PigStorage() AS (ngram:chararray, year:int,count:int);
yearData = GROUP data BY year;
maxYearData = FOREACH yearData GENERATE
group AS groupId, MAX(data.count) AS maxCount;
joinResult = JOIN maxYearData BY
(groupId,maxCount), data by (year,count);
result = FOREACH joinResult GENERATE
$0 AS year, $1 AS count, $2 AS ngram;
STORE result into 'hdfs:///result';
```

7.4 Case Study: Batch Analysis of News Articles

In this section, we will describe a case study on a system for batch analysis of news articles
aggregated from multiple news websites. The system computes the sentiment of each news
article and finds the trending topics.

Given the analysis requirements of this system, let us map the system to one of the
analytics patterns proposed in Chapter-1. Since the system processes news articles in batch
model, we suggest the use of the Alpha pattern. Figure 7.10(a) shows a realization of Alpha
pattern for this system, with the specific tools and frameworks that can be used. The system
uses MapReduce and Pig for batch analysis, such as computing the most common word and

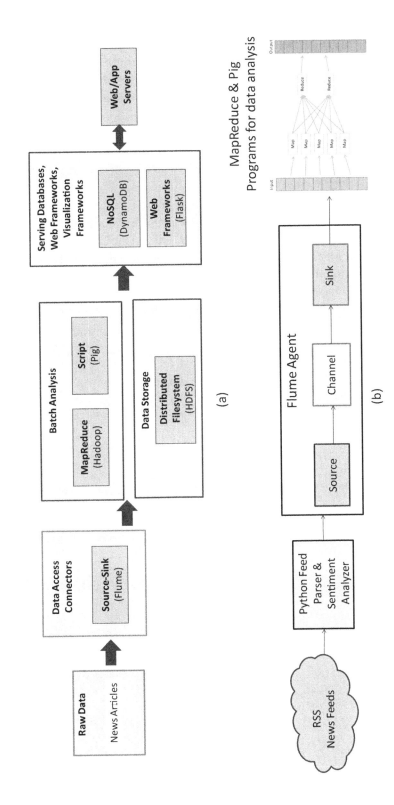

Figure 7.10: (a) A realization of Alpha pattern for batch analysis of news articles (b) Architecture of the system

most common phrase among all news articles. Figure 7.10(b) shows the architecture of the news analysis system.

To collect news articles from different websites, the Python program shown in Box 7.8 is used. In this program, the RSS (Rich Site Summary) feed links for different news websites are provided. An RSS feed parsing library called *feedparser* is used. The Python program runs continuously to collect RSS feeds every five minutes and computes sentiment scores of the news headlines. The output of the Python program is a CSV file which has the following columns: sentiment analysis score, news headline, URL, source, and timestamp.

To compute the sentiments, we use the AFINN [18] sentiment lexicon, which is a list of over 2400 English words rated for sentiment which is an integer between minus five (negative) and plus five (positive).

The CSV files generated by the Python program are then moved to HDFS for further analysis. For this, the Apache Flume framework is used. The Flume configuration used includes a spool directory source and an HDFS sink. The CSV files generated by the Python program are ingested from the spool directory to HDFS using Flume. Box 7.9 shows the Flume configuration used. With the aggregated dataset in HDFS, MapReduce and Pig programs are used to perform computation for all of the application features such as dividing news into categories based on sentiment scores, analyzing hourly news traffic, and determining trending words and topics. A Flask web application is used to display the results.

■ Box 7.8: Python program for aggregating news articles

```
import feedparser
import threading
import sys
import time
import subprocess
from datetime import datetime

refresh_time = 300 #in seconds

rss_feeds = [
('http://rss.cnn.com/rss/cnn_topstories.rss', 'CNN'),
('http://rss.nytimes.com/services/xml/rss/nyt/HomePage.xml',
'The New York Times'),
('http://www.wsj.com/xml/rss/3_7085.xml', 'Wall Street Journal'),
('http://www.news.gatech.edu/rss/all', 'Georgia Tech News')]

csv_file = open("Output.csv","a")

sentiments={}
file = open('AFINN-111.txt')
lines = file.readlines()
for line in lines:
s = line.split("\t")
sentiments[s[0]] = s[1].strip()
file.close()
```

```python
def get_sentiment_score(phrase):
   phrase = phrase.strip()
   total = 0.0
   for word in phrase.split():
      word = word.lower()
      for char in `[!@#$)(*<>=+/:;&%#|{},.? `]-˝:
         word = word.replace(char,``)
      if word in list(sentiments):
         total = total + float(sentiments[word])
   return total


last_round_headlines = []
this_round_headlines = []

def get_headlines(rss_feed):
   feed = feedparser.parse(rss_feed[0])
   for entry in feed.entries:
      title = entry.title.encode(`utf-8`)
      this_round_headlines.append(title)
      if title not in last_round_headlines:
         score = get_sentiment_score(title)
         title = title.replace(`,`,``)
         #Format:  # score, title, link, source, timestamp
         to_print = "" + str(score) + ", " + title + ", "
          + entry.link.encode(`utf-8`) + ", " + rss_feed[1] +
          ", " + str(datetime.now())
         csv_file.write(to_print)


while True:
   for rss_feed in rss_feeds:
      t = threading.Thread(target=get_headlines, args = (rss_feed,))
      t.start()
   time.sleep(refresh_time)
   last_round_headlines = list(this_round_headlines)
   this_round_headlines = list()
```

■ **Box 7.9: Flume configuration**

```
agent.sources = pstream
agent.channels = memoryChannel
agent.channels.memoryChannel.type = memory
agent.channels.memoryChannel.capacity = 10000000
agent.channels.memoryChannel.transactionCapacity = 10000000
agent.sources.pstream.channels = memoryChannel
agent.sources.pstream.type = spooldir
agent.sources.pstream.spoolDir = test
agent.sinks = hdfsSink
agent.sinks.hdfsSink.type = hdfs
agent.sinks.hdfsSink.channel = memoryChannel
agent.sinks.hdfsSink.hdfs.path = /spooldirtest
```

```
agent.sinks.hdfsSink.hdfs.fileType = DataStream
agent.sinks.hdfsSink.hdfs.writeFormat = Text
agent.sinks.hdfsSink.hdfs.batchSize = 10000000
agent.sinks.hdfsSink.hdfs.rollCount = 0
agent.sinks.hdfsSink.hdfs.rollInterval = 0
agent.sinks.hdfsSink.hdfs.rollSize = 0
agent.sinks.hdfsSink.hdfs.fileSuffix = .csv
```

Box 7.10 shows a MapReduce program for finding the most common two-word phrase from the input.

■ Box 7.10: MapReduce program for finding the most common two-word phrase from the input

```python
from mrjob.job import MRJob
import string

stop_words = ["for","of","the","in","a",
     "to","is","news", "breaking", "and",
     "you", "by", "your", "on", "at",
     "as", "this", "it", "with", "from"]

exclude = set(string.punctuation)

#----- Load Ignore Words Dict ---
stopFile = open('StopWords.txt')
lines = stopFile.readlines()
for line in lines:
    s = line.split("\t")
    stop_words.append(s)
stopFile.close()

class MyMRJob(MRJob):
   def mapper(self, _, line):
      #Get data
      data=line.split(',')
      sentiment = data[0].strip()
      headline = data[1].strip()
      headline = headline.lower()
      words = headline.split()

      good_words = []
      for word in words:
         good_words.append(word)

      # Create phrases
      phrases = []
      for i in range(0, len(good_words) - 1):
         word1 = good_words[i]
         word2 = good_words[i+1]
         if word1 in stop_words:
            continue
         if word2 in stop_words:
            continue
```

```
            phrase = '%s %s' %(word1, word2)
            phrases.append(phrase)

        link = data[2].strip()
        for phrase in phrases:
            yield phrase, (1, sentiment, link)

    def reducer(self, key, list_of_values):
        totalCount = 0.0
        totalSentiment = 0.0
        list_of_links = []
        for item in list_of_values:
            #Skip if the link has already been processed
            if item[2] in list_of_links:
                continue

            #Add count
            totalCount = totalCount + item[0]
            #Add sentiment
            totalSentiment = totalSentiment + float(item[1])
            #Append links
            list_of_links.append(item[2])

        avgSentiment = totalSentiment / totalCount
        yield None, (totalCount, key, avgSentiment, list_of_links)

    def reducer2(self, _, list_of_values):
        #Print top 25
        count = 0
        for item in sorted(list_of_values, reverse = True):
            if count > 25:
                break
            print item
            count = count + 1

    def steps(self):
        return [self.mr(mapper=self.mapper,
        reducer=self.reducer), self.mr(reducer=self.reducer2)]

if __name__ == '__main__':
    MyMRJob.run()
```

Box 7.11 shows a Pig program for finding the most common word from the news.

■ **Box 7.11: Pig program for finding the most common word from the news**

```
data = LOAD 'data.csv' USING PigStorage(',') as
(sentiment:float, headline:chararray, link:chararray);
/* Remove any duplicates */
data = DISTINCT data;

/* Group by each headline*/
headlines = group data BY headline;
```

```
words = FOREACH data GENERATE flatten(TOKENIZE(headline)) as wordTuple;
C = group words by wordTuple;

/* Get count, organize by count, limit to the top 50 */
wordCount = foreach C generate COUNT(words) as count, group as word;
OUT = ORDER wordCount by count DESC;
OUT = LIMIT OUT 50;
STORE OUT into 'mostCommonWords.txt';
```

7.5 Apache Oozie

Many batch analysis applications require more than one MapReduce job to be chained to
perform data analysis. This can be accomplished using Apache Oozie system. Oozie is a
workflow scheduler system that allows managing Hadoop jobs. With Oozie, you can create
workflows which are a collection of actions (such as MapReduce jobs) arranged as Direct
Acyclic Graphs (DAG). Control dependencies exist between the actions in a workflow. Thus,
an action is executed only when the preceding action is completed. An Oozie workflow
specifies a sequence of actions that need to be executed using an XML-based Process
Definition Language called Hadoop Process Definition Language (hPDL). Oozie supports
various types of actions such as Hadoop MapReduce, Hadoop file system, Pig, Java, Email,
Shell, Hive, Sqoop, SSH and custom actions.

7.5.1 Oozie Workflows for Data Analysis

Let us look at an example of analyzing log data. Assuming that the data received has the
following structure (including time stamp and the status/error code):

```
#timestamp, status/error "2014-07-01 20:03:18",115
"2014-07-01 20:04:15",106
:
"2014-07-01 20:10:15",110
```

The goal of the analysis job is to find the counts of each status/error code and produce an
output with a structure as shown below:

```
#status/error, count 111, 6
112, 7
113, 12
```

Figure 7.11 shows a representation of the Oozie workflow comprising a Hadoop streaming
MapReduce job action and Email actions that notify the success or failure of the job.

Boxes 7.12 and 7.13 show the map and reduce programs which are executed in the
workflow. The map program parses the status/error code from each line in the input and emits
key-value pairs where the key is the status/error code and value is 1. The reduce program
receives the key-value pairs emitted by the map program aggregated by the same key. For
each key, the reduce program calculates the count and emits key-value pairs where the key is
the status/error code and the value is the count.

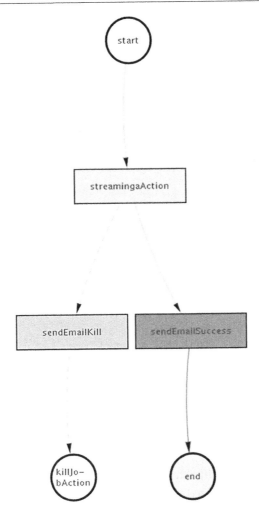

Figure 7.11: Oozie workflow

■ **Box 7.12: Map program for computing counts of status/error codes**

```
#!/usr/bin/env python
import sys

#Data format
#"2014-07-01 20:03:18",115

# input comes from STDIN (standard input)
for line in sys.stdin:
    # remove leading and trailing whitespace
    line = line.strip()
    # split the line into words
    data = line.split(',')
    print '%s\t%s' % (data[1], 1)
```

■ **Box 7.13: Reduce program for computing counts of status/error codes**

```python
#!/usr/bin/env python
from operator import itemgetter
import sys

current_key = None
current_count = 0
key = None

# input comes from STDIN
for line in sys.stdin:
    line = line.strip()

    key, count = line.split('\t', 1)
    count = int(count)

    if current_key == key:
        current_count += count
    else:
        if current_key:
            unpackedKey = current_key.split(',')
            print '%s%s' % (current_key, current_count)
        current_count = count
        current_key = key

if current_key == key:
    unpackedKey = current_key.split(',')
    print '%s\t%s' % (current_key, current_count)
```

Box 7.14 shows the specification for the Oozie workflow shown in Figure 7.11. Oozie workflow has been parameterized with variables within the workflow definition. The values of these variables are provided in the job properties file shown in Box 7.15

■ **Box 7.14: Oozie workflow for computing counts of status/error codes**

```xml
<workflow-app name="PythonOozieApp" xmlns="uri:oozie:workflow:0.1">
 <start to="streamingaAction"/>
  <action name="streamingaAction">
<map-reduce>
    <job-tracker>${jobTracker}</job-tracker>
    <name-node>${nameNode}</name-node>
    <prepare>
    <delete path="${outputDir}"/>
    </prepare>
    <streaming>
     <mapper>python Mapper.py</mapper>
     <reducer>python Reducer.py</reducer>
    </streaming>
    <configuration>
<property>
<name>oozie.libpath</name>
```

```
      <value>${oozieLibPath}/mapreduce-streaming</value>
    </property>
      <property>
       <name>mapred.input.dir</name>
       <value>${inputDir}</value>
      </property>
      <property>
       <name>mapred.output.dir</name>
       <value>${outputDir}</value>
      </property>
<property>
       <name>mapred.reduce.tasks</name>
       <value>1</value>
      </property>
    </configuration>
<file>${appPath}/Mapper.py#Mapper.py</file>
<file>${appPath}/Reducer.py#Reducer.py</file>
  </map-reduce>
<ok to="sendEmailSuccess"/>
<error to="sendEmailKill"/>
  </action>

<action name="sendEmailSuccess">
  <email xmlns="uri:oozie:email-action:0.1">
    <to>${emailToAddress}</to>
    <subject>Status of workflow ${wf:id()}</subject>
    <body>The workflow ${wf:id()} completed successfully</body>
  </email>
  <ok to="end"/>
  <error to="end"/>
 </action>
 <action name="sendEmailKill">
  <email xmlns="uri:oozie:email-action:0.1">
   <to>${emailToAddress}</to>
   <subject>Status of workflow ${wf:id()}</subject>
   <body>The workflow ${wf:id()} had issues and was killed.
The error message is:  ${wf:errorMessage(wf:lastErrorNode())}</body>
  </email>
  <ok to="killJobAction"/>
  <error to="killJobAction"/>
 </action>

  <kill name="killJobAction">
   <message>"Killed job due to error:
${wf:errorMessage(wf:lastErrorNode())}"</message>
  </kill>
 <end name="end" />
</workflow-app>
```

■ **Box 7.15: Job properties file for Oozie workflow**

```
nameNode=hdfs://master:54310
jobTracker=master:54311
```

```
queueName=default

oozie.libpath=${nameNode}/user/hduser/share/lib
oozie.use.system.libpath=true
oozie.wf.rerun.failnodes=true

oozieProjectRoot=${nameNode}/user/hduser/oozieProject
appPath=${oozieProjectRoot}/pythonApplication
oozie.wf.application.path=${appPath}
oozieLibPath=${oozie.libpath}

inputDir=${oozieProjectRoot}/pythonApplication/data/
outputDir=${appPath}/output
```

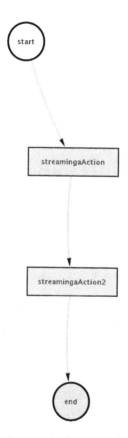

Figure 7.12: Oozie workflow for computing status/error code with maximum count

Let us now look at a more complicated workflow which has two MapReduce jobs. Extending the example described earlier in this section, let us say we want to find the status/error code with the maximum count. The MapReduce job in the earlier workflow computed the counts for each status/error code. A second MapReduce job, which consumes the output of the first MapReduce job computes the maximum count. The map and reduce programs for the second MapReduce job are shown in Boxes 7.16 and 7.17.

Figure 7.12 shows a DAG representation of the Oozie workflow for computing status/error code with maximum count. The specification of the workflow is shown in Box 7.18.

■ Box 7.16: Map program for computing status/error code with maximum count

```python
#!/usr/bin/env python
import sys

#Data format
#"2014-07-01 20:03:18",115

# input comes from STDIN (standard input)
for line in sys.stdin:
    # remove leading and trailing whitespace
    line = line.strip()
    # split the line into words
    data = line.split('\t')

    #For aggregation by minute
    print '%s\t%s' % (data[0], data[1])
```

■ Box 7.17: Reduce program for computing status/error code with maximum count

```python
#!/usr/bin/env python
from operator import itemgetter
import sys

current_key = None
current_count = 0
key = None
maxcount=0
maxcountkey=None

# input comes from STDIN
for line in sys.stdin:
    # remove leading and trailing whitespace
    line = line.strip()

    # parse the input we got from mapper.py
    key, count = line.split('\t', 1)

    # convert count to int
    count = int(count)

    if count>maxcount:
        maxcount=count
        maxcountkey=key
        print '%s\t%s' % (maxcountkey, maxcount)
```

■ Box 7.18: Oozie workflow for computing status/error code with maximum count

```
<workflow-app name="PythonOozieApp" xmlns="uri:oozie:workflow:0.1">
 <start to="streamingaAction"/>
   <action name="streamingaAction">
<map-reduce>
    <job-tracker>${jobTracker}</job-tracker>
    <name-node>${nameNode}</name-node>
    <prepare>
     <delete path="${outputDir}"/>
    </prepare>
    <streaming>
     <mapper>python Mapper.py</mapper>
     <reducer>python Reducer.py</reducer>
    </streaming>
    <configuration>
<property>
<name>oozie.libpath</name>
    <value>${oozieLibPath}/mapreduce-streaming</value>
   </property>
     <property>
     <name>mapred.input.dir</name>
     <value>${inputDir}</value>
    </property>
     <property>
     <name>mapred.output.dir</name>
     <value>${outputDir}</value>
    </property>
<property>
     <name>mapred.reduce.tasks</name>
     <value>1</value>
    </property>
   </configuration>
<file>${appPath}/Mapper.py#Mapper.py</file>
<file>${appPath}/Reducer.py#Reducer.py</file>
  </map-reduce>
    <ok to="streamingaAction2"/>
    <error to="killJobAction"/>
  </action>

<action name="streamingaAction2">
<map-reduce>
    <job-tracker>${jobTracker}</job-tracker>
    <name-node>${nameNode}</name-node>
    <streaming>
     <mapper>python Mapper1.py</mapper>
     <reducer>python Reducer1.py</reducer>
    </streaming>
    <configuration>
<property>
<name>oozie.libpath</name>
    <value>${oozieLibPath}/mapreduce-streaming</value>
   </property>
```

```
         <property>
          <name>mapred.input.dir</name>
          <value>${outputDir}</value>
         </property>
         <property>
          <name>mapred.output.dir</name>
          <value>${outputDir}/output2</value>
         </property>
<property>
          <name>mapred.reduce.tasks</name>
          <value>1</value>
         </property>
      </configuration>
<file>${appPath}/Mapper1.py#Mapper1.py</file>
<file>${appPath}/Reducer1.py#Reducer1.py</file>
    </map-reduce>
     <ok to="end"/>
     <error to="killJobAction"/>
    </action>

    <kill name="killJobAction">
     <message>"Killed job due to error:
${wf:errorMessage(wf:lastErrorNode())}"</message>
    </kill>
  <end name="end" />
</workflow-app>
```

Figure 7.13 shows a screenshot of the Oozie web console which can be used to monitor the status of Oozie workflows.

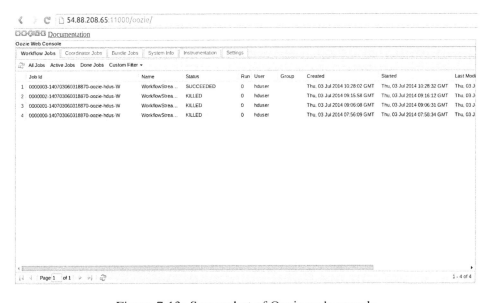

Figure 7.13: Screenshot of Oozie web console

7.6 Apache Spark

Apache Spark is an open source cluster computing framework for data analytics [62]. Spark supports in-memory cluster computing and promises to be faster than Hadoop. Spark supports various high-level tools for data analysis such as Spark Streaming for streaming jobs, Spark SQL for analysis of structured data, MLlib machine learning library for Spark, and GraphX for graph processing. Spark allows real-time, batch and interactive queries and provides APIs for Scala, Java and Python languages.

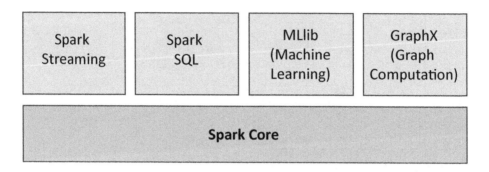

Figure 7.14: Spark tools

- **Spark Core**: Spark Core provides common functionality (such as task scheduling and input/output), which is used by other Spark components. Spark provides a data abstraction called resilient distributed dataset (RDD) which is a collection of elements partitioned across the nodes in a Spark cluster. The RDD elements can be operated on in parallel in the cluster. RDDs are immutable and distributed collection of objects.
- **Spark Streaming**: Spark Streaming is a Spark component for analysis of streaming data such as sensor data, click stream data, web server logs, etc.
- **Spark SQL**: Spark SQL is a Spark component that enables interactive querying of data using SQL queries. Spark SQL is described in detail in Chapter-9 where we describe tools for interactive querying.
- **Spark MLlib**: Spark MLlib is Spark's machine learning library that provides implementations of commonly used machine learning algorithms for clustering, classification, regression, collaborative filtering and dimensionality reduction.
- **Spark GraphX**: Spark GraphX is a component for performing graph computations. GraphX provides implementations of common graph algorithms such as PageRank, connected components, and triangle counting.

Figure 7.15 shows the components of a Spark cluster. Each Spark application consists of a driver program and is coordinated by a *SparkContext* object. Spark supports various cluster managers including Spark's standalone cluster manager, Apache Mesos and Hadoop YARN. The cluster manager allocates resources for applications on the worker nodes. The executors which are allocated on the worker nodes run the application code as multiple tasks. Applications are isolated from each other and run within their own executor processes on the worker nodes.

Spark comes with a spark-ec2 script (in the spark/ec2 directory) which makes it easy to setup Spark cluster on Amazon EC2. With spark-ec2 script you can easily launch, manage

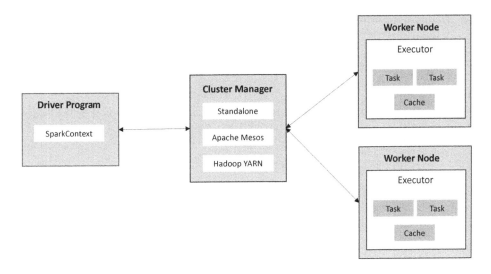

Figure 7.15: Components of a Spark cluster

and shutdown Spark cluster on Amazon EC2. To start a Spark cluster use the following command:

```
■ ./spark-ec2 -k <keypair> -i <key-file> -s <num-slaves>
launch <cluster-name> -instance-type=<INSTANCE_TYPE>
```

Spark cluster setup on EC2 is configured to use HDFS as its default filesystem. To analyze contents of a file, the file should be first copied to HDFS using the following command:

```
■ bin/hadoop fs -put file.txt file.txt
```

Spark supports a shell mode with which you can interactively run commands for analyzing data. To launch the Spark Python shell, run the following command:

```
■ ./bin/pyspark
```

When you launch a PySpark shell, a SparkContext is created with the variable name *sc*.

Creating RDDs
RDDs can be created either by parallelizing existing collections or by loading an external dataset as shown in box below:

```
■ #Create RDD from a local file
lines = sc.textFile("file:///root/spark/README.md")

#Create RDD by parallelizing an existing collection
data = sc.parallelize([1, 2, 2, 3, 3, 4, 5])
```

7.6.1 Spark Operations

Spark RDDs support two types of operations:

- **Transformations**: Transformations are used to create a new dataset from an existing one.
- **Actions**: Actions return a value to the driver program after running a computation on the dataset.

Transformations

Let us look at some commonly used transformations with examples. For the examples, we will use the three datasets as shown below:

```
lines = sc.textFile("file:///root/spark/README.md")

data1 = sc.parallelize([1, 2, 2, 3, 3, 4, 5])
data2 = sc.parallelize([3, 4, 5, 6, 7, 8])
```

map

The *map* transformation takes as input a function which is applied to each element of the dataset and maps each input item to another item.

```
#map transformation example
lineLengths = lines.map(lambda s:  len(s))
lineLengths.take(5)
[14, 0, 78, 72, 73]
```

filter

The *filter* transformation generates a new dataset by filtering the source dataset using the specified function.

```
#filter transformation example
filteredLines = lines.filter(lambda line:  line.find('Spark')>0)
filteredLines.take(3)
[u'# Apache Spark', u'rich set of higher-level tools including Spark SQL
for SQL and structured', u'and Spark Streaming for stream processing.']
```

reduceByKey

The *reduceByKey* transformation when applied on dataset containing key-value pairs, aggregates values of each key using the function specified.

```
# reduceByKey transformation example
splitLines = lines.flatMap(lambda line:  line.split())
words=splitLines.map(lambda word:  (word, 1))

counts=words.reduceByKey(lambda a, b:  a+b)
counts.take(5)
[(u'all', 1), (u'when', 1), (u'"local"', 1),
(u'including', 3), (u'computation', 1)]
```

flatMap

The *flatMap* transformation takes as input a function which is applied to each element of the dataset. The *flatMap* transformation can map each input item to zero or more output items.

```
■ #flatMap transformation example
splitLines = lines.flatMap(lambda line:  line.split())
splitLines.take(10)
[u'#', u'Apache', u'Spark', u'Spark', u'is',
u'a', u'fast', u'and', u'general', u'cluster']
```

sample

The *sample* transformation samples the data with or without replacement.

```
■ #sample transformation example
datasample = data1.sample(False, 0.5)
datasample.collect()
[3, 3, 4]
```

union

The *union* transformation generates a new dataset from the union of two datasets.

```
■ #union transformation example
data = data1.union(data2)
data.collect()
[1, 2, 2, 3, 3, 4, 5, 3, 4, 5, 6, 7, 8]
```

intersection

The *intersection* transformation generates a new dataset from the intersection of two datasets.

```
■ #intersection transformation example
data = data1.intersection(data2)
data.collect()
[4, 5, 3]
```

join

The *join* transformation generates a new dataset by joining two datasets containing key-value pairs.

```
■ #join transformation example
a=sc.parallelize([('John', 1), ('Tom', 2), ('Ben', 3)])
b=sc.parallelize([('John', 'CA'), ('Tom', 'GA'), ('Ben', 'VA')])
c=a.join(b)
c.collect()
[('Ben', (3, 'VA')), ('John', (1, 'CA')), ('Tom', (2, 'GA'))]
```

Transformations are *lazy* and not computed till an action requires a result to be returned to the driver program. By computing transformations in a lazy manner, Spark is able to perform operations in a more efficient manner as the operations can be grouped together. Spark API allows chaining together transformations and actions.

Actions

Let us look at some commonly used actions with examples:

reduce

The *reduce* action aggregates the elements in a dataset using the specified function.

```
#reduce transformation example
lineLengths = lines.map(lambda s:  len(s))
totalLength = lineLengths.reduce(lambda a, b:  a + b)
3526
```

collect

The *collect* action is used to return all the elements of the result as an array.

```
#Map transformation example
lineLengths = lines.map(lambda s:  len(s))
lineLengths.collect()
[14, 0, 78, 72, 73, ...  , 70]
```

count

The *count* action returns the number of elements in a dataset.

```
#count transformation example
lines.count()
98
```

first

The *first* action returns the first element in a dataset.

```
#Map transformation example
lines.first()
u'# Apache Spark'
```

take

The *take* action returns the first *n* elements in a dataset.

```
#Map transformation example
lines.take(3)
[u'# Apache Spark', u'', u'Spark is a fast and general
cluster computing system for Big Data.  It provides']
```

takeSample

The *takeSample* action returns a sample containing a specified number of elements from a dataset with or without replacement.

```
#takeSample transformation example
data1.takeSample(False, 2)
[2, 2]
```

saveAsTextFile

The *saveAsTextFile* action writes the elements in a dataset to a text file either on the local filesystem or HDFS.

```
■ #saveAsTextFile transformation example
lines.saveAsTextFile('/path/to/file')
```

saveAsSequenceFile
The *saveAsSequenceFile* action writes the elements in a dataset to Hadoop SequenceFile on
the local filesystem or HDFS.

```
■ #saveAsSequenceFile transformation example
data.saveAsSequenceFile('/path/to/file')
```

Let us now look at a standalone Spark application that computes word counts in a file.
Box 7.19 shows a Python program for computing word count. The program uses the map
and reduce functions. The *flatMap* and *map* transformation take as input a function which
is applied to each element of the dataset. While the *flatMap* function can map each input
item to zero or more output items, the *map* function maps each input item to another item.
The transformations take as input, functions which are applied to the data elements. The
input functions can be in the form of Python lambda expressions or local functions. In the
word count example *flatMap* takes as input a lambda expression that splits each line of the
file into words. The *map* transformation outputs key value pairs where the key is a word
and value is 1. The *reduceByKey* transformation aggregates values of each key using the
function specified (*add* function in this example). Finally, the *collect* action is used to return
all the elements of the result as an array.

■ **Box 7.19: Apache Spark Python program for computing word count**

```
from operator import add
from pyspark import SparkContext

sc = SparkContext(appName="WordCountApp")
lines = sc.textFile("file.txt")
counts = lines.flatMap(lambda x:
x.split(' ')).map(lambda x:   (x, 1)).reduceByKey(add)

output = counts.collect()

for (word, count) in output:
   print "%s:  %i" % (word, count)
```

7.7   Search

7.7.1   Apache Solr

Apache Solr is a scalable and open-source framework for searching data. Solr is built on
Apache Lucene, which is an open source library for indexing and search. To enable searching
of documents, Solr creates an index of the documents. Solr can index documents in XML,
JSON, CSV and binary formats. Solr provides a REST-like web service that can be used for
indexing and querying.

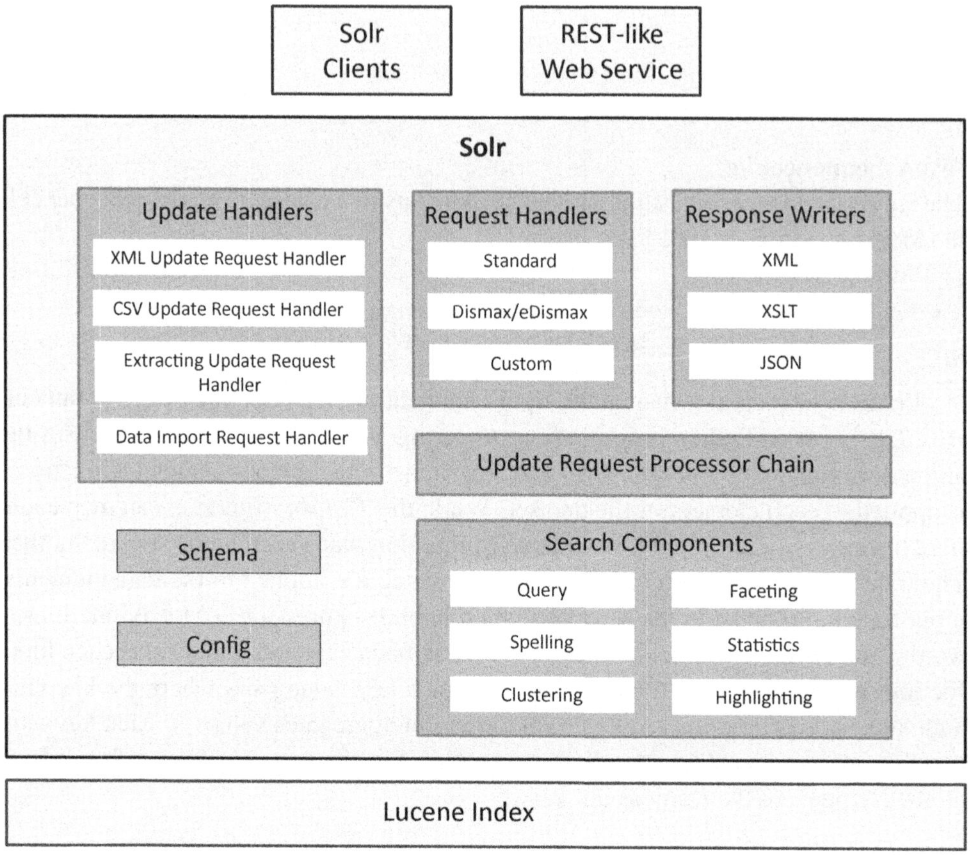

Figure 7.16: Apache Solr components

Figure 7.16 shows the components of Solr. Solr using Lucene for building and maintaining
an inverted index which contains mappings from the search terms to the documents. While
Lucene manages the index structure and executes the queries, Solr is used to define the
structure of the index. With Solr, the index structure can be defined within an XML file
(*schema.xml*), which contains definitions of the various fields and the data types used in the
index. Solr provides dynamic fields which can be used to automatically define the field types
without explicitly defining them in the index schema. Solr runs as a Java web application and
provides a REST-like web service based on HTTP. Solr can also be accessed using Solr clients
available for different programming languages such as Python, Java, PHP and Ruby. The Solr
Update Handlers process the requests and update the index. Request types supported by the
update handlers include add, delete, commit and optimize. When new documents are added
in the index, they are visible in search only after they have been committed to the index.
Solr provides normal-commit (or hard-commit), soft-commit and auto-commit options for
committing changes to the index. Normal-commit, commits all the changes to Lucene index
files to the disk. In soft-commit, all the changes are committed to the Lucene data structures
but the changes are not committed to the disk. Soft-commit is used for the near real-time
search feature, discussed later in this section. The auto-commit option allows the changes to

be committed on a regular basis or when the number of uncommitted documents become greater than a threshold. The Solr *Request Handlers* process the incoming requests which can be either query requests or index update requests. The Solr *Response Writers* generate the response in the desired formats (such as XML, CSV, JSON). Solr provides various *Search Components*, which provide implementations of search features such as faceting, highlighting, etc., described later in this section. All the update requests are run through a chain of plugins called the *Update Request Processor Chain*. Figure 7.16 shows the Solr components involved in the indexing and querying processes.

Solr provides a deployment functionality called SolrCloud which makes it easier to setup clusters of Solr servers. SolrCloud provides distributed indexing and search capabilities. SolrCloud uses Zookeeper for centralized configuration and coordination. SolrCloud enables load balancing and fail-over for queries and highly-available and fault-tolerant Solr deployments. Each Solr instance can have multiple indexes. Solr can scale to index millions of documents and handle queries from millions of users.

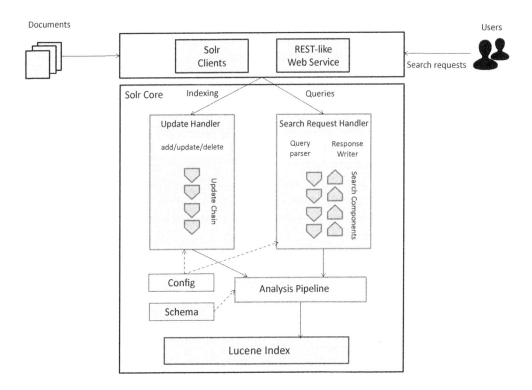

Figure 7.17: Indexing and Querying in Apache Solr

Let us look at some of the key-features of Solr:

- **Faceting**: Faceting is a feature in Solr that allows the results to be grouped based on a specific field or defined criteria. With faceting, users can refine search results. For example, faceting can be used in a search system for an eCommerce application to group products based on price, vendor, color, size, etc.
- **Auto-Suggest**: The auto-suggest feature, also called auto-complete or type-ahead search, provides suggestions to the users as they type in the queries. Auto-suggest

provides a list of suggested queries based on the documents indexed.

- **Spell Check**: Spell check feature in Solr enables spelling corrections in the queries by providing query suggestions based on similar terms in the index.
- **Highlighting**: The hit highlighting features enables highlighting specific portions of the documents that match the user's query. The matching portions are included in the query response and formatting clues are included to highlighting the matching portion.
- **Clustering**: Clustering groups the related documents in the search results and assigns labels to the groups. Clustering prevents multiple documents with similar content being returned separately in the search results. The similar documents in the search results are grouped in a process called *online-clustering*. Solr also supports *offline-clustering* of documents in the index.
- **Spatial Search**: Solr supports spatial search which enables filtering search results based on location. Solr can index spatial data such a latitude/longitude,
- **Pagination and Ranking**: Solr provides pagination of search results. When the user searches for a term, only the top-N results are returned for the first page. The results are ranked based on a relevance score. The benefit of pagination is that instead of returning all matching documents, only a subset of the documents are returned on a particular page, which speeds up the response.
- **Results Grouping**: Solr supports grouping the results based on a grouping field so that instead of returning separate documents, the documents are grouped together and the top documents in each group are returned. For example, while searching for a collection of books, the results can be grouped by the genre field. The results will then contain all the unique genres and the top books in each genre.
- **Near Real-time Search**: Near real-time search feature in Solr enables searching of documents immediately after being indexed. This feature is useful for applications with dynamically changing content such as news and social media applications.
- **MoreLikeThis**: This feature enables users to query for documents which are similar to the documents returned for a search query.

Solr Examples

In this section, we will describe examples of indexing and querying data with Solr. To setup Solr, obtain the latest release from the Solr website. For the examples, we will create a SolrCloud deployment on a local machine using the commands shown below:

```
■ wget http://apache.arvixe.com/lucene/solr/5.2.1/solr-5.2.1.tgz
tar -xzf solr-5.2.1.tgz
cd solr-5.2.1/

bin/solr start -e cloud -noprompt
```

When Solr starts, you can access the admin user interface at: http://localhost:8983/solr/.

Before we can start using Solr for querying data, we need to index some data. Box 7.20 shows a sample JSON file that we will index. This file contains product details about four mobile phones.

■ Box 7.20: Sample JSON file to index

```json
[
{
   "id" :  "1",
   "name" :  "HTC Desire 816",
   "brand" :  "HTC",
   "display_t" :  "5.5 inch S-LCD Display",
   "memory_s" :  "8 GB",
   "price_f" : 150.00,
   "color" :  "black",
   "features" : ["Android 4.4 Kit Kat OS","13 MP Rear Facing BSI Camera",
"5 MP Front Facing"]
},

{
   "id" :  "2",
   "name" :  "LG Tribute",
   "brand" :  "LG",
   "display_t" :  "4.5 inch Capacitive Display",
   "memory_s" :  "8 GB",
   "price_f" : 65.00,
   "color" :  "black",
   "features" : ["Android 4.4 Kit Kat OS",
"5 MP Rear Facing FSI Camera"]
},

{
   "id" :  "3",
   "name" :  "Samsung Galaxy S5 White",
   "brand" :  "Samsung",
   "display_t" :  "5.1inch Full HD Super AMOLED",
   "memory_s" :  "16 GB",
   "price_f" : 499.99,
   "color" :  "white",
   "features" : ["Android 4.4 Kit Kat OS","16 megapixel camera",
"2.5 GHz quad-core processor"]
},

{
   "id" :  "4",
   "name" :  "Kyocera Hydro Vibe",
   "brand" :  "Kyocera",
   "display_t" :  "4.5 inch qHD IPS screen",
   "memory_s" :  "8 GB",
   "price_f" : 49.90,
   "color" :  "black",
   "features" : ["Andriod 4.3 Jelly Bean OS",
"8 MP Rear Facing BSI Camera", "2 MP Front Facing"]
}

]
```

Solr provides a utility called *post* for indexing. The basic unit of data indexed is called a document. A document is a collection of fields. Each field in the document is either indexed or stored or both. An indexed field is one which is searchable and sortable, but the field is not returned in the search results. During the indexing process, the indexed fields undergo an analysis phase in which various transformations are applied. A stored field is one which is returned in the search results. Stored fields are saved as is without undergoing analysis.

Solr requires a schema (defined in schema.xml), which includes the field definitions and information on how the fields should be analyzed in the indexing process. While it is recommended to define the schema explicitly for fine-grained control over the indexing process, Solr also provides the option of *Dynamic* fields which allows Solr to index fields that are not explicitly defined in the schema. Dynamic fields have wild cards in their names, for example, fields that end with '_i' are treated as integer fields, fields that end with '_s' are treated as string fields, fields that end with '_f' are treated as float fields, and so on.

The box below shows how to index the JSON file. A new collection named *products* is created with the indexed JSON file.

```
■  /solr-5.2.1$ bin/post -c products products.json

java -classpath /home/ubuntu/solr-5.2.1/dist/solr-core-5.2.1.jar
-Dauto=yes -Dc=products -Ddata=files org.apache.solr.util.SimplePostTool
products.json SimplePostTool version 5.0.0
Posting files to [base] url http://localhost:8983/solr/products/update..
Entering auto mode.  File endings considered are xml,json,csv,
pdf,doc,docx, ppt,pptx,xls,xlsx,odt,odp,ods,ott,otp,ots,rtf,htm,
html,txt,log POSTing file products.json (application/json) to [base]
1 files indexed.
COMMITting Solr index changes to
http://localhost:8983/solr/products/update...
Time spent:  0:00:00.071
```

Once the documents have been indexed, Solr can be queried either using the Solr admin dashboard or via REST clients. Figure 7.18 shows an example of querying Solr from the admin dashboard.

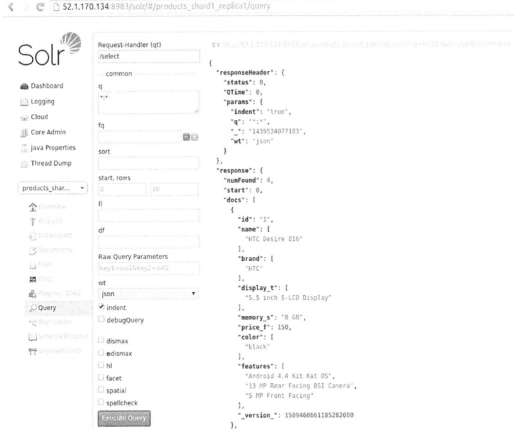

Figure 7.18: Querying from Apache Solr dashboard

The box below shows an example of querying Solr using the CURL utility. In this query, we query for all the documents in the *products* collection (by setting q = *:*) and specify the response type as JSON (by setting wt = json). The JSON response is also shown.

```
 $ curl "http://localhost:8983/solr/products/select?q=*%3A*&wt=json
&indent=true"
{
"responseHeader":{
   "status":0,
   "QTime":1,
   "params":{
    "indent":"true",
    "q":"*:*",
    "wt":"json"}},
"response":{"numFound":4,"start":0,"docs":[
    {
     "id":"1",
     "name":["HTC Desire 816"],
     "brand":["HTC"],
     "display_t":["5.5 inch S-LCD Display"],
     "memory_s":"8 GB",
```

```
        "price_f":150.0,
        "color":["black"],
        "features":["Android 4.4 Kit Kat OS",
         "13 MP Rear Facing BSI Camera",
         "5 MP Front Facing"],
        "_version_":1509468909469696000},
      {
        "id":"2",
        "name":["LG Tribute"],
        "brand":["LG"],
        "display_t":["4.5 inch Capacitive Display"],
        "memory_s":"8 GB",
        "price_f":65.0,
        "color":["black"],
        "features":["Android 4.4 Kit Kat OS",
         "5 MP Rear Facing FSI Camera"],
        "_version_":1509468909473890304},
      {
        "id":"3",
        "name":["Samsung Galaxy S5 White"],
        "brand":["Samsung"],
        "display_t":["5.1inch Full HD Super AMOLED"],
        "memory_s":"16 GB",
        "price_f":499.99,
        "color":["white"],
        "features":["Android 4.4 Kit Kat OS",
         "16 megapixel camera",
         "2.5 GHz quad-core processor"],
        "_version_":1509468909474938880},
      {
        "id":"4",
        "name":["Kyocera Hydro Vibe"],
        "brand":["Kyocera"],
        "display_t":["4.5 inch qHD IPS screen"],
        "memory_s":"8 GB",
        "price_f":49.9,
        "color":["black"],
        "features":["Andriod 4.3 Jelly Bean OS",
         "8 MP Rear Facing BSI Camera",
         "2 MP Front Facing"],
        "_version_":1509468909475987456}]
}}
```

The box below shows an example of querying for a specific term.

```
■ $ curl "http://localhost:8983/solr/products/select?q=htc&wt=json
&indent=true"
{
"responseHeader":{
   "status":0,
   "QTime":2,
   "params":{
    "indent":"true",
    "q":"htc",
```

```
      "wt":"json"}},
  "response":{"numFound":1,"start":0,"docs":[
      {
        "id":"1",
        "name":["HTC Desire 816"],
        "brand":["HTC"],
        "display_t":["5.5 inch S-LCD Display"],
        "memory_s":"8 GB",
        "price_f":150.0,
        "color":["black"],
        "features":["Android 4.4 Kit Kat OS",
         "13 MP Rear Facing BSI Camera",
         "5 MP Front Facing"],
         "_version_":1509468909469696000}]
  }}
```

Let us look at an example of Faceting, which allows the results to be grouped based on a specific field or defined criteria. The box below shows an example of arranging the results into subsets using the price field. The response shows the number of products for each price.

```
■ $ curl "http://localhost:8983/solr/products/select?q=*:*&wt=json
&indent=on&rows=0&facet=true&facet.field=price_f"
{
"responseHeader":{
   "status":0,
   "QTime":1,
   "params":{
     "facet":"true",
     "indent":"on",
     "q":"*:*",
     "facet.field":"price_f",
     "wt":"json",
     "rows":"0"}},
  "response":{"numFound":4,"start":0,"docs":[]
},
"facet_counts":{
   "facet_queries":{},
   "facet_fields":{
     "price_f":[
       "49.9",1,
       "65.0",1,
       "150.0",1,
       "499.99",1]},
   "facet_dates":{},
   "facet_ranges":{},
   "facet_intervals":{},
   "facet_heatmaps":{}}}
```

Solr also allows partitioning the results using range facets. The box below shows an example of range facet where the range start value, end value and range gap is specified. The response shows the number of products in each range.

```
■ $ curl "http://localhost:8983/solr/products/select?q=*:*&wt=json
&indent=on&rows=0&facet=true&facet.range=price_f
&f.price_f.facet.range.start=0.0&f.price_f.facet.range.end=500.0
&f.price_f.facet.range.gap=100"
{
"responseHeader":{
   "status":0,
   "QTime":2,
   "params":{
    "facet":"true",
    "indent":"on",
    "q":"*:*",
    "f.price_f.facet.range.end":"500.0",
    "facet.range":"price_f",
    "wt":"json",
    "f.price_f.facet.range.gap":"100",
    "f.price_f.facet.range.start":"0.0",
    "rows":"0"}},
"response":{"numFound":4,"start":0,"docs":[]
},
"facet_counts":{
   "facet_queries":{},
   "facet_fields":{},
   "facet_dates":{},
   "facet_ranges":{
    "price_f":{
      "counts":[
       "0.0",2,
       "100.0",1,
       "200.0",0,
       "300.0",0,
       "400.0",1],
      "gap":100.0,
      "start":0.0,
      "end":500.0}},
   "facet_intervals":{},
   "facet_heatmaps":{}}}
```

The box below shows an example of adding a new document to the index using the Solr web service.

```
■ curl http://localhost:8983/solr/products/update/json?commit=true -d
'[{"id" :  "5",
"name" :  "Samsung Galaxy S4",
"brand" :  "Samsung",
"display_t" :  "5 inch Super AMOLED",
"memory_s" :  "16 GB",
"price_f" :  329.90,
"color" :  "white",
"features" :  ["Andriod 4.3 Jelly Bean OS","13 MP Rear Facing Camera"]}]'

{"responseHeader":{"status":0,"QTime":4}}
```

You can retrieve a document using the ID as shown in box below.

```
■ curl http://localhost:8983/solr/products/get?id=5
{
"doc":
{
   "id":"5",
   "name":["Samsung Galaxy S4"],
   "brand":["Samsung"],
   "display_t":["5 inch Super AMOLED"],
   "memory_s":"16 GB",
   "price_f":329.9,
   "color":["white"],
   "features":["Andriod 4.3 Jelly Bean OS",
    "13 MP Rear Facing Camera"],
   "_version_":1509469873669931008}}
```

Summary

In this chapter you learned how to use tools and frameworks for batch processing of data including: Hadoop-MapReduce, Pig, Oozie, Spark, and Solr. Apache Hadoop is an open source framework for distributed batch processing of big data. MapReduce is a parallel data processing model for processing and analysis of massive scale data. MapReduce model has two phases: Map and Reduce. In the Map phase, data is read from a distributed file system, partitioned among a set of computing nodes in the cluster, and sent to the nodes as a set of key-value pairs. The Map tasks process the input records independently of each other and produce intermediate results as key-value pairs. The intermediate results are stored on the local disk of the node running the Map task. When all the Map tasks are completed, the Reduce phase begins in which the intermediate data with the same key is aggregated. We described the next generation Hadoop architecture and the YARN cluster manager. Next, we described the Hadoop FIFO, Fair and Capacity schedulers. We introduced Pig, which is a high-level data processing language. Pig makes it easy for developers to write data analysis scripts, which are translated into MapReduce programs by the Pig compiler. The Apache Oozie workflow scheduler system was described. Next, we introduced the Apache Spark framework and described various transformations and actions that can be performed with Spark. Finally, we described the Apache Solr framework for searching data.

8 - Real-time Analysis

This chapter covers

- Real-time Analysis frameworks
- Apache Storm
- Apache Spark

In this chapter we describe the Apache Storm and Spark Streaming frameworks for implementing real-time data analytics applications.

8.1 Stream Processing

8.1.1 Apache Storm

Apache Storm is a framework for distributed and fault-tolerant real-time computation [65]. Storm can be used for real-time processing of streams of data. Storm can ingest data from a variety of sources such as publish-subscribe messaging frameworks (such as Kafka or Kinesis), messaging queues (such as RabbitMQ, ZeroMQ or SQS) and other custom connectors described in Chapter-5. Storm is a scalable and distributed framework, and offers reliable processing of messages. Storm has been designed to run indefinitely and process streams of data in real-time. The processing latencies with Storm are in the order of milliseconds.

Concepts

- **Topology**: A computation job on the Storm cluster, called a "topology", is a graph of computation. A Storm topology comprises multiple worker processes that are distributed on the cluster. Each worker process runs a subset of the topology. A topology is composed of two types of nodes; Spouts and Bolts. Figure 8.1 shows some examples of these Storm topologies. The nodes in a topology are connected by directed edges. Each node receives a stream of data from other nodes and emits a new stream.
- **Tuples**: The nodes in a topology consume data which is in the form of tuples. Each node receives data tuples from the previous node and emits tuples which are processed further by the downstream nodes. A tuple is an ordered list of values. Tuples can contain primitive data types such as integers, floats, doubles, strings, booleans, shorts, longs, etc, and also custom types (with custom serializers provided).
- **Stream**: Stream is an unbounded sequence of tuples. The nodes in a topology receive streams, process them and emit new streams. The output streams can be consumed and processed by any downstream nodes in the topology. In complex topologies, as shown in Figure 8.1(b), a node can emit or ingest multiple streams.
- **Spout**: Spout is a type of a node in a topology, which is a source of streams. Spouts receive data from external sources and emit them into the topology as streams of tuples. Spouts do not process the tuples; they simply emit the tuples which are consumed by the bolts in the topology.
- **Bolt**: Bolt is a type of a node in a topology that processes tuples. Bolts receive streams of tuples, process them and emit output streams. Bolts can receive streams either from spouts or other bolts. Bolts can perform various types of data processing operations such as filtering, aggregation, joins, custom functions, etc. Storm topologies are designed such that each bolt performs simple transformations on the data stream. Complex transformations are broken down into simpler transformations, which are performed by multiple bolts. Since the different bolts process data in parallel, Storm can achieve low latencies for data processing.
- **Workers**: Spouts and bolts have multiple worker processes. Each worker process

itself has multiple threads of execution (called tasks). These tasks process the data in parallel.

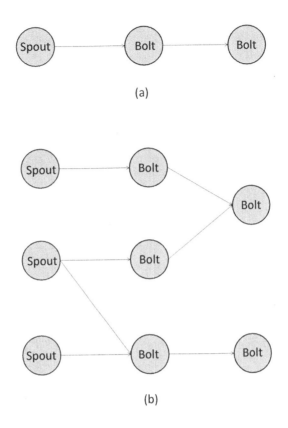

Figure 8.1: Storm topology examples

Stream Groupings

Since the bolts in a topology can have multiple tasks (threads of execution), some mechanism is required to define how the streams should be partitioned among the tasks. This partitioning is defined in terms of stream groupings. Stream groupings define how the tuples emitted by a spout or bolt are distributed among the tasks of a downstream bolt.

Storm supports the following types of stream groupings:

- **Shuffle Grouping**: In shuffle grouping, tuples are randomly distributed across the tasks such that each task gets an equal number of tuples.
- **Field Grouping**: In field grouping, a grouping field is specified by which the tuples in a stream are grouped. Tuples with the same value of the grouping field are always sent to the same task.
- **All Grouping**: In all grouping, the stream is broadcast to all the tasks in the bolt. This type of grouping is used where the stream is to be replicated to all tasks in the destination bolt.
- **Global Grouping**: In global grouping, the entire stream is sent to a particular task of the destination bolt (task with the lowest ID).

- **Direct Grouping**: In direct grouping, the sender node (spout or bolt) decides which task in the destination bolt should receive the stream.

Figure 8.2 shows the various types of stream groupings.

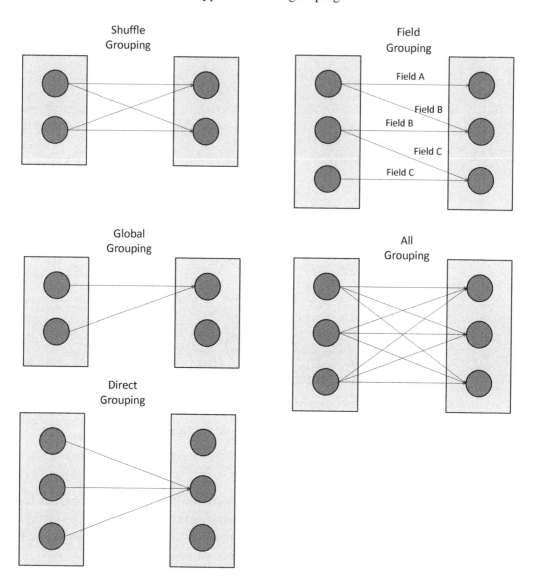

Figure 8.2: Stream groupings in Storm

Architecture

Figure 8.3 shows the components of a Storm cluster. A Storm cluster consists of the Nimbus, Supervisor and Zookeeper components. Nimbus is responsible for distributing topology code and tasks around the cluster, launching workers across the cluster, and monitoring the execution of topologies. A Storm cluster has one or more Supervisor nodes on which the worker processes run. Nimbus sends signals to supervisors to start or stop processes.

Supervisor nodes communicate with Nimbus through Zookeeper. Zookeeper is a high performance distributed coordination service for maintaining configuration information, naming, providing distributed synchronization and group services [66]. Zookeeper is required for coordination of the Storm cluster. Zookeeper maintains the operational state of the cluster.

Storm topologies include implementations of spouts and bolts and the topology definitions. Topologies are packaged as JAR files and submitted to the Nimbus node for execution. The Nimbus uploads the topology to all supervisors and signals the supervisors to launch worker processes. The spout and bolt tasks (threads of execution) are assigned to the worker processes on the supervisor nodes. The topologies are monitored by the Nimbus node. If a worker on a supervisor fails, the supervisor restarts it. If a supervisor fails the Nimbus re-assigns the tasks to other supervisors. If the Nimbus dies, the worker processes are not affected as the state information is maintained by Zookeeper. The Nimbus and Supervisor daemons are run under supervision (using tools such as monit, supervisord), so that they can be restarted if they die.

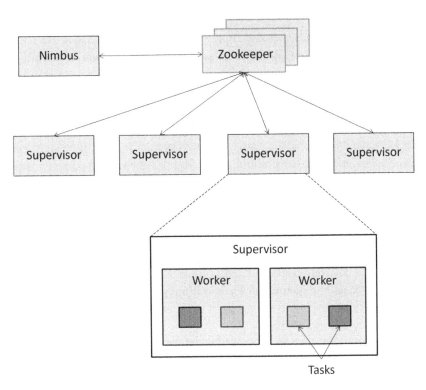

Figure 8.3: Storm cluster components

Reliable Processing

Storm provides reliable processing of tuples. Storm guarantees that each tuple emitted by a spout is processed. Within a topology, a tuple which is emitted by a spout is processed by the bolts resulting in the creation of multiple tuples which are based on the original tuple. This results in a tuple tree as shown in Figure 8.4. Bolts in a topology acknowledge the processing of tuples to the upstream bolts or spouts. If all bolts in a tuple tree acknowledge that a tuple has been successfully processed, the spout marks the tuple processing to be completed, performs cleanup and sends an acknowledgment to the external data source. If

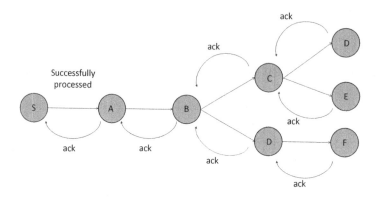

Figure 8.4: Tuple tree

any bolt in the tuple tree indicates that tuple processing failed (or timed-out), the spout marks the tuple processing as failed. When tuple processing fails, the spout re-emits the tuple.

8.2   Storm Case Studies

8.2.1   Real-time Twitter Sentiment Analysis

In this section, we will describe a case study on a system for real-time sentiment analysis of Twitter feeds. Given the analysis requirements of this system, let us map the system to one of the analytics patterns proposed in Chapter-1. Since the system processes social media feeds in real-time, we can use the Beta pattern. Figure 8.5(a) shows a realization of Beta pattern for this system, with the specific tools and frameworks that can be used. For this system, we will use the Apache Storm and Apache Kafka frameworks. Figure 8.5(b) shows the components of the real-time sentiment analysis system including:

- **Listener**: The listener component connects to Twitter with the streaming API and retrieves tweets in real-time. A Python library called *tweepy* is used for retrieving the tweets containing specific keywords. The listener publishes the tweets to a Kafka topic managed by a Kafka Broker.
- **Storm Spout**: Storm Spout contains a Kafka consumer which retrieves the tweets from the Kafka topic and emits tuples (containing tweets) to be processed by the Storm Bolt.
- **Storm Bolt**: Storm Bolt analyzes the tweets and computes their sentiment using a sentiment lexicon.
- **DynamoDB**: The timestamped tweets and their sentiments are stored by the Storm Bolt to an Amazon DynamoDB table.
- **Flask Web App**: The Flask web application retrieves the tweets and their sentiments from DynamoDB and displays them.

Let us look at the steps involved in building the real-time sentiment analysis system along with the implementations of the various components.

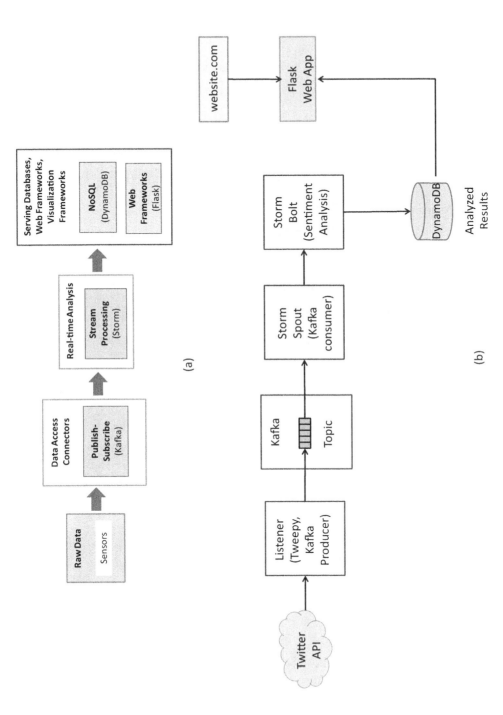

Figure 8.5: (a) A realization of Beta pattern for real-time sentiment analysis of Twitter feeds (b) Architecture of the system

Create Kafka Topic

The listener component publishes the tweets to a Kafka topic. To create Kafka topic, follow the commands below:

```
■ #Creating a Kafka Topic
cd /usr/hdp/2.2.0.0-2041/kafka
bin/kafka-topics.sh -create -zookeeper
   ip-10-179-181-24.ec2.internal:2181 -replication-factor 1
   -partitions 1 -topic mytopic

bin/kafka-topics.sh -list -zookeeper ip-10-179-181-24.ec2.internal:2181

(Change the DNS in the above commands to the
DNS of the instance on which Kafka is setup)
```

Figure 8.6: Creating DynamoDB table to store tweets and their sentiments

Create DynamoDB Table

In this case study, we will use Amazon DynamoDB database for storing the analyzed results. To use DynamoDB we need to create a new table as shown in Figure 8.6.

Getting Twitter App Keys

To connect to the Twitter streaming API, the listener requires Twitter application keys. You can register for a Twitter developer account and create a new application at: https://dev.twitter.com/apps

Note down the application access token, access token secret, consumer key and consumer secret from the application details page as shown in Figure 8.7.

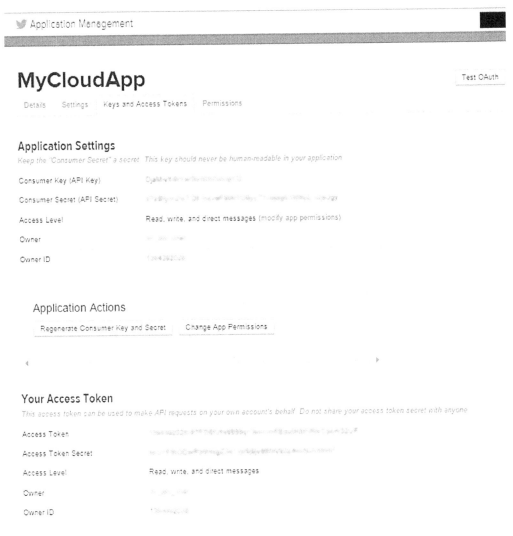

Figure 8.7: Getting Twitter application credentials from Twitter developer account

Implement Listener

The listener component connects to Twitter with the streaming API, retrieves tweets in real-time and publishes the tweets to a Kafka topic. Box 8.1 shows a Python implementation of the listener component.

■ Box 8.1: Python implementation of listener that receives tweets

```
from tweepy.streaming import StreamListener
from tweepy import OAuthHandler
from tweepy import Stream
```

```
import time
import datetime
from kafka.client import KafkaClient
from kafka.producer import SimpleProducer

#Connect to Kafka
client = KafkaClient("ip-172-31-60-0.ec2.internal:6667")
producer = SimpleProducer(client)


#Get Twitter API keys from Twitter developer account
access_token = "<Enter>"
access_token_secret = "<Enter>"
consumer_key = "<Enter>"
consumer_secret = "<Enter>"


def publish(data):
   producer.send_messages('mytopic', data.encode())


class StdOutListener(StreamListener):

   def on_data(self, data):
     publish(data)

   def on_error(self, status):
     print status

if __name__ == '__main__':
   print 'Listening...'
   #This handles Twitter authetification and
   #the connection to Twitter Streaming API
   #sets callback on data
   l = StdOutListener()
   auth = OAuthHandler(consumer_key, consumer_secret)
   auth.set_access_token(access_token, access_token_secret)
   stream = Stream(auth, l)

   #This line filter Twitter Streams to capture data by the keywords
   stream.filter(track=['basketball'])
```

Implement Storm Spout and Bolt

Box 8.2 shows a Python implementation of the Storm Spout. The Spout retrieves tweets from the Kafka topic and emits them as tuples into the topology.

■ Box 8.2: Python implementation of Spout

```
from storm import Spout, emit, log
from kafka.client import KafkaClient
from kafka.consumer import KafkaConsumer
from kafka.producer import SimpleProducer
```

```
client = KafkaClient("ip-172-31-60-0.ec2.internal:6667")
consumer = KafkaConsumer("tweetsent",
   metadata_broker_list=['ip-172-31-60-0.ec2.internal:6667'])

#gets the tweet
def getData():
data = consumer.next().value
return data

class MySpout(Spout):
   def nextTuple(self):
      data = getData()
      emit([data])


MySpout().run()
```

Box 8.3 shows a Python implementation of the Storm Bolt, which computes the tweet sentiments and stores the results in a DynamoDB table.

■ Box 8.3: Python implementation of Bolt

```
import storm
from datetime import date
import time
import datetime
import boto.dynamodb2
from boto.dynamodb2.table import Table
import json
import re

ACCESS_KEY="<Enter>"
SECRET_KEY="<Enter>"
REGION="us-east-1"


#Connect to DynamoDB
conn = boto.dynamodb2.connect_to_region(REGION,
         aws_access_key_id=ACCESS_KEY,
         aws_secret_access_key=SECRET_KEY)

TERMS={}
#----- Load Sentiments Dict ---
sent_file = open('AFINN-111.txt')
sent_lines = sent_file.readlines()
for line in sent_lines:
   s = line.split("")
   TERMS[s[0]] = s[1]

sent_file.close()



#----- Find Sentiment -------
```

```python
def findsentiment(tweet):
   sentiment=0.0

   if tweet.has_key('text'):
      text = tweet['text']
      text=re.sub('[!@#$)(*<>=+/:;&%#|{},.? ']', '', text)
      splitTweet=text.split()

      for word in splitTweet:
         if TERMS.has_key(word):
            sentiment = sentiment+ float(TERMS[word])

   return sentiment

def analyzeData(data):
   #Add your code for data analysis here
   tweet = json.loads(data)
   sentiment= findsentiment(tweet)
   return sentiment

class MyBolt(storm.BasicBolt):
   def process(self, tup):
      now = datetime.datetime.now()
      data = tup.values[0]

      output = analyzeData(data)
      tweet=json.loads(data)
      today = date.today()
      timestampp=now.strftime("%H:%M:%S")
      #Store analyzed results in DynamoDB
      table=Table('twittersentiment',connection=conn)
      item = table.put_item(data={
                  'date':str(today),
                  'timestamp':str(timestampp),
                  'tweet':  tweet['text'],
                  'sentiment':str(output)
                  },overwrite=True)


MyBolt().run()
```

Though Storm Spouts and Bolts can be implemented in Python (and other languages), there is no direct way of implementing Storm topologies with Python. Box 8.4 shows a Java implementation of the Storm topology.

■ Box 8.4: Storm topology implementation

```java
package com.mycompany.app;
import backtype.storm.Config;
import backtype.storm.LocalCluster;
import backtype.storm.StormSubmitter;
import backtype.storm.task.ShellBolt;
import backtype.storm.spout.ShellSpout;
```

```java
import backtype.storm.topology.IRichBolt;
import backtype.storm.topology.IRichSpout;
import backtype.storm.topology.OutputFieldsDeclarer;
import backtype.storm.topology.TopologyBuilder;
import backtype.storm.tuple.Fields;
import java.util.Map;


public class App {

public static class SensorSpout extends ShellSpout implements IRichSpout
{
   public SensorSpout() {
      super("python", "myspout.py");
   }

   @Override
   public void declareOutputFields(OutputFieldsDeclarer declarer) {
      declarer.declare(new Fields("word"));
   }

   @Override
   public Map<String, Object> getComponentConfiguration() {
      return null;
   }
}

public static class SensorBolt extends ShellBolt implements IRichBolt {
   public SensorBolt() {
      super("python", "mybolt.py");
   }

   @Override
   public void declareOutputFields(OutputFieldsDeclarer declarer) {
      declarer.declare(new Fields("word"));
   }

   @Override
   public Map<String, Object> getComponentConfiguration() {
      return null;
   }
}


public static void main(String[] args) throws Exception {

   TopologyBuilder builder = new TopologyBuilder();

   builder.setSpout("spout", new SensorSpout(), 5);
   builder.setBolt("analysis",
        new SensorBolt(), 8).shuffleGrouping("spout");

   Config conf = new Config();
   conf.setDebug(true);
```

```
   if (args != null && args.length > 0) {
      conf.setNumWorkers(3);
      StormSubmitter.submitTopology(args[0], conf,
         builder.createTopology());
   }
   else {
      conf.setMaxTaskParallelism(3);

      LocalCluster cluster = new LocalCluster();
      cluster.submitTopology("mytopology", conf,
         builder.createTopology());

      Thread.sleep(10000);

      cluster.shutdown();
   }
}

}
```

Build Storm Project

Storm projects are packaged as JAR files. The box below shows a directory tree of a Storm
project. The Spout and Bolt Python files are included in the multilang/resources folder, and
the topology implementation is in the App.java file.

```
■ #Storm Project Directory Tree
/home/ubuntu/storm-project
|- multilang
|    '- resources
|        |- mybolt.py
|        |- myspout.py
|        '- storm.py
|- pom.xml
|- src
|    |- main
|    |    '- java
|    |        '- com
|    |            '- mycompany
|    |                '- app
|    |                    |- App.java
'- target
    '- storm-project-jar-with-dependencies.jar
```

```
■ #Build Storm Project
cd /home/ubuntu/storm-project
mvn clean package
```

The Storm project JAR file (storm-project-jar-with-dependencies.jar) will be generated within
storm-project/target folder.

Implement Web Application

Finally, we implement a web application to present the sentiment analysis results. Box 8.5 shows a Python implementation of the web application using the Python Flask web framework.

■ **Box 8.5: Flask web application for visualizing tweet sentiments**

```python
from flask import Flask
import urllib2
import boto.dynamodb2
from boto.dynamodb2.table import Table

app = Flask(__name__)
from datetime import date
today = date.today()

#-----Connect to DynamoDB------
ACCESS_KEY="<Enter>"
SECRET_KEY="<Enter>"
REGION="us-east-1"


conn_db = boto.dynamodb.connect_to_region(REGION,
aws_access_key_id=ACCESS_KEY,
aws_secret_access_key=SECRET_KEY)

table = conn_db.get_table('twittersentiment')
#-----------------------

@app.route('/')
def tweet_home():

   #Scan DynamoDB table
   results=table.scan()

   html = '<html><body><table width=80% border=1 align="center">'+
       '<tr><td><strong>Timestamp</strong></td>
       <td><strong>Date</strong></td>
       <td><strong>Tweet</strong></td>
       <td><strong>Sentiment</strong></td>
       </tr>'


   for result in results:
      html+='<tr><td>'+result['timestamp']+'</td><td>'+
      result['date']+'</td><td>'+result['tweet']+'</td><td>'+
      result['sentiment']+'</td></tr>'

   html+='</table></body></html>'

   return html

if __name__ == '__main__':
   app.run(host='0.0.0.0')
```

Submit Storm Topology

To submit and run the Storm topology, run the following command on the Storm cluster:

```
■ #Submit Storm Topology
storm jar
/home/ubuntu/storm-project/target/storm-project-jar-with-dependencies.jar
com.mycompany.app.App mytopology
```

Topology summary

Name	Id	Owner	Status	Uptime	Num workers	Num executors	Num tasks	Scheduler Info
mytopology	mytopology-14-1426736997		ACTIVE	3m 14s	2	16	16	

Topology actions

Activate Deactivate Rebalance Kill

Topology stats

Window	Emitted	Transferred	Complete latency (ms)	Acked	Failed
10m 0s	420	420	0.000	440	0
3h 0m 0s	420	420	0.000	440	0
1d 0h 0m 0s	420	420	0.000	440	0
All time	420	420	0.000	440	0

Spouts (All time)

Id	Executors	Tasks	Emitted	Transferred	Complete latency (ms)	Acked	Failed	Error Host	Error Port	Last error
spout	5	5	420	420	0.000	0	0			

Figure 8.8: Screenshot of Storm Topology page

Component summary

Id	Topology	Executors	Tasks
spout	mytopology	5	5

Spout stats

Window	Emitted	Transferred	Complete latency (ms)	Acked	Failed
10m 0s	420	420	0.000	0	0
3h 0m 0s	420	420	0.000	0	0
1d 0h 0m 0s	420	420	0.000	0	0
All time	420	420	0.000	0	0

Output stats (All time)

Stream	Emitted	Transferred	Complete latency (ms)	Acked	Failed
default	420	420	0	0	0

Executors (All time)

Id	Uptime	Host	Port	Emitted	Transferred	Complete latency (ms)	Acked	Failed
[12-12]	3m 39s	ip-172-31-60-0.ec2.internal	6700	80	80	0.000	0	0

Figure 8.9: Screenshot of Storm Spout page

After submitting the topology, run the listener and the Flask web application. You can view the status of the Storm topology, Spout and Bolt from the Storm UI pages as shown in Figures 8.8, 8.9 and 8.10. You will be able to see the tweets along with the computed sentiments in the DynamoDB dashboard as shown in Figures 8.11 and the web application as shown in Figures 8.12.

Bolt stats

Window	Emitted	Transferred	Execute latency (ms)	Executed	Process latency (ms)	Acked	Failed
10m 0s	0	0	0.130	460	9567.454	440	0
3h 0m 0s	0	0	0.130	460	9567.454	440	0
1d 0h 0m 0s	0	0	0.130	460	9567.454	440	0
All time	0	0	0.130	460	9567.454	440	0

Input stats (All time)

Component	Stream	Execute latency (ms)	Executed	Process latency (ms)	Acked	Failed
spout	default	0.130	460	0.130	440	0

Output stats (All time)

Stream	Emitted	Transferred

Executors

Figure 8.10: Screenshot of Storm Bolt page

Figure 8.11: DynamoDB table showing analyzed tweets

Timestamp	Date	Data	Prediction
06:49:16	2015-03-27	Under Armour Men's Micro G Torch Basketball Shoes in Blue in Sizes 6.5 to 14 http://t.co/H3lByAulXV http://t.co/GBo28vKuKH	0.0
06:49:17	2015-03-27	Under Armour Men's Micro G Torch Basketball Shoes in Blue in Sizes 6.5 to 14 http://t.co/H3lByAulXV http://t.co/XYmt9JXcFJ	0.0
06:49:18	2015-03-27	Under Armour Men's Micro G Torch Basketball Shoes in Blue in Sizes 6.5 to 14 http://t.co/H3lByAulXV http://t.co/FUW9iYRnhp	0.0
06:49:19	2015-03-27	Under Armour Men's Micro G Torch Basketball Shoes in Blue in Sizes 6.5 to 14 http://t.co/H3lByAulXV http://t.co/FUW9iYRnhp	0.0
06:49:20	2015-03-27	Great Range of Baseball and Basketball Shirts at: http://t.co/TYLIXEvrrb	0.0
06:49:23	2015-03-27	'Happy' dancing kid steals the spotlight at high school basketball tournament – http://t.co/PLSiJc50t6 http://t.co/A2EQ2K5FKW	-2.0
06:49:27	2015-03-27	"@iamannaceline: Pag nandito si Bugoy Cariño sa lugar namin. normal lang sya, nag lalaro pa nga ng basketball kasama mga tambay eh hahahaha"	0.0
06:49:28	2015-03-27	"@CardinMorgane: Dans l'indifférence générale @EsbvaLm remporte L'eurocup 🏀 #BasketBall bravo à elles" @bbarbusse @mc_naves @generalifrance	0.0
06:49:29	2015-03-27	RT @FoxNews: Late UNC basketball coach Smith left former lettermen $200 each http://t.co/aOSYTajOJ7 http://t.co/bEzdygMOpD	0.0

Figure 8.12: Screenshot of Flask web application showing tweets and the computed sentiments

8.2.2   Real-time Weather Data Analysis

Let us look at the another case study on a system for real-time analysis of weather data to make predictions on the occurrence of fog or haze in a specific location. The system determines whether fog or haze is expected based on various parameters including current temperature, humidity, wind, and pressure. The dataset used in this case study was obtained from National Oceanic and Atmospheric Administration (NOAA). The NOAA dataset is used to train a Support Vector Machine (SVM) based machine learning classifier. To test the system, historical data regarding temperature, humidity, wind, and pressure for a particular location is fed to the system (as synthetic real-time data).

Given the analysis requirements of this system, let us map the system to one of the analytics patterns proposed in Chapter-1. Since the system processes weather data in real-time, we can use the Beta pattern. Figure 8.13(a) shows a realization of Beta pattern for this system, with the specific tools and frameworks that can be used. For this system, we will use the Apache Storm and Apache Kafka frameworks. Figure 8.13(b) shows the system architecture. The system includes the following components:

- **Listener**: The listener component connects to the weather data source and obtains the current temperature, humidity, wind, and pressure data.
- **Kafka**: The listener publishes data to a Kafka topic.
- **Storm Spout**: Storm Spout subscribes to the Kafka topic and receives all published messages from the listener. The spout receives this data and emits tuples containing the hourly observations.
- **Storm Bolt**: Storm Bolt receives the data and loads the SVM models from the pickle files. The SVM models are used to predict for fog and haze.
- **Cassandra Database**: The predictions along with timestamps are stored in a Cassandra database.
- **Flask Web App**: The Flask web application is used to visualize the results.

Dataset

The data used for both testing and training the machine learning classifier as well as the real-time data is from the NOAA U.S. Local Climatological Data. The specific dataset used was the Quality Controlled Local Climatological Data (QCLCD).

Listener

Box 8.6 shows a python implementation of the listener component. The listener connects to the weather data source. For this case study, the listener used data from NOAA. The listener used data from the same months but for a different year from the data used to train the classifier. Listener replays data from three CSV files: PositiveFog.csv, PositiveHaze.csv, and NegativeFogHaze.csv. The listener publishes a new data entry to Kafka every 5 seconds to simulate periodically receiving data from real sensors.

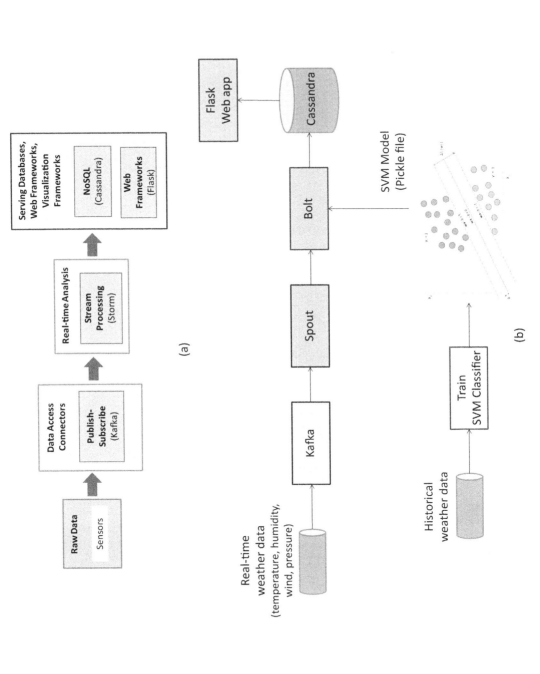

Figure 8.13: (a) A realization of Beta pattern for real-time analysis of weather data (b) Architecture of the system

▪ Box 8.6: Python implementation of Listener

```python
from random import randrange
import time
import datetime
from kafka.client import KafkaClient
from kafka.consumer import SimpleConsumer
from kafka.producer import SimpleProducer
import csv
import json
import time

#Connect to Kafka
#change to private DNS
client = KafkaClient("127.0.0.1:6667")
producer = SimpleProducer(client)

def is_number(s):
   try:
      float(s)     except ValueError:
      return False
   return True

def sysTest(filename):
   f = open(filename)
   csv_f = csv.reader(f)
   tList=[]
   tClass=[]
   counter=0
   for row in csv_f:
      new_list=[]
      if counter < 2:
         counter=counter+1
         continue
      for item in row:
         if not(is_number(item)):
            continue
         new_list.append(float(item))
      #print new_list
      if len(new_list)!=5:
         continue
      dataSend=json.dumps(new_list).encode('utf-8')
      producer.send_messages('weather',dataSend)
      time.sleep(5)
      print dataSend
      print type(dataSend)
   f.close()


if __name__ == '__main__':
   print 'Publishing...'
   sysTest('PositiveFog.csv')
   sysTest('PositiveHaze.csv')
   sysTest('NegativeFogHaze.csv')
```

Prediction Model

The NOAA dataset is used to train two SVM-based machine learning classifiers, one for fog and one for haze. The SVM's are trained on positive hourly data (fog or haze did occur) and negative hourly data. The training data is structured in three CSV files: FogTrain.csv, HazeTrain.csv, and NegativeTrain.csv. FogTrain.csv has positive data for hourly observations of fog, HazeTrain.csv has positive data for hourly observations of haze, and NegativeTrain.csv has negative data for hourly observations of haze and fog. Once both SVMs are trained, they are stored in pickle files: svmHaze.pkl and svmFog.pkl. These files are used within the Storm Bolt for making predictions. Box 8.7 shows the python code for training SVM classifiers for fog and haze. We use the Python scikit-learn machine learning library for building the SVM models.

■ **Box 8.7: Python code for training SVM Classifier**

```
from sklearn import svm
import csv
import numpy as np
from sklearn.externals import joblib

def is_number(s):
  try:
     float(s) # for int, long and float
  except ValueError:
     return False

  return True


def svmTrain():
  f = open('PositiveHaze.csv')
  csv_f = csv.reader(f)
  tList=[]
  tClass=[]
  counter=0
  for row in csv_f:
     new_list=[]
     if counter < 2:
       counter=counter+1
       continue
     for item in row:
       if not(is_number(item)):
          continue
       new_list.append(float(item))
     print new_list
     if len(new_list)!=5:
       print "ERROR"
       continue
     tList.append(new_list)
     tClass.append(1)

  f.close()
```

```python
f=open('NegativeHazeAndNegativeFog.csv')
csv_f=csv.reader(f)
counter=0
for row in csv_f:
    new_list=[]
    if counter < 2:
        counter=counter+1
        continue
    for item in row:
        if not(is_number(item)):
            continue
        new_list.append(float(item))
    print new_list
    if len(new_list)!=5:
        print "ERROR"
        continue
    tList.append(new_list)
    tClass.append(0)


f.close();
f=open('PositiveFog.csv')
csv_f= csv.reader(f)
tFogList=[]
tFogClass=[]
counter=0

for row in csv_f:
    new_list=[]
    if counter < 2:
        counter=counter+1
        continue
    for item in row:
        if not(is_number(item)):
            continue
        new_list.append(float(item))
    print new_list
    if len(new_list)!=5:
        continue
        exit(2)
    tFogClass.append(1)
    tFogList.append(new_list)

f.close()
f=open('NegativeHazeAndNegativeFog.csv')
csv_f=csv.reader(f)
counter=0
for row in csv_f:
    new_list=[]
    if counter < 2:
        counter=counter+1
        continue
    for item in row:
        if not(is_number(item)):
            continue
```

```
            new_list.append(float(item))
        print new_list
        if len(new_list)!=5:
           continue
        tFogClass.append(0)
        tFogList.append(new_list)

    svmThunder = svm.SVC()

    svmThunder.fit(tList,tClass)

    svmFog = svm.SVC()

    svmFog.fit(tFogList,tFogClass)

    joblib.dump(svmThunder, 'svmHaze.pkl')
    joblib.dump(svmFog, 'svmFog.pkl' )


if __name__ == '__main__':
    svmTrain()
```

Storm Spout

The Storm Spout subscribes to the Kafka topic and receives messages published by the listener. The Spout emits this data as a stream of tuples into the Storm topology to be processed by the Bolt. Box 8.8 shows a Python implementation of the Storm Spout.

■ **Box 8.8: Python implementation of Storm Spout**

```
from storm import Spout, emit, log
from kafka.client import KafkaClient
from kafka.consumer import KafkaConsumer
from kafka.producer import SimpleProducer
from kafka.consumer import SimpleConsumer

client = KafkaClient("127.0.0.1:6667")
consumer = KafkaConsumer("weather",
   metadata_broker_list=['127.0.0.1:6667'])

def getData():
   data = consumer.next().value
   data = data.replace('[',"").replace(']',"").split(',')
   data = [ float(x) for x in data ]
   return data

class SensorSpout(Spout):
   def nextTuple(self):
      data = getData()
      emit([data])

SensorSpout().run()
```

Storm Bolt

The Storm Bolt receives the data emitted by the Spout and loads the trained SVM classifiers
for fog and haze from the pickle files. The input data is passed to these classifiers to predict
for fog and haze. To store the predictions along with timestamps, a Cassandra database is
used. Cassandra is an open source distributed database management system designed for
large data applications. Box 8.9 shows a Python implementation of the Storm bolt.

■ Box 8.9: Python implementation of Bolt

```
import storm
import json
import re
from cassandra.cluster import Cluster
import blist
from sklearn import svm
from sklearn.externals import joblib
import datetime
#------- Load Clf files -------
svmFog = joblib.load('svmFog.pkl')
svmHaze = joblib.load('svmHaze.pkl')

#----- Connect to Cassandra -----
cluster = Cluster(['127.0.0.1'])
session = cluster.connect('predictions')

def analyzeData(data):
   fog_predict = svmFog.predict(data)
   haze_predict = svmHaze.predict(data)
   return [str(fog_predict[0]), str(haze_predict[0])]

class SensorBolt(storm.BasicBolt):
   def process(self, tup):
      data = tup.values[0]

      output = analyzeData(data)
      result = "Result:  "+ str(output)
      timestamp= datetime.datetime.now().strftime("%Y-%m-%d %H:%M:%S")

      #Store analyzed results in Cassandra
      session.execute(
      """
      INSERT INTO data(timestamp, fog_prediction, haze_prediction)
      VALUES (%s, %s, %s)
      """,
      (timestamp, output[0], output[1])
      )

      storm.emit([result])

SensorBolt().run()
```

Web Application

Box 8.10 shows the Python code for the Flask web application that pulls the data from the Cassandra database and shows it in a table.

■ **Box 8.10: Flask web application code**

```
from flask import Flask
import urllib2
app = Flask(__name__)
import blist

from cassandra.cluster import Cluster

cluster = Cluster(['127.0.0.1'])
session = cluster.connect('predictions')

@app.route('/')
def tweet_home():


   html = '<html><body><table width=80% border=1 align="center">'+
        '<tr><td><strong>Timestamp</strong></td>'+
        '<td><strong>Fog Prediction</strong></td>'+
        '<td><strong>Haze Prediction</strong></td></tr>'

   data = session.execute('SELECT * FROM data')
   for each in data:
      html+='<td>'+each.timestamp+'</td><td>'+
      each.fog_prediction+'</td><td>'+
      each.haze_prediction+'</td></tr>'

   html+='</table></body></html>'

   return html

if __name__ == '__main__':
   app.run(host='0.0.0.0')
```

To run the system, run the listener and web application Python programs and submit the Storm topology. You will be able to see the fog/haze predictions from the Cassandra shell as shown in Figures 8.14 and the web application as shown in Figures 8.15.

8.3   In-Memory Processing

8.3.1   Apache Spark

We described Spark architecture and Spark operations in the previous chapter and how Spark can be used for batch processing of data. In this section, we will describe the Spark Streaming component for analysis of streaming data such as sensor data, clickstream data, web server logs, etc. The streaming data is ingested and analyzed in micro-batches. Spark Streaming enables scalable, high throughput and fault-tolerant stream processing. Spark Streaming provides a high-level abstraction called DStream (discretized stream). DStream

```
cqlsh:predictions> select * from data;

 timestamp              | fog_prediction | haze_prediction
------------------------+----------------+----------------
 2015-04-16 21:07:03 |              0 |              0
 2015-04-16 21:07:28 |              0 |              0
 2015-04-16 21:06:10 |              0 |              0
 2015-04-16 21:05:37 |              0 |              0
 2015-04-16 21:06:58 |              0 |              0
 2015-04-16 21:07:01 |              0 |              1
 2015-04-16 21:05:15 |              0 |              0
 2015-04-16 21:04:49 |              0 |              0
 2015-04-16 21:06:00 |              0 |              0
 2015-04-16 21:05:40 |              0 |              0
 2015-04-16 21:04:38 |              0 |              0
 2015-04-16 21:06:39 |              0 |              0
 2015-04-16 21:06:35 |              0 |              0
 2015-04-16 21:05:53 |              0 |              0
 2015-04-16 21:04:27 |              0 |              0
 2015-04-16 21:05:39 |              0 |              0
 2015-04-16 21:04:30 |              0 |              0
 2015-04-16 21:07:33 |              0 |              0
 2015-04-16 21:07:19 |              0 |              0
 2015-04-16 21:05:19 |              0 |              0
 2015-04-16 21:04:52 |              0 |              0
 2015-04-16 21:04:56 |              0 |              0
 2015-04-16 21:04:09 |              0 |              0
 2015-04-16 21:07:29 |              0 |              0
 2015-04-16 21:04:21 |              0 |              0
 2015-04-16 21:04:51 |              0 |              0
```

Figure 8.14: Screenshot of Cassandra shell showing fog/haze predictions

Timestamp	Fog Prediction	Haze Prediction
2015-04-16 21:07:03	0	0
2015-04-16 21:07:28	0	0
2015-04-16 21:06:10	0	0
2015-04-16 21:05:37	0	0
2015-04-16 21:06:58	0	0
2015-04-16 21:07:52	0	0
2015-04-16 21:07:01	0	1
2015-04-16 21:05:15	0	0
2015-04-16 21:04:49	0	0
2015-04-16 21:06:00	0	0
2015-04-16 21:07:56	0	0
2015-04-16 21:05:40	0	0
2015-04-16 21:08:10	0	0
2015-04-16 21:04:38	0	0
2015-04-16 21:06:39	0	0
2015-04-16 21:06:35	0	0
2015-04-16 21:05:53	0	0
2015-04-16 21:07:47	0	0
2015-04-16 21:08:06	0	0
2015-04-16 21:04:27	0	0
2015-04-16 21:05:39	0	0
2015-04-16 21:04:30	0	0
2015-04-16 21:07:33	0	0
2015-04-16 21:07:19	0	0
2015-04-16 21:05:19	0	0
2015-04-16 21:04:52	0	0
2015-04-16 21:04:56	0	0

Figure 8.15: Screenshot of Flask web application showing fog/haze predictions

is a sequence of RDDs. Spark can ingest data from various types of data sources such as publish-subscribe messaging frameworks, messaging queues, distributed file systems and custom connectors. The data ingested is converted into DStreams. Figure 8.16 shows the Spark Streaming components.

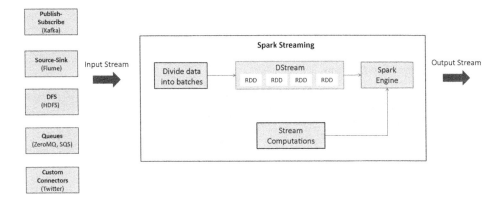

Figure 8.16: Spark Streaming

Just like operations for RDDs described in the previous chapter, Spark provides operations for DStreams. Figure 8.17 shows a DStream, which is composed of RDDs, where each RDD contains data from a certain time interval. The DStream operations are translated into operations on the underlying RDDs. DStream transformations such as *map*, *flatMap*, *filter*, *reduceByKey* are stateless as the transformation are applied to the RDDs in the DStream separately.

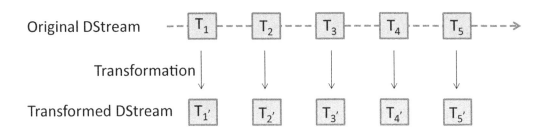

Figure 8.17: Spark DStream transformation

Spark also supports stateful operations such as windowed operations and *updateStateByKey* operation. Stateful operations require *checkpointing* for fault tolerance purposes. For stateful operations, a checkpoint directory is provided to which RDDs are checkpointed periodically. Figure 8.18 shows an example of a window operation. Window operations allow the computations to be done over a sliding window of data. For window operations, a window length and a slide interval in specified. In the example in Figure 8.18, the window length is 3 and slide interval is 2.

Window Operations

Let us look at some commonly used window operations:

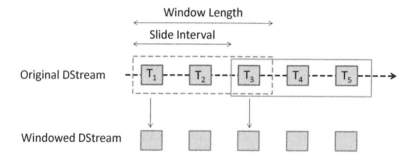

Figure 8.18: Spark DStream window transformation

window

The *window* operation returns a new DStream from a sliding window over the source DStream.

```
■ #Format:  window(windowLength, slideInterval)
# Example:  Return a new DStream with RDDs containing last
# 8 seconds of data, every 4 seconds
windowStream = sourceStream.window(8,4)
```

countByWindow

The *countByWindow* operation counts the number of elements in a window over the DStream.

```
■ #Format:  countByWindow(windowDuration, slideDuration)
# Example:  Count the number of elements in a sliding window with
# window duration of 10 and slide interval of 4 seconds
count = sourceStream.countByWindow(10,4)
```

reduceByWindow

The *reduceByWindow* operation aggregates the elements in a sliding window over a stream using the specified function.

```
■ #Format:  reduceByWindow(func, windowLength, slideInterval)
# Example:  In a text data stream compute the running line lenghts
# with window duration of 10 and slide interval of 4 seconds
totalLength = lineLengths.reduceByWindow(lambda a, b:  a + b, 10, 4)
```

reduceByKeyAndWindow

The *reduceByKeyAndWindow* operation when applied on DStream containing key-value pairs, aggregates values of each key in a sliding window over a stream using the specified function. The *reduceByKeyAndWindow* operation has two forms. In one form the reduced value over a new window is calculated by applying the specified function over the whole window. In the other form, the reduced value over a new window is calculated by applying the function to the new values which entered the window and an inverse function over the values which left the window.

```
■ #Format:  reduceByKeyAndWindow(func, windowLength,
slideInterval, numPartitions)

# Example:  Count the number of words in a text stream
# with a sliding window of duration 10 seconds
and slide interval of 4 seconds

words = textStream.flatMap(lambda line:  line.split(" ")).map(lambda word:  (word,
1))
counts = reduceByKeyAndWindow(lambda a, b:  a + b, 10, 4)

# Alternative and optimized implementation
#Format:  reduceByKeyAndWindow(func, invFunc, windowLength,
slideInterval, numPartitions)

counts = reduceByKeyAndWindow(lambda a, b:  a + b,
lambda a, b:  a - b, 10, 4)
```

countByValueAndWindow

The *reduceByKeyAndWindow* operation when applied on DStream containing key-value pairs, returns a new DStream with key-value pairs where the value is the count for each key (number of elements) in the sliding window.

```
■ #Format:  countByValueAndWindow(windowLength,
slideInterval, numPartitions)
# Example:  Count the number of elements for each key in a sliding
window with # window duration of 10 and slide interval of 4 seconds
count = sourceStream.countByValueAndWindow(10,4)
```

updateStateByKey

Another type of stateful operation is the *updateStateByKey* operation which maintains and tracks the state for each key in a dataset. The *updateStateByKey* operation requires a state to be defined and an update function for updating the state using the previous state and the new values.

```
■ #Format:  updateStateByKey(func)
# Example:  Compute a running count of number of words
# in a text stream counts = lines.flatMap(lambda line:  line.split(" "))
.map(lambda word:  (word, 1))
.updateStateByKey(updateFunc)
```

8.4   Spark Case Studies

In this section we present two case studies on real-time sensor data analysis and one case study on real-time sentiment analysis of Twitter tweets. The first case study is about a system for detecting forest fires by analysis of sensor data collected from a number of IoT devices deployed in a forest. The second case study is about a smart parking system that detects the empty slots in a parking lot.

Given the analysis requirements of both the systems, let us map the systems to one of the analytics patterns proposed in Chapter-1. Since these systems processes sensor data in real-time, we can use the Beta pattern. Figure 8.19 shows a realization of Beta pattern for the forest fire detection and smart parking systems, with the specific tools and frameworks that can be used.

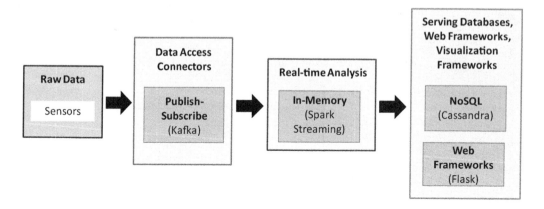

Figure 8.19: A realization of Beta pattern for forest fire detection and smart parking systems

8.4.1 Real-time Sensor Data Analysis

This case study is about real-time sensor data analysis for a forest fire detection system. The system has multiple end-nodes which are deployed in a forest. The end-nodes are equipped with sensors for measuring temperature, humidity, light and carbon monoxide (CO) at various locations in a forest. Each end node sends data independently to a Kafka topic. The system uses Spark for data analysis and making predictions.

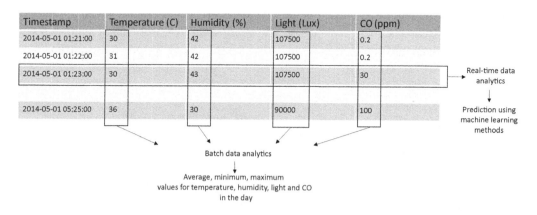

Figure 8.20: Format of data collected for forest fire detection

Figure 8.20 shows an example of the data collected for forest fire detection. Each row in the table shows a time-stamped readings of temperature, humidity, light and CO sensors. By analyzing the sensor readings in real-time (each row of the table), predictions can be made about the occurrence of a forest fire. The sensor readings can also be aggregated on various timescales (minute, hourly, daily or monthly) to determine the mean, maximum and minimum readings. This data can help in developing prediction models.

Filtering Data

Let us look at a Spark Streaming application for filtering sensor data. The Python code for the Spark application is shown in Box 8.11. A StreamingContext is created by specifying the underlying SparkContext and a batch interval for creating small batches of data for analysis. This example uses the Spark's Kafka utilities to create a DStream. The DStream is transformed with map and filter operations.

■ **Box 8.11: Apache Spark Python program for filtering sensor readings**

```
#Data format:
#"2014-06-25 10:47:44",26,36,2860,274

from pyspark import SparkContext
from pyspark.streaming import StreamingContext
from pyspark.streaming.kafka import KafkaUtils

sc = SparkContext(appName="FilterSensorData")
scc = StreamingContext(sc,1)

#Replace with DNS of instance running Zookeeper
zkQuorum = "ip-172-31-33-135.ec2.internal:2181"
topic = "forestfire"

kvs = KafkaUtils.createStream(ssc, zkQuorum,
     "spark-streaming-consumer", topic:1)
lines = kvs.map(lambda x:   x[1])

splitlines = lines.map(lambda line:   line.split(','))
filteredlines = splitlines.filter(lambda line:   int(line[1])>20 and
     int(line[2])>20 and int(line[3])>6000
     and int(line[4])>200)

filteredlines.pprint()

ssc.start()
ssc.awaitTermination()
```

8.4.2   Real-Time Parking Sensor Data Analysis for Smart Parking System

In this case study, we describe a system for real-time analysis of parking sensor data in a smart parking lot for dynamic pricing of parking spots. The system analyzes parking data from the various sensors located in a parking lot and dynamically varies the pricing for each parking spot based on occupancy. The occupancy rate of the parking lots are calculated, and a dynamic pricing model is used to compute the price. The processed data can be stored in a database for further historical and usage pattern analysis.

For the purpose of this case study we will use a synthetic data generator which generates data with the format as shown below:

```
■ Parking Lot ID, Parking Spot ID, Timestamp, Occupied
Example:
5235, 20, 20:30, True
```

In an ideal scenario, each parking sensor would transmit the data every few seconds. For this case study, we generate the start and end time for each parking spot only. The duration of the parking sessions is chosen from a probability distribution function. Box 8.12 shows the Python code for generating synthetic parking sensor data. The sensor data is sent to a Kafka topic.

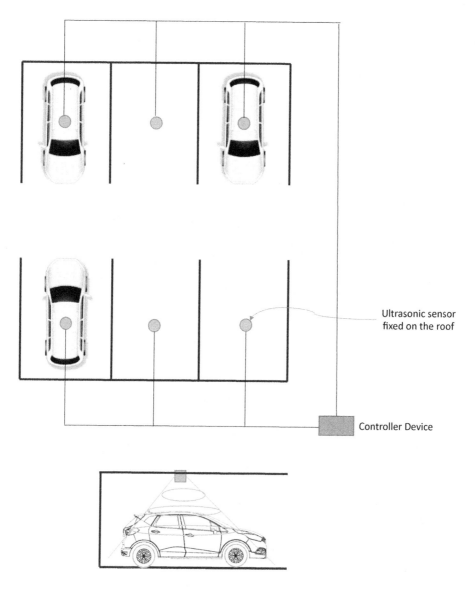

Figure 8.21: Smart parking system

■ Box 8.12: Python program for generating synthetic parking sensor data

```python
import signal
import sys
import random
from kafka.client import KafkaClient
from kafka.consumer import SimpleConsumer
from kafka.producer import SimpleProducer

#Connect to kafka
client = KafkaClient('ip-172-31-39-49.ec2.internal:6667')
producer = SimpleProducer(client)

class sensorMessage(object):
   def __init__(self,lotId,spotId,timeStamp,occupied):
      self.lotId      =    lotId
      self.spotId     =    spotId
      self.timeStamp  =    timeStamp
      self.occupied   =    occupied

   def getKey(self):
      return self.timeStamp

class parkingLot(object):
   def __init__(self,lotId):
      self.emptySpots = range(1,101)
      self.lotId = lotId

   def getLotId(self):
      return self.lotId

   def getEmptySpotId(self):
      if(len(self.emptySpots) != 0):
         return random.choice(self.emptySpots)
      else:
         return 0

class timeStamp(object):
   def __init__(self):
      self.hours      = range(0,24,1)
      self.minutes    = range(0,60,1)
      self.offset     = [1,1,1,1,1,2,2,4,4,8,8,8,8,8,8,8,8,6]

   def getTime(self):
      hour_start    = random.choice(self.hours)
      min_start     = random.choice(self.minutes)
      min_end = min_start
      hour_end = (hour_start + random.choice(self.offset)) % 24
      return (str(hour_start) + ":" + str(min_start),str(hour_end) +
":" + str(min_end))

def startParkingSession(lotId,spotId,timestamp):
   return sensorMessage(lotId,spotId,timestamp,True)
```

```python
def endParkingSession(lotId,spotId,timestamp):
    return sensorMessage(lotId,spotId,timestamp,False)

parkingMessages = []

lots = [parkingLot(1),parkingLot(2),parkingLot(3)]

timeObj = timeStamp()

for i in range(0,200000):
    lot      = random.choice(lots)
    lotId    = lot.getLotId()
    spotId   = lot.getEmptySpotId()

    if spotId == 0:
        continue

    startTime,endTime = timeObj.getTime()

    parkingMessages.append(startParkingSession(lotId,spotId,startTime))
    parkingMessages.append(endParkingSession(lotId,spotId,endTime))

parkingMessages.sort(key = lambda msg:msg.getKey())

for msg in parkingMessages:
    x = str(msg.lotId), str(msg.spotId), str(msg.timeStamp),
        str(msg.occupied)
    producer.send_messages("smartparking",bytes(x))
```

We use Spark Streaming for real-time analysis of parking sensor data. The Spark Streaming instance connects to Kafka by creating a new Data Stream called DStream. Spark Streaming creates micro batches of data received from Kafka. The batch interval is set to 250ms. Thus, every 250ms, the set of sensor data is combined into one RDD. The Spark program counts the total number of occupied slots in each parking lot and computes the dynamic price based on a simple gradient heuristic. The results are stored in a Cassandra database. Box 8.13 shows the Python code for the Spark Streaming application that analyzes the parking data. The program calculates the occupancy ratio for each parking lot.

■ **Box 8.13: Spark Streaming application for parking data analysis**

```python
import random
import sys
import uuid
from cassandra.cluster import Cluster
from pyspark import SparkContext
from pyspark.streaming import StreamingContext
from pyspark.streaming.kafka import KafkaUtils
from operator import add
from kafka.client import KafkaClient
from kafka.consumer import SimpleConsumer
from kafka.producer import SimpleProducer
from pyspark.sql import SQLContext
```

```
from pyspark.sql.types import Row, StructField,
   StructType, StringType, IntegerType
import datetime
from datetime import timedelta


timestamp = datetime.datetime.utcnow()
client = KafkaClient('ip-172-31-39-49.ec2.internal:6667')
producer = SimpleProducer(client)

cluster = Cluster()
session = cluster.connect('test')
baseRate = 2
totalSlots = 500.0


def printel(x):
   global timestamp
   l = x.collect()
   if len(l) !=3:
   return
   print l
   for lot,cars in l:
      lotid= lot.strip("'")
   occrate = ( cars / totalSlots) * 100

   if occrate > 100:
      occrate = 100
         price = -1
      else:
         price = 2 + (occrate/100) * 20

      session.execute("INSERT INTO smartpark (key,lotid,
         occrate,time,price) VALUES (%s,%s,%s,%s,%s)", [uuid.uuid4(),
         int(lotid),occrate,str(timestamp)[:-7],price])
      seconds = random.randint(1800,2400)
      timestamp = timestamp + datetime.timedelta(0,seconds)


sc = SparkContext(appName="SmartParking")
sqlContext = SQLContext(sc)
ssc = StreamingContext(sc, 0.250)

# Replace with DNS of instance running Zookeeper
zkQuorum = "ip-172-31-39-49.ec2.internal:2181"
topic = "smartparking"

kvs = KafkaUtils.createStream(ssc, zkQuorum, "spark-streaming-consumer",
topic: 1)
lines = kvs.map(lambda x:  x[1])

lines = lines.map(lambda line:  line.encode('ascii','ignore'))
lines = lines.map(lambda line:  line.split(","))
lines = lines.map(lambda line:  (line[0][1:]   ,1
```

```
        if line[3][2:-2] == "True" else 0)).reduceByKey(add)

lines.foreachRDD(lambda rdd:  printel(rdd))
ssc.start()
ssc.awaitTermination()
```

Box 8.14 shows the Python code for the Flask web application that displays the occupancy ratio for different parking lots and Figure 8.22 shows a screenshot of the web application.

■ Box 8.14: Python code for the Flask web application

```
from flask import Flask, render_template
from cassandra.cluster import Cluster


cluster = Cluster()
app = Flask(__name__)

@app.route('/')
def index():
   session = cluster.connect('test')
   lot1 = session.execute('Select occrate, price from smartpark where
         lotid = 1 limit 1')

   lot2 = session.execute('Select occrate, price from smartpark where
         lotid = 2 limit 1')

   lot3 = session.execute('Select occrate, price from smartpark where
         lotid = 3 limit 1')

   return render_template('index.html', price1=str(lot1[0].price),
      price2=str(lot2[0].price), price3=str(lot3[0].price),
      occrate1=str(lot1[0].occrate), occrate2=str(lot2[0].occrate),
      occrate3=str(lot3[0].occrate))

@app.route('/ParkingLot/<pid>')
def ParkingLot(pid=1):
   session = cluster.connect('test')
   lot = session.execute('Select occrate,price from smartpark where
      lotid = %s limit 30', [int(pid)])

   return render_template('plot.html', pid=pid,
      price=lot[0].price, occrate= lot[0].occrate, lot=lot)


if __name__ == '__main__':
   app.run(host='0.0.0.0', debug = True)
```

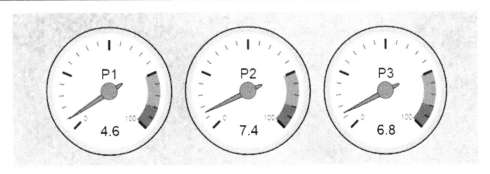

Figure 8.22: Smart parking web application showing occupancy ratio for different parking lots

8.4.3   Real-time Twitter Sentiment Analysis

In this section, we will describe a case study on a system for real-time sentiment analysis of Twitter feeds using Spark Streaming. Figure 8.23 shows a realization of Beta pattern for this system, with the specific tools and frameworks that can be used.

The components of this system include:

- **Listener**: The listener component connects to Twitter with the streaming API and retrieves tweets in real-time. A Python library called *tweepy* is used for retrieving the tweets containing specific keywords. The listener publishes the tweets to a Kafka topic managed by a Kafka Broker.
- **Spark Streaming**: The Spark Streaming component creates a DStream by connecting to the Kafka topic and computes their sentiment using a sentiment lexicon.
- **SQS**: The timestamped tweets and their sentiments are pushed by the Spark Streaming component to an SQS queue.
- **DynamoDB**: The analyzed tweets are also stored in an Amazon DynamoDB table.
- **Flask Web App**: The Flask web application retrieves the tweets from the SQS queue and displays them.

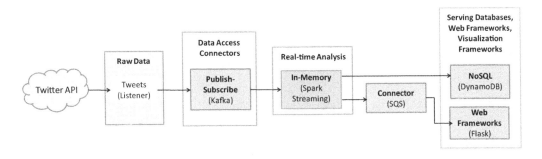

Figure 8.23: A realization of Beta pattern for real-time Twitter sentiment analysis

Box 8.15 shows the Python code for the Listener component that retrieves the tweets using the Twitter API and publishes the tweets to a Kafka topic. The *keywords_list* in this program contains the list of keywords related to which the Tweets are retrieved. For this case study, we use the keyword - 'cricket'.

▪ Box 8.15: Listener component for fetching Tweets and publishing to Kafka

```python
from tweepy.streaming import StreamListener
from tweepy import OAuthHandler
from tweepy import Stream
from random import randrange
import time
import datetime
from kafka import KafkaProducer
import httplib
import json

#Variables that contains the user credentials to access Twitter API
access_token = "<enter>"
access_token_secret = "<enter>"
consumer_key = "<enter>"
consumer_secret = "<enter>"

#List of keywords to filter
keywords_list = ['cricket']

#Connect to Kafka
producer = KafkaProducer(bootstrap_servers=['127.0.0.1:6667'])

#This is a function publishes data to a Kafka topic
def publish(data):
 tweet = json.loads(data)
 if("retweeted" in tweet.keys()):
 if(tweet['retweeted'] == False):
  print tweet['text']

  #Send tweet to a topic named Cricket
  producer.send('Cricket', data.encode("utf"))

#This is a basic listener that just prints received tweets to stdout.
class StdOutListener(StreamListener):
 def on_data(self, data):
 publish(data)
 return True

 def on_error(self, status):
  print status

if __name__ == '__main__':
 #This handles Twitter authetification and
 #the connection to Twitter Streaming API
 l = StdOutListener()
 auth = OAuthHandler(consumer_key, consumer_secret)
 auth.set_access_token(access_token, access_token_secret)
 while True:
  try:
   stream = Stream(auth, l)
  stream.filter(track=keywords_list,languages =['en'])
```

```
except httplib.IncompleteRead:
 print "Incomplete Read!!!!"
 pass
```

Box 8.16 shows the Python code for the Spark Streaming application that computes the tweet sentiments. To enable integration with Kafka in the Spark Streaming application we use the KafkaUtils library. A DStream is set up to consume the stream of tweets from the Kafka topic (to which the listener published the tweets). The streams of tweets are partitioned into separate RDDs using the *map* function in order to perform parallel transformations on their respective elements (each single tweet).

Using the *foreachRDD* method, as well as the *foreach* method, the program first breaks the collection of RDDs into separate RDDs, then passes each element of the discrete RDD to a custom function to reformat the tweet, parse the tweet, compute sentiment, and finally push the processed data to an Amazon SQS queue for web consumption, as well as a DynamoDB database for storage.

To compute the sentiments, we use the AFINN [18] sentiment lexicon, which is a list of over 2400 English words rated for sentiment which is an integer between minus five (negative) and plus five (positive).

■ **Box 8.16: Spark Streaming application for sentiment analysis of tweets**

```
import boto.dynamodb2
from boto.dynamodb2.table import Table
import boto.sqs
from boto.sqs.message import Message
import cPickle as pickle
import json
from pyspark import SparkContext
from pyspark.streaming import StreamingContext
from pyspark.streaming.kafka import KafkaUtils
import random
from random import randint
import string
import time
import datetime
from datetime import datetime as newdatetime
import pytz

# Create connection to DynamoDB service
conn_dynamo = boto.dynamodb2.connect_to_region(REGION,
aws_access_key_id=ACCESS_KEY,
aws_secret_access_key=SECRET_KEY)

# Retrieve handle to DynamoDB table
table1=Table('tweets',connection=conn_dynamo)

# Create connection to SQS service
conn_sqs = boto.sqs.connect_to_region(REGION,
aws_access_key_id=ACCESS_KEY,
aws_secret_access_key=SECRET_KEY)
```

```
# Retrieve handle to queue
q1 = conn_sqs.get_all_queues(prefix='cricket')

TERMS={}

#----- Load Sentiments Dict ---
sent_file = open('AFINN-111.txt')
sent_lines = sent_file.readlines()
for line in sent_lines:
s = line.split("\t")
TERMS[s[0]] = s[1]

sent_file.close()


#----- Find Sentiment -------
def findsentiment(tweet):
 sentiment=0.0

 if tweet.has_key('text'):
  text = tweet['text']
  text=re.sub('[!@#$)(*=+/:;&%#|{},.? `]', "", text)
  splitTweet=text.split()

  for word in splitTweet:
   if TERMS.has_key(word):
    sentiment = sentiment+ float(TERMS[word])

 return sentiment

#---Send analyzed Tweet to SQS and DynamoDB---
def send_results(words):
 tweet = json.loads(words)

 sentimentScore = findsentiment(tweet)

 datas={}
 datas['timestamp'] =str(newdatetime.strptime(tweet['created_at'],
  '%a %b %d %H:%M:%S +0000 %Y').replace(tzinfo=pytz.UTC))[:-6]

 datas['id_str'] = tweet['id_str']
 datas['sentiment'] = sentimentScore
 datas['tweet_name'] = tweet['user']['name']
 datas['tweet_text'] = tweet['text']
 datas['tweet_user_id'] = tweet['user']['screen_name']

 p = pickle.dumps(json.loads(json.dumps(datas)))
 m = Message()
 m.set_body(p)
 status = q1[0].write(m)

 item = table1.put_item(data=datas)
```

```
# Create a local StreamingContext
sc = SparkContext("local[2]", "NetworkWordCount")
ssc = StreamingContext(sc, 5)

cricket_kvs = KafkaUtils.createStream(ssc, '127.0.0.1',
    "spark-streaming-consumer", {'Cricket':  1})

cricket_lines = cricket_kvs.map(lambda x:  x[1])

cricket_lines.pprint()

cricket_lines.foreachRDD(lambda rdd:  rdd.foreach(send_results))

# Start the computation
ssc.start()

# Wait for the computation to terminate
ssc.awaitTermination()
```

   Box 8.17 shows the Python code for the Flask web application. Due to space constraints, we have included only the Python code for the Flask web application and omitted the HTML and JavaScript code for the user interface. Figure 8.24 shows a screenshot of the Flask web application that displays the analyzed tweets.

■ **Box 8.17: Flask web application to displays analyzed Tweets**

```
from flask import Flask, jsonify, abort, request, make_response, url_for
from flask.ext.cors import CORS
import sqlite3
import json
import random
from random import randint
import string
import datetime
import boto.sqs
from boto.sqs.message import Message
import cPickle as pickle
from time import sleep

app = Flask(__name__, static_url_path="")
cors = CORS(app, resources={r"/api/*":  {"origins":  "*"}})

#Create connection to SQS service
conn_sqs = boto.sqs.connect_to_region(REGION,
aws_access_key_id=ACCESS_KEY,
aws_secret_access_key=SECRET_KEY)

# Retrieve handle to queue
q1 = conn_sqs.get_all_queues(prefix='weather')

@app.route('/api/update', methods=['GET'])
def get_updates():
  topics = {}
```

```
tweets = []
flag = False
data1 = {'empty':  'null'}

count = q1[0].count()
if count > 0:
 m = q1[0].read()
 bod = m.get_body()
 data1 = pickle.loads(str(bod))
 q1[0].delete_message(m)

    topics['Cricket'] = data1
print topics
return jsonify(topics)


if __name__ == '__main__':
 app.run(debug=True, host='0.0.0.0')
```

Figure 8.24: Screenshot of Flask web application to show analyzed tweets

8.4.4 Windowed Analysis of Tweets

This case study is about the windowed analysis of tweets. For this case study, the same listener component as described in the previous section can be used. The listener sends tweets to a Kafka topic. Box 8.18 shows the code for a Spark streaming application for analysis of tweets. This application uses the *reduceByKeyAndWindow* operation to find the number of positive, negative and neutral tweets received in the last 30 seconds every 10 seconds.

■ **Box 8.18: Spark Streaming application for windowed analysis of tweets**

```python
from pyspark import SparkContext
from pyspark.streaming import StreamingContext
from pyspark.streaming.kafka import KafkaUtils

#Load Sentiments Dictionary
sent_file = open('AFINN-111.txt')
sent_lines = sent_file.readlines()
for line in sent_lines:
    s = line.split("")
    TERMS[s[0]] = s[1]
sent_file.close()


def findsentiment(tweet):
    sentiment=0.0
    if tweet.has_key('text'):
        text = tweet['text']
        splitTweet=text.split()

        for word in splitTweet:
            if TERMS.has_key(word):
                sentiment = sentiment+ float(TERMS[word])

    return sentiment

def analyzeData(data):
    tweet = json.loads(data)
    sentiment= findsentiment(tweet)
    if sentiment>0:
        return ("Positive", 1)
    elif sentiment<0:
        return ("Negative", 1)
    else:
        return ("Neutral", 1)

sc = SparkContext(appName="SentimentAnalysis")
scc = StreamingContext(sc,1)

#Replace with DNS of instance running Zookeeper
zkQuorum = "ip-172-31-33-135.ec2.internal:2181"
topic = "tweets"

kvs = KafkaUtils.createStream(ssc, zkQuorum,
```

```
"spark-streaming-consumer", topic:1)
tweets = kvs.map(lambda x:  x[1])

sentiments = tweets.map(analyzeData)

windowedSentiments = sentiments.reduceByKeyAndWindow(lambda x,
          y:  x + y, lambda x, y:  x - y, 30, 10)

windowedSentiments.pprint()

ssc.start()
ssc.awaitTermination()
```

Summary

In this chapter we described the Apache Storm and Spark Streaming frameworks, for real-time data analytics. Storm is a framework for distributed and fault-tolerant real-time computation. Storm is a scalable and distributed framework, and offers reliable processing of messages. A computation job on the Storm cluster is called a topology. Spout is a type of a node in a topology, which is a source of streams. Bolt is a type of a node in a topology that processes tuples. Spouts and bolts have multiple worker processes and each worker has multiple tasks. We described various types of stream groupings for partitioning of streams among the tasks. We described the roles of Nimbus, Supervisor and Zookeeper, in Storm cluster. In the second part of the chapter, we described the Spark Streaming framework, which enables scalable, high throughput and fault-tolerant stream processing. Spark Streaming provides a high-level abstraction called DStream. Spark can ingest data from various types of data sources and the data ingested is converted into DStreams. Spark supports DStream transformations which are stateless, and also stateful operations such as windowed operations. Case studies of real-time social media, weather and sensor data analysis using Storm and Spark were described.

9 - Interactive Querying

This chapter covers

- Interactive Querying frameworks
- SparkSQL
- Hive
- Amazon Redshift
- Google BigQuery

Interactive querying is useful when your analytics application demands flexibility to query data on demand. This chapter describes tools and frameworks for interactive querying of big data. These include Spark SQL, Hive, Google BigQuery and Amazon RedShift. These tools and frameworks allow users to query data by writing statements in SQL-like languages.

9.1 Spark SQL

Spark SQL is a component of Spark which enables interactive querying. Spark SQL can interactively query structured and semi-structured data using SQL-like queries. Spark SQL provides a programming abstraction called DataFrames. A DataFrame is a distributed collection of data organized into named columns. DataFrames can be created from existing RDDs, structured data files (such as text files, Parquet, JSON, Apache Avro), Hive tables and also from external databases. Spark provides a Data Sources API, which allows accessing structured data though Spark SQL.

Let us look at examples of using Spark SQL for interactive querying of data from the Spark shell. To launch the Spark Python shell use the command shown in box below:

```
bin/pyspark
```

Spark SQL provides an SQLContext, which is the entry point for Spark SQL. SQLContext provides functionality for creating a DataFrame, registering DataFrame as a table and executing SQL statements over a table. SQLContext can be created from a SparkContext as shown in the box below.

```
from pyspark.sql import SQLContext, Row
sqlContext = SQLContext(sc)
from pyspark.sql.types import *
```

Let us look at an example where we create and use a DataFrame. We will use the Google N-Gram dataset [29] in this example. The dataset file is in CSV format and contains data on bigrams with the following columns: Bigram, Year, Count, Pages, Books. In this example, an RDD is first created by loading the dataset file. The lines in the file are split to obtain the individual columns which are then converted into *Row* objects by passing the list of key-value pairs to the *Row* class. SQLContext provides a *createDataFrame* function to convert the RDD of *Row* objects to a DataFrame by inferring the data types.

```
lines = sc.textFile("file:///home/hadoop/
googlebooks-eng-us-all-2gram-20090715-50.csv")

parts = lines.map(lambda l:  l.split(""))

ngrams = parts.map(lambda x:  Row(ngram=x[0],
year=int(x[1]), ngramcount=int(x[2]), pages=int(x[3]), books=int(x[4])))

schemaNGrams = sqlContext.createDataFrame(ngrams)
```

To view the rows in the created DataFrame, the *show* function can be used which prints the first N rows to the console (default N=20).

```
»> schemaNGrams.show()

+---+----+-------+---+---+
|books| ngram|ngramcount|pages|year|
+---+----+-------+---+---+
|   1|  !  09|        1|  1|1829|
|   3|  !  09|        3|  3|1879|
|   2|  !  09|        2|  2|1911|
|   4|  !  09|        4|  4|1941|
|   4|  !  09|        4|  4|1969|
|  12|  !  09|       17| 17|1994|
|   1|!  13.5|        1|  1|1936|
|   1|!  1430|        1|  1|1861|
|   1|!  1430|        1|  1|1959|
|   2|!  16th|        3|  3|1854|
|   1|!  16th|        1|  1|1959|
|   2|!  1791|        2|  2|1856|
|   1|!  1791|        1|  1|1968|
|   1|!  1847|        1|  1|1859|
|   2|!  1847|        2|  2|1909|
|   2|!  1847|        2|  2|1962|
|   2|!  1944|        2|  2|1945|
|   2|!  1944|        8|  8|1977|
|   1|!  1944|        1|  1|2007|
|   2|!  23rd|        2|  2|1957|
+---+----+-------+---+---+
```

To view the schema of the DataFrame the *printSchema* function can be used as shown below:

```
»> schemaNGrams.printSchema()
root
|- books:  long (nullable = true)
|- ngram:  string (nullable = true)
|- ngramcount:  long (nullable = true)
|- pages:  long (nullable = true)
|- year:  long (nullable = true)
```

An alternative method of creating a DataFrame is to specify the schema as shown in the example below. An RDD of tuples is first created, and the schema is defined using *StructType*. Finally, the schema is applied to the RDD of tuples to create the DataFrame.

```
ngrams = parts.map(lambda x:  (x[0], x[1], x[2], x[3], x[4]))
schemaString = "ngram year ngramcount pages books"
fields = [StructField(field_name, StringType(), True)
for field_name in schemaString.split()]
schema = StructType(fields)
schemaNGrams = sqlContext.createDataFrame(ngrams, schema)
```

Having looked at methods of creating DataFrames, now let us look at some examples of querying data. The box below shows an example of the *filter* function which filters rows using the given condition. In this example, we filter all N-grams which have a count greater than five.

```
■ schemaNGrams.filter(schemaNGrams['ngramcount'] > 5).show()

+---+-----+-------+---+---+
|books| ngram|ngramcount|pages|year|
+---+-----+-------+---+---+
|  12|  !  09|   17|  17|1994|
|   2| !  1944|    8|   8|1977|
|  11|  !  28|   15|  15|1866|
|  10|  !  28|   10|  10|1891|
|  32|  !  28|   37|  37|1916|
|  14|  !  28|   14|  14|1941|
|  41|  !  28|   48|  47|1966|
|  57|  !  28|   76|  76|1991|
|  15|  !  56|   15|  15|1979|
|  54|  !  56|   61|  61|2004|
|   3| !  936|   16|  15|1943|
|   6| !  936|    9|   9|1973|
|  14|  !  ANNE|  108|  95|1916|
|   4|  !  ANNE|   35|  26|1941|
|   6|  !  ANNE|   28|  26|1969|
|   6|  !  AS|    6|   6|1892|
|   6|  !  AS|    6|   6|1943|
|   6|  !  AS|    7|   7|1968|
|  10|  !  AS|   17|  15|1993|
|  17|! Abort|   24|  21|2004|
+---+-----+-------+---+---+
```

The *groupBy* function can be used to group the DataFrame using the specified columns. Aggregations (such as avg, max, min, sum, count) can then be applied to the grouped DataFrame. The box below shows an example of grouping the N-Grams by year and then applying the count aggregations to find the total number of N-Grams in each year.

```
■ schemaNGrams.groupBy("year").count().show()

+---+---+
|year|count|
+---+---+
|1831|  79|
|1832|  57|
|1833|  56|
|1834|  47|
|1835|  71|
|1836|  66|
|1837|  74|
|1838|  56|
|1839|  63|
|1840|  66|
```

```
|1841|  71|
|1842|  54|
|1843|  87|
|1844|  81|
|1845|  91|
|1846|  95|
|1847|  72|
|1848|  76|
|1849| 101|
|1850| 104|
+---+---+
```

Spark SQL allows registering a DataFrame as a temporary table for querying the data using SQL-like queries. With the created DataFrame (schemaNGrams) a temporary table (ngrams) is created using *registerTempTable* function. An SQL query for filtering all N-grams which have count greater than five is shown below:

```
■ schemaNGrams.registerTempTable("ngrams")

result = sqlContext.sql("SELECT ngram, ngramcount
FROM ngrams WHERE ngramcount >= 5").show()
+----+-------+
| ngram|ngramcount|
+----+-------+
| !   09|   17|
|!  1944|    8|
| !  28|   15|
| !  28|   10|
| !  28|   37|
| !  28|   14|
| !  28|   48|
| !  28|   76|
| !  56|    5|
| !  56|    5|
| !  56|   15|
| !  56|   61|
| ! 936|   16|
| ! 936|    9|
|! ANNE|  108|
|! ANNE|   35|
|! ANNE|   28|
| ! AS|    5|
| ! AS|    6|
| ! AS|    6|
+----+-------+
```

The box below shows an example of an SQL query that uses the GROUP BY clause to group the N-Grams by the year column and COUNT statement to count the number of N-Grams in each year. The results are ordered by the count of N-Grams.

```
■ result = sqlContext.sql("SELECT year, COUNT(*) AS cnt FROM
ngrams GROUP BY year ORDER BY cnt DESC").show()

+---+--+
|year|cnt|
+---+--+
|2007|470|
|2002|450|
|2000|447|
|2003|446|
|2006|445|
|2001|445|
|1997|441|
|2004|440|
|1988|437|
|1999|436|
|2005|435|
|1991|432|
|1998|421|
|1995|415|
|1996|410|
|1987|408|
|1994|402|
|1990|397|
|1978|390|
|1986|390|
+---+--+
```

The box below shows an example of finding the N-Gram with the maximum count (most popular N-Gram) in each year. The GROUP BY clause is used to group the N-Grams by the year, and the MAX clause is used to find the maximum count.

```
■ result = sqlContext.sql("SELECT ngram, year, MAX(ngramcount) AS
maxCount FROM ngrams GROUP BY ngram, year").show()

+----------+---+-----+
|    ngram|year|maxCount|
+----------+---+-----+
|    ) î|1900|    2|
|    ) $15|1939|    3|
|    ( HCOa|1989|    1|
|  """ THERE'S"|1894|    3|
|""" obliterate"|1969|  10|
|  ' Mulberry|1839|    1|
|  ) refinery|1951|    3|
|    & RH|1982|   13|
| & Covington|1955|    1|
|    "|1942|  208|
|    ( 1260|1887|   13|
| """ Rain's"|1956|    3|
|  """ khaki"|1912|    5|
| """ Miinchner"|1919|    5|
```

```
|   """ effects"|1960|   329|
|   ( Menin|2001|    4|
|   ( FVR|1966|    1|
|   ! Branch|1881|    1|
|   """ muchas"|1911|    4|
|   """ Days"|1887|   40|
+----------+---+-----+
```

9.1.1 Case Study: Interactive Querying of Weather Data

In this section we present a case study on a system for interactive querying of weather data. We will use the NCDC weather dataset [52] for this case study. NCDC provides access to daily data from the U.S. Climate Reference Network / U.S. Regional Climate Reference Network (USCRN/USRCRN) via FTP.

Given the analysis requirements of this system, let us map the system to one of the analytics patterns proposed in Chapter-1. Since the system allows interactive querying of weather data, we can use the Delta pattern. Figure 9.1 shows a realization of Delta pattern for this system, with the specific tools and frameworks that can be used. In this section we describe the use of Spark SQL for interactive querying of the weather dataset. The use of Hive for querying the same dataset is described in the next section.

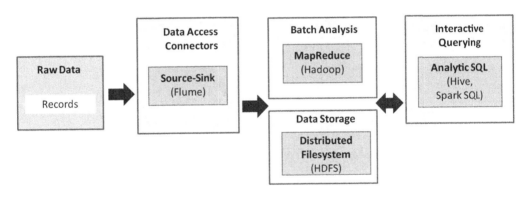

Figure 9.1: A realization of Delta pattern for interactive querying of weather data

To move the weather data to HDFS from an external source, we can use a source-sink connector such as Flume. Since the dataset used in this case study is in the form of a single text file, we simple move the text file into HDFS using the HDFS command line tools. The box below shows the Python code for creating a DataFrame from the dataset using *createDataFrame* function which converts the RDD of Row objects to a DataFrame by inferring the data types.

```
■ from pyspark.sql import SQLContext, Row
sqlContext = SQLContext(sc)
from pyspark.sql.types import *

lines = sc.textFile("file:///home/hadoop/
CRND0103-2014-VA_Cape_Charles_5_ENE_T.txt")
parts = lines.map(lambda l: l.split(" "))
```

```
weatherdata = parts.map(lambda x:  Row(WBANNO=int(x[0]),
LST_DATE=int(x[1]),
CRX_VN=float(x[2]),
LONGITUDE=float(x[3]),
LATITUDE=float(x[4]),
T_DAILY_MAX=float(x[5]),
T_DAILY_MIN=float(x[6]),
T_DAILY_MEAN=float(x[7]),
T_DAILY_AVG=float(x[8]),
P_DAILY_CALC=float(x[9]),
SOLARAD_DAILY=float(x[10]),
SUR_TEMP_DAILY_TYPE=x[11],
SUR_TEMP_DAILY_MAX=float(x[12]),
SUR_TEMP_DAILY_MIN=float(x[13]),
SUR_TEMP_DAILY_AVG=float(x[14]),
RH_DAILY_MAX=float(x[15]),
RH_DAILY_MIN=float(x[16]),
RH_DAILY_AVG=float(x[17]),
SOIL_MOISTURE_5_DAILY=float(x[18]),
SOIL_MOISTURE_10_DAILY=float(x[19]),
SOIL_MOISTURE_20_DAILY=float(x[20]),
SOIL_MOISTURE_50_DAILY=float(x[21]),
SOIL_MOISTURE_100_DAILY=float(x[22]),
SOIL_TEMP_5_DAILY=float(x[23]),
SOIL_TEMP_10_DAILY=float(x[24]),
SOIL_TEMP_20_DAILY=float(x[25]),
SOIL_TEMP_50_DAILY=float(x[26]),
SOIL_TEMP_100_DAILY=float(x[27]) ))

schemaWeather = sqlContext.createDataFrame(weatherdata)
schemaWeather.registerTempTable("weather")
```

The box below shows the schema of the created DataFrame.

```
■ »> schemaWeather.printSchema()
root
|- WBANNO: string (nullable = true)
|- LST_DATE: string (nullable = true)
|- CRX_VN: string (nullable = true)
|- LONGITUDE: string (nullable = true)
|- LATITUDE: string (nullable = true)
|- T_DAILY_MAX: string (nullable = true)
|- T_DAILY_MIN: string (nullable = true)
|- T_DAILY_MEAN: string (nullable = true)
|- T_DAILY_AVG: string (nullable = true)
|- P_DAILY_CALC: string (nullable = true)
|- SOLARAD_DAILY: string (nullable = true)
|- SUR_TEMP_DAILY_TYPE: string (nullable = true)
|- SUR_TEMP_DAILY_MAX: string (nullable = true)
|- SUR_TEMP_DAILY_MIN: string (nullable = true)
|- SUR_TEMP_DAILY_AVG: string (nullable = true)
|- RH_DAILY_MAX: string (nullable = true)
|- RH_DAILY_MIN: string (nullable = true)
```

```
|- RH_DAILY_AVG: string (nullable = true)
|- SOIL_MOISTURE_5_DAILY: string (nullable = true)
|- SOIL_MOISTURE_10_DAILY: string (nullable = true)
|- SOIL_MOISTURE_20_DAILY: string (nullable = true)
|- SOIL_MOISTURE_50_DAILY: string (nullable = true)
|- SOIL_MOISTURE_100_DAILY: string (nullable = true)
|- SOIL_TEMP_5_DAILY: string (nullable = true)
|- SOIL_TEMP_10_DAILY: string (nullable = true)
|- SOIL_TEMP_20_DAILY: string (nullable = true)
|- SOIL_TEMP_50_DAILY: string (nullable = true)
|- SOIL_TEMP_100_DAILY: string (nullable = true)
```

The box below shows an example of an SQL query for fetching the station WBAN number, date and maximum daily temperature sorted in descending order. The LIMIT clause is used to limit the number of rows returned.

```
■ # Sort by maximum temperature
result = sqlContext.sql("SELECT WBANNO, LST_DATE, T_DAILY_MAX FROM
weather ORDER BY T_DAILY_MAX DESC LIMIT 10").show()
+----+-----+-------+
|WBANNO|LST_DATE|T_DAILY_MAX|
+----+-----+-------+
| 3739|20140618| 33.4|
| 3739|20140708| 33.1|
| 3739|20140902| 32.9|
| 3739|20140702| 32.6|
| 3739|20140901| 32.1|
| 3739|20140709| 32.0|
| 3739|20140619| 31.8|
| 3739|20140906| 31.7|
| 3739|20140707| 31.6|
| 3739|20140617| 31.5|
```

The box below shows an example of an SQL query for finding the maximum temperature observed in the entire year.

```
■ # Max Temp observed in entire year
result = sqlContext.sql("SELECT WBANNO, MAX(T_DAILY_MAX) AS
maxTemp FROM weather GROUP BY WBANNO").show()

+----+-----+
|WBANNO|maxTemp|
+----+-----+
| 3739| 33.4|
+----+-----+
```

The box below shows an example of an SQL query for finding the minimum temperature observed in the entire year. Note the use of WHERE clause to filter out missing values (set to -9999.0).

```
■ # Min Temp observed in entire year
result = sqlContext.sql("SELECT WBANNO, MIN(T_DAILY_MIN) AS
```

```
minTemp FROM weather WHERE T_DAILY_MIN <> -9999.0
GROUP BY WBANNO").show()


+----+-----+
|WBANNO|minTemp|
+----+-----+
| 3739| -15.1|
+----+-----+
```

9.2 Hive

Apache Hive is a data warehousing framework built on top of Hadoop. Hive provides an SQL-like query language called Hive Query Language, for querying data residing in HDFS. Hive organizes data into tables like a relational database. While the table data resides on HDFS, Hive includes a Metastore which stores table metadata (such as table schema). Hive tables are serialized and stored in HDFS. For each table, Hive has a directory on HDFS. Tables are divided into partitions which speed up queries. Partitions are further divided into buckets. Hive converts the SQL-like queries into series of jobs which are executed on the Hadoop cluster. Hive can use either MapReduce or Apache Tez as the execution engines.

Hive provides a shell for creating tables and querying data. The Hive shell can be launched with the *hive* command. The box below shows an example of creating a Hive table from Hive shell.

```
■ # Creating Hive table
hive> CREATE TABLE weatherdata
(station INT, country STRING, timestamp INT, temperature FLOAT, humidity
FLOAT);
```

Additional options such as the row format, storage format, partitions and buckets can also be specified while creating a table as shown in the example below:

```
■ # Creating Hive table
hive> CREATE TABLE weatherdata
(station INT, timestamp INT, temperature FLOAT, humidity FLOAT)
PARTITIONED BY(country STRING)
CLUSTERED BY(station) SORTED BY(timestamp) INTO 4 BUCKETS
ROW FORMAT DELIMITED
FIELDS TERMINATED BY '\t'
STORED AS TEXTFILE;
```

Tables can be partitioned by one or more columns. When a table is partitioned, Hive creates a separate data directory for each distinct value combination in the partition columns. Tables can be stored as plain textfiles, SequenceFiles or in ORC file format. Tables or partitions can be further divided into buckets by specifying CLUSTERED BY columns. The data can be sorted within buckets by specifying the SORT BY columns.

For the examples in this section, we will use Apache Hue, which an open source Web interface for analyzing data with Hadoop. With Hue, you can create Hive tables, compose and execute Hive queries from the web interface.

Figure 9.2 shows how to create a Metastore table from the Hue web interface. The data file can either be uploaded directly from the wizard or if the file already exists on HDFS, the

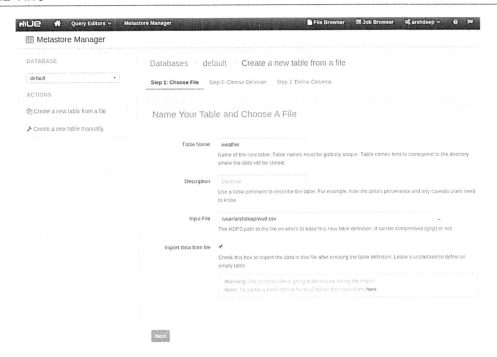

Figure 9.2: Creating Hive table from Hue - step 1

Figure 9.3: Creating Hive table from Hue - step 2

file path is specified. For the examples in this section, we will use weather dataset for the city of Atlanta for the year 2014, obtained from Weather Underground [31]. In the next step, the delimiter for the dataset file is specified as shown in Figure 9.3.

In the next step, the column names and the data types for the columns are specified as shown in Figure 9.4.

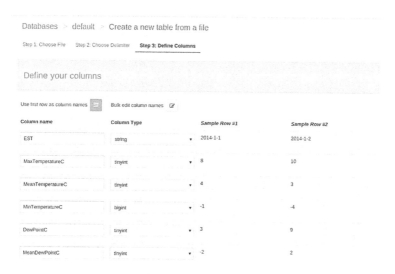

Figure 9.4: Creating Hive table from Hue - step 3

Upon completion of the table creation wizard, you can view the columns of the table along with the data types as shown in Figure 9.5.

Databases > default > weather

Columns   Sample   Properties

	Name	Type
0	est	string
1	maxtemperaturec	tinyint
2	meantemperaturec	tinyint
3	mintemperaturec	bigint
4	dewpointc	tinyint
5	meandewpointc	tinyint
6	mindewpointc	bigint
7	maxhumidity	tinyint
8	meanhumidity	tinyint
9	minhumidity	tinyint
10	maxsealevelpressurehpa	smallint
11	meansealevelpressurehpa	smallint
12	minsealevelpressurehpa	smallint
13	maxvisibilitykm	tinyint
14	meanvisibilitykm	tinyint
15	minvisibilitykm	bigint
16	maxwindspeedkmh	tinyint
17	meanwindspeedkmh	tinyint
18	maxgustspeedkmh	tinyint
19	precipitationmm	float
20	cloudcover	tinyint
21	events	string
22	winddirdegrees	smallint

Figure 9.5: Hive table created from Hue

Let us now look at examples of some SQL queries that can be executed from the Hive query editor in Hue. Figure 9.6 shows an SQL query for retrieving ten records from the table. The query output can also be seen in the figure.

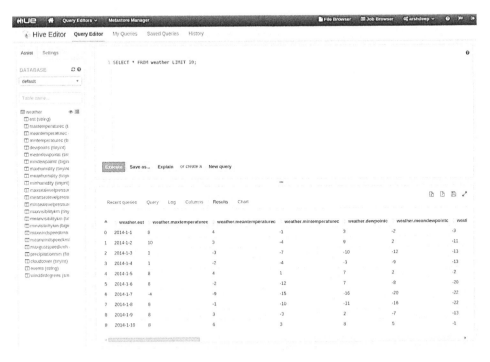

Figure 9.6: Querying data with Hive

Figure 9.7 shows an SQL query for finding the maximum, minimum and mean temperature in the entire year.

Figure 9.7: Querying data with Hive

Figure 9.8 shows an SQL query for finding the ten most wet days in the year, ordered by the precipitation.

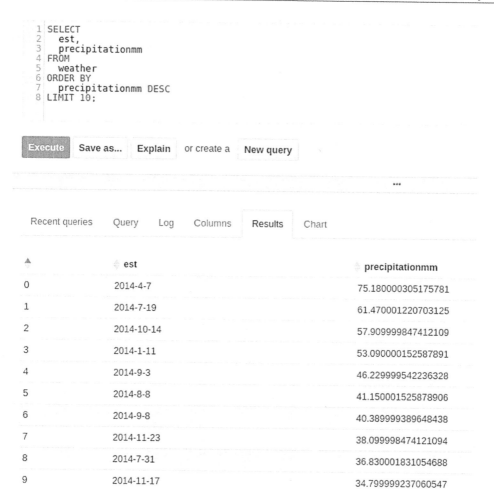

Figure 9.8: Querying data with Hive

9.3 Amazon Redshift

Amazon Redshift is a fast, massive-scale managed data warehouse service. Redshift specializes in handling queries on datasets of sizes up to a petabyte or more through the use of a Massively Parallel Processing (MPP) architecture, which parallelizes SQL queries across all resources in the Redshift cluster. Redshift provides a columnar storage and advanced data compression which enable very fast searches on keys.

A Redshift data warehouse comprises *clusters* which include a collection of *nodes*. Redshift is highly scalable and allows additional nodes to be added or removed from the cluster while remaining operational. Redshift is a fully managed data warehouse and provides features such as automated backups, fault tolerance, security, and restorations.

To begin working with Redshift, first a data cluster must be created using either the Redshift dashboard or Redshift API. Figure 9.9 shows a screenshot of the wizard for creating a Redshift cluster. A unique name for the cluster and a database must be specified.

In the next step, the node type and cluster type needs to be specified as shown in Figure 9.10.

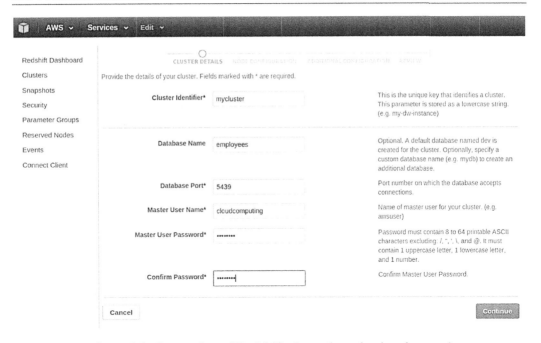

Figure 9.9: Screenshot of Redshift cluster launch wizard - step 1

Figure 9.10: Screenshot of Redshift cluster launch wizard - step 2

In the next step, additional configuration for the cluster is specified as shown in Figure 9.11. Figure 9.12 shows the review page of the cluster launch wizard.

When the cluster is launched, you can view the cluster details from the Redshift dashboard as shown in Figure 9.13.

To connect to the Redshift cluster, you will need to configure a security group to authorize access. In the security group for the launched cluster add a custom TCP rule and enable port 5439 (which is the default port for Redshift).

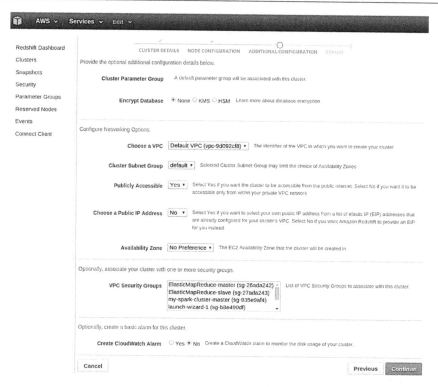

Figure 9.11: Screenshot of Redshift cluster launch wizard - step 3

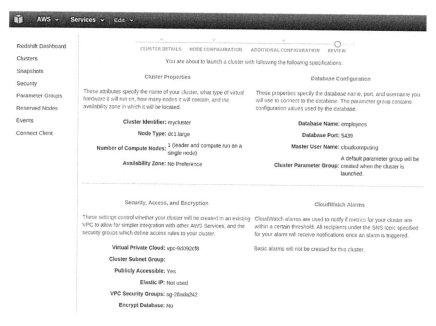

Figure 9.12: Screenshot of Redshift cluster launch wizard - step 4

You can now connect to the Redshift cluster and execute SQL queries from an SQL client. For the examples in this chapter, we will use SQL Workbench/J client. To setup SQL

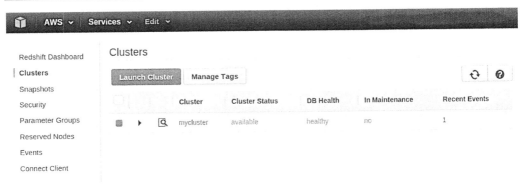

Figure 9.13: Screenshot of Redshift dashboard showing the details of the cluster

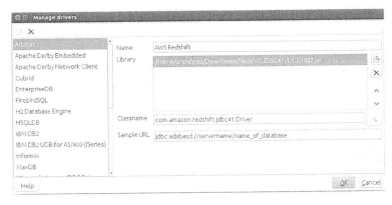

Figure 9.14: Screenshot of SQL WorkBench - adding Redshift driver

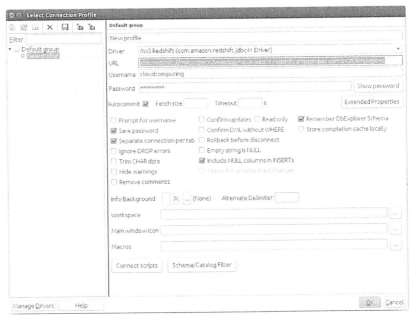

Figure 9.15: Screenshot of SQL WorkBench - connecting to Redshift cluster

Workbench/J client to connect to Redshift, download the Redshift JDBC driver from the Redshift dashboard and add the driver to SQL Workbench/J from the manage drivers dialog as shown in Figure 9.14.

In SQL Workbench/J, create a new connection profile and copy the JDBC URL of the Redshift cluster in the connection profile dialog as shown in Figure 9.15. You can obtain the JDBC URL of the Redshift cluster from the Redshift dashboard.

For the examples, we will use a dataset of employees [30]. Box 9.1 shows the SQL statements for creating the database tables.

■ Box 9.1: SQL statements for creating database tables

```
CREATE TABLE employees (
    emp_no    INT          NOT NULL,
    birth_date VARCHAR(14)           NOT NULL,
    first_name VARCHAR(20)    NOT NULL,
    last_name VARCHAR(20)     NOT NULL,
    gender    VARCHAR(10)     NOT NULL,
    hire_date VARCHAR(14)            NOT NULL,
    PRIMARY KEY (emp_no)
);
CREATE TABLE departments (
    dept_no      VARCHAR(10)    NOT NULL,
    dept_name VARCHAR(40)    NOT NULL,
    PRIMARY KEY (dept_no),
    UNIQUE (dept_name)
);
CREATE TABLE dept_manager (
    dept_no      VARCHAR(10)    NOT NULL,
    emp_no    INT            NOT NULL,
    from_date    VARCHAR(14)    NOT NULL,
    to_date      VARCHAR(14)    NOT NULL,
    FOREIGN KEY (emp_no) REFERENCES employees (emp_no) ,
    FOREIGN KEY (dept_no) REFERENCES departments (dept_no),
    PRIMARY KEY (emp_no,dept_no)
);
CREATE TABLE dept_emp (
    emp_no    INT            NOT NULL,
    dept_no      VARCHAR(10)    NOT NULL,
    from_date VARCHAR(14)    NOT NULL,
    to_date      VARCHAR(14)    NOT NULL,
    FOREIGN KEY (emp_no) REFERENCES employees (emp_no) ,
    FOREIGN KEY (dept_no) REFERENCES departments (dept_no),
    PRIMARY KEY (emp_no,dept_no)
);
CREATE TABLE titles (
    emp_no    INT            NOT NULL,
    title      VARCHAR(50)    NOT NULL,
    from_date VARCHAR(14)    NOT NULL,
    to_date      VARCHAR(14),
    FOREIGN KEY (emp_no) REFERENCES employees (emp_no),
    PRIMARY KEY (emp_no,title, from_date)
);
```

```
CREATE TABLE salaries (
   emp_no     INT           NOT NULL,
   salary     INT           NOT NULL,
   from_date VARCHAR(14)     NOT NULL,
   to_date    VARCHAR(14)     NOT NULL,
   FOREIGN KEY (emp_no) REFERENCES employees (emp_no),
   PRIMARY KEY (emp_no, from_date)
);
```

Figure 9.16 shows the execution of the SQL statements for creating tables in SQL WorkBench/J.

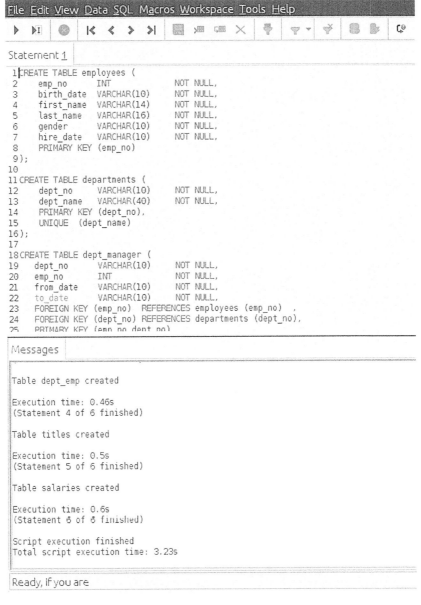

Figure 9.16: Screenshot of SQLWorkBench - creating tables

The dataset files for the individual tables (in CSV format) are copied to an Amazon S3 bucket. To load the data to the Redshift cluster, the SQL COPY command is used as shown in Box 9.2.

■ **Box 9.2: Loading data into tables**

```
copy departments FROM 's3://abahgacloud/departments.csv'
credentials 'aws_access_key_id=<enter-key>;
aws_secret_access_key=<enter-secret>'
delimiter ',';


COPY employees FROM 's3://abahgacloud/employees.csv'
credentials 'aws_access_key_id=<enter-key>;
aws_secret_access_key=<enter-secret>'
delimiter ',';


COPY dept_manager FROM 's3://abahgacloud/dept_manager.csv'
credentials 'aws_access_key_id=<enter-key>;
aws_secret_access_key=<enter-secret>'
delimiter ',';


COPY dept_emp FROM 's3://abahgacloud/dept_emp.csv'
credentials 'aws_access_key_id=<enter-key>;
aws_secret_access_key=<enter-secret>'
delimiter ',';


COPY titles FROM 's3://abahgacloud/titles.csv'
credentials 'aws_access_key_id=<enter-key>;
aws_secret_access_key=<enter-secret>'
delimiter ',';


COPY salaries FROM 's3://abahgacloud/salaries.csv'
credentials 'aws_access_key_id=<enter-key>;
aws_secret_access_key=<enter-secret>'
delimiter ',';
```

With the data loaded into the database, you can now query the data using SQL statements. Figure 9.17 shows the SQL SELECT statements to get a subset of rows from all the tables in the Employees database. Figure 9.18 shows the execution details of a query in the Redshift dashboard.

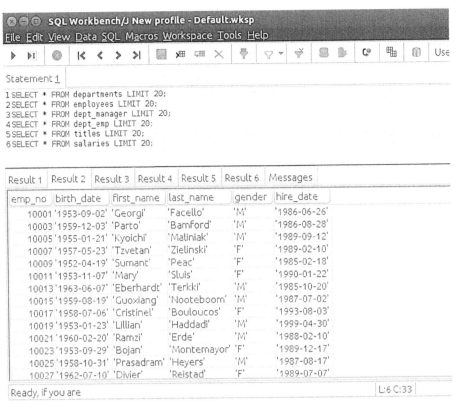

Figure 9.17: Screenshot of SQLWorkBench - querying data

Figure 9.18: Screenshot of Redshift dashboard showing query execution details

Now, let us look at some more advanced SQL queries. Box 9.3 shows an SQL query for retrieving the salaries (and the effective dates) for an employee with ID 10009.

■ **Box 9.3: Get all the salaries and the effective dates for employee with ID 10009**

```
SELECT first_name, last_name, salary, from_date, to_date
FROM employees, salaries
WHERE employees.emp_no=salaries.emp_no
AND employees.emp_no='10009';

'Sumant'    'Peac'   60929   '1985-02-18'   '1986-02-18'
'Sumant'    'Peac'   64780   '1987-02-18'   '1988-02-18'
'Sumant'    'Peac'   69042   '1989-02-17'   '1990-02-17'
'Sumant'    'Peac'   71434   '1991-02-17'   '1992-02-17'
'Sumant'    'Peac'   76518   '1993-02-16'   '1994-02-16'
'Sumant'    'Peac'   80944   '1995-02-16'   '1996-02-16'
'Sumant'    'Peac'   85875   '1997-02-15'   '1998-02-15'
'Sumant'    'Peac'   90668   '1999-02-15'   '2000-02-15'
'Sumant'    'Peac'   94443   '2001-02-14'   '2002-02-14'
'Sumant'    'Peac'   64604   '1986-02-18'   '1987-02-18'
'Sumant'    'Peac'   66302   '1988-02-18'   '1989-02-17'
'Sumant'    'Peac'   70889   '1990-02-17'   '1991-02-17'
'Sumant'    'Peac'   74612   '1992-02-17'   '1993-02-16'
'Sumant'    'Peac'   78335   '1994-02-16'   '1995-02-16'
'Sumant'    'Peac'   82507   '1996-02-16'   '1997-02-15'
'Sumant'    'Peac'   89324   '1998-02-15'   '1999-02-15'
'Sumant'    'Peac'   93507   '2000-02-15'   '2001-02-14'
'Sumant'    'Peac'   94409   '2002-02-14'   '9999-01-01'
```

Box 9.4 shows an SQL query for finding most recent salary of the employee with ID 10009.

■ **Box 9.4: Find most recent salary of the employee with ID 10009**

```
SELECT first_name, last_name, salary
FROM employees, salaries
WHERE employees.emp_no=salaries.emp_no
AND employees.emp_no='10009'
AND to_date=(
   SELECT MAX(to_date)
   FROM salaries
   WHERE emp_no = '10009'
);

'Sumant'    'Peac'    94409
```

Box 9.5 shows an SQL query for retrieving the details of the manager of the department with ID d009.

■ **Box 9.5: Get details of the manager of the department with ID d009**

```
SELECT * FROM employees
WHERE emp_no = (
   SELECT emp_no
   FROM dept_manager
   WHERE dept_no = 'd009'
   AND to_date = (
      SELECT max(from_date)
      FROM dept_manager
      WHERE dept_no = 'd009'
   )
);


111939   '1960-03-25'   'Yuchang'   'Weedman'   'M'   '1989-07-10'
```

Box 9.6 shows an SQL query for retrieving all the titles held and the effective dates, for the employee with ID 10009.

■ **Box 9.6: Get all the titles held and the effective dates for the employee with ID 10009**

```
SELECT first_name, last_name, title, from_date, to_date
FROM employees, titles
WHERE employees.emp_no=titles.emp_no
AND employees.emp_no='10009';

'Sumant'   'Peac'   'Engineer'           '1990-02-18'   '1995-02-18'
'Sumant'   'Peac'   'Assistant Engineer'  '1985-02-18'   '1990-02-18'
'Sumant'   'Peac'   'Senior Engineer'     '1995-02-18'   '9999-01-01'
```

9.4   Google BigQuery

Google BigQuery is a service for querying massive datasets. BigQuery allows querying datasets using SQL-like queries. The BigQuery queries are run against append-only tables that use the processing power of Google's infrastructure for speeding up queries. To query data, it is first loaded into BigQuery using the BigQuery console or BigQuery command line tool or BigQuery API. Data can be either in CSV or JSON format. The uploaded data can be queried using BigQuery's SQL dialect.

The primary difference between Amazon Redshift and Google BigQuery is that while Redshift offers a standard SQL database which has a Massively Parallel Processing (MPP) architecture and needs to be provisioned before it can be used, BigQuery is an online service which does not require users to provision the service. BigQuery is an always available service to which the users can load data and then query the data. For Redshift, the users are charged based on the number of nodes provisioned and the hours for which the nodes run. BigQuery, in contrast to Redshift, charges users for the amount of data stored and the amount of data consumed at the query time.

Figure 9.19 shows a screenshot of the BigQuery wizard for loading data. A dataset ID and table ID is specified in the first step.

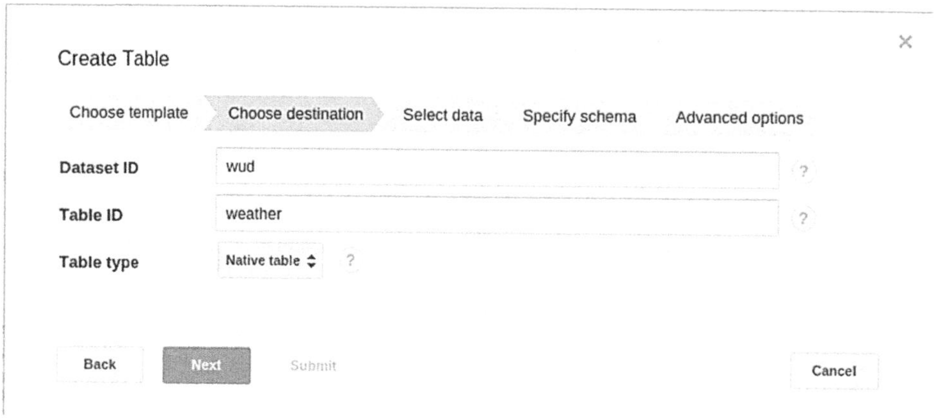

Figure 9.19: Screenshot of BigQuery dashboard - creating table - step 1

Figure 9.20 shows the next step in which the format of the source file (CSV or JSON) is specified. The data file can either be uploaded directly from the wizard or if the file already exists on Google Cloud Storage, the file URI is specified. For the examples in this section, we will use weather dataset for the city of Atlanta for the year 2014, obtained from Weather Underground [31].

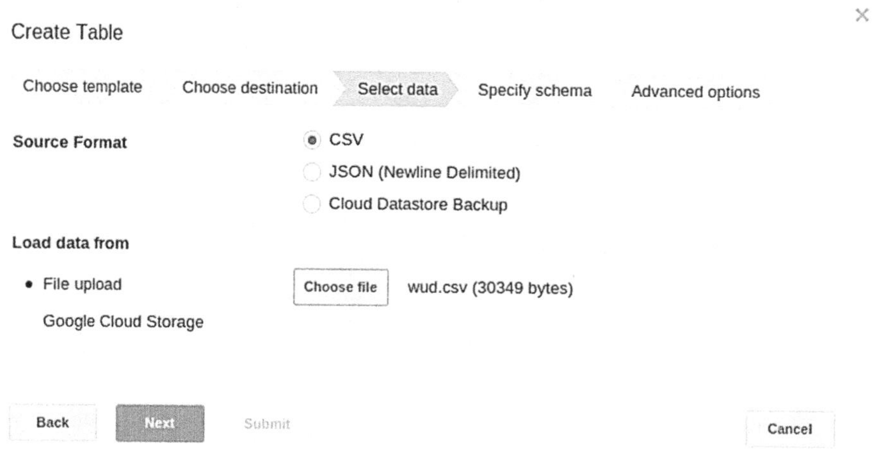

Figure 9.20: Screenshot of BigQuery dashboard - creating table - step 2

In the next step, the schema of the table is specified as shown in Figure 9.21.

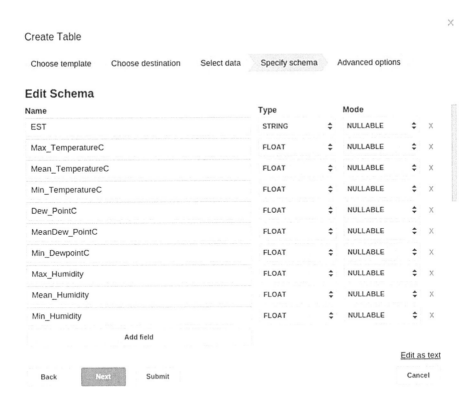

Figure 9.21: Screenshot of BigQuery dashboard - creating table - step 3

In the last step, the field delimiter used in the dataset file, the number of header lines to skip and other advanced options are specified as shown in Figure 9.22.

Figure 9.22: Screenshot of BigQuery dashboard - creating table - step 4

With the data loaded into BigQuery table, the table details can seen from the BigQuery dashboard as shown in Figure 9.23.

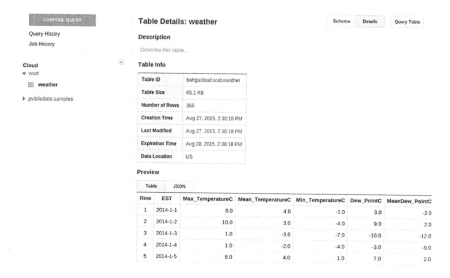

Figure 9.23: Screenshot of BigQuery dashboard showing table details

Let us now look at examples of some SQL queries that can be executed from the BigQuery dashboard. Figure 9.24 shows an SQL query for retrieving ten records from the table. The query output can also be seen in the figure.

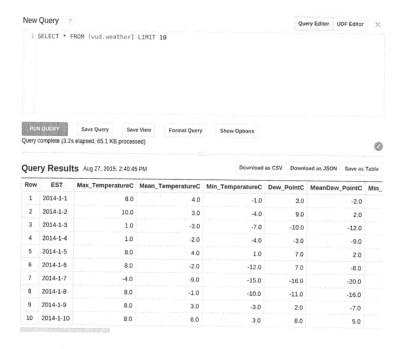

Figure 9.24: Screenshot of BigQuery dashboard showing query results

Figure 9.25 shows an SQL query for finding the maximum, minimum and mean temperature in the entire year.

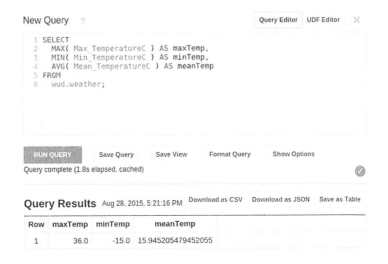

Figure 9.25: Screenshot of BigQuery dashboard showing query results

Figure 9.25 shows an SQL query for finding the ten most wet days in the year, ordered by the precipitation.

Figure 9.26: Screenshot of BigQuery dashboard showing query results

Till now we looked at BigQuery examples which used the BigQuery web interface. BigQuery also provides an API for creating datasets and querying data. Box 9.7 shows the Python program for creating a BigQuery dataset. The *jobs*().*insert* method of the Google BigQuery API is used for inserting a new dataset. The request body of this method contains properties such as configuration, load, and schema. In this example, the data is loaded from a CSV file. The schema property specifies the schema of the CSV file. The *jobs*().*insert* method returns immediately, therefore, the *jobs.get* is called to get the job status.

■ **Box 9.7: Python program for creating a BigQuery dataset**

```
import json
import uuid
from googleapiclient.discovery import build
from oauth2client.client import GoogleCredentials

credentials = GoogleCredentials.get_application_default()
bigquery_service = build('bigquery', 'v2', credentials=credentials)

PROJECT_ID = 'mycloud'
DATASET_ID = 'wud'
TABLE_ID = 'weather'

job_data = {
  'jobReference':  {
    'projectId':  PROJECT_ID,
    'job_id':  str(uuid.uuid4())
  },
  'configuration':  {
    'load':  {
      'sourceUris':  ['gs://abahga/wud.csv'],
      'schema':  {
        'fields':  [
          {
          'name':  'EST',
          'type':  'STRING'
          },
          {
          'name':  'Max_TemperatureC',
          'type':  'FLOAT'
          },
          {
          'name':  'Mean_TemperatureC',
          'type':  'FLOAT'
          },
          {
          'name':  'Min_TemperatureC',
          'type':  'FLOAT'
          },
          {
          'name':  'Dew_PointC',
          'type':  'FLOAT'
          },
```

```
                {
                'name':   'MeanDew_PointC',
                'type':   'FLOAT'
                },
                {
                'name':   'Max_Humidity',
                'type':   'FLOAT'
                },
                {
                'name':   'Mean_Humidity',
                'type':   'FLOAT'
                },
                {
                'name':   'Min_Humidity',
                'type':   'FLOAT'
                },
                {
                'name':   'Max_Sea_Level_PressurehPa',
                'type':   'FLOAT'
                },
                {
                'name':   'Mean_Sea_Level_PressurehPa',
                'type':   'FLOAT'
                },
                {
                'name':   'Min_Sea_Level_PressurehPa',
                'type':   'FLOAT'
                },
                {
                'name':   'Max_VisibilityKm',
                'type':   'FLOAT'
                },
                {
                'name':   'Mean_VisibilityKm',
                'type':   'FLOAT'
                },
                {
                'name':   'Min_VisibilitykM',
                'type':   'FLOAT'
                },
                {
                'name':   'Max_Wind_SpeedKmph',
                'type':   'FLOAT'
                },
                {
                'name':   'Mean_Wind_SpeedKmph',
                'type':   'FLOAT'
                },
                {
                'name':   'Max_Gust_SpeedKmph',
                'type':   'FLOAT'
                },
                {
                'name':   'Precipitationmm',
```

```
               'type':    'FLOAT'
            },
            {
               'name':    'CloudCover',
               'type':    'FLOAT'
            },
            {
               'name':    'Events',
               'type':    'FLOAT'
            },
            {
               'name':    'WindDirDegrees',
               'type':    'FLOAT'
            }

         ]
      },
      'destinationTable':   {
         'projectId':   PROJECT_ID,
         'datasetId':   DATASET_ID,
         'tableId':   TABLE_ID
      }
    }
  }
}

insertResponse = bigquery_service.jobs().insert(projectId=PROJECT_ID,
   body=job_data).execute(num_retries=5)

print insertResponse

while True:
  job = bigquery_service.jobs().get(projectId=PROJECT_ID,
  jobId=insertResponse['jobReference']['jobId']).execute()
  print job['status']['state']
  if 'DONE' == job['status']['state']:
    print 'Done!'
    break

  print 'Loading data...'
  time.sleep(10)
```

Box 9.8 shows the Python program for querying a dataset with BigQuery. The *jobs().query*
method of the Google BigQuery API is used for querying the dataset. This method runs a
BigQuery SQL query synchronously and returns query results.

■ Box 9.8: Python program for querying a dataset with BigQuery

```
import json
import uuid
from googleapiclient.discovery import build
from oauth2client.client import GoogleCredentials
```

```
credentials = GoogleCredentials.get_application_default()
bigquery_service = build('bigquery', 'v2', credentials=credentials)

PROJECT_ID = 'mycloud'

query_data = {'query':'SELECT EST, Precipitationmm
FROM [wud.weather] ORDER BY Precipitationmm DESC LIMIT 10 ;'}

query_response = bigquery_service.jobs().query(projectId=PROJECT_ID,
body=query_data).execute()

print query_response

print 'Query Results:'
for row in query_response['rows']:
  result_row = []
  for field in row['f']:
    result_row.append(field['v'])
  print ('').join(result_row)
```

Summary

In this chapter, we described tools and frameworks for interactive querying of big data including Spark SQL, Hive, Google BigQuery and Amazon RedShift, along with examples of querying. Spark SQL is a component of Spark which enables interactive querying. Spark SQL is useful for querying structured and semi-structured data using SQL-like queries. Hive is a data warehousing framework built on top of Hadoop. Hive provides an SQL-like query language called Hive Query Language, for querying data residing in HDFS. Amazon Redshift is a fast, massive-scale managed data warehouse service. Redshift specializes in handling queries on datasets of sizes up to a petabyte or more through the use of a Massively Parallel Processing (MPP) architecture, which parallelizes SQL queries across all resources in the Redshift cluster. Google BigQuery allows querying datasets using SQL-like queries. The BigQuery queries are run against append-only tables that use the processing power of Google's infrastructure for speeding up queries.

10 - Serving Databases & Web Frameworks

This chapter covers

- Serving Databases - SQL and NoSQL
- MySQL
- DynamoDB
- MongoDB
- Cassandra
- Python Web Framework - Django

In the first part of this chapter, we describe various options for serving databases for big data applications. A comparison of the relational and non-relational NoSQL databases for this purpose is provided. Implementation examples of various databases are also provided. In the second part of the chapter, we describe the Django Python web framework which can be used for developing web applications to present the analysis results to the users.

10.1   Relational (SQL) Databases

A relational database is a database that conforms to the relational model that was popularized by IBM's Edgar Codd in 1970 [34]. A relational database has a collection of relations (or tables). A relation is a set of tuples (or rows). Each relation has a fixed schema that defines the set of attributes (or columns in a table) and the constraints on the attributes. Each tuple in a relation has the same attributes (columns). The tuples in a relation can have any order and the relation is not sensitive to the ordering of the tuples. Each attribute has a domain, which is the set of possible values for the attribute. Relations can be modified using insert, update and delete operations. Every relation has a primary key that uniquely identifies each tuple in the relation. An attribute can be made a primary key if it does not have repeated values in different tuples. That is, no two tuples can have the same value for the primary key attribute.

A relational database has various constraints described as follows:

- **Domain Constraint:** Domain constraints restrict the domain of each attribute or the set of possible values for the attribute. Domain constraints specify that the value of each attribute must be a value from the domain of the attribute.
- **Entity Integrity Constraint:** Entity integrity constraint states that no primary key value can be null. Since primary key is used to identify uniquely each tuple in a relation, having a null value for a primary key value will make it impossible to identify tuples in the relation.
- **Referential Integrity Constraint:** Referential integrity constraints are required to maintain consistency among the tuples in two relations. Referential integrity requires every value of one attribute of a relation to exist as a value of another attribute in another relation. In other words, tuples in a relation that refers to another relation must refer to tuples that exist in the other relation.
- **Foreign Key:** For cross-referencing between multiple relations foreign keys are used. Foreign key is a key in a relation that matches the primary key of another relation.

Relational databases support at least one comprehensive sub-language, the most popular being the Structured Query Language (SQL). Relational databases provide ACID guarantees that are a set of properties that guarantee that database transactions are processed reliably, described as follows:

- **Atomicity:** Atomicity property ensures that each transaction is either "all or nothing". In other words, an atomic transaction ensures that all parts of the transaction complete or the database state is left unchanged. Partially completed transactions in the event of system outages can lead to an invalid state. Atomicity ensures that the transaction is indivisible and is either committed or aborted.
- **Consistency:** Consistency property ensures that each transaction brings the database from one valid state to another. In other words, the data in a database always conforms to the defined schema and constraints.

Pros	Cons
Well-defined consistency model. An application that runs on one relational database (such as MySQL) can be easily changed to run on other relational databases (eg. Microsoft SQL server). The underlying model remains unchanged.	Performance is the major constraint for relational databases. The performance depends on the number of relations and the size of the relations. Scaling out relational database deployments is difficult.
Provide ACID guarantees.	Limited support for complex data structures. Eg. if the data is naturally organized in a hierarchical manner and stored as such, the hierarchical approach can allow quick analysis of data.
Relational integrity maintained through entity and referential integrity constraints.	A complete knowledge of the database structure is required to create ad hoc queries.
Well suited for Online Transaction Processing (OLTP) applications.	Most relation database systems are expensive.
Sound theoretical foundation (based on relational model) which has been tried and tested for several years. Stable and standardized databases available.	Some relational databases have limits on the size of the fields.
The database design and normalization steps are well defined and the underlying structure is well understood.	Integrating data from multiple relational database systems can be cumbersome.

Table 10.1: Pros and Cons of relational databases

- **Isolation:** Isolation property ensures that the database state obtained after a set of concurrent transactions is the same as would have been if the transactions were executed serially. This provides concurrency control, i.e. the results of incomplete transactions are not visible to other transactions. The transactions are isolated from each other until they finish.
- **Durability:** Durability property ensures that once a transaction is committed, the data remains as it is, i.e. it is not affected by system outages such as power loss. Durability guarantees that the database can keep track of changes and can recover from abnormal terminations.

Table 10.1 lists some pros and cons of relational databases.

10.1.1 MySQL

MySQL is an open source Relational Database Management System (RDBMS). MySQL is one of the most widely used RDBMS and a good choice to be a serving database for data analytics applications where the data is structured.

Let us look at an example of using MySQL for a reference application that maintains a record of employees in a company. Figure 10.1 shows the Entity-relationship (ER) diagram for the reference application which graphically represents the entities and their relationships to each other. The ER diagram shows three entities - Employee, Department and Project. Note that a one-to-one relationship exists between Employee and Department entities, whereas a many-to-many relationship exists between Employee and Project.

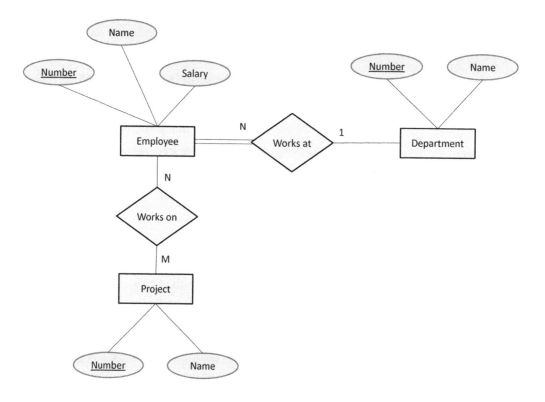

Figure 10.1: Entity-relationship (ER) diagram for the reference application

To map the ER model represented in the ER diagram to a relation model we follow the following rules:

- For each regular entity in the ER model, create a relation (table).
- Make the attributes of the entity as the attributes of the table (or columns in a table). Choose one of the key attributes of the entity as the primary key for the relation.
- For 1:1 relationship between two entities (say P and Q), include as a foreign key in one of the relations, say the relation for entity P, the primary key of the other relation Q.
- For 1:N relationship between two entities (say R and S), include as a foreign key in relation for entity S (where S is the entity on the N side of the relationship), the primary key of relation for entity R.
- For a M:N relationship between two entities (say U and V), create a new relation and in that relation include as foreign keys, the primary keys of the relations for entities U and V. If the M:N relationship has any simple attributes, include those as well in the new relation.

Following the above rules, we come up with the relations (tables) and their attributes (columns in the tables). Box 10.1 shows the 'CREATE TABLE' SQL statements for creating the tables.

■ **Box 10.1: SQL statements for creating tables**

```
CREATE TABLE department (
number varchar(50) NOT NULL PRIMARY KEY,
name varchar(200) NULL
);

CREATE TABLE employee (
number varchar(100) NOT NULL PRIMARY KEY,
name varchar(100) NOT NULL,
salary varchar(20) NOT NULL,
department_id varchar(20) REFERENCES department (number),
);

CREATE TABLE project (
number varchar(20) NOT NULL PRIMARY KEY,
name varchar(100) NOT NULL
);

CREATE TABLE workson (
id INT(6) UNSIGNED AUTO_INCREMENT PRIMARY KEY,
employee_id varchar(20) NOT NULL REFERENCES employee (number),
project_id varchar(20) NOT NULL REFERENCES project (number)
);
```

After creating the tables, data can be inserted into the tables using the 'INSERT INTO' SQL statements as shown in Box 10.2.

■ **Box 10.2: SQL statements for inserting data into tables**

```
INSERT INTO department VALUES ("1001", "ECE");

INSERT INTO employee (number, name,
salary,department_id) VALUES ("5001",
"Alex", "50000", "1001");

INSERT INTO project VALUES ("201", "Cloud");

INSERT INTO workson(employee_id,project_id)
VALUES ("5001", "201");
```

Finally, the data can be queried using the SELECT statements as shown in Box 10.3.

■ **Box 10.3: SQL statements for querying tables**

```
# Retrieve all employees
SELECT * FROM employee;

# Retrieve top 3 employees with highest salary
SELECT * FROM employee ORDER BY salary DESC LIMIT 3;
```

```
# Retrieve all employees in department 'ECE'
SELECT e.name, e.number, d.name FROM
employee e, department d WHERE d.name='ECE' ;

# Count the number of employees working on 'IoT' project
SELECT COUNT(*) FROM project p, workson w WHERE p.name='IoT' ;
```

10.2   Non-Relational (NoSQL) Databases

In Chapter-4, we described various types of Non-Relational (NoSQL) databases. Unlike relational databases, NoSQL databases do not provide ACID guarantees. Most NoSQL databases offer 'eventual' consistency, which means that given a sufficiently long period of time over which no updates are made, all updates can be expected to propagate eventually through the system and the replicas will be consistent. Some authors have referred to the term BASE (Basically Available, Soft state, Eventual consistency) guarantees for NoSQL databases as opposed to ACID guarantees provided by relational databases.

Pros	Cons
Easy to scale-out. Higher performance for massive scale data as compared to relational databases. Allows sharing of data across multiple servers.	Do not provide ACID guarantees, therefore less suitable for applications such as transaction processing that require strong consistency.
Most solutions are either open-source or cheaper as compared to relational databases.	No fixed schema. There is no common data storage model. Different solutions have different data storage models.
High availability and fault tolerance provided by data replication.	Limited support for aggregation (SUM, AVG, COUNT, GROUP BY) as compared to relational databases.
Support complex data structures and native programming objects.	Performance for complex joins is poor as compared to relational databases.
No fixed schema. Support unstructured data.	No well defined approach for database design, since different solutions have different data storage models.
Very fast retrieval of data. Suitable for real-time applications.	Lack of a consistent model can lead to solution lock-in, i.e., migrating from one solution to other may require significant remodeling of the application.
Most solutions provide support for MapReduce programming model for processing massive scale data.	

Table 10.2: Pros and Cons of non-relational databases

The driving force behind the NoSQL databases is the need for databases that can achieve the performance-related measures of high scalability, fault tolerance, and availability. These databases can be distributed on a large cluster of machines. Fault tolerance is provided by storing multiple replicas of data on different machines. For, example with a replication factor set equal to N for a NoSQL database, each record has N replicas on different machines. Table 10.2 lists some pros and cons of non-relational databases.

10.2.1 Amazon DynamoDB

We described Amazon DynamoDB in Chapter-4. In this section, we will describe an example of using DynamoDB for a reference application that retrieves and stores weather data for different cities. The first step is to create a DynamoDB table from the DynamoDB dashboard as shown Figure 10.2. A DynamoDB table can either have a simple primary key which is composed of a hash attribute (or partition key) or a composite primary key which is composed of a hash attribute and a range attribute (or sort key). The hash attribute is used to build an unordered hash index and the range attribute is used to build an ordered range index.

Figure 10.2: Creating DynamoDB table - step-1

In the next step, you can specify additional indexes as shown in Figure 10.3. DynamoDB gives the option to define one or more secondary indexes on a table. Two types of secondary indexes are supported - global secondary index and local secondary index. A global secondary index can be created with hash and range key attributes which are different from the primary key. Whereas a local secondary index can be created from the same hash attribute as for the primary key but a different range attribute.

In the next step, you can specify the provisioned throughput capacity as shown in Figure 10.4. DynamoDB provides a consistent and predictable performance by allowing the users to specify the provisioned throughput capacity while creating or updating a table. The provisioned throughput is defined in terms of read and write capacity units. A read

Create Table
                                                                          Cancel ⊠

PRIMARY KEY   ADD INDEXES   PROVISIONED   ADDITIONAL OPTIONS   SUMMARY
                    (optional)   THROUGHPUT CAPACITY   (optional)

Add Indexes (optional)

An index is a data structure that maintains an alternate hash and range key. You can use it to Query an item the same way you use the table hash and range key. ⓘ

Index Type:*	Global Secondary Index ▼ ⓘ
Index Hash Key:*	● String ○ Number ○ Binary [ ] ⓘ
Index Range Key:	● String ○ Number ○ Binary [ ] ⓘ
Index Name:*	[ ] ⓘ
Projected Attributes:*	All Attributes ▼ ⓘ
	[Add Index To Table]

Table Indexes

Index Type	Index Hash Key	Index Range Key	Index Name	Projected Attributes	
		No Indexes exist. Enter values and click 'Add Index To Table' to create one.			

> ⚠ Local Secondary Indexes can only be defined at table creation time, and cannot be removed or modified later. Global Secondary Indexes can be defined at table creation time, or later. Please see Secondary Indexes, Global Index Guidelines, and Local Index Guidelines for more information and other considerations.

Back   [Continue ▷]   Help ⧉

Figure 10.3: Creating DynamoDB table - step-2

capacity unit is one strongly consistent read or two eventually consistent reads per second for items as large as 4 KB. A write capacity unit represents one write per second for items as large as 1 KB. For example, if you want to read 100 items per seconds (where each item is up to 4 KB in size), a read capacity of 100 must be provisioned. For items larger than 4 KB, the read capacity is calculated by rounding up to the next multiple of 4. For example, to read 100 items per second where each item is of 6 KB, a read capacity of 200 must be provisioned. Similarly, for writes, if an item is greater than 1 KB, the write capacity is calculated by rounding up to the next 1 KB. In the next step, you can specify any throughput alarm notifications for the table as shown in Figure 10.5.

For the reference weather data application we will use the PyOwm Python library to fetch data from OpenWeatherMap (OWM) [35]. OpenWeatherMap is an online service that provides a free API for weather data. Box 10.4 shows the Python code for fetching the current weather data and weather forecast for a list of cities and writing the data to DynamoDB tables. In this example, a connection is first established with DynamoDB service and a handle to an existing table is retrieved. To write data to DynamoDB, the *table.put_item* function is used.

■ **Box 10.4: Python program for retrieving weather data and writing to DynamoDB**

```
import pyowm
import boto.dynamodb2
from boto.dynamodb2.table import Table
import time
from datetime import date
import datetime
```

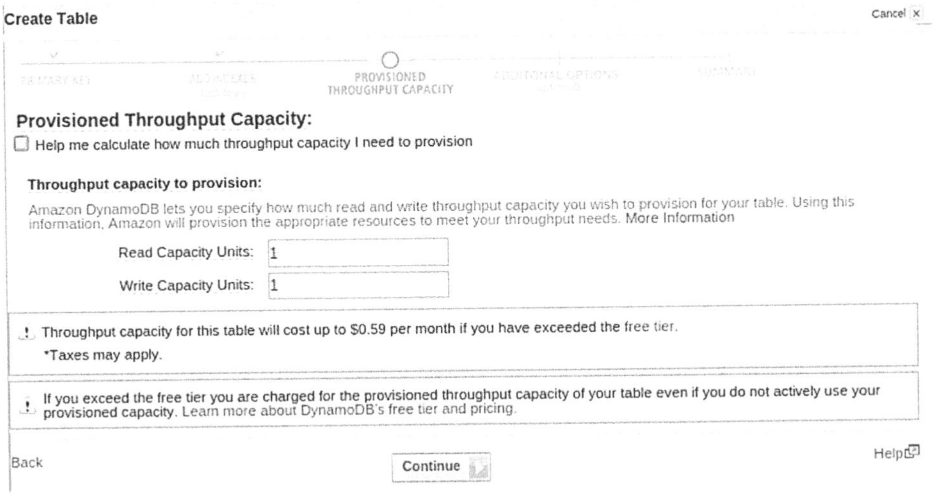

Create Table   Cancel ✕

○
PROVISIONED
THROUGHPUT CAPACITY

Provisioned Throughput Capacity:

☐ Help me calculate how much throughput capacity I need to provision

Throughput capacity to provision:

Amazon DynamoDB lets you specify how much read and write throughput capacity you wish to provision for your table. Using this information, Amazon will provision the appropriate resources to meet your throughput needs. More Information

Read Capacity Units: `1`

Write Capacity Units: `1`

⚠ Throughput capacity for this table will cost up to $0.59 per month if you have exceeded the free tier.

   *Taxes may apply.

ℹ If you exceed the free tier you are charged for the provisioned throughput capacity of your table even if you do not actively use your provisioned capacity. Learn more about DynamoDB's free tier and pricing.

Back   Continue   Help

Figure 10.4: Creating DynamoDB table - step-3

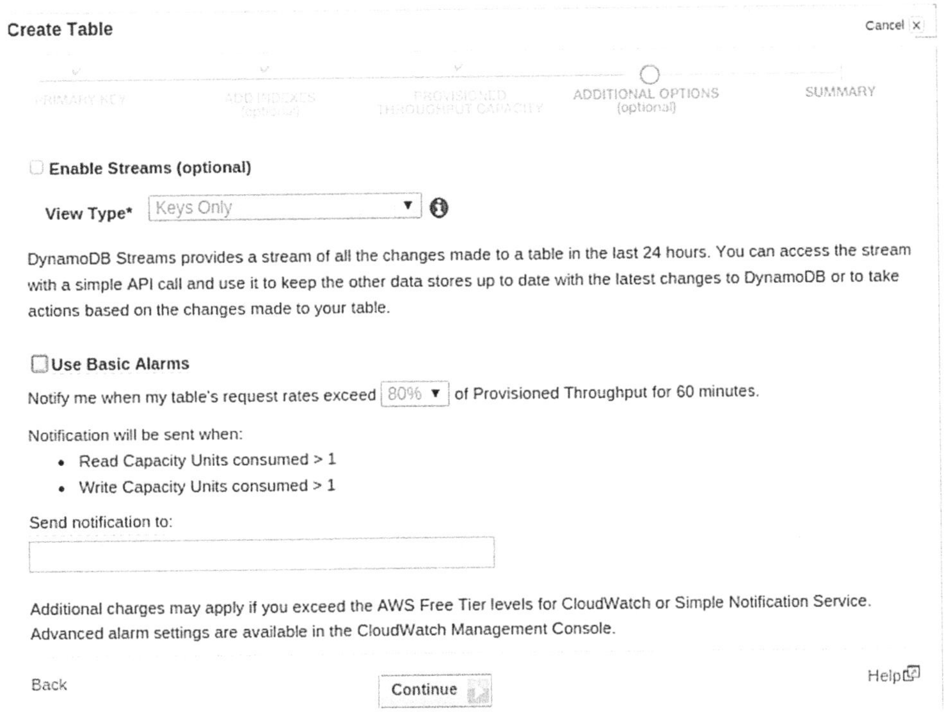

Create Table   Cancel ✕

○
ADDITIONAL OPTIONS
(optional)

PRIMARY KEY   ADD INDEXES   PROVISIONED   ADDITIONAL OPTIONS   SUMMARY
                   (optional)   THROUGHPUT CAPACITY   (optional)

☐ **Enable Streams (optional)**

View Type* `Keys Only ▼` ℹ

DynamoDB Streams provides a stream of all the changes made to a table in the last 24 hours. You can access the stream with a simple API call and use it to keep the other data stores up to date with the latest changes to DynamoDB or to take actions based on the changes made to your table.

☐ **Use Basic Alarms**

Notify me when my table's request rates exceed `80% ▼` of Provisioned Throughput for 60 minutes.

Notification will be sent when:
- Read Capacity Units consumed > 1
- Write Capacity Units consumed > 1

Send notification to:

Additional charges may apply if you exceed the AWS Free Tier levels for CloudWatch or Simple Notification Service. Advanced alarm settings are available in the CloudWatch Management Console.

Back   Continue   Help

Figure 10.5: Creating DynamoDB table - step-4

```
import cPickle

PYOWM_KEY='<enter>'
owm = pyowm.OWM(PYOWM_KEY)

REGION="us-east-1"
```

```python
print "Connecting to DynamoDB"

conn = boto.dynamodb2.connect_to_region(REGION,
aws_access_key_id='<enter>',
aws_secret_access_key='<enter>')


table=Table('weather',connection=conn)


places=['New York,US', 'Los Angeles,US',
  'Chicago,US', 'Houston,US', 'Philadelphia,US',
  'Phoenix,US', 'San Antonio,US', 'San Diego,US',
  'Dallas,US', 'San Jose,US']

for place in places:
 print place
 observation = owm.weather_at_place(place)
 w= observation.get_weather()

 item = table.put_item(data={
   'city':place,
   'time':  str(w.get_reference_time(timeformat='iso')),
   'currentTemperature':  str(w.get_temperature(unit='celsius')['temp']),
   'weatherStatus':  str(w.get_detailed_status()),
   'cloudCoverage':  str(w.get_clouds()),
   'rainVolume':  str(w.get_rain()),
   'windSpeed':  str(w.get_wind()['speed']),
   'humidity':  str(w.get_humidity()),
   'pressure':  str(w.get_pressure()['press'])
 })


forecastTable=Table('forecast',connection=conn)

for place in places:
 print place
 fc = owm.daily_forecast(place, limit=7)
 f = fc.get_forecast()
 forecast_list=[]
 for w in f.get_weathers():
  forecast_dict={}
  t=w.get_reference_time()
  forecast_dict['date'] =
  datetime.datetime.fromtimestamp(t).strftime('%Y-%m-%d')
  forecast_dict['tempMin']= w.get_temperature(unit='celsius')['min']
  forecast_dict['tempMax']= w.get_temperature(unit='celsius')['max']

  rain= w.get_rain()
  if rain.has_key('all'):
   forecast_dict['rain'] = rain['all']
  else:
   forecast_dict['rain'] = 0
```

```
    forecast_dict['status']= w.get_detailed_status()
    forecast_list.append(forecast_dict)

item = forecastTable.put_item(data={
  'city':place,
  'forecastList':  cPickle.dumps(forecast_list)
},overwrite=True)
```

Box 10.5 shows the Python example for reading data from DynamoDB. DynamoDB supports two types of read operations - Query and Scan. Query operation allows you to query a table by providing a hash key attribute name and value. Additionally, a range key attribute and value can be specified along with a comparison operator to refine the results. The Scan operation can be used to read all the items in a table.

■ **Box 10.5: Python program for reading data from DynamoDB**

```
import boto.dynamodb2
from boto.dynamodb2.table import Table

REGION="us-east-1"

conn = boto.dynamodb2.connect_to_region(REGION,
aws_access_key_id='<enter>',
aws_secret_access_key='<enter>')

table=Table('weather',connection=conn)

#Scan table
all_items=table.scan()

for item in all_items:
 print item.items()

#Query for a particular city
results = table.query_2(city__eq='New York,US')

for r in results:
 print r['time']
 print r['currentTemperature']
 print r['weatherStatus']
 print r['pressure']
 print r['humidity']
 print r['windSpeed']
 print r['rainVolume']
 print r['cloudCoverage']
```

Figures 10.6 and 10.7 show examples of scanning and querying a DynamoDB table from the DynamoDB dashboard.

city	time	cloudCoverage	currentTemperature	humidity	pressure	rainVolume	weatherStatus	windSpeed
Chicago,US	2015-10-13 06:40:26+00	90	11.92	50	1001	0	overcast clouds	6.2
Chicago,US	2015-10-13 06:48:10+00	90	11.95	50	1002	0	overcast clouds	5.1
New York,US	2015-10-13 06:36:35+00	75	12.99	77	1006	0	mist	2.1
New York,US	2015-10-13 06:58:33+00	1	13.05	87	1005	0	mist	1.75
San Antonio,US	2015-10-13 06:40:28+00	1	25.83	57	1012	0	clear sky	2.75
San Antonio,US	2015-10-13 06:55:00+00	1	25.55	88	1012	0	clear sky	2.1
Dallas,US	2015-10-13 06:39:49+00	1	20.81	27	1014	0	clear sky	3.1
Dallas,US	2015-10-13 06:56:36+00	1	20.6	37	1014	0	clear sky	3.1
Los Angeles,US	2015-10-13 06:41:22+00	1	26.93	39	1013	0	clear sky	1.5
Los Angeles,US	2015-10-13 06:49:13+00	1	26.99	39	1013	0	clear sky	1.5

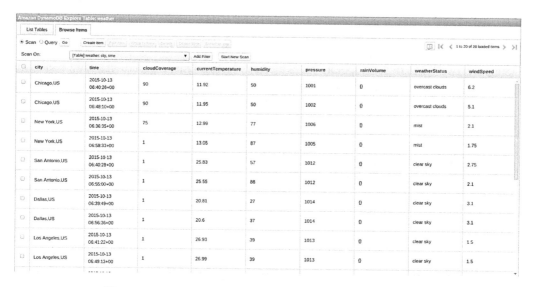

Figure 10.6: Scanning table from DynamoDB Dashboard

city	time	cloudCoverage	currentTemperature	humidity	pressure	rainVolume	weatherStatus	windSpeed
Dallas,US	2015-10-13 06:39:49+00	1	20.81	27	1014	0	clear sky	3.1
Dallas,US	2015-10-13 06:56:36+00	1	20.6	37	1014	0	clear sky	3.1

Figure 10.7: Querying table from DynamoDB Dashboard

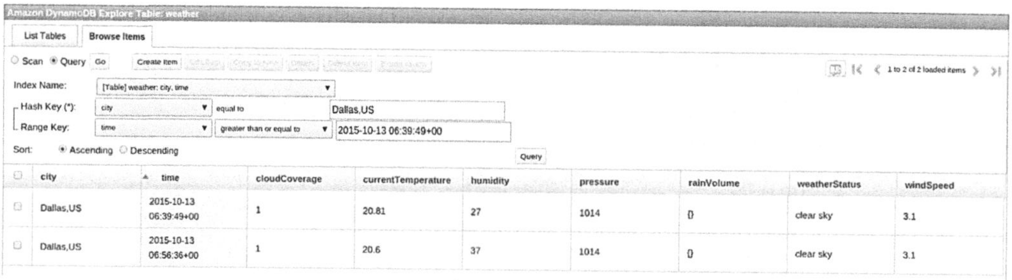

10.2.2 Cassandra

Cassandra is a scalable, highly available, fault tolerant open source non-relational database system. Cassandra has a distributed, decentralized and peer-to-peer architecture where all the nodes have the same role. The data stored is replicated across multiple nodes in a cluster and the database performance can scale linearly by the addition of new nodes. The Cassandra data model is similar to the HBase model described in Chapter-4. The basic unit of data storage is a *Column* which has a name, value and timestamp. A *Row* has multiple columns and is identified by a unique row key. A *ColumnFamily* has multiple rows and is analogous to a table in a relational database. Different rows in a ColumnFamily can have different sets of columns, and columns can be added anytime. A *Keyspace* in Cassandra is analogous to a database in a relational database system. Keyspace contains operational elements such as the replication strategy and replication factor.

Box 10.6 shows the commands for setting up and running Cassandra.

■ **Box 10.6: Setting up Cassandra**

```
#Download Cassandra distribution
wget http://www.eu.apache.org/dist/cassandra/2.1.10/
apache-cassandra-2.1.10-bin.tar.gz
tar -xzf apache-cassandra-2.1.10-bin.tar.gz
cd apache-cassandra-2.1.10

#Run Cassandra
bin/cassandra -f

#Run CQL shell
bin/cqlsh
```

Cassandra provides a query language called Cassandra Query Language (CQL) which is similar to SQL. The CQL shell can be used to interact with Cassandra.

In this section, we will describe an example of using Cassandra for the reference weather data application. Box 10.7 shows the CQL statements for creating tables for storing current weather data and weather forecasts.

■ **Box 10.7: Creating Cassandra tables**

```
#Create keyspace
CREATE KEYSPACE weatherkeyspace
WITH REPLICATION = { 'class' : 'SimpleStrategy', 'replication_factor' :
1 };

#Use keyspace
USE weatherkeyspace;

#Create tables
CREATE TABLE weathernew (
  city text,
  time text,
  currentTemperature float,
```

```
  weatherStatus text,
  cloudCoverage text,
  rainVolume text,
  windSpeed float,
  humidity float,
  pressure float,
  PRIMARY KEY (city, time)
);


CREATE TABLE forecast (
  city text,
  forecastList text,
  PRIMARY KEY (city)
);
```

Box 10.8 shows Python code for fetching the current weather data and weather forecast for a list of cities and writing the data to Cassandra tables.

■ Box 10.8: Python program for retrieving weather data and writing to Cassandra

```
import pyowm
import time
from datetime import date
import datetime
import cPickle
from cassandra.cluster import Cluster

PYOWM_KEY='<enter>'
owm = pyowm.OWM(PYOWM_KEY)

## create Cassandra instance
cluster = Cluster()

## establish Cassandra connection, using local default
session = cluster.connect('weatherkeyspace')
places=['New York,US', 'Los Angeles,US', 'Chicago,US',
'Houston,US', 'Philadelphia,US', 'Phoenix,US',
'San Antonio,US', 'San Diego,US', 'Dallas,US', 'San Jose,US']

for place in places:
 print place
 observation = owm.weather_at_place(place)
 w= observation.get_weather()

 rain= w.get_rain()
 if rain.has_key('all'):
  rainVolume = rain['all']
 else:
  rainVolume = 0


 statement="INSERT INTO weathernew (city, time,
  currentTemperature, weatherStatus, cloudCoverage,
```

```
         rainVolume, windSpeed, humidity, pressure) VALUES('" +
    str(place)+"', '"+ str(w.get_reference_time(timeformat='iso'))+
    "', "+ str(w.get_temperature(unit='celsius')['temp'])+", '"+
    str(w.get_detailed_status())+"', '"+ str(w.get_clouds())+"', '"+
    str(rainVolume) +"', "+ str(w.get_wind()['speed'])+", "+
    str(w.get_humidity())+", "+ str(w.get_pressure()['press'])+")"

    session.execute(statement)

for place in places:
  print place
  fc = owm.daily_forecast(place, limit=7)
  f = fc.get_forecast()
  forecast_list=[]
  for w in f.get_weathers():
   forecast_dict={}
   t=w.get_reference_time()
   forecast_dict['date'] =
   datetime.datetime.fromtimestamp(t).strftime('%Y-%m-%d')
   forecast_dict['tempMin']= w.get_temperature(unit='celsius')['min']
   forecast_dict['tempMax']= w.get_temperature(unit='celsius')['max']

   rain= w.get_rain()
   if rain.has_key('all'):
     forecast_dict['rain'] = rain['all']
   else:
     forecast_dict['rain'] = 0
   forecast_dict['status']= w.get_detailed_status()
   forecast_list.append(forecast_dict)

  statement="INSERT INTO forecast (city, forecastList)
   VALUES('"+str(place)+"', '"+
   cPickle.dumps(forecast_list).encode("hex") +"')"

  session.execute(statement)
```

Figure 10.8 shows a screenshot of a query executed in CQL shell.

```
cqlsh:weatherkeyspace> SELECT * FROM weather;

 city            | time                | cloudcoverage | currenttemperature | humidity | pressure | rainvolume | weatherstatus           | windspeed
-----------------+---------------------+---------------+--------------------+----------+----------+------------+-------------------------+----------
      Dallas,US  | 2015-10-16 08:23:01+00 |            20 |              22.23 |       38 |     1020 |          0 |              few clouds |       2.1
      Dallas,US  | 2015-10-16 09:59:50+00 |             1 |              21.15 |       43 |     1022 |          0 |               clear sky |       7.2
     Phoenix,US  | 2015-10-16 08:20:50+00 |             1 |              26.79 |       37 |     1013 |          0 |               clear sky |       2.5
     Phoenix,US  | 2015-10-16 09:56:45+00 |             1 |              25.79 |       34 |     1013 |          0 |               clear sky |       1.5
    New York,US  | 2015-10-16 08:19:31+00 |            75 |              10.41 |       71 |     1013 |          0 |            broken clouds |       3.6
    New York,US  | 2015-10-16 09:50:11+00 |            40 |              10.43 |       71 |     1013 |          0 |          scattered clouds |       2.6
   San Diego,US  | 2015-10-16 08:20:22+00 |            90 |              21.84 |       88 |     1013 |          0 |                    mist |       2.6
   San Diego,US  | 2015-10-16 09:55:20+00 |            90 |              21.56 |       88 |     1013 |          0 | light intensity drizzle |       2.6
 San Antonio,US  | 2015-10-16 08:24:58+00 |             1 |              17.64 |       77 |     1021 |          0 |               clear sky |       1.5
 San Antonio,US  | 2015-10-16 08:25:13+00 |            40 |              17.07 |       82 |     1021 |          0 |          scattered clouds |       2.1
 Los Angeles,US  | 2015-10-16 08:25:13+00 |            20 |              19.91 |       83 |     1013 |          0 |              few clouds |       2.6
 Los Angeles,US  | 2015-10-16 09:59:08+00 |            75 |              19.92 |       88 |     1013 |          0 |                    mist |         1
     Chicago,US  | 2015-10-16 08:21:29+00 |             1 |               5.98 |       61 |     1021 |          0 |               clear sky |       3.6
     Chicago,US  | 2015-10-16 09:54:23+00 |             1 |               6.04 |       52 |     1022 |          0 |               clear sky |       3.1
     Houston,US  | 2015-10-16 08:20:23+00 |             1 |              17.04 |       88 |     1019 |          0 |                     fog |       1.4
     Houston,US  | 2015-10-16 09:57:16+00 |             1 |              16.33 |       88 |     1019 |          0 |                     fog |       1.4
Philadelphia,US  | 2015-10-16 08:18:25+00 |            20 |               8.84 |       87 |     1014 |          0 |              few clouds |      4.55
Philadelphia,US  | 2015-10-16 09:52:39+00 |             0 |               0.92 |       87 |     1014 |          0 |               clear sky |       1.5
    San Jose,US  | 2015-10-16 08:14:35+00 |             1 |              16.28 |       82 |     1014 |          0 |               clear sky |       2.6
    San Jose,US  | 2015-10-16 09:49:21+00 |             1 |              16.74 |       82 |     1015 |          0 |               clear sky |      0.75

(20 rows)
```

Figure 10.8: Querying Cassandra table from CQL shell

10.2.3 MongoDB

We described MongoDB in Chapter-4. In this section, we will describe an example of using MongoDB for the reference weather data application. MongoDB provides a shell which can be used for performing various database operations. Box 10.9 shows some examples of various database operations using the MongoDB shell.

■ Box 10.9: Using MongoDB shell commands

```
#Launch MongoDB shell
mongo localhost:27017


#Switch to new database named weatherdb
> use weatherdb
switched to db weatherdb


#Insert a document
> post = {
  "city" :  "New York,US",
  "windSpeed" :  "5.7",
  "currentTemperature" :  "12.01",
  "time" :  "2015-10-23 09:15:00+00",
  "cloudCoverage" :  "20",
  "rainVolume" :  "{u'1h': 0.25}",
  "humidity" :  "54",
  "pressure" :  "1021",
  "weatherStatus" :  "light rain"
}
> db.collection.insert(post)
WriteResult({ "nInserted" :  1 })

# Retrieve all documents
> db.collection.find()
{ "_id" :  ObjectId("5629fee545c8be72b82fc60e"), "city" :  "New York,US",
"windSpeed" :  "5.7", "currentTemperature" :  "12.01",
"time" :  "2015-10-23 09:15:00+00", "cloudCoverage" :  "20",
"rainVolume" :  "{u'1h': 0.25}", "humidity" :  "54",
"pressure" :  "1021", "weatherStatus" :  "light rain" }

{ "_id" :  ObjectId("5629ff4d45c8be72b82fc60f"), "city" :  "Chicago,US",
"windSpeed" :  "4.6", "currentTemperature" :  "10.98",
"time" :  "2015-10-23 09:01:04+00", "cloudCoverage" :  "90",
"rainVolume" :  "{}", "humidity" :  "66", "pressure" :  "1024",
"weatherStatus" :  "overcast clouds" }

# Retrieve documents matching the query
> db.collection.find({"city" :  "New York,US"})
{ "_id" :  ObjectId("5629fee545c8be72b82fc60e"), "city" :  "New York,US",
"windSpeed" :  "5.7", "currentTemperature" :  "12.01",
"time" :  "2015-10-23 09:15:00+00", "cloudCoverage" :  "20",
"rainVolume" :  "{u'1h': 0.25}", "humidity" :  "54",
"pressure" :  "1021", "weatherStatus" :  "light rain" }

#Show current database name
```

```
> db
weatherdb

#Show collections in the database
> show collections
collection
system.indexes
```

Box 10.10 shows the Python code for fetching the current weather data and weather forecast for a list of cities and writing the data to MongoDB.

■ **Box 10.10: Python program for retrieving weather data and writing to MongoDB**

```
import pyowm
import time
from datetime import date
import datetime
import cPickle
from pymongo import MongoClient

PYOWM_KEY='<enter>'
owm = pyowm.OWM(PYOWM_KEY)

client = MongoClient('mongodb://root:password@hostname:53688/weather')
db = client['weather']
weather_collection = db['current']
forecast_collection = db['forecast']


places=['New York,US','Los Angeles,US',
'Chicago,US','Houston,US', 'Philadelphia,US',
'Phoenix,US', 'San Antonio,US','San Diego,US',
'Dallas,US','San Jose,US']

for place in places:
 print place
 observation = owm.weather_at_place(place)
 w= observation.get_weather()

 item = {
  'city':place,
  'time':  str(w.get_reference_time(timeformat='iso')),
  'currentTemperature':  str(w.get_temperature(unit='celsius')['temp']),
  'weatherStatus':  str(w.get_detailed_status()),
  'cloudCoverage':  str(w.get_clouds()),
  'rainVolume':  str(w.get_rain()),
  'windSpeed':  str(w.get_wind()['speed']),
  'humidity':  str(w.get_humidity()),
  'pressure':  str(w.get_pressure()['press'])
 }

 weather_collection.insert_one(item)
```

```
for place in places:
 print place
 fc = owm.daily_forecast(place, limit=7)
 f = fc.get_forecast()
 forecast_list=[]
 for w in f.get_weathers():
  forecast_dict={}
  t=w.get_reference_time()
  forecast_dict['date'] =
  datetime.datetime.fromtimestamp(t).strftime('%Y-%m-%d')
  forecast_dict['tempMin']= w.get_temperature(unit='celsius')['min']
  forecast_dict['tempMax']= w.get_temperature(unit='celsius')['max']

  rain= w.get_rain()
  if rain.has_key('all'):
   forecast_dict['rain'] = rain['all']
  else:
   forecast_dict['rain'] = 0
  forecast_dict['status']= w.get_detailed_status()
  forecast_list.append(forecast_dict)

 item = {
  'city':place,
  'forecastList':  forecast_list
 }

 forecast_collection.insert_one(item)
```

10.3   Python Web Application Framework - Django

Django is an open source web application framework for developing web applications in
Python [61]. A web application framework, in general, is a collection of solutions, packages
and best practices that allow development of web applications and dynamic websites. Django
is based on the Model-Template-View architecture and provides a separation of the data
model from the business rules and the user interface. Django provides a unified API to
a database backend. Thus, web applications built with Django can work with different
databases without requiring any code changes. Django consists of an object-relational
mapper, a web templating system, and a regular-expression-based URL dispatcher.

   Given the separation of the models, views and templates, flexibility to use different
databases, combined with the powerful capabilities of the Python language and the Python
ecosystem, Django is one of the most suitable web application frameworks for big data
analytics and cloud applications.

10.3.1   Django Architecture

Django adopts a Model-Template-View (MTV) architecture. The roles of model, template
and view are as follows:

Model
The model acts as a definition of stored data and handles the interactions with the database.
A Django model is a Python class that outlines the variables and methods for a particular

type of data.

Template

In a typical Django web application, the template is simply an HTML page with a few extra placeholders. Django's template language can be used to create various forms of text files (XML, email, CSS, Javascript, CSV, etc.)

View

The view ties the model to the template. The view is where you write the code that generates the web pages. View determines what data is to be displayed, retrieves the data from the database and passes the data to the template.

For describing the implementation of the model, template and view components of a Django application we will use a reference application that maintains a record of employees in a company. The ER diagram for the application for the reference application was described earlier in the chapter.

10.3.2   Starting Development with Django

Django can be installed with the following commands:

```
# Installing Django
sudo apt-get install python-pip
sudo pip install Django==1.8.5
```

In this section, you will learn how to start developing web applications with Django.

Creating a Django Project and App

Box 10.11 provides the commands for creating a Django project and an application within a project.

When you create a new Django project the following files are created:
- __init__.py: This file tells Python that this folder is a Python package
- manage.py: This file contains an array of functions for managing the project
- settings.py: This file contains the project settings
- urls.py: This file contains the URL patterns that map URLs to pages

A Django project can have multiple applications. Apps are where you write the code that makes your web application function. Each project can have multiple apps and each app can be part of multiple projects.

When a new application is created a new directory for the application is created which has multiple files including:
- model.py: This file contains the description of the models for the application
- views.py: This file contains the application views

■ Box 10.11: Creating a new Django project and an app in the project

```
#Create a new project
django-admin.py startproject myproject
```

```
#Create an application within the project
python mangage.py startapp myapp

#Starting development server
python manage.py runserver

#Django uses port 8000 by default
#The project can be viewed at the URL:
#http://localhost:8000
```

Django comes with a built-in, lightweight Web server that can be used for development purposes. When the Django development server is started the default project can be viewed at the URL: http://localhost:8000.

Configuring a Database

Till now you have learned how to create a new Django project and an app within the project. Most web applications have a database backend. Developers have a wide choice of databases that can be used for web applications including both relational and non-relational databases. Django provides a unified API for database backends thus giving the freedom to choose the database. Django supports various relational database engines including MySQL, PostgreSQL, Oracle and SQLite3. Support for non-relational databases such as MongoDB can be added by installing additional engines (e.g. Django-MongoDB engine for MongoDB).

Let us look at an example of setting up a MySQL database with a Django project. The first step in setting up a database is to install and configure a database server. After installing the database, the next step is to specify the database settings in the setting.py file in the Django project.

Box 10.12 shows the commands to setup MySQL. Box 10.13 shows the database setting to use MySQL with a Django project.

■ Box 10.12: Setting up MySQL database

```
#Install MySQL
sudo apt-get install mysql-server mysql-client
sudo mysqladmin -u root -h localhost password 'mypassword'
```

■ Box 10.13: Configuring MySQL with Django - settings.py

```
DATABASES = {
    'default': {
        'ENGINE': 'django.db.backends.mysql',
        'NAME': '<database-name>',
        'USER': 'root'
        'PASSWORD': 'mypassword'
        'HOST': '<hostname>', # set to empty for localhost
        'PORT': '<port>', #set to empty for default port
    }
}
```

Defining a Model

Model acts as a definition of the data in the database. Box 10.14 shows the Python code for the Django models for the reference application. The various database tables for this application are defined as Classes in the Django model. Each class that represents a database table is a subclass of *django.db.models.Model* class which contains all the functionality that allows the models to interact with the database. To sync the models with the database simply run the following command:

>python manage.py syncdb

When the *syncdb* command is run the first time, it creates all the tables defined in the Django model in the configured database.

■ **Box 10.14: Django model for reference application**

```python
from django.db import models
from django.contrib.auth.models import User
from django.conf import settings

class Department(models.Model):
 name = models.CharField(verbose_name="Name",
  max_length=1000,blank = True,null=True)

 number = models.CharField(verbose_name="Number",
  max_length=1000,blank = True,primary_key=True)

 def __unicode__(self):
   return str(self.name)+" - "+str(self.number)

class Project(models.Model):
 name = models.CharField(verbose_name="Name",
  max_length=1000,blank = True,null=True)

 number = models.CharField(verbose_name="Number",
  max_length=1000,blank = True,primary_key=True)

 def __unicode__(self):
   return str(self.name)+" - "+str(self.number)
 def project_ids(self):
   return "project_"+str(self.id)

class Employee (models.Model):

 name = models.CharField(verbose_name="Name",
  max_length=1000,blank = True,null=True)

 number = models.CharField(verbose_name="Number",
  max_length=1000,blank = True,primary_key=True)

 salary = models.CharField(verbose_name="Salary",
  max_length=1000,blank = True,null=True)
```

```
department= models.ForeignKey(Department, null=True,blank=True,
  related_name='departmentname', default="null")

project=models.ManyToManyField(Project,through='WorksOn')

def __unicode__(self):
  return str(self.name)+" - "+str(self.number)+
   " - "+str(self.department.number)


class WorksOn(models.Model):
employee = models.ForeignKey(Employee)
project = models.ForeignKey(Project)

def __unicode__(self):
  return str(self.employee.name)+" - "+str(self.project.name)
```

Django Admin Site

Django provides an administration system that allows you to manage the project without writing additional code. The admin system reads the Django model and provides an interface that can be used to add content to the project. The Django admin site is enabled by adding *django.contrib.admin* and *django.contrib.admindocs* to the INSTALLED_APPS section in the settings.py file. The admin site also requires URL pattern definitions in the urls.py file described later in the URLs sections.

To define the application models which can be edited in the admin interface, a new file named admin.py is created in the application folder as shown in Box 10.15.

■ Box 10.15: Enabling admin for Django models

```
from django.contrib import admin
from django.contrib.auth.models import User

from myapp.models import Department,
 Employee, Project, WorksOn

admin.site.register(Department)
admin.site.register(Employee)
admin.site.register(Project)
admin.site.register(WorksOn)
```

Figure 10.9 shows a screenshot of the Django admin interface. You can see all the tables corresponding to the Django models in this screenshot. Figures 10.10, 10.11, 10.12 and 10.13 show how to add new items in the Department, Employee, Project and WorksOn tables using the admin site.

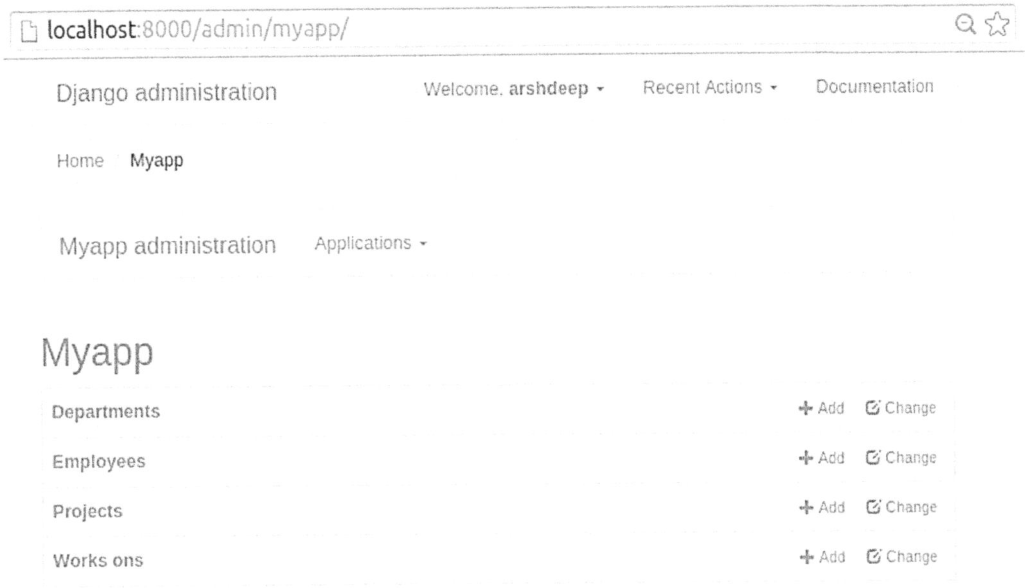

localhost:8000/admin/myapp/

Django administration · Welcome, **arshdeep** ▾ · Recent Actions ▾ · Documentation

Home · **Myapp**

Myapp administration · Applications ▾

Myapp

Departments	✚ Add · ✎ Change
Employees	✚ Add · ✎ Change
Projects	✚ Add · ✎ Change
Works ons	✚ Add · ✎ Change

Figure 10.9: Screentshot of Django admin site

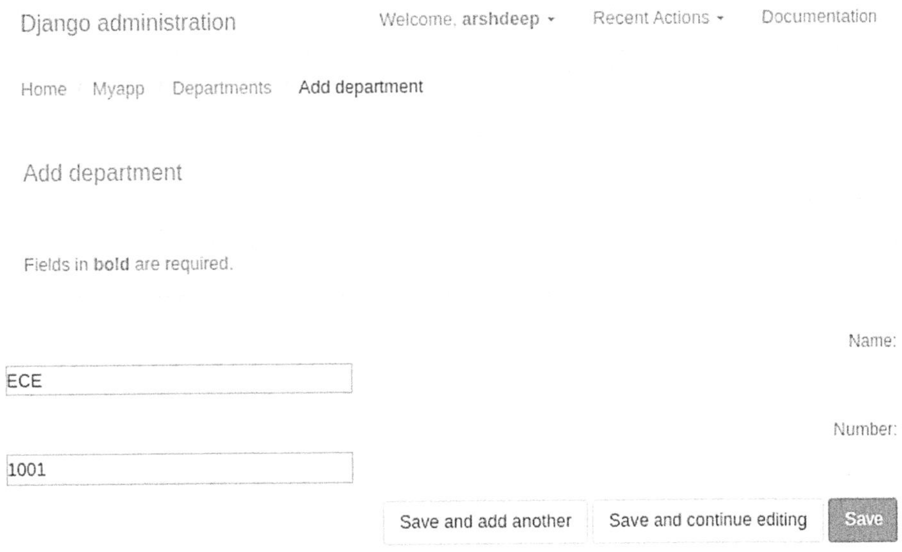

Django administration · Welcome, **arshdeep** ▾ · Recent Actions ▾ · Documentation

Home · Myapp · Departments · **Add department**

Add department

Fields in **bold** are required.

Name:

ECE

Number:

1001

Save and add another · Save and continue editing · **Save**

Figure 10.10: Django admin site - adding new items to department table

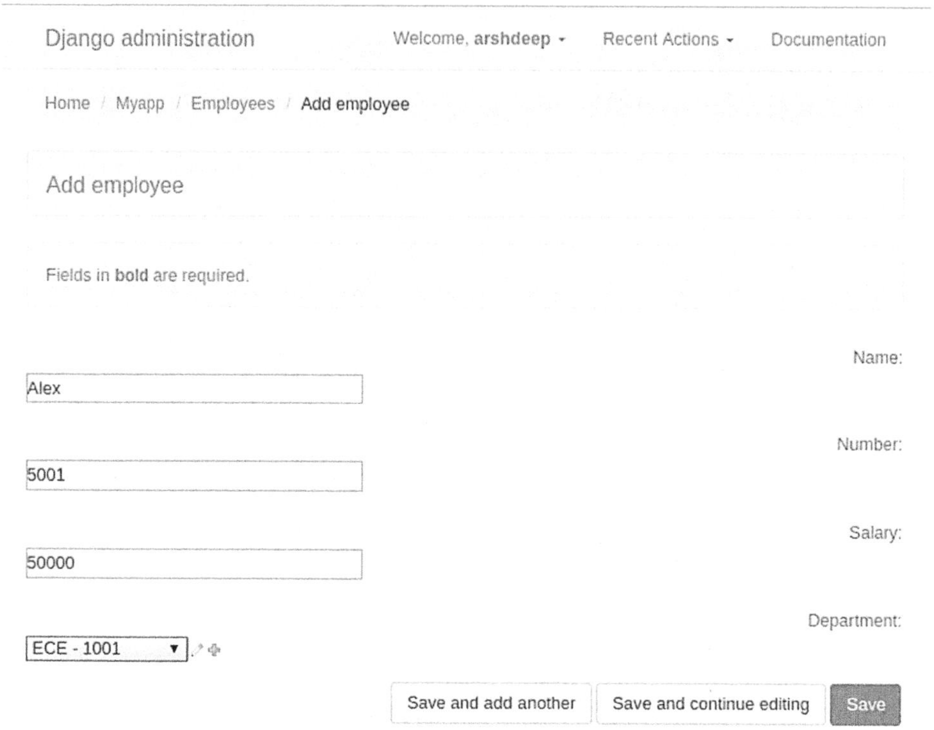

Django administration   Welcome, **arshdeep** ▾   Recent Actions ▾   Documentation

Home / Myapp / Employees / **Add employee**

Add employee

Fields in **bold** are required.

Name:

| Alex |

Number:

| 5001 |

Salary:

| 50000 |

Department:

| ECE - 1001   ▼ | ⸜ ✛

Save and add another   Save and continue editing   Save

Figure 10.11: Django admin site - adding new items to employee table

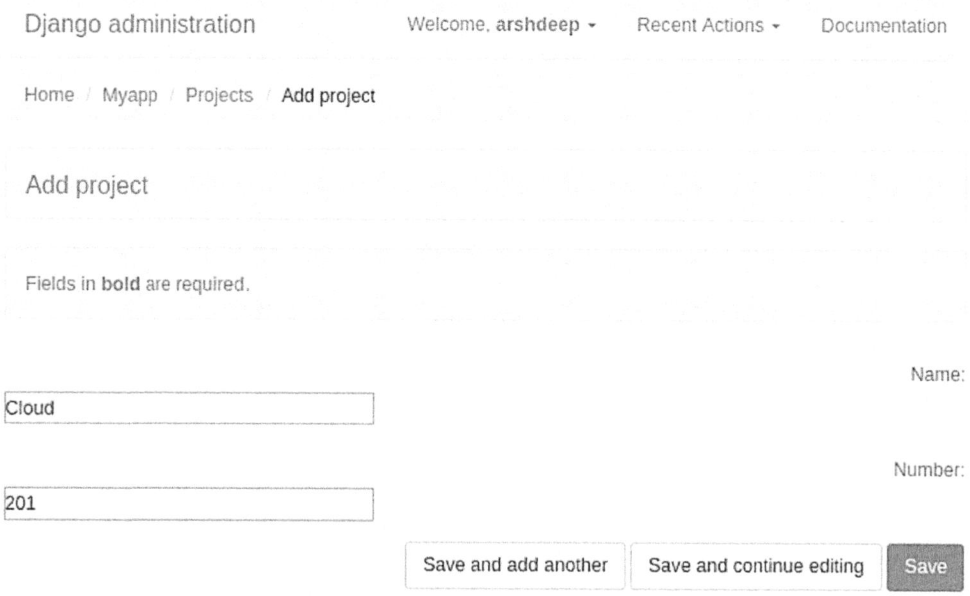

Django administration   Welcome, **arshdeep** ▾   Recent Actions ▾   Documentation

Home / Myapp / Projects / **Add project**

Add project

Fields in **bold** are required.

Name:

| Cloud |

Number:

| 201 |

Save and add another   Save and continue editing   Save

Figure 10.12: Django admin site - adding new items to project table

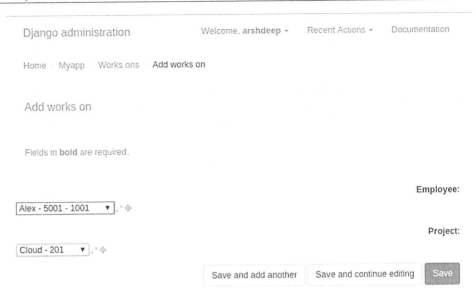

Figure 10.13: Django admin site - adding new items to works-on table

Defining a View

View contains the logic that glues the model to the template. The view determines the data to be displayed in the template, retrieves the data from the database and passes it to the template. Conversely, the view also extracts the data posted in a form in the template and inserts it into the database. Typically, each page in a web application has a separate view, which is a Python function in the views.py file. Views can also perform additional tasks such as authentication, sending emails, etc.

Box 10.16 shows the source code for the Django views for the reference application. The views correspond to the web pages that display the list of employees, employee details, department details and project details.

In the views, the Django's built in object-relational mapping API is used to retrieve the data from the database tables. The object-relational mapping API allows the developers to write generic code for interacting with the database without worrying about the underlying database engine. So the same code for database interactions works with different database backends. You can optionally choose to use a Python library specific to the database backend used (e.g. MySQLdb for MYSQL, PyMongo for MongoDB, etc.) to write database-backed specific code.

In the views shown in Box 10.16, the *table.objects.all* query returns a QuerySet with all the entries in a table. To retrieve specific entries, you can use *table.objects.filter(* * kwargs)* to filter out queries that match the specified condition. For example, the query *Employee.objects.filter(number =' 123')* returns the details of the employee with employee-number 123. To render the retrieved entries in the template, the *render_to_response* function is used. This function renders a given template with a given context dictionary and returns an *HttpResponse* object with that rendered text.

■ Box 10.16: Django view for reference application

```python
from django.shortcuts import render_to_response
from django.template import RequestContext
from django.shortcuts import render
from django.shortcuts import redirect
from django.contrib.auth import authenticate, login
from django.contrib.auth import logout
from django.contrib.auth.decorators import login_required
from django.contrib.auth.models import User
from myapp.models import Department, Employee, Project, WorksOn

def logout_view(request):
 logout(request)
 return redirect('/')


def home(request):
 if request.method == 'POST':
  username = request.POST['username']
  password = request.POST['password']
  user = authenticate(username=username, password=password)
  if user is not None:
   if user.is_active:
    login(request, user)
    username = request.user.username
    authorusername = str(request.user.username)


 if request.user.is_authenticated():
  authorusername = str(request.user.username)

  employeecount = Employee.objects.all().count()
  departmentcount = Department.objects.all().count()
  projectcount = Project.objects.all().count()

  return render_to_response('index.html',{
   'authorusername': authorusername, 'employeecount':employeecount,
    'departmentcount':departmentcount, 'projectcount':projectcount},
   context_instance=RequestContext(request))

 return redirect('/accounts/login')

@login_required
def employees(request):
  if request.user.is_authenticated():
  authorusername = str(request.user.username)
 employees = Employee.objects.all()
 project_list=[]
 len_e=len(employees)
 for it in range(len(employees)):
  temp1=employees[it].project.all()
  for items3 in temp1:
```

```
      project_list.append((items3.name,employees[it].number))
  return render_to_response('employees.html',{
     'authorusername':  authorusername,'employees':employees,
     'len':len_e,'project_list':project_list},
     context_instance=RequestContext(request))

@login_required
def employeedetail(request, query):
  if request.user.is_authenticated():
   authorusername = str(request.user.username)

  employee = Employee.objects.filter(number=query).get()
  project_list=employee.project.all()
  return render_to_response('employeedetail.html',{
   'authorusername':  authorusername,'employee':employee,
   'project_list':project_list},
   context_instance=RequestContext(request))

@login_required
def departmentdetail(request, query):
  if request.user.is_authenticated():
   authorusername = str(request.user.username)

  department = Department.objects.filter(number=query).get()
  employee_count = Employee.objects.filter(department__pk=query).count()
  return render_to_response('departmentdetail.html',{
   'authorusername':  authorusername,'department':department,
   'employee_count':employee_count},
   context_instance=RequestContext(request))

@login_required
def projectdetail(request, query):
  if request.user.is_authenticated():
   authorusername = str(request.user.username)

  project = Project.objects.filter(number=query).get()
  employee_count = Employee.objects.filter(project__pk=query).count()
  return render_to_response('projectdetail.html',{
   'authorusername':  authorusername,'project':project,
   'employee_count':employee_count},
   context_instance=RequestContext(request))
```

Defining a Template

A Django template is typically an HTML file (though it can be any text file such as XML, email, CSS, JavaScript, CSV, etc.). Django templates allow separation of the presentation of data from the actual data by using placeholders and associated logic (using template tags). A template receives a context from the view and presents the data in context variables in the placeholders.

Boxes 10.17, 10.18, 10.19 and 10.20 show the templates for the reference application. The data is retrieved from the database in the view and passed to the template in the form of a context dictionary. The *for* tags in the template loop over each item in a sequence and the items are inserted with the placeholder tags (variable name surrounded by braces, e.g.

{{entry.email}}). Template tag is any text that is surrounded by curly braces and percent signs (e.g. {% for entry in student_entries %}). Django's template language offers basic tags such as *for*, *if*, etc. and a number of built-in filters for modifying the output of variables. Filters are attached to variables using a pipe character (|). For example the filter *join* in {{entry.courses.all|join:", "}} joins a list with a string.

■ **Box 10.17: Django template for showing employees list**

```
<html lang="en">
 <head>
 <title> Dashboard</title>
 <!- Bootstrap Core CSS ->
 <link href="/static/css/bootstrap.min.css" rel="stylesheet">
 </head>
 <body>
 <div id="page-wrapper">
 <div class="container-fluid">
 <!- Page Heading ->
 <div class="row">
  <div class="col-lg-12">
   <h1 class="page-header">
   Employees
   </h1>
  </div>
 </div>
 <!- /.row ->
 </div>
 <!- /.row ->
 <div class="row">
 <div class="col-lg-6">
  <div class="panel panel-default">
  <div class="panel-heading">
   <h3 class="panel-title">Employees List</h3>
  </div>
  <div class="panel-body">
   <div class="table-responsive">
    <table class="table table-bordered table-hover table-striped">
     <thead>
      <tr>
       <th>Employee No.</th>
       <th>Name</th>
       <th>Salary</th>
       <th>Department</th>
      </tr>
     </thead>
     <tbody>
     {% for employee in employees%}
     <tr>
     <td>
<a href="/employee/{{employee.number}}/">{{employee.number}}</a></td>
       <td>{{employee.name}}</td>
       <td>{{employee.salary}}</td>
       <td><a href="/department/{{employee.department.number}}/">
```

```
{{employee.department.name}}</a></td>
     </tr>
     {% endfor %}
     </tbody>
    </table>
   </div>
   <!- /.row ->
  </div>
  </div>
  <!- /#page-wrapper ->
 </div>
 <!- /#wrapper ->
 <!- jQuery ->
 <script src="/static/js/jquery.js"></script>
 <!- Bootstrap Core JavaScript ->
 <script src="/static/js/bootstrap.min.js"></script>
 </body>
 </html>
```

■ **Box 10.18: Django template for showing employee details**

```
<html lang="en">
 <head>
 <title> Dashboard</title>
 <!- Bootstrap Core CSS ->
 <link href="/static/css/bootstrap.min.css" rel="stylesheet">
 </head>
 <body>
 <div id="wrapper">
 <div id="page-wrapper">
 <div class="container-fluid">
  <!- Page Heading ->
  <div class="row">
   <div class="col-lg-12">
    <h1 class="page-header">
     {{employee.name}}
    </h1>
   </div>
  </div>
  <!- /.row ->
  </div>
  <!- /.row ->
  <div class="row">
  <div class="col-lg-6">
   <div class="panel panel-default">
    <div class="panel-heading">
     <h3 class="panel-title">Employee Detail</h3>
    </div>
    <div class="panel-body">
     <div class="table-responsive">
      <table class="table table-bordered table-hover table-striped">
       <tbody>
```

```
     <tr>
      <td>Name</td>
      <td>{{employee.name}}</td>
     </tr>
     <tr>
      <td> Number</td>
      <td>{{employee.number}}</td>
     </tr>
     <tr>
      <td>Salary</td>
      <td>{{employee.salary}}</td>
     </tr>
     <tr>
      <td>Projects</td>
      <td>
       {% for project in project_list%}
       <a href="/project/{{project.number}}/">{{project.name}}</a><br>
       {% endfor %}
      </td>
     </tr>
    </tbody>
   </table>
  </div>
  <!- /.row ->
 </div>
 </div>
 <!- /#page-wrapper ->
</div>
<!- /#wrapper ->
<!- jQuery ->
<script src="/static/js/jquery.js"></script>
<!- Bootstrap Core JavaScript ->
<script src="/static/js/bootstrap.min.js"></script>
</body>
</html>
```

■ **Box 10.19: Django template for showing project details**

```
<html lang="en">
<head>
 <title>Dashboard</title>
 <!- Bootstrap Core CSS ->
 <link href="/static/css/bootstrap.min.css" rel="stylesheet">
</head>
<body>
 <div id="wrapper">
 <div id="page-wrapper">
 <div class="container-fluid">
  <!- Page Heading ->
  <div class="row">
   <div class="col-lg-12">
    <h1 class="page-header">
```

```
   {{project.name}}
  </h1>
 </div>
</div>
<!- /.row ->
</div>
<!- /.row ->
<div class="row">
<div class="col-lg-6">
 <div class="panel panel-default">
  <div class="panel-heading">
   <h3 class="panel-title"> Project Details</h3>
  </div>
  <div class="panel-body">
   <div class="table-responsive">
    <table class="table table-bordered table-hover table-striped">
     <tbody>
      <tr>
       <td>Name</td>
       <td>{{project.name}}</td>
      </tr>
      <tr>
       <td>Number</td>
       <td>{{project.number}}</td>
      </tr>
       <td>Total Employees Working on the Project</td>
       <td>{{employee_count}}</td>
      </tr>
     </tbody>
    </table>
   </div>
   <!- /.row ->
  </div>
 </div>
 <!- /#page-wrapper ->
</div>
<!- /#wrapper ->
<!- jQuery ->
<script src="/static/js/jquery.js"></script>
<!- Bootstrap Core JavaScript ->
<script src="/static/js/bootstrap.min.js"></script>
</body>
</html>
```

■ **Box 10.20: Django template for showing department details**

```
<html lang="en">
 <head>
  <title> Dashboard</title>
  <!- Bootstrap Core CSS ->
  <link href="/static/css/bootstrap.min.css" rel="stylesheet">
 </head>
```

```html
<body>
<div id="wrapper">
<div id="page-wrapper">
<div class="container-fluid">
<!- Page Heading ->
<div class="row">
<div class="col-lg-12">
<h1 class="page-header">
{{department.name}}
</h1>
</div>
</div>
<!- /.row ->
</div>
<!- /.row ->
<div class="row">
<div class="col-lg-6">
<div class="panel panel-default">
<div class="panel-heading">
<h3 class="panel-title">Department Detail</h3>
</div>
<div class="panel-body">
<div class="table-responsive">
<table class="table table-bordered table-hover table-striped">
<tbody>
<tr>
<td>Name</td>
<td>{{department.name}}</td>
</tr>
<tr>
<td>Number</td>
<td>{{department.number}}</td>
</tr>
<tr>
<td>Total Employees in Department</td>
<td>{{employee_count}}</td>
</tr>
</tbody>
</table>
</div>
<!- /.row ->
</div>
<!- /.container-fluid ->
</div>
<!- /#page-wrapper ->
</div>
<!- /#wrapper ->
<!- jQuery ->
<script src="/static/js/jquery.js"></script>
<!- Bootstrap Core JavaScript ->
<script src="/static/js/bootstrap.min.js"></script>
</body>
</html>
```

Defining the URL Patterns

URL Patterns are a way of mapping the URLs to the views that should handle the URL requests. The URLs requested by the user are matched with the URL patterns and the view corresponding to the pattern that matrices the URL is used to handle the request. Box 10.21 shows an example of the URL patterns for the reference application. As seen in this example, the URL patterns are constructed using regular expressions. The simplest regular expression (r'$^$ $') corresponds to the root of the website or the home page. More complex URLs allow capturing values. For example the pattern:

url(r'$^$ employee/(?P<query>\w+)', 'myapp.views.employeedetail')

captures the employee number from the URL to the variable *query* and passes it to the *employeedetail* view.

■ **Box 10.21: Example of a URL configuration**

```
from django.conf.urls import patterns, include, url
from myapp import views
from django.contrib import admin

admin.autodiscover()

urlpatterns = patterns('',
url(r'^$', 'myapp.views.home', name='home'),
url(r'^employees/$', 'myapp.views.employees', name='employees'),
url(r'^employee/(?P<query>\w+)/$', 'myapp.views.employeedetail'),
url(r'^department/(?P<query>\w+)/$', 'myapp.views.departmentdetail'),
url(r'^project/(?P<query>\w+)/$', 'myapp.views.projectdetail'),
url(r'^admin/doc/', include(django.contrib.admindocs.urls)),
url(r'^admin/', include(admin.site.urls)),
)
```

Figures 10.14, 10.15, 10.16 and 10.17 show the various pages of the reference application which are rendered from the templates shown in Boxes 10.17, 10.18, 10.19 and 10.20.

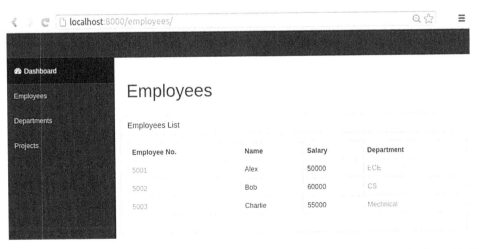

Figure 10.14: Screenshot of employees list page rendered from template in Box 10.17

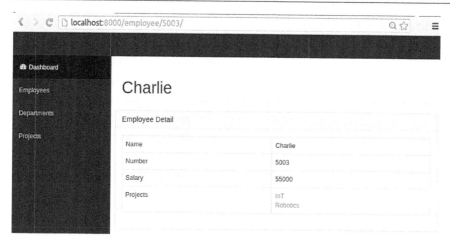

Figure 10.15: Screenshot of employee details page rendered from template in Box 10.18

Figure 10.16: Screenshot of project details page rendered from template in Box 10.19

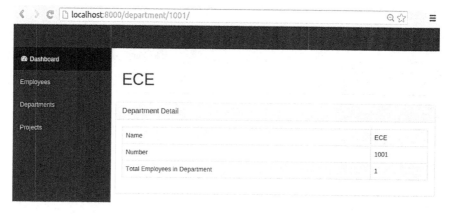

Figure 10.17: Screenshot of department details page rendered from template in Box 10.20

10.4   Case Study: Django application for viewing weather data

Let us look at a case study of a Django application that displays the current weather data and weather forecast for different cities. In the sections on DynamoDB, Cassandra and MongoDB we described examples of obtaining weather data using the OpenWeatherMap API and writing the data to the respective databases. Let us now build a Django web application that retrieves the weather data from these databases and presents the data in a web page. We will describe three alternative implementations based on DynamoDB, Cassandra and MongoDB. Box 10.22 shows the source code for the Django view that retrieves weather data from DynamoDB tables and renders it in the Django template.

■ **Box 10.22: Django view for retrieving weather data from DynamoDB**

```
from django.shortcuts import render_to_response
from django.template import RequestContext
import boto.dynamodb2
from boto.dynamodb2.table import Table
import cPickle
import pyowm

REGION="us-east-1"

conn = boto.dynamodb2.connect_to_region(REGION,
aws_access_key_id='<enter>',
aws_secret_access_key='<enter>')


table=Table('weather',connection=conn)
forecastTable=Table('forecast',connection=conn)

PYOWM_KEY='<enter>'
owm = pyowm.OWM(PYOWM_KEY)

def home(request):
  if request.method == 'POST':
   city=request.POST.get('city')
  else:
   city = 'New York,US'

  results = table.query_2(city__eq=city, reverse=True, limit=1)
  for r in results:
   time=r['time']
   temp=r['currentTemperature']
   status=r['weatherStatus']
   pressure=r['pressure']
   humidity=r['humidity']
   wind=r['windSpeed']
   rain=r['rainVolume']
   clouds=r['cloudCoverage']

  results = forecastTable.query_2(city__eq=city)
```

```
for r in results:
 data = str(r['forecastList'])

forecast_list = cPickle.loads(data)

return render_to_response('index.html',{
  'city':city,'time':time, 'temp':temp, 'status':status,
  'pressure':pressure, 'humidity':humidity,
  'wind':wind, 'rain':rain, 'clouds':clouds,
  'forecast_list':forecast_list},
 context_instance=RequestContext(request))
```

Box 10.23 shows the source code for the Django view that retrieves weather data from Cassandra tables and renders it in the Django template.

■ Box 10.23: Django view for retrieving weather data from Cassandra

```
from django.shortcuts import render_to_response
from django.template import RequestContext
import cPickle
import pyowm
from cassandra.cluster import Cluster
PYOWM_KEY='<enter>'
owm = pyowm.OWM(PYOWM_KEY)

## create Cassandra instance
cluster = Cluster()

## establish Cassandra connection, using local default
session = cluster.connect('weatherkeyspace')


def home(request):
 if request.method == 'POST':
  city=request.POST.get('city')
 else:
  city = 'New York,US'

 results = session.execute('SELECT * FROM weather
   WHERE city='+city+'ORDER BY time DESC LIMIT 1')
 for r in results:
  time=r[1]
  temp=r[2]
  status=r[3]
  pressure=r[4]
  humidity=r[5]
  wind=r[6]
  rain=r[7]
  clouds=r[8]

 results = session.execute('SELECT * FROM forecast
   WHERE city='+city+'')

 for r in results:
```

```
   data = r[1]

 forecast_list = cPickle.loads(data.decode("hex"))

 return render_to_response('index.html',{
   'city':city,'time':time, 'temp':temp,
   'status':status, 'pressure':pressure, 'humidity':humidity,
   'wind':wind, 'rain':rain, 'clouds':clouds,
   'forecast_list':forecast_list},
   context_instance=RequestContext(request))
```

Box 10.24 shows the source code for the Django view that retrieves weather data from
MongoDB and renders it in the Django template.

■ Box 10.24: Django view for retrieving weather data from MongoDB

```
from django.shortcuts import render_to_response
from django.template import RequestContext
import pyowm
from pymongo import MongoClient

client = MongoClient('mongodb://root:password@hostname:53688/weather')
db = client['weather']
weather_collection = db['current']
forecast_collection = db['forecast']

PYOWM_KEY='<enter>'
owm = pyowm.OWM(PYOWM_KEY)

def home(request):
 if request.method == 'POST':
  city=request.POST.get('city')
 else:
  city = 'New York,US'

 results = weather_collection.find({"city":
  city}).sort("_id",-1).limit(1)
 for r in results:
  time=r['time']
  temp=r['currentTemperature']
  status=r['weatherStatus']
  pressure=r['pressure']
  humidity=r['humidity']
  wind=r['windSpeed']
  rain=r['rainVolume']
  clouds=r['cloudCoverage']

 results = forecast_collection.find({"city":  city})

 for r in results:
  data = r['forecastList']

 forecast_list = data
```

```
return render_to_response('index.html',{
   'city':city, 'time':time, 'temp':temp,
   'status':status, 'pressure':pressure, 'humidity':humidity,
   'wind':wind, 'rain':rain, 'clouds':clouds,
   'forecast_list':forecast_list},
context_instance=RequestContext(request))
```

Box 10.25 shows the source code of the Django template for the weather application and
Figure 10.18 shows a screenshot of the web page rendered from the template.

■ **Box 10.25: Django template for weather application**

```
<html lang="en">
 <head>
 <title> Dashboard</title>
 <!- Bootstrap Core CSS ->
 <link href="/static/css/bootstrap.min.css" rel="stylesheet">
 <!- Morris Charts CSS ->
 <link href="/static/css/plugins/morris.css" rel="stylesheet">
 <!-[if lt IE 9]>
 <script src="/static/js/html5shiv.js"></script>
 <script src="/static/js/respond.min.js"></script>
 <![endif]->
 <script src="/static/js/raphael-min.js"></script>
 <script src="/static/js/jquery-1.8.2.min.js"></script>
 <script src="/static/js/morris-0.4.1.min.js"></script>
 </head>
<body>
<div id="wrapper">
 <div id="page-wrapper">
  <div class="container-fluid">
   <!- Page Heading ->
   <div class="row">
    <div class="col-lg-12">
     <h1 class="page-header">
      {{city}}
     </h1>
    </div>
   </div>
   <!- /.row ->
   <div class="row">
    <div class="col-lg-4">
     <div class="panel panel-default">
     <div class="panel-heading">
      <h3 class="panel-title">Current Weather</h3>
     </div>
     <div class="panel-body">
      <div class="table-responsive">
       <table class="table table-bordered table-hover table-striped">
        <tbody>
         <tr>
          <td>Temperature</td>
          <td>{{temp}} &#176;C</td>
         </tr>
```

```
   <tr>
    <td>Humidity</td>
    <td>{{humidity}} %</td>
   </tr>
   <tr>
    <td>Pressure</td>
    <td>{{pressure}} hpa</td>
   </tr>
   <tr>
    <td>Wind</td>
    <td>{{wind}} meter/sec</td>
   </tr>
   <tr>
    <td>Cloud Coverage</td>
    <td>{{clouds}} %</td>
   </tr>
   <tr>
    <td>Status</td>
    <td>{{status}}</td>
   </tr>
   <tr>
    <td>Last Updated Time</td>
    <td>{{time}}</td>
   </tr>
   </tbody>
   </table>
  </div>
 </div>
</div>
</div>
<div class="col-lg-4">
 <div class="panel panel-green">
  <div class="panel-heading">
   <h3 class="panel-title">Search</h3>
  </div>
  <div class="panel-body">
   <form method="post" action="/">{%csrf_token%}
    <input type="text" name="city" id="city" placeholder="City" />
    <input type="submit" value="Search" />
   </form>
  </div>
 </div>
</div>
</div>
<!- /.row ->
<div class="row">
 <div class="col-lg-4">
  <div class="panel panel-green">
   <div class="panel-heading">
    <h3 class="panel-title">Forecast - Temperature</h3>
   </div>
   <div class="panel-body">
    <script>
     $(function() {
```

```
    Morris.Line({
     element:  'morris-line-chart',
     data:  [
      {% for f in forecast_list %}
    { y:  '{{f.date}}', 'a':  {{f.tempMax}}, 'b':  {{f.tempMin}} },
      {% endfor %}
     ],
     xkey:  'y',
     ykeys:  ['a', 'b'],
     xLabels:'day',
     lineColors:  ['red','blue'],
     labels:  ['Maximum Temperature', 'Minimum Temperature']
     });
     });
    </script>
    <div id="morris-line-chart"></div>
   </div>
  </div>
 </div>
 <div class="col-lg-4">
  <div class="panel panel-yellow">
   <div class="panel-heading">
    <h3 class="panel-title">Forecast - Rain</h3>
   </div>
   <div class="panel-body">
    <script>
     $(function() {
     Morris.Line({
      element:  'morris-line-chart1',
      data:  [
       {% for f in forecast_list %}
     { y:  '{{f.date}}', 'a':  {{f.rain}} },
       {% endfor %}
      ],
      xkey:  'y',
      ykeys:  ['a'],
      xLabels:'day',
      labels:  ['Rain'],
      lineColors:  ['green']
      });
      });
    </script>
    <div id="morris-line-chart1"></div>
   </div>
  </div>
 </div>
 </div>
 <!- /.row ->
 </div>
 <!- /.container-fluid ->
</div>
<!- /#page-wrapper ->
</div>
<!- /#wrapper ->
```

```
<!- jQuery ->
<script src="/static/js/jquery.js"></script>
<!- Bootstrap Core JavaScript ->
<script src="/static/js/bootstrap.min.js"></script>
</body>
</html>
```

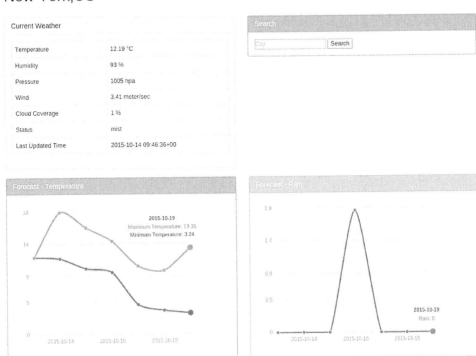

Figure 10.18: Screenshot of Django application for displaying weather data

Summary

In this chapter we provide a comparison of relational and non-relational NoSQL databases and also examples of some popular databases which can be used as serving databases for big data applications. Relational databases have a well defined consistent model and fixed schemas for the relations. Relational databases provide Atomicity, Consistency, Isolation and Durability (ACID) guarantees. Non-relational databases do not have fixed schemas and not provide ACID guarantees. Non-relational databases are more scalable as compared to relational databases and have distributed, highly available and fault tolerant architectures. We described examples of using MySQL, DynamoDB, Cassandra and MongoDB as serving databases. Next, we described the Django Python web framework which can be used for developing web applications to present the analysis results to the users. Django adopts a model-template-view architecture and offers a unified API to the database backend. We also described examples of creation the models, views and templates for a reference application.

Part III

ADVANCED TOPICS

11 - Analytics Algorithms

This chapter covers

- Machine Learning tools and frameworks
- Spark MLlib
- H2O
- Clustering Algorithms
- Classification Algorithms
- Regression Algorithms
- Recommendation Systems

In this chapter, you will learn algorithms for big data analytics including clustering, classification, regression and recommendation. For the examples in this chapter, we will use Spark MLlib and H2O machine learning frameworks.

11.1 Frameworks

11.1.1 Spark MLlib

Spark MLlib is the Spark's machine learning library which provides implementations of various machine learning algorithms including classification, regression, clustering, collaborative filtering and dimensionality reduction. The MLlib APIs are built on top of the Spark's resilient distributed datasets (RDDs). MLlib also provides high-level data types such as Vector, LabeledPoint, Rating and Matrix, which are backed by RDDs. The benefit of using MLlib over machine learning libraries is that it provides parallel implementations of machine learning algorithms and can process large distributed datasets. Spark MLlib provides APIs for Python, Scala, and Java programming languages. Figure 11.1 shows the various components of Spark MLlib.

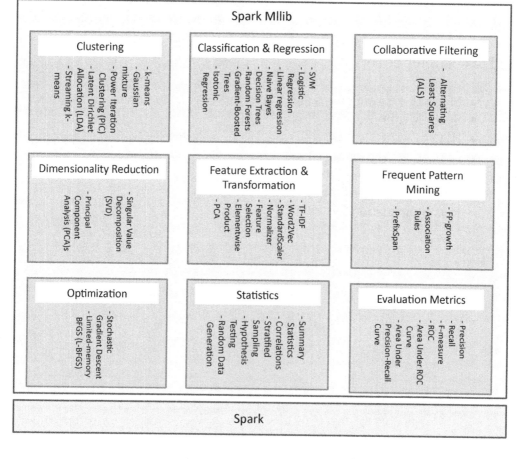

Figure 11.1: Spark MLlib components

11.1.2   H2O

H2O is an open source predictive analytics framework which provides implementations of various machine learning algorithms for clustering, classification, and dimensionality reduction. Figure 11.2 shows the various components of H2O framework. H2O provides APIs for Python, Scala, R and Java programming languages. H2O also provides a notebook-style web interface called H2O which allows users to import data from various sources, build machine learning models and make predictions using the models. H2O can either run as a standalone cluster or on top of existing Hadoop or Spark clusters. H2O's Sparkling Water library integrates the H2O machine learning engine with Spark. H2O can connect to various sources of data such as HDFS, S3, SQL, and NoSQL.

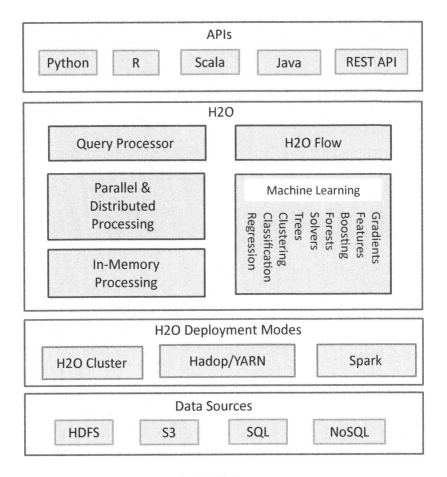

Figure 11.2: H2O components

Setting up H2O

H2O can be either run as a standalone cluster or on top of a Hadoop cluster. To setup a standalone cluster of H2O, download the latest H2O release from http://h2o.ai/download/ and follow the commands shown in the box below:

```
■ unzip h2o-3.2.0.5.zip
cd h2o-3.2.0.5
java -jar h2o.jar
```

To run H2O on a Hadoop cluster, download an H2O release specific to your Hadoop version and follow the commands shown in the box below:

```
■ unzip h2o-3.2.0.5-hdp2.2.zip
cd h2o-3.2.0.5-hdp2.2
hadoop jar h2odriver.jar -nodes 1 -mapperXmx 6g -output hdfsOutputDir
```

The above command will launch an H2O cluster with one node and 6GB memory. The URL of the H2O Flow UI can be obtained from the output as shown below:

```
■ Determining driver host interface for mapper->driver callback...
[Possible callback IP address:  172.31.2.74]
[Possible callback IP address:  127.0.0.1]
Using mapper->driver callback IP address and port:  172.31.2.74:41892
(You can override these with -driverif and -driverport.)
Memory Settings:  mapreduce.map.java.opts:  -Xms1g -Xmx1g -XX:PermSize=256m
-verbose:gc -XX:+PrintGCDetails
-XX:+PrintGCTimeStamps -Dlog4j.defaultInitOverride=true
Extra memory percent:   10
mapreduce.map.memory.mb:   1126
15/10/01 05:58:35 INFO impl.TimelineClientImpl:
Timeline service address:  http://ip-172-31-2-74.ec2.internal:8188/ws/v1/timeline/
15/10/01 05:58:35 INFO client.RMProxy:
Connecting to ResourceManager at ip-172-31-2-74.ec2.internal/172.31.2.74:8050
15/10/01 05:58:36 INFO mapreduce.JobSubmitter:  number of splits:1
15/10/01 05:58:36 INFO mapreduce.JobSubmitter:
Submitting tokens for job:  job_1443678868179_0002
15/10/01 05:58:37 INFO impl.YarnClientImpl:
Submitted application application_1443678868179_0002
15/10/01 05:58:37 INFO mapreduce.Job:  The url to track the job:
http://ip-172-31-2-74.ec2.internal:8088/proxy/application_1443678868179_0002/
Job name 'H2O_87495' submitted
JobTracker job ID is 'job_1443678868179_0002'
For YARN users, logs command is
'yarn logs -applicationId application_1443678868179_0002'
Waiting for H2O cluster to come up...
H2O node 172.31.2.74:54321 requested flatfile
Sending flatfiles to nodes...
[Sending flatfile to node 172.31.2.74:54321]
H2O node 172.31.2.74:54321 reports H2O cluster size 1
H2O cluster (1 nodes) is up
(Note:  Use the -disown option to exit the driver after cluster formation)

Open H2O Flow in your web browser:  http://172.31.2.74:54321

(Press Ctrl-C to kill the cluster)
Blocking until the H2O cluster shuts down...
```

Figure 11.3 shows a screenshot of the H2O Flow UI.

Figure 11.3: H2O Flow UI

11.2 Clustering

Clustering is the process of grouping similar data items together such that data items that are more similar to each other (with respect to some similarity criteria) than other data items are put in one cluster. Clustering big data is of much interest, and happens in applications such as:

- Clustering social network data to find a group of similar users
- Clustering electronic health record (EHR) data to find similar patients.
- Clustering sensor data to group similar or related faults in a machine
- Clustering market research data to group similar customers
- Clustering clickstream data to group similar users

Clustering is achieved by clustering algorithms that belong to a broad category algorithms called unsupervised machine learning. Unsupervised machine learning algorithms find the patterns and hidden structure in data for which no training data is available.

11.2.1 K-Means

K-means is a clustering algorithm that groups data items into k clusters, where k is user defined. Each cluster is defined by a centroid point. All points in a cluster are closer (with respect to some distance measure) to their centroid as compared to the centroids of neighboring clusters. K-means clustering begins with a set of k centroid points which are either randomly chosen from the dataset or chosen using some initialization algorithm such as canopy clustering. The algorithm proceeds by finding the distance between each data point in the dataset and the centroid points. Based on the distance measure, each data point is assigned to the cluster belonging to the closest centroid. In the next step the centroids are recomputed by taking the mean value of all the data points in a cluster. This process is repeated till the centroids no longer move more than a specified threshold. The k-means clustering algorithm is shown in Box 11.1.

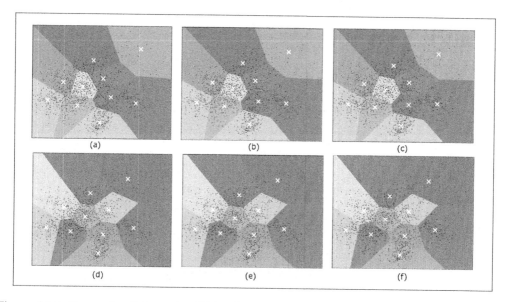

Figure 11.4: Example of clustering 300 points with k-means: (a) iteration 1, (b) iteration 2, (c) iteration 3, (d) iteration 5, (e) iteration 10, (f) iteration 100.

▪ Box 11.1: k-means clustering algorithm

Start with k centroid points

while the centroids no longer move beyond a threshold or maximum number of iterations reached:
    for each point in the dataset:
        for each centroid:
            find the distance between the point and the centroid
            assign the point to the cluster belonging to the nearest centroid
        for each cluster:
            recompute the centroid point by taking mean value of all points in the cluster

Figure 11.4 shows an example of clustering 300 data points. The centroid points are recomputed after each iteration, and as seen in this figure there is little movement of centroids after ten iterations.

There are various distance measures that can be used for clustering algorithms including:

- **Euclidean distance measure:** This is the simplest of all distance measures. The Euclidean distance between points p and q in N-dimensional space is given as:

$$d(p,q) = \sqrt{\sum_{i=1}^{N}(p_i - q_i)^2} \qquad (11.1)$$

- **Cosine distance measure:** Cosine distance measure finds the cosine of angle between two vectors (vectors drawn from the origin to the points).

$$d = cos(\theta) = \frac{A.B}{||A||||B||} \qquad (11.2)$$

- **Manhattan distance measure:** Manhattan distance measure is the sum of the absolute differences of the coordinates of two points given as:

$$d(p,q) = \left| \sum_{i=1}^{N}(p_i - q_i) \right| \qquad (11.3)$$

Let us look at an example of k-means clustering using H2O framework. For this example, we will use the Wine dataset from the UCI Machine learning repository [39]. This dataset has results of a chemical analysis of wines grown in Italy. The chemical analysis determined the quantities of 13 constituents (such as alcohol, malic acid, magnesium, etc.) found in three types of wines.

Using the wine dataset and ignoring the class labels (types of wines) let us try to cluster the data to identify patterns in the data using H2O. Launch an H2O cluster using the following command:

```
■ java -jar h2o.jar
```

When the H2O cluster is launched with the above command the output will include a URI of the H2O Flow UI (default for local machine is http://localhost:54321). With the H2O cluster launched, let us import the data into H2O from the H2O Flow UI as shown in Figure 11.5. You can either use the H2O importFiles command or choose the import files option from the H2O Flow UI menu. Enter the path to the data file and press the import button.

The next step is to parse the imported file. Click the Parse button after importing the file. Figure 11.6 shows setting up the parser. In this step, you can specify various parsing options such as the data types for each column, the type of parser to use (CSV, XLS, etc.), the separator used, etc. For most data parsing, H2O automatically recognizes the data type. After selecting the parse options, click the Parse button to parse the file. The data from the parsed file is stored in an H2O frame. Figure 11.7 shows the H2O frame created by parsing the dataset file.

With the data imported and parsed, let us now build a k-means clustering model. Click the Build Model button in the actions of the parsed frame or choose the Build Model option from the menu. Figure 11.8 shows the various options for the model. Select the algorithm

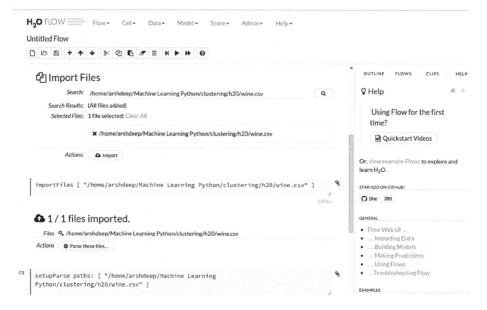

Figure 11.5: Importing dataset files using H2O Flow UI

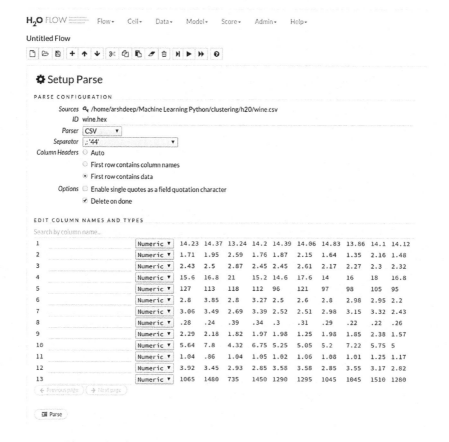

Figure 11.6: Parsing the dataset file using H2O Flow UI

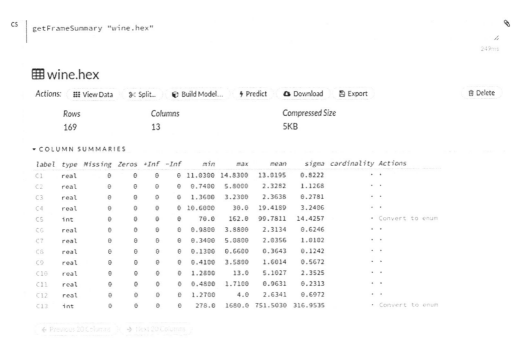

Figure 11.7: Viewing the H2O frame created from parsed dataset file

type to be K-means, training frame as wine.hex, and enter the number of clusters (k=3) and maximum iterations (max_iterations=100). After specifying the model options, click the Build Model button to build the model.

Figure 11.9 shows the details of the k-means model built from the Wine dataset. The model summary shows the various model statistics such as the number of clusters, number of categorical columns, number of iterations, etc. The centroid statistics and cluster means can also be seen in the model output.

While it is convenient to use the H2O Flow UI for analyzing the data, for datasets that require additional processing you can implement Python programs that use the H2O Python APIs. Let us look at a Python implementation of clustering data with k-means using the H2O Python API. Box 11.2 shows a Python program for k-means clustering using H2O. In this program, we import the H2O python library and then initialize H2O. This will launch a new H2O cluster. The *import_frame* is used to import the data into an H2O frame. With the data imported, we use the *kmeans* function to build a k-means clustering model.

■ **Box 11.2: Python program for k-means clustering using H2O**

```
import h2o

h2o.init()

data = h2o.import_frame(path="/home/ubuntu/wine.data.txt")

data.describe()
```

H₂O FLOW ═══   Flow ▾   Cell ▾   Data ▾   Model ▾   Score ▾   Admin ▾   Help ▾

Untitled Flow

CS | assist buildModel, null, training_frame: "wine.hex"

🎁 Build a Model

Select an algorithm: K-means ▼

PARAMETERS

model_id kmeans-e784b377-1fbd-4427-8c98-c	Destination id for this model; auto-generated if not specified
training_frame wine.hex ▼	Training frame
validation_frame (Choose...) ▼	Validation frame
nfolds 0	Number of folds for N-fold cross-validation
ignored_columns Search...	

Showing page 1 of 1.

- ☐ C1 REAL
- ☐ C2 REAL
- ☐ C3 REAL
- ☐ C4 REAL
- ☐ C5 INT
- ☐ C6 REAL
- ☐ C7 REAL
- ☐ C8 REAL
- ☐ C9 REAL
- ☐ C10 REAL
- ☐ C11 REAL

☑ All   ☐ None   ← Previous 100   → Next 100

Only show columns with more than ⓪ % missing values.

ignore_const_cols ☑	Ignore constant columns
k* 3	Number of clusters
user_points (Choose...) ▼	User-specified points
max_iterations 100	Maximum training iterations
init Furthest ▼	Initialization mode

ADVANCED

fold_column (Choose...) ▼	Column with cross-validation fold index assignment per observation
score_each_iteration ☐	Whether to score during each iteration of model training
standardize ☑	Standardize columns

EXPERT

seed 8873118635855	RNG Seed

▣ Build Model

Figure 11.8: Building a k-means clustering model using H2O Flow UI

```
model = h2o.kmeans(x=data[1:], k=3,
init="Random", seed=2, standardize=True)

total_within_sumofsquares = model.tot_withinss()
number_of_clusters = len(model.centers())
number_of_dimensions = len(model.centers()[0])
number_of_rows = sum(model.size())
```

Let us repeat the clustering example using Spark MLlib. Box 11.3 shows a Python program for clustering data using Spark MLlib. Spark MLlib includes a parallel implementation of k-means which can be used for clustering big data. This program can be run in the PySpark shell. In this program we implement a *parseVector* function which takes each line of the

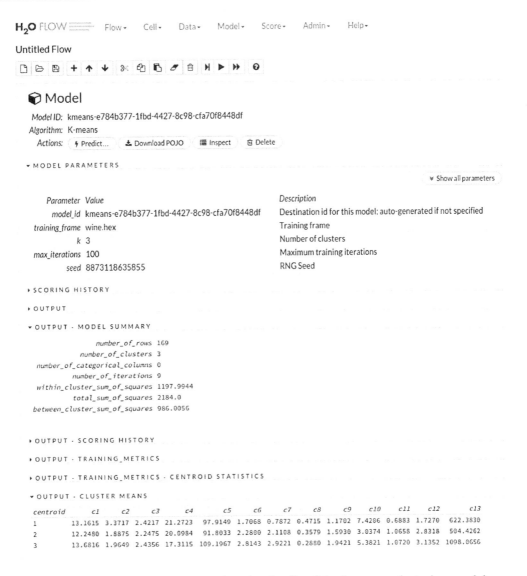

Figure 11.9: H2O Flow UI showing the details of the k-means clustering model

input file, splits the line into individual columns separated by commas, converts the values to floats and returns a Python numpy array. The *KMeans* class of the MLlib clustering module is used to build a k-means clustering model. After the model has been built, the *clusterCenters* method of the KMeans class can be used to view the cluster centers.

■ **Box 11.3: Python program for k-means clustering using Spark MLlib**

```python
import numpy as np
from pyspark import SparkContext
from pyspark.mllib.clustering import KMeans


def parseVector(line):
    return np.array([float(x) for x in line.split(',')])


sc = SparkContext(appName="KMeans")

lines = sc.textFile('file:///home/hadoop/wine.data.txt')

data = lines.map(parseVector)

k = 3

model = KMeans.train(data, k)

print("Final centers:  " + str(model.clusterCenters))
```

11.3   Case Study: Song Recommendation System

In this section, we will describe a case study on building a music recommendation system using Apache Spark. While most of the song recommendation systems use collaborative filtering, which requires access to user profile data such as the songs played by users and the song ratings given the users, in the absence of such information, it becomes difficult to recommend songs to a user. For the purpose of this case study we will use a content-based filtering approach which does not require information about the users, instead, it leverages the properties of the songs for recommending new songs to the users.

For this case study, we will use the Million Songs Dataset [44]. The dataset contains the information about a million contemporary songs such as the song metadata, artist metadata and acoustic features of the songs. The dataset files are available in HDF5 format. For this case study, we will use a subset of the data. Box 11.4 shows the Python code for reading an H5 file and extracting the metadata fields of interest into a CSV file.

■ **Box 11.4: Python program for reading H5 files and exporting meta-data to CSV**

```python
import hdf5_getters as GETTERS
import csv

h5 = GETTERS.open_h5_file_read("input.h5")
c = csv.writer(open("data.csv", "w+"))

all_artist_id = []
all_artist_names = []
all_songs_id = []
all_songs_names = []
```

```
all_tempo = []
all_loudness = []
all_key_confidence = []
all_mode_confidence = []
all_song_hottness=[]
all_year =[]

artist_id = GETTERS.get_artist_id(h5)
all_artist_id.append(artist_id)

artist_name = GETTERS.get_artist_name(h5)
all_artist_names.append(artist_name)

song_id = GETTERS.get_song_id(h5)
all_songs_id.append(song_id)

song_name = GETTERS.get_title(h5)
all_songs_names.append(song_name)

loudness = GETTERS.get_loudness(h5)
all_loudness.append(loudness)

song_hottness = GETTERS.get_song_hotttnesss(h5)
all_song_hottness.append(song_hottness)

tempo = GETTERS.get_tempo(h5)
all_tempo.append(tempo)

key_confidence = GETTERS.get_key_confidence(h5)
all_key_confidence.append(key_confidence)

mode_confidence = GETTERS.get_mode_confidence(h5)
all_mode_confidence.append(mode_confidence)

year=GETTERS.get_year(h5)
all_year.append(year)

for k in range(len(list(all_artist_names))):
    artist_id=list(all_artist_id)[k]
    artist_name=list(all_artist_names)[k]
    song_id=list(all_songs_id)[k]
    song_name=list(all_songs_names)[k]
    loudness=list(all_loudness)[k]
    tempo=list(all_tempo)[k]
    key_confidence=list(all_key_confidence)[k]
    mode_confidence=list(all_mode_confidence)[k]
    year=list(all_year)[k]

    c.writerow([artist_id, artist_name, song_id, song_name,
      loudness, tempo,key_confidence, mode_confidence, year])
```

The box below shows the format and a sample of the meta-data extracted into a CSV file from the original dataset.

```
#Sample of data extracted into CSV
Artist ID, Artist Name, Song ID, Song Name, Loudness, Song Hottness, Tempo, Key Confidence, Mode Confidence,
Year
ARE26EG1187B990AEF, Sunscreem, SOICLQB12A8C13637C, Exodus, -8.955, 0.79, 130.201, 0.625, 0.558, 1995
```

Box 11.5 shows a Spark program for finding the top 10 songs and top 10 artists in each year. This program takes as input the CSV file generated in the previous step. The map transformation was used to split the comma separated values into words. The blank lines are then filtered out. The next step is to map the comma separated values into (artist_id, artist_name, artist_hotness, year) and (song_id, song_name, song_hotness, year). There are artists with multiple songs, so the distinct() transformation is used to find the unique artists so that they are not repeated while calculating top artists. Next, a for loop is used to calculate the top artists and songs for each year. The next step is to change the keys from artist_id and song_id to artist_hotness and song_hotness which was done with another map transformation. However, some of the songs had the song_hotness value as NaN. So these values had to be filtered out. The *sortByKey* operator is used to arrange the entries in descending order of hotness values and the *take* operator is used to return a list of top 10 songs and artists.

■ **Box 11.5: Spark program for finding the top 10 songs and top 10 artists in each year**

```
from pyspark import SparkContext

sc = SparkContext("local", "Simple App")

step1=sc.textFile("file:///output_csv.csv")
step2=step1.map(lambda line:  line.split(",")).filter(lambda line:
len(line)>1)

step3=step2.map(lambda line:  ((str(line[1].encode('utf-8')),
   str(line[0].encode('utf-8')))))

step4=step2.map(lambda line:  ((line[1].encode('utf-8'),
   line[0].encode('utf-8'),float(line[4]),int(line[9])))).distinct()

for i in range (10)
   inp_year = 1990 + i

   step5=step4.filter(lambda line:  line[3]==inp_year).map(lambda
      line:  ((float(line[2]),(line[0],line[1],line[3])))))

   step6=step5.sortByKey(False)

   #Emit top 10 artists
   topArtists=step6.take(10)

   step8=step2.map(lambda line:  ((line[3].encode('utf-8'),
         line[2].encode('utf-8'),float(line[5]),int(line[9])))).distinct()

   step9=step8.filter(lambda line:  line[3]==inp_year).map(lambda line:
         ((float(line[2]),(line[0],line[1],line[3])))).filter(lambda
```

```
       line:    not math.isnan(line[0]))

 step10=step9.sortByKey(False)

 #Emit top 10 songs
 topSongs=step10.take(10)

sc.stop
```

To recommend similar songs, the songs are first clustered into 10 clusters. Songs in a particular cluster are more correlated/similar to each other as compared to the songs in other clusters. Spark's MLlib provides an implementation of the K-Means clustering algorithm. After clustering the songs, we append the corresponding cluster information of each song into the CSV file which also has the song metadata. The cluster centers are stored in a pickle file. Figure 11.10 shows the steps involved in song recommendation.

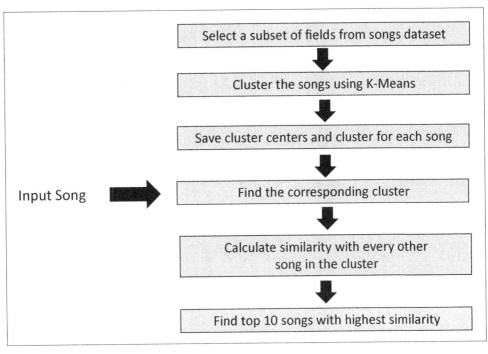

Figure 11.10: Steps involved in song recommendation

For recommending a song, the user provides a song-ID as input. The system then looks up the CSV file containing cluster information to find the corresponding cluster and loads the pickle file to find the corresponding cluster center. The next step is to find every other song in the corresponding cluster apart from the user input song and compute the Euclidean distance between each song and the user input song. Note that, after clustering the search space is significantly reduced and this search can potentially be performed in real time. The songs in the cluster are then sorted according to their Euclidean distance with the user input song and top 10 songs are selected for displaying to the user.

Box 11.6 shows the Spark program for clustering the songs, and Box 11.7 shows the Spark program for recommending similar songs.

■ **Box 11.6: Spark program for clustering the songs**

```python
from pyspark import SparkContext
from pyspark.mllib.clustering import KMeans
from math import sqrt
import sys
import pickle

sc = SparkContext("local", "App")

def closestPoint(p,centers):
    bestIndex = 0
    closest = float("+inf")
    for i in range(len(centers)):
        tempDist = np.sum((p - centers[i]) ** 2)
        if tempDist < closest:
            closest = tempDist
            bestIndex = i
    return bestIndex

Parseddata=sc.textFile("file:///data.csv").map(lambda line:
line.split(",")).filter(lambda line:
len(line)>1).map(lambda line:
(float(line[4]),float(line[5]),float(line[6]),float(line[7])))

clusters = KMeans.train(Parseddata, 10, maxIterations=100,
    runs=100, initializationMode="random")

print str(clusters.clusterCenters)

cc=clusters.clusterCenters
pickle.dump(cc,open("cluster_centers.p","wb"))

PD1 = sc.textFile("file:///data.csv").map(lambda line:
line.split(",")).filter(lambda line:   len(line)>1).map(lambda p:
(p[0].encode('utf-8'),p[1].encode('utf-8'),p[2].encode('utf-8'),
p[3].encode('utf-8'),float(p[4]),float(p[5]),float(p[6]),
float(p[7]),closestPoint([float(p[4]),float(p[5]),
float(p[6]),float(p[7])],cc),p[8].encode('utf-8')))

PD1.saveAsTextFile("file:///data_clustered.txt")

logData = sc.textFile("file:///data_updated.csv").cache()

sc.stop()
```

■ **Box 11.7: Spark program for recommending similar songs**

```python
from pyspark import SparkContext
from operator import add
from pyspark.mllib.clustering import KMeans
import numpy as np
```

```python
from numpy import array
from math import sqrt
import sys
import pickle
import re
import datetime
sc = SparkContext("local", "Simple App")

def g(x):
    print x

def line_strip(p):
   a = p[0].encode('ascii')
   b = p[1].encode('ascii')
   c = (p[2].encode('ascii')).strip(" ")
   d = p[3].encode('ascii')
   e=float(p[4])
   f=float(p[5])
   g=float(p[6])
   h=float(p[7])
   i=int(p[8].encode('ascii'))
   k = p[9].encode('ascii')
   j=(a,b,c,d,e,f,g,h,i,k)
   return j

def euclid_dist(p,user_point,center):
   a=user_point-center
   b=p-center

   c=np.array([(user_point[0]/center[0]-1),(user_point[1]/center[1]-1),
       (user_point[2]/center[2]-1),(user_point[3]/center[3]-1)])

   d=np.array([(p[0]/center[0]-1),(p[1]/center[1]-1),
       (p[2]/center[2]-1),(p[3]/center[3]-1)])

   dist1=np.linalg.norm(c)
   dist2= np.linalg.norm(d)
   dot=np.dot(c,d)
   cosine=dot/dist1/dist2
   similarity=np.sqrt(cosine*cosine+(dist1-dist2)*(dist1-dist2))
   return str(similarity)

PD4_read=sc.textFile("file:////data.csv")
PD4_read_count=PD4_read.count()
PD4_iter=PD4_read.map(lambda line:  line.split(",")).filter(lambda
line:  len(line)>1).map(lambda line:line_strip(line)).collect()

for item in range(len(PD4_iter)):
   input_user=PD4_iter[itcm][2]

   PD4_read2=PD4_read.map(lambda line:  line.split(",")).filter(lambda
      line:  len(line)>1).map(lambda line:line_strip(line))

   PD4_filt=PD4_read2.filter(lambda line:(line[2]==input_user))
```

```
PD4_filt.foreach(g)
CF=PD4_filt.collect()

Cl_found=CF[0][8]
print 'Cluster Found=',Cl_found
cc = pickle.load(open("cluster_centers.p", "rb" ))
print 'Cluster Center=',cc[Cl_found][0],',',
    cc[Cl_found][1],',',cc[Cl_found][2],',',
    cc[Cl_found][3],'',type(Cl_found)

PD6=PD4_read2.filter(lambda line:
(line[8]==Cl_found)).filter(lambda line:(line[2]!=input_user))

PD7=PD6.map(lambda p:(euclid_dist(np.asarray((p[4],p[5],p[6],p[7])),
    np.asarray((CF[0][4],CF[0][5],CF[0][6],CF[0][7])),cc[Cl_found]),
    (p[0],p[1],p[2],p[3]))).sortByKey().collect()

post = {"name":  (CF[0][3]).encode('ascii'),
        "artist":(CF[0][1]).encode('ascii'),
        "spark-id":(CF[0][2]).encode('ascii'),
        "year":(CF[0][9]).encode('ascii'),
        "tags":   ["mongodb", "python", "pymongo"],
        "date":   datetime.datetime.utcnow()}
post["similar"]=[]

print 'Similar Songs are '

for item in range(10):
    song = {"name":  (PD7[item][1][3]).encode('ascii'),
        "artist":(PD7[item][1][1]).encode('ascii'),
        "spark-id":(PD7[item][1][2]).encode('ascii')}
    post["similar"].append(song)

print post

sc.stop()
```

11.4   Classification & Regression

Classification is the process of categorizing objects into predefined categories. Classification is achieved by classification algorithms that belong to a broad category of algorithms called supervised machine learning. Supervised learning involves inferring a model from a set of input data and known responses to the data (training data) and then using the inferred model to predict responses to new data. There are various types of classification approaches for big data analytics including:

- **Binary classification:** Binary classification involves categorizing the data into two categories. For example, classifying the sentiment of a news article into positive or negative, classifying the state of a machine into good or faulty, classifying the health test into positive or negative, etc.
- **Multi-class classification:** Multi-class classification involves more than two classes into which the data is categorized. For example, gene expression classification problem involves multiple classes.

- **Document classification:** Document classification is a type of multi-class classification approach in which the data to the classified is in the form of text document. For example, classifying news articles into different categories such as politics, sports, etc.

Regression

While in classification, the response variable is categorical and unordered (for example yes/no or positive/negative in binary classification) in Regression, the response variable takes continuous values. Regression involves modeling the relationship between a dependent variable (response variable) and one or more independent variables. For example, in linear regression a dependent variable y is modeled as a linear combination of the independent variables. In regression, the goal is to learn a function $h(x)$ from the training set, which can predict the values of y. The function $h(x)$ is called the hypothesis. For linear regression,

$$h(x) = \sum_{i=0}^{n} \theta_i x_i$$

where $\theta_0, \theta_1, ..., \theta_n$ are the parameters.

11.4.1 Performance Evaluation Metrics

For a binary classification problem (with two classes *Positive* and *Negative*) we can have four possible cases: (1) For a *Positive* class if the prediction is *Positive* then this is a *TruePositive*, (2) For a *Positive* class if the prediction is *Negative* then this is a *FalseNegative*, (3) For a *Negative* class if the prediction is *Negative* then this is a *TrueNegative*, (4) For a *Negative* class if the prediction is *Positive* then this is a *FalsePositive*, The performance of classification algorithms can be evaluated using the following metrics:

- **True Positive Rate (TPR)/ Sensitivity / Recall:** True Positive Rate (TPR) also called Sensitivity or Recall is the fraction of the positives which are classified correctly.

$$TPR = \frac{TruePositive}{(TruePositive + FalseNegative)} \tag{11.4}$$

- **True Negative Rate (TNR)/ Specificity:** True Negative Rate (TPR) also called Specificity is the fraction of the negatives which are classified correctly.

$$TNR = \frac{TrueNegative}{(TrueNegative + FalsePositive)} \tag{11.5}$$

- **False Positive Rate (FPR):** False Positive Rate (FPR) is defined as,

$$FPR = \frac{FalsePositive}{(FalsePositive + TrueNegative)} \tag{11.6}$$

- **Precision:** Precision is the fraction of objects that are classified correctly. Precision is defined as,

$$Precision = \frac{TruePositive}{(TruePositive + FalsePositive)} \tag{11.7}$$

- **Accuracy:** Accuracy is defined as,

$$Accuracy = \frac{(TruePositive + TrueNegative)}{(TruePositive + TrueNegative + FalsePositive + FalseNegative)}$$
(11.8)

- **F1-score:** F1-score is a measure of accuracy that considers both precision and recall. F1-score is the harmonic means of precision and recall given as,

$$F1 - Score = \frac{2(Precision)(Recall)}{(Precision + Recall)}$$
(11.9)

- **Receiver Operating Characteristics (ROC) Curve:** ROC curve is the plot of the True Positive Rate (TPR) versus the False Positive Rate (FPR). For different values of the discrimination threshold (threshold for the probability above which we choose a positive class), we get a number of pairs of (TPR, FPR) values.
- **Area Under Curve (AUC):** AUC is the area under the ROC curve.
- **Mean Squared Error (MSE):** Mean Squared Error is the mean of the sum of the square of the errors between the estimated and actual values.

$$MSE = \frac{1}{n}\sum_{i=1}^{n}(h(x^{(i)}) - y^{(i)})^2$$
(11.10)

- **Coefficient of Determination (R^2):** Coefficient of Determination also called R^2 or R-Squared, is a measure of how well the model is able to explain the variation of the data. R^2 is defined as,

$$R^2 = 1 - \frac{\sum_{i=1}^{n}(y^{(i)} - h(x^{(i)}))^2}{\sum_{i=1}^{n}(y^{(i)} - \mu)^2} = 1 - \frac{SSE}{SST}$$
(11.11)

where SSE is the residual sum of squares and SST is the total sum of squares. R^2 varies between 0 and 1. R^2=1 means that the model explains all the variability of the data around its mean.

11.4.2 Naive Bayes

Naive Bayes is a probabilistic classification algorithm based on the Bayes theorem with a naive assumption about the independence of feature attributes. Given a class variable C and feature variables $F_1, ..., F_n$, the conditional probability (posterior) according to Bayes theorem is given as,

$$P(C|F_1, ..., F_n) = \frac{P(F_1, ..., F_n|C)P(C)}{P(F_1, ..., F_n)}$$
(11.12)

where, $P(C|F_1, ..., F_n)$ is the posterior probability, $P(F_1, ..., F_n|C)$ is the likelihood and $P(C)$ is the prior probability and $P(F_1, ..., F_n)$ is the evidence. Naive Bayes makes a naive assumption about the independence every pair of features given as,

$$P(F_1, ..., F_n|C) = \prod_{i=1}^{n} P(F_i|C) \qquad (11.13)$$

In practice, since the evidence $P(F_1, ..., F_n)$ is constant for a given input and does not depend on the class variable C, only the numerator of the posterior probability is important for classification. Therefore we get,

$$P(C|F_1, ..., F_n) \propto P(C) \prod_{i=1}^{n} P(F_i|C) \qquad (11.14)$$

With this simplification, classification can then be done as follows,

$$C = argmax_C P(C) \prod_{i=1}^{n} P(F_i|C) \qquad (11.15)$$

There are different versions of Naive Bayes which differ in the naive assumption made. Some of them include:

- **Gaussian Naive Bayes:** Gaussian Naive Bayes assumes the likelihood $P(F_1, ..., F_n|C)$ as,

$$P(F_1, ..., F_n|C) = \prod_{i=1}^{n} P(F_i|C) \qquad (11.16)$$

where,

$$P(F_i|C) = \frac{1}{\sqrt{2\pi\sigma_C^2}} exp\left(\frac{-(F_i - \mu_C)^2}{2\pi\sigma_C^2}\right) \qquad (11.17)$$

where μ is the mean and σ_C is the standard deviation for values in F_i in class C. Gaussian Naive Bayes is suitable for problems in which the feature variables have continuous values which are assumed to have a Gaussian distribution.

- **Multinomial Naive Bayes:** Multinomial Naive Bayes uses multinomial distribution for each of the feature variables. This is suitable for problems which have discrete features such as document classification.

- **Bernoulli Naive Bayes:** Bernoulli Naive Bayes is also suitable for problems which have discrete features. The likelihood in Bernoulli Naive Bayes is as follows,

$$P(F_i|C) = P(i|CF_i(1 - P(i|C))(1 - F_i) \qquad (11.18)$$

where each feature is assumed to be binary valued.

Let us look at an example of Naive Bayes classification using H2O framework. For this example, we will use the UCI Parkinsons dataset [43]. This dataset is composed of a range of biomedical voice measurements. Each column represents a particular voice measure. The status column has a value 1 for people who have Parkinsons disease and 0 for people who do not have the disease. We will use the training dataset to train a Naive Bayes model and then use the model to make predictions for the test dataset. (i.e. classify people into two categories: those who have Parkinsons disease and those who do not have the disease).

The first step is to import the dataset file into H2O from the H2O Flow UI as shown in Figure 11.11.

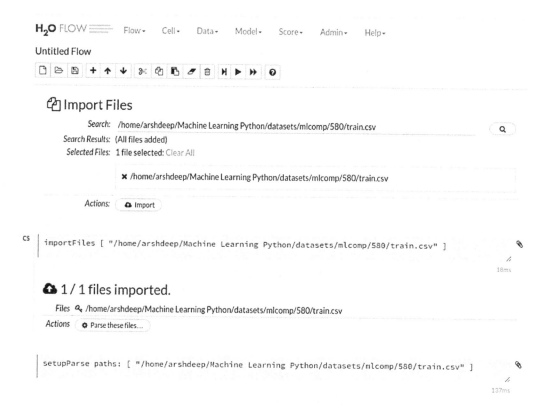

Figure 11.11: Importing dataset files using H2O Flow UI

Figure 11.12: Parsing the dataset file using H2O Flow UI

Next, we parse the dataset file as shown in Figure 11.12. In this step, you can specify various parsing options. After selecting the parse options, click the Parse button to parse the file. The data from the parsed file is stored in an H2O frame. Figure 11.13 shows the H2O frame created by parsing the dataset file.

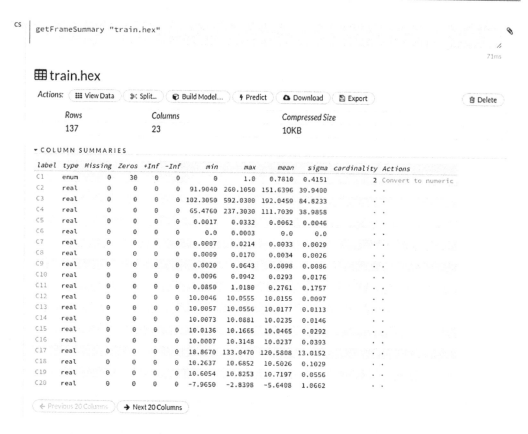

CS | getFrameSummary "train.hex"

71ms

⊞ train.hex

Actions: ⠿ View Data   ✂ Split...   ◉ Build Model...   ⚡ Predict   ⬇ Download   📄 Export   🗑 Delete

Rows	Columns	Compressed Size
137	23	10KB

▾ COLUMN SUMMARIES

label	type	Missing	Zeros	+Inf	-Inf	min	max	mean	sigma	cardinality	Actions
C1	enum	0	30	0	0	0	1.0	0.7810	0.4151	2	Convert to numeric
C2	real	0	0	0	0	91.9040	260.1050	151.6396	39.9400		· ·
C3	real	0	0	0	0	102.3050	592.0300	192.0459	84.8233		· ·
C4	real	0	0	0	0	65.4760	237.3030	111.7039	38.9858		· ·
C5	real	0	0	0	0	0.0017	0.0332	0.0062	0.0046		· ·
C6	real	0	0	0	0	0.0	0.0003	0.0	0.0		· ·
C7	real	0	0	0	0	0.0007	0.0214	0.0033	0.0029		· ·
C8	real	0	0	0	0	0.0009	0.0170	0.0034	0.0026		· ·
C9	real	0	0	0	0	0.0020	0.0643	0.0098	0.0086		· ·
C10	real	0	0	0	0	0.0096	0.0942	0.0293	0.0176		· ·
C11	real	0	0	0	0	0.0850	1.0180	0.2761	0.1757		· ·
C12	real	0	0	0	0	10.0046	10.0555	10.0155	0.0097		· ·
C13	real	0	0	0	0	10.0057	10.0556	10.0177	0.0113		· ·
C14	real	0	0	0	0	10.0073	10.0881	10.0235	0.0146		· ·
C15	real	0	0	0	0	10.0136	10.1665	10.0465	0.0292		· ·
C16	real	0	0	0	0	10.0007	10.3148	10.0237	0.0393		· ·
C17	real	0	0	0	0	18.8670	133.0470	120.5808	13.0152		· ·
C18	real	0	0	0	0	10.2637	10.6852	10.5026	0.1029		· ·
C19	real	0	0	0	0	10.6054	10.8253	10.7197	0.0556		· ·
C20	real	0	0	0	0	-7.9650	-2.8398	-5.6408	1.0662		· ·

← Previous 20 Columns   → Next 20 Columns

Figure 11.13: Viewing the frame created from the parsed dataset file

With the data imported and parsed, let us now build a Naive Bayes classification model. Click the Build Model button in the actions of the parsed frame or choose the Build Model option from the menu. Figure 11.14 shows the various options for the model. Select the algorithm type to be Naive Bayes, training frame as train.hex and response column as C1. After specifying the model options, click the Build Model button to build the model.

```
cs   assist buildModel, null, training_frame: "train.hex"
```

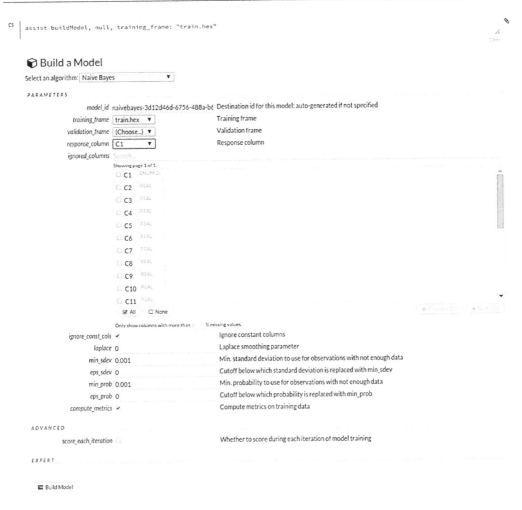

Figure 11.14: Building a Naive Bayes model using H2O Flow UI

Figure 11.15 shows the details of the Naive Bayes model. The model summary shows the various model statistics such as mean squared error (MSE), coefficient of determination (R^2) and area under the curve (AUC).

Next, import and parse the test dataset in the same way as we imported and parsed the training dataset. To make the predictions for the test dataset, enter the *predict* command or choose the predict option from the menu and then select the model and test frame and then click the Predict button, as shown in Figure 11.16.

Figure 11.17 shows the prediction summary including the plot of true positive rate (TPR) and false positive rate (FPR) called the receiver operating characteristic (ROC) curve. Finally, the prediction frame can be exported (as a CSV file) as shown in Figure 11.18.

⬢ Model

Model ID: naivebayes-3d12d46d-6756-488a-b67f-bf629394464b
Algorithm: Naive Bayes
Actions: (⚡ Predict...) (⬇ Download POJO) (☰ Inspect) (🗑 Delete)

▸ MODEL PARAMETERS

▸ OUTPUT

▾ OUTPUT - MODEL SUMMARY

number_of_response_levels 2
  min_apriori_probability 0.2190
  max_apriori_probability 0.7810

▾ OUTPUT - TRAINING_METRICS

            model   naivebayes-3d12d46d-6756-488a-b67f-bf629394464b
   model_checksum   9030698936015077376
            frame   train.hex
  frame_checksum   -3892016302790028800
     description   ·
  model_category   Binomial
    scoring_time   1441791309838
     predictions   ·
             MSE   0.303731
              r2   -0.775925
          logloss   4.065928
             AUC   0.858879
            Gini   0.717757

▾ DOMAIN

domain
-1
1

Figure 11.15: Viewing details of the Naive Bayes model

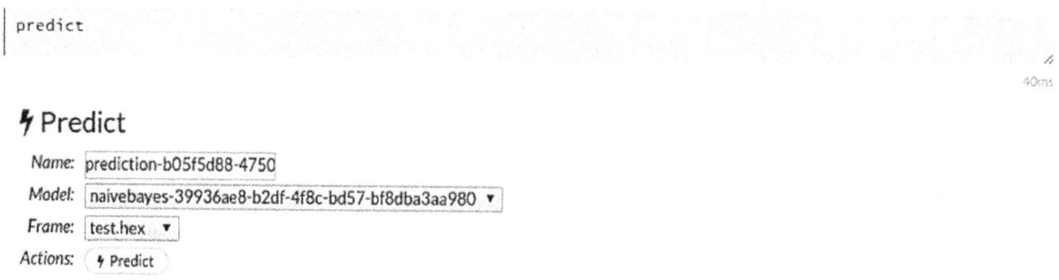

predict
                                                                    ⁄
                                                                 40ms

⚡ Predict

Name: [prediction-b05f5d88-4750]
Model: [naivebayes-39936ae8-b2df-4f8c-bd57-bf8dba3aa980 ▾]
Frame: [test.hex ▾]
Actions: (⚡ Predict)

Figure 11.16: Making predictions for the test data

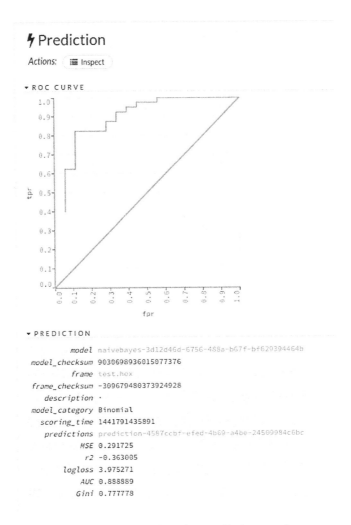

Figure 11.17: Viewing the prediction results

Figure 11.18: Viewing and exporting the prediction frame

Let us look at a Python implementation of Naive Bayes classification using the H2O Python API. Box 11.8 shows a Python program for Naive Bayes classification. The *import_frame* function is used to import the training and test data. Next, we specify the response columns in the training and test frames. We use the *naive_bayes* function to build a Naive Bayes model. To this function we pass the training data without response column (x=train[1:]), response column in the training data (y=train[0]), test data without response column (validation_x= test[1:]) and the response column in the test data (validation_y=test[0]). With the model built, we can then use the *show()* function to view the model summary, *predict* function to make predictions, and *model_performance* function to view the performance of the model with the test data. To export the prediction frame into a CSV file, the *download_csv* function can be used.

■ **Box 11.8: Python program for Naive Bayes classification using H2O**

```
import h2o

h2o.init()

train = h2o.import_frame(path=h2o.locate("/home/ubuntu/train.csv"))
test = h2o.import_frame(path=h2o.locate("/home/ubuntu/test.csv"))


train[0] = train[0].asfactor()
test[0] = test[0].asfactor()

model = h2o.naive_bayes(x=train[1:], y=train[0], validation_x= test[1:],
validation_y=test[0])

model.show()

prediction = model.predict(test)

prediction.head()

perf = model.model_performance(test)
perf.show()

print 'Confusion Matrix: '
print (perf.confusion_matrix())

print 'Precision: '
print (perf.precision())

print 'Accuracy: '
print (perf.accuracy())

print 'AUC: '
print (perf.auc())

h2o.download_csv(prediction, 'prediction.csv')
```

Box 11.9 shows the output of the Python program for Naive Bayes classification.

▪ Box 11.9: Output of program for Naive Bayes classification using H2O

```
>>> model.show()

Model Details
=============
H2OBinomialModel : Naive Bayes
Model Key: NaiveBayes_model_python_1441787876875_21

Model Summary:

 number_of_response_levels min_apriori_probability max_apriori_probability
 ------------------- ----------------- -----------------
    2          0.218978      0.781022


ModelMetricsBinomial: naivebayes
** Reported on train data.  **

MSE: 0.303730509167
R²: -0.775924587712
LogLoss:  4.06592781328
AUC: 0.858878504673
Gini:  0.717757009346

Confusion Matrix (Act/Pred) for max f1 @ threshold = 2.32859177356e-09:

   -1 1 Error Rate
--- --- -- ----- --------
-1  12 18 0.6   (18.0/30.0)
1   1  106 0.0093 (1.0/107.0)
Total 13 124 0.1387 (19.0/137.0)

Maximum Metrics:

 metric         threshold value   idx
------------------ ------- ----- ---
 max f1          2.32859e-09 0.917749 87
 max f2          1.89463e-10 0.963964 90
 max f0point5     2.96126e-07 0.889101 67
 max accuracy     1.14672e-08 0.861314 83
 max precision     1    1     0
 max absolute_MCC   2.32859e-09 0.551268 87
 max min_per_class_accuracy 5.64389e-06 0.766355 52


ModelMetricsBinomial: naivebayes
** Reported on validation data.  **

MSE: 0.291725313697
R²: -0.36300549344
LogLoss:  3.97527089485
AUC: 0.888888888889
Gini:  0.777777777778

Confusion Matrix (Act/Pred) for max f1 @ threshold = 9.23991456735e-09:

   -1 1 Error Rate
--- --- -- ----- -------
-1  10 8 0.4444 (8.0/18.0)
1   1  39 0.025  (1.0/40.0)
Total 11 47 0.1552 (9.0/58.0)
```

```
Maximum Metrics:

metric          threshold value   idx
----------------- -------- ----- ---
max f1          9.23991e-09 0.896552 30
max f2          5.78867e-10 0.952381 33
max f0point5      1.31851e-05 0.916667 18
max accuracy      1.31851e-05 0.844828 18
max precision     0.0441224 0.961538 9
max absolute_MCC    1.31851e-05 0.675148 18
max min_per_class_accuracy 1.31851e-05 0.825   18



>>> prediction
First 10 rows and first 3 columns:
predict    p-1    p1
------ ------- -------
  1 4.04867e-06 0.999996
  1 0.0174331 0.982567
  1 1    9.23991e-09
  1 3.86239e-67 1
  1 1.39996e-27 1
  1 1.10407e-17 1
  1 1    9.9068e-08
 -1 1    1.92925e-09
 -1 1    5.84447e-10
  1 1    1.04785e-08



>>> perf = model.model_performance(test)
>>> perf.show()

ModelMetricsBinomial: naivebayes
** Reported on test data.  **

MSE: 0.291725313697
R^2:  -0.36300549344
LogLoss:  3.97527089485
AUC: 0.888888888889
Gini:  0.777777777778

Confusion Matrix (Act/Pred) for max f1 @ threshold = 9.23991456735e-09:

   -1 1 Error Rate
--- --- -- ----- -------
-1  10 8 0.4444 (8.0/18.0)
1   1  39 0.025 (1.0/40.0)
Total 11 47 0.1552 (9.0/58.0)

Maximum Metrics:

metric          threshold value   idx
----------------- -------- ----- ---
max f1          9.23991e-09 0.896552 30
max f2          5.78867e-10 0.952381 33
max f0point5      1.31851e-05 0.916667 18
max accuracy      1.31851e-05 0.844828 18
max precision     0.0441224 0.961538 9
max absolute_MCC    1.31851e-05 0.675148 18
max min_per_class_accuracy 1.31851e-05 0.825   18

>>> print 'Precision: '
```

```
Precision:
>>> print (perf.precision())
[[0.04412240492341057, 0.9615384615384616]]
>>>
>>> print 'Accuracy:  '
Accuracy:
>>> print (perf.accuracy())
[[1.3185115335693565e-05, 0.8448275862068966]]
>>>
>>> print 'AUC: '
AUC:
>>> print (perf.auc())
0.888888888889
```

Let us now look at a Naive Bayes classification example using Spark MLlib. For this example, we will use the Wine dataset from the UCI Machine learning repository [39] which includes results of a chemical analysis of wines. The chemical analysis determined the quantities of 13 constituents (such as alcohol, malic acid, magnesium, etc.) found in three types of wines.

Box 11.10 shows a Python program for Naive Bayes classification using Spark MLlib. This program can be run in the PySpark shell. In this program we implement a *parseLine* function which takes each line of the input file, splits the line into individual columns separated by commas, converts the values to floats and returns a Python numpy array. In this function, we also change the wine labels from 1.0, 2.0 and 3.0 to 0.0, 1.0 and 2.0 as the Spark's implementation of Naive Bayes expects the labels from 0 to N-1 where N is the total number of classes in the data.

The *NaiveBayes* class of the MLlib classification module is used to build a Naive Bayes model. After the model has been built, the *predict* method of the NaiveBayes class can be used to make the predictions. Finally, we compare the labels in the test dataset and the predicted labels and compute the test error and the accuracy of the model.

■ **Box 11.10: Python program for Naive Bayes classification using Spark MLlib**

```
from pyspark.context import SparkContext
from pyspark.mllib.classification import NaiveBayes
from pyspark.mllib.linalg import Vectors
from pyspark.mllib.regression import LabeledPoint

def parseLine(line):
   parts = line.split(',')
   label = float(parts[0])
   if label==1.0:
      label =0.0
   if label==2.0:
      label = 1.0
   if label==3.0:
      label = 2.0
   features = Vectors.dense([float(x) for x in parts[1:]])
   return LabeledPoint(label, features)

sc = SparkContext(appName="NBExample")
```

```
trainingData = sc.textFile('file:///home/hadoop/wine.data.txt').map(parseLine)

testData = sc.textFile('file:///home/hadoop/wine.test.txt').map(parseLine)

model = NaiveBayes.train(trainingData, 1.0)

predictions = model.predict(testData.map(lambda x:  x.features))

labelsAndPredictions = testData.map(lambda lp:
lp.label).zip(predictions)

testErr = labelsAndPredictions.filter(lambda v_p:
v_p[0] != v_p[1]).count()/float(testData.count())

print('Test Error = ' + str(testErr))
# Test Error = 0.333333333333

predictionAndLabel = testData.map(lambda p :  (model.predict(p.features),
p.label))

predictionAndLabel.take(10)
#[(0.0, 0.0), (0.0, 0.0), (1.0, 1.0), (1.0, 1.0), (2.0, 1.0), (1.0, 2.0),
(1.0, 2.0), (2.0, 2.0), (2.0, 2.0)]

accuracy = 1.0 * predictionAndLabel.filter(lambda (x, v):
x == v).count() / testData.count()

print accuracy
#0.666666666667

sc.stop()
```

11.4.3 Generalized Linear Model

While ordinary linear regression models are used for modeling response variables which are continuous, normally distributed and have constant variance, Generalized Linear Models (GLM) are a generalization of ordinary linear regression models that allows response variables which are discrete, non-normally distributed and/or non-constant variance. Generalized Linear Models are useful for modeling quantities which vary over a wide range (e.g. house prices), categorical and unordered data (e.g. classifying whether a tumor is benign or malignant) and ordinal data (e.g. movie ratings on a scale of 0 to 10), where the exact numerical value has no significance other than ranking (in other words, a movie A with rating 8 is better than a movie B with rating 4, but it does not imply that movie A is twice as better than movie B).

A Generalized Linear Model has three components:

- **Random Component**: The random component of a GLM is a probability distribution of the response variable (y) from the exponential family.
- **Systematic Component**: The random component of a GLM is a linear predictor η which includes the independent variables and the model parameters,
  $$\eta = \beta_0 + \beta_1 x_1 + ... + \beta_n x_n = \mathbf{X}\boldsymbol{\beta}$$
- **Link Function**: The link function specifies the relationship between the expected

value of the response variable ($E(y)$) and the linear predictor (η),

$$E(\mathbf{Y}) = \mu = g^{-1}(\eta)$$

Linear regression is a special case of a Generalized Linear Model where the random component (probability distribution of the response variable) is a normal distribution; the systematic component predicts continuous values and the link function is an identity function.

$$\eta = \mathbf{X}\boldsymbol{\beta} = g(\mu) = \mu$$

Logistic regression is a special case of a Generalized Linear Model where the random component is a Bernoulli distribution, the systematic component predicts categorical values and the link function is a Logit function.

$$\eta = \mathbf{X}\boldsymbol{\beta} = g(\mu) = ln\left(\frac{\mu}{1-\mu}\right)$$

In logistic regression, the predicted values are probabilities which are restricted to (0,1) through the Logit function.

Regression

Let us look at an example of Linear regression using H2O framework. For this example, we will use the UCI Wine Quality dataset [40]. This dataset includes data on physicochemical tests for red and white variants of a Portuguese wine. There are 11 input variables (such as fixed acidity, volatile acidity, citric acid, etc.), and the output variable is a quality score between 0 and 10.

The first step is to import the dataset file into H2O from the H2O Flow UI as shown in Figure 11.19.

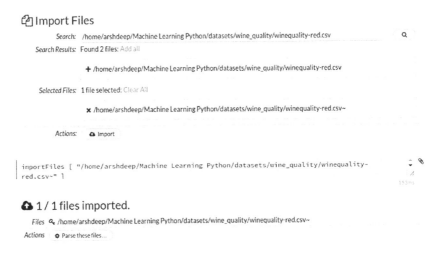

Figure 11.19: Importing dataset file from the H2O Flow UI

Next step is to parse the dataset file. Click the Parse button after importing the file. Figure 11.20 shows how to set up the parser. In this step, you can specify various parsing options. After selecting the parse options, click the Parse button to parse the file.

⚙ Setup Parse

PARSE CONFIGURATION

Sources 🔍 /home/arshdeep/Machine Learning Python/datasets/wine_quality/winequality-red.csv~
ID winequality_red_csv_.hex
Parser [CSV ▼]
Separator [;: '59' ▼]
Column Headers ○ Auto
       ● First row contains column names
       ○ First row contains data
Options ☐ Enable single quotes as a field quotation character
       ☑ Delete on done

EDIT COLUMN NAMES AND TYPES

Search by column name...

#	Column	Type									
1	fixed acidity	Numeric ▼	7.4	7.8	7.8	11.2	7.4	7.4	7.9	7.3	7.8
2	volatile acidity	Numeric ▼	0.7	0.88	0.76	0.28	0.7	0.66	0.6	0.65	0.58
3	citric acid	Numeric ▼	0	0	0.04	0.56	0	0	0.06	0	0.02
4	residual sugar	Numeric ▼	1.9	2.6	2.3	1.9	1.9	1.8	1.6	1.2	2
5	chlorides	Numeric ▼	0.076	0.098	0.092	0.075	0.076	0.075	0.069	0.065	0.073
6	free sulfur dioxide	Numeric ▼	11	25	15	17	11	13	15	15	9
7	total sulfur dioxide	Numeric ▼	34	67	54	60	34	40	59	21	18
8	density	Numeric ▼	0.9978	0.9968	0.997	0.998	0.9978	0.9978	0.9964	0.9946	0.9968
9	pH	Numeric ▼	3.51	3.2	3.26	3.16	3.51	3.51	3.3	3.39	3.36
10	sulphates	Numeric ▼	0.56	0.68	0.65	0.58	0.56	0.56	0.46	0.47	0.57
11	alcohol	Numeric ▼	9.4	9.8	9.8	9.8	9.4	9.4	9.4	10	9.5
12	quality	Numeric ▼	5	5	5	6	5	5	5	7	7

(← Previous page) (→ Next page)

(⬛ Parse)

Figure 11.20: Parsing the imported dataset file using H2O Flow UI

The data from the parsed file is stored in an H2O frame. Figure 11.21 shows the H2O frame created by parsing the dataset file.

The data is split into training and test frames as shown in Figure 11.22. In the next step, we build a GLM model. Figure 11.23 shows the various options for the model. Select the algorithm type to be Generalized Linear Model, training frame (wine_frame_0.750) and family (random component for GLM) to be Gaussian. Choose the family default option for the link function, which will automatically select the default link function for the selected family (Gaussian family). After specifying the model options, click the Build Model button to build the model.

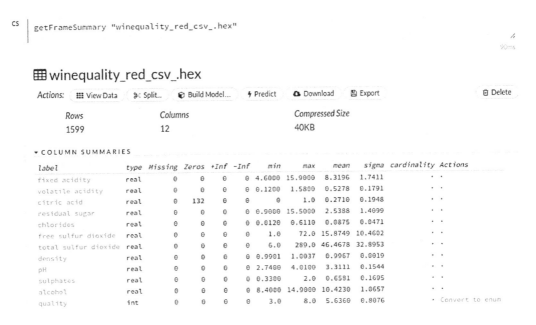

Figure 11.21: Viewing the H2O frame created from the parsed dataset file

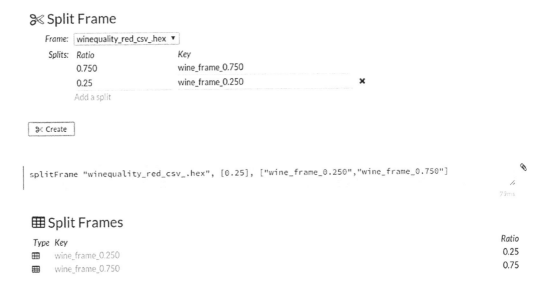

Figure 11.22: Splitting the H2O frame into training and test frames

📦 Build a Model

Select an algorithm: [Generalized Linear Model ▼]

PARAMETERS

model_id	glm-a32eae26-880d-4acd-ad5!	Destination id for this model; auto-generated if not specified
training_frame	[wine_frame_0.750 ▼]	Training frame
validation_frame	[(Choose...) ▼]	Validation frame
nfolds	0	Number of folds for N-fold cross-validation
response_column	[quality ▼]	Response column
ignored_columns	Search	

Showing page 1 of 1.
☐ volatile acidity   REAL
☐ citric acid   REAL
☐ residual sugar   REAL
☐ chlorides   REAL
☐ free sulfur dioxide   REAL
☐ total sulfur dioxide   REAL
☐ density   REAL
☐ pH   REAL
☐ sulphates   REAL
☐ alcohol   REAL
☐ quality   INT

☑ All   ☐ None   ← Previous 100   → Next 100

Only show columns with more than 0   % missing values.

ignore_const_cols	☑	Ignore constant columns
family	[gaussian ▼]	Family. Use binomial for classification with logistic regression, others are for regression problems.
solver	[IRLSM ▼]	Auto will pick solver better suited for the given dataset, in case of lambda search solvers may be changed during computation. IRLSM is fast on on problems with small number of predictors and for lambda-search with L1 penalty, L_BFGS scales better for datasets with many columns.
alpha	0.3	distribution of regularization between L1 and L2.
lambda	0.002	regularization strength
lambda_search	☐	use lambda search starting at lambda max, given lambda is then interpreted as lambda min
standardize	☑	Standardize numeric columns to have zero mean and unit variance
non_negative	☐	Restrict coefficients (not intercept) to be non-negative
beta_constraints	[(Choose...) ▼]	beta constraints

ADVANCED

fold_column	[(Choose...) ▼]	Column with cross-validation fold index assignment per observation
score_each_iteration	☐	Whether to score during each iteration of model training
offset_column	[(Choose...) ▼]	Offset column
weights_column	[(Choose...) ▼]	Column with observation weights
max_iterations	-1	Maximum number of iterations
link	[family_default ▼]	

Figure 11.23: Building a GLM model from H2O Flow UI

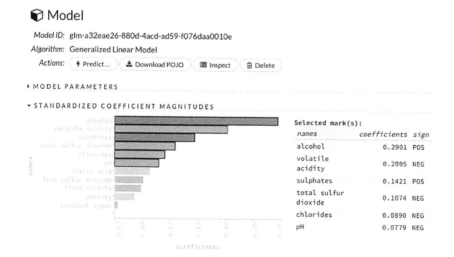

📦 Model

Model ID: glm-a32eae26-880d-4acd-ad59-f076daa0010e

Algorithm: Generalized Linear Model

Actions: ⚡ Predict...   ⬇ Download POJO   ☰ Inspect   🗑 Delete

▸ MODEL PARAMETERS

▾ STANDARDIZED COEFFICIENT MAGNITUDES

Selected mark(s):

names	coefficients	sign
alcohol	0.2901	POS
volatile acidity	0.2005	NEG
sulphates	0.1421	POS
total sulfur dioxide	0.1074	NEG
chlorides	0.0890	NEG
pH	0.0779	NEG

Figure 11.24: Viewing GLM model details

Figure 11.24 shows the model summary including the standardized coefficient magnitudes for the linear regression model. To make the predictions for the test dataset, enter the *predict* command or choose the predict option from the menu, then select the model and test frame, and then click the Predict button. Figure 11.25 shows the prediction summary. Finally, the prediction frame can be exported (as a CSV file) as shown in Figure 11.26.

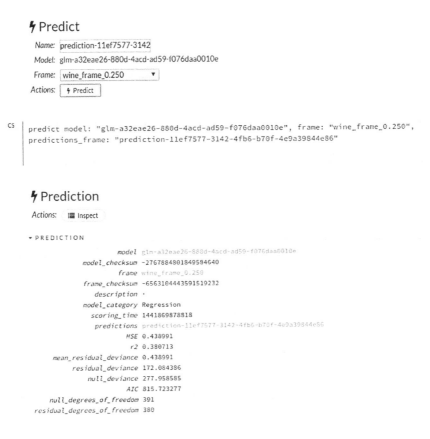

Figure 11.25: Making predictions with GLM model

Figure 11.26: Exporting the prediction frame from H2O Flow UI

Box 11.11 shows a Python implementation of the same example using H2O's Python library and Box 11.12 shows the program output.

■ **Box 11.11: Python program for GLM regression using H2O**

```
import h2o

h2o.init()

data = h2o.import_frame(path=h2o.locate("/home/ubuntu/winequality.csv"))

data_split = data.split_frame(ratios = [0.75,0.25])
train = data_split[0]
test = data_split[1]

train[11] = train[11].asfactor()
test[11] = test[11].asfactor()

model = h2o.glm(x=train[0:11], y=train[11],
    validation_x= test[0:11], validation_y=test[11],
    family='gaussian', link='identity')

model.show()

prediction = model.predict(test)

prediction.head()

perf = model.model_performance(test)
perf.show()

h2o.download_csv(prediction, '/home/ubuntu/prediction.csv')
```

■ **Box 11.12: Output of program for GLM regression using H2O**

```
>>> model.show()
Model Details
=============
H2ORegressionModel : Generalized Linear Model
Model Key:  GLM_model_python_1441864435922_77

ModelMetricsRegressionGLM: glm
** Reported on train data.  **

MSE: 0.407159182645
R²:  0.378282135573
Mean Residual Deviance:  0.407159182645
Null degrees of freedom:  1198
Residual degrees of freedom:  1187
Null deviance:  785.217681401
Residual deviance:  488.183859991
AIC: 2351.25188426

ModelMetricsRegressionGLM: glm
** Reported on validation data.  **

MSE: 0.459194439276
R²:  0.274000886521
```

```
Mean Residual Deviance:  0.459194439276
Null degrees of freedom:  399
Residual degrees of freedom:  388
Null deviance:  258.264326472
Residual deviance:  183.67777571
AIC: 849.838209107


>>> prediction = model.predict(test)

>>>prediction.head()
First 10 rows and first 1 columns:
predict
------
5.16886
5.56495
6.16603
6.28652
5.15812
6.12444
6.12444
6.12444
5.42637
6.12444

>>> perf = model.model_performance(test)
>>> perf.show()

ModelMetricsRegressionGLM: glm
** Reported on test data.  **

MSE: 0.459194439276
R2:  0.274000886521
Mean Residual Deviance:  0.459194439276
Null degrees of freedom:  399
Residual degrees of freedom:  388
Null deviance:  258.264326472
Residual deviance:  183.67777571
AIC: 849.838209107
```

Classification

Let us look at an example of GLM classification (Logistic Regression model) using H2O framework. For this example, we will use the UCI Parkinsons dataset. Import and parse the dataset in the same manner as shown in the Naive Bayes classification example (Figures 11.11 and 11.12).

With the data imported and parsed, let us now build a GLM classification model. Click the Build Model button in the actions of the parsed frame or choose the Build Model option from the menu. Figure 11.27 shows the various options for the model. Select the algorithm type to be Generalized Linear Model, the training frame, and the family (random component for GLM) to be Binomial. Choose the family default option for the link function, which will automatically select the default link function for the selected family (Binomial family). After specifying the model options, click the Build Model button to build the model. Figures 11.28 and 11.29 show the details of the GLM model including the ROC curve and standardized coefficient magnitudes.

Next, import and parse the test dataset in the same way as we imported and parsed the training dataset. To make the predictions for the test dataset, enter the *predict* command or

🗃 Build a Model

Select an algorithm: | Generalized Linear Model   ▼ |

PARAMETERS

model_id	glm-fed8c8cd-256:	Destination id for this model; auto-generated if not specified
training_frame	train1.hex ▼	Training frame
validation_frame	test.hex ▼	Validation frame
nfolds	0	Number of folds for N-fold cross-validation
response_column	C1 ▼	Response column
ignored_columns	Search...	

Showing page 1 of 1.

☐ C1   ENUM(2)
☐ C2   REAL
☐ C3   REAL
☐ C4   REAL
☐ C5   REAL
☐ C6   REAL
☐ C7   REAL
☐ C8   REAL
☐ C9   REAL
☐ C10   REAL
☐ C11   REAL

☑ All   ☐ None   ← Previous 100   → Next 100

Only show columns with more than 0 % missing values.

ignore_const_cols	☑	Ignore constant columns
family	binomial ▼	Family. Use binomial for classification with logistic regression, others are for regression problems.
solver	AUTO ▼	Auto will pick solver better suited for the given dataset, in case of lambda search solvers may be changed during computation. IRLSM is fast on on problems with small number of predictors and for lambda-search with L1 penalty, L_BFGS scales better for datasets with many columns.
alpha		distribution of regularization between L1 and L2.
lambda		regularization strength
lambda_search	☐	use lambda search starting at lambda max, given lambda is then interpreted as lambda min

Figure 11.27: Building a GLM model from H2O Flow UI

choose the predict option from the menu, then select the model and test frame, and then click
the Predict button. Figure 11.30 shows the prediction summary. Finally, the prediction frame
can be exported (as a CSV file) as shown in Figure 11.31.

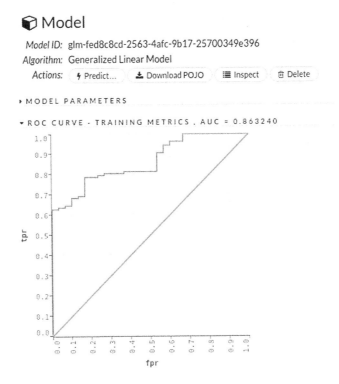

Figure 11.28: Viewing GLM model details

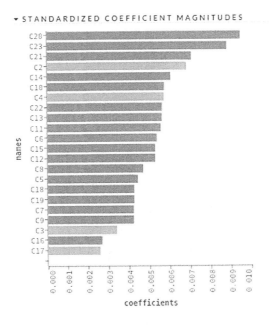

Figure 11.29: Viewing GLM model details

⚡ Predict

Name: `prediction-02735903-d762`

Model: glm-fed8c8cd-2563-4afc-9b17-25700349e396

Frame: `test.hex ▼`

Actions: ⚡ Predict

```
predict model: "glm-fed8c8cd-2563-4afc-9b17-25700349e396", frame: "test.hex",
predictions_frame: "prediction-02735903-d762-4696-a883-c82a80e5a54e"
```
227ms

⚡ Prediction

Actions: ☰ Inspect

▾ PREDICTION

model	glm-fed8c8cd-2563-4afc-9b17-25700349e396
model_checksum	3698391112080226816
frame	test.hex
frame_checksum	-309679480373924928
description	·
model_category	Binomial
scoring_time	1442482485083
predictions	prediction-02735903-d762-4696-a883-c82a80e5a54e
MSE	0.213617
r2	0.081935
logloss	0.616407
AUC	0.918056
Gini	0.836111
residual_deviance	71.503238
null_deviance	74.448375
AIC	117.503238
null_degrees_of_freedom	57
residual_degrees_of_freedom	35

Figure 11.30: Making predictions using GLM model

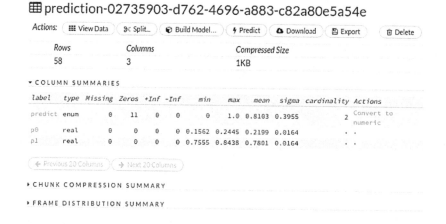

⊞ prediction-02735903-d762-4696-a883-c82a80e5a54e

Actions: ☰ View Data   ✂ Split...   ⬡ Build Model...   ⚡ Predict   ☁ Download   🖺 Export   🗑 Delete

Rows	Columns	Compressed Size
58	3	1KB

▾ COLUMN SUMMARIES

label	type	Missing	Zeros	+Inf	-Inf	min	max	mean	sigma	cardinality	Actions
predict	enum	0	11	0	0	0	1.0	0.8103	0.3955	2	Convert to numeric
p0	real	0	0	0	0	0.1562	0.2445	0.2199	0.0164	·	·
p1	real	0	0	0	0	0.7555	0.8438	0.7801	0.0164	·	·

(← Previous 20 Columns) (→ Next 20 Columns)

▸ CHUNK COMPRESSION SUMMARY

▸ FRAME DISTRIBUTION SUMMARY

Figure 11.31: Exporting the prediction frame

Box 11.13 shows a Python implementation of the same example using H2O's Python library and Box 11.14 shows the program output.

■ **Box 11.13: Python program for GLM classification using H2O**

```
import h2o

h2o.init()

train = h2o.import_frame(path=h2o.locate("/home/ubuntu/train.csv"))
test = h2o.import_frame(path=h2o.locate("/home/ubuntu/train.csv"))

train[0] = train[0].asfactor()
test[0] = test[0].asfactor()

model = h2o.glm(x=train[1:], y=train[0],
   validation_x= test[1:], validation_y=test[0],
   family='binomial', link='logit')

model.show()

prediction = model.predict(test)

prediction.head()

perf = model.model_performance(test)
perf.show()

print 'Confusion Matrix:  '
print (perf.confusion_matrix())

print 'Precision:  '
print (perf.precision())

print 'Accuracy:  '
print (perf.accuracy())

print 'AUC: '
print (perf.auc())

h2o.download_csv(prediction, '/home/ubuntu/prediction.csv')
```

■ **Box 11.14: Output of program for GLM classification using H2O**

```
>>> model.show()
Model Details
=============
H2OBinomialModel :  Generalized Linear Model
Model Key:  GLM_model_python_1442483162375_2

GLM Model:

family:  binomial
```

```
link:  logit
regularization:  Elastic Net (alpha = 0.5, lambda = 0.04384 )
number_of_predictors_total:  22
number_of_active_predictors:  10
number_of_iterations:  6
training_frame:  py0cdd7344-bfca-42a5-a122-7d4db9da9615

ModelMetricsBinomialGLM: glm
** Reported on train data.  **


MSE: 0.10081486084
R²:  0.410531425821
LogLoss:  0.3256156667
Null degrees of freedom:  136
Residual degrees of freedom:  127
Null deviance:  144.017560202
Residual deviance:  89.2186926758
AIC: 109.218692676
AUC: 0.893769470405
Gini:  0.78753894081


Confusion Matrix (Act/Pred) for max f1 @ threshold = 0.439216360065:

   -1 1 Error Rate
--- --- -- ----- --------
-1   15 15 0.5   (15.0/30.0)
1    0  107 0   (0.0/107.0)
Total 15 122 0.1095 (15.0/137.0)

Maximum Metrics:

metric         threshold value  idx
----------------- ------- ----- ---
max f1          0.439216  0.934498 121
max f2          0.439216  0.972727 121
max f0point5     0.734741  0.903491 94
max accuracy     0.480394  0.890511 119
max precision    0.998257  1    0
max absolute_MCC   0.439216  0.662212 121
max min_per_class_accuracy 0.748936  0.766667 89


ModelMetricsBinomialGLM: glm
** Reported on validation data.  **

MSE: 0.104925736208
R²:  0.509763643607
LogLoss:  0.337658509376
Null degrees of freedom:  57
Residual degrees of freedom:  48
Null deviance:  74.4483748993
Residual deviance:  39.1683870876
AIC: 59.1683870876
AUC: 0.927777777778
Gini:  0.855555555556


Confusion Matrix (Act/Pred) for max f1 @ threshold = 0.568524772441:

   -1 1 Error Rate
--- --- -- ----- -------
-1   12 6 0.3333 (6.0/18.0)
1    0  40 0   (0.0/40.0)
Total 12 46 0.1034 (6.0/58.0)
```

```
Maximum Metrics:

metric              threshold value   idx
----------------    --------- -----   ---
max f1              0.568525   0.930233 45
max f2              0.568525   0.970874 45
max f0point5        0.767793   0.914634 30
max accuracy        0.568525   0.896552 45
max precision       0.999028   1     0
max absolute_MCC    0.568525   0.761387 45
max min_per_class_accuracy 0.749704   0.8   34


>>> prediction = model.predict(test)
>>> prediction.head()
First 10 rows and first 3 columns:
predict    p0   p1
------    -------  -----
   1  0.0329049 0.967095
   1  0.0378409 0.962159
   1  0.412367 0.587633
   1  0.00664681 0.993353
   1  0.0211856 0.978814
   1  0.08681   0.91319
   1  0.431475 0.568525
  -1  0.715825 0.284175
  -1  0.743189 0.256811
  -1  0.83547   0.16453


>>> perf = model.model_performance(test)
>>> perf.show()

ModelMetricsBinomialGLM: glm
** Reported on test data.   **

MSE: 0.104925736208
R^2:  0.509763643607
LogLoss:  0.337658509376
Null degrees of freedom:  57
Residual degrees of freedom:  48
Null deviance:  74.4483748993
Residual deviance:  39.1683870876
AIC: 59.1683870876
AUC: 0.927777777778
Gini:  0.855555555556


Confusion Matrix (Act/Pred) for max f1 @ threshold = 0.568524772441:

   -1 1 Error Rate
--- --- -- ----- -------
-1  12 6 0.3333 (6.0/18.0)
1   0  40 0   (0.0/40.0)
Total 12 46 0.1034 (6.0/58.0)

Maximum Metrics:

metric              threshold value   idx
----------------    --------- -----   ---
max f1              0.568525   0.930233 45
max f2              0.568525   0.970874 45
max f0point5        0.767793   0.914634 30
max accuracy        0.568525   0.896552 45
max precision       0.999028   1     0
max absolute_MCC    0.568525   0.761387 45
```

```
max min_per_class_accuracy 0.749704   0.8   34
>>>
>>> print 'Confusion Matrix:  '
Confusion Matrix:
>>> print (perf.confusion_matrix())

Confusion Matrix (Act/Pred) for max f1 @ threshold = 0.568524772441:

   -1 1 Error Rate
--- --- -- ----- -------
-1   12 6 0.3333 (6.0/18.0)
1    0  40 0    (0.0/40.0)
Total 12 46 0.1034 (6.0/58.0)

>>>
>>> print 'Precision:  '
Precision:
>>> print (perf.precision())
[[0.9990275569821115, 1.0]]
>>>
>>> print 'Accuracy:  '
Accuracy:
>>> print (perf.accuracy())
[[0.568524772440684, 0.896551724137931]]
>>>
>>> print 'AUC: '
AUC:
>>> print (perf.auc())
0.927777777778
```

Let us now repeat the same example using Spark MLlib. Box 11.15 shows a Python program for GLM classification (logistic regression model) using Spark MLlib. This program can be run in the PySpark shell. In this program we implement a *parseLine* function which takes each line of the input file, splits the line into individual columns separated by commas, converts the values to floats and returns LabeledPoints. The *LogisticRegressionWithLBFGS* class of the MLlib classification module is used to build a Logistic Regression model. After the model has been built, the *predict* method of the LogisticRegressionWithLBFGS class can be used to make the predictions. Finally, we compare the labels in the test dataset and the predicted labels and compute the test error. The predictions can be saved to a text file using the *saveAsTextFile* function.

■ **Box 11.15: Python program for GLM classification (logistic regression) using Spark MLlib**

```
from pyspark.context import SparkContext
from pyspark.mllib.classification import LogisticRegressionWithLBFGS
from pyspark.mllib.linalg import Vectors
from pyspark.mllib.regression import LabeledPoint

def parseLine(line):
   parts = line.split(',')
   label = float(parts[0])
   if label==-1.0:
      label =0.0
   features = Vectors.dense([float(x) for x in parts[1:]])
```

```
    return LabeledPoint(label, features)

sc = SparkContext(appName="GLMExample")

trainingData = sc.textFile('file:///home/hadoop/train.csv').map(parseLine)

testData = sc.textFile('file:///home/hadoop/test.csv').map(parseLine)

model = LogisticRegressionWithLBFGS.train(trainingData)

predictions = model.predict(testData.map(lambda x:  x.features))

labelsAndPredictions = testData.map(lambda lp:
            lp.label).zip(predictions)

testErr = labelsAndPredictions.filter(lambda v_p:
        v_p[0] != v_p[1]).count()/ float(testData.count())

print('Test Error = ' + str(testErr))

labelsAndPredictions.saveAsTextFile('file:///home/hadoop/prediction.txt')
sc.stop()
```

11.4.4 Decision Trees

Decision Trees are a supervised learning method that use a tree created from simple decision rules learned from the training data as a predictive model. The predictive model is in the form of a tree that can be used to predict the value of a target variable based on several attribute variables. Each node in the tree corresponds to one attribute in the dataset on which the "split" is performed. Each leaf in a decision tree represents a value of the target variable. The learning process involves recursively splitting on the attributes until all the samples in the child node have the same value of the target variable or splitting further results in no further information gain. To select the best attribute for splitting at each stage, different metrics can be used. The two most popular metrics used to determine the best attribute for splitting are:

- **Information Gain:** Information content of a discrete random variable X with probability mass function (PMF), $P(X)$, is defined as,

$$I(X) = -\log_2 P(X) \tag{11.19}$$

Information gain is defined based on the entropy of the random variable which is defined as,

$$H(X) = E[I(X)] = E[-\log_2 P(X)] = -\sum_i \log_2 P(x_i) \tag{11.20}$$

Entropy is a measure of uncertainty in a random variable and choosing the attribute with the highest information gain results in a split that reduces the uncertainty the most at that stage.

- **Gini Coefficient:** Gini coefficient measures the inequality, i.e. how often a randomly chosen sample that is labeled based on the distribution of labels, would be labeled incorrectly. Gini coefficient is defined as,

$$G(X) = 1 - \sum_i P(x_i)^2 \tag{11.21}$$

There are different algorithms for building decisions trees, the popular ones being ID3 and C4.5. Let us look at the steps involved in the ID3 algorithm:

- Attributes are discrete. If not, discretize the continuous attributes.
- Calculate the entropy of every attribute using the dataset.
- Choose the attribute with the highest information gain.
- Create branches for each value of the selected attribute.
- Repeat with the remaining attributes.

The ID3 algorithm can result in over-fitting to the training data and can be expensive to train especially for continuous attributes. The C4.5 algorithm is an extension of the ID3 algorithm. C4.5 supports both discrete and continuous attributes. To support continuous attributes, C4.5 finds thresholds for the continuous attributes and then splits based on the threshold values. C4.5 prevents over-fitting by pruning trees after they have been created. Pruning involves removing or aggregating those branches which provide little discriminatory power.

Let us now look at a Decision Tree classification example using Spark MLlib. For this example, we will use the UCI Parkinsons dataset. Box 11.16 shows a Python program for Decision Tree classification using Spark MLlib. This program can be run in the PySpark shell. In this program we implement a *parseLine* function which takes each line of the input file, splits the line into individual columns separated by commas, converts the values to floats and returns a Python numpy array. In this function, we also change the wine labels from -1.0, 1.0 to 0.0 and 1.0 as the Spark expects the labels from 0 to N-1 where N is the total number of classes in the data.

The *DecisionTree* class of the MLlib classification module is used to build a Decision Tree model. After the model has been built, the *predict* method of the DecisionTree class can be used to make the predictions. Finally, we compare the labels in the test dataset and the predicted labels and compute the test error of the model.

■ Box 11.16: Python program for Decision Tree classification using Spark MLlib

```
import sys

from pyspark.context import SparkContext
from pyspark.mllib.tree import DecisionTree, DecisionTreeModel
from pyspark.mllib.linalg import Vectors
from pyspark.mllib.regression import LabeledPoint

def parseLine(line):
   parts = line.split(',')
   label = float(parts[0])
   if label==1.0:
      label =1
   if label==-1.0:
      label = 0
   features = Vectors.dense([float(x) for x in parts[1:]])
   return LabeledPoint(label, features)

sc = SparkContext(appName="DTExample")
```

```
trainingData = sc.textFile('file:///home/hadoop/train.csv').map(parseLine)

testData = sc.textFile('file:///home/hadoop/test.csv').map(parseLine)


model = DecisionTree.trainClassifier(trainingData, numClasses=3,
categoricalFeaturesInfo=, impurity='gini', maxDepth=5, maxBins=32)

predictions = model.predict(testData.map(lambda x:  x.features))

labelsAndPredictions = testData.map(lambda lp:
lp.label).zip(predictions)

labelsAndPredictions.take(10)
#[(1.0, 1.0), (1.0, 1.0), (1.0, 1.0), (1.0, 1.0), (1.0, 1.0),
(1.0, 1.0), (1.0, 0.0), (0.0, 0.0), (0.0, 0.0), (0.0, 0.0)]


testErr = labelsAndPredictions.filter(lambda v_p:
v_p[0] != v_p[1]).count()/ float(testData.count())

print('Test Error = ' + str(testErr))
#Test Error = 0.155172413793

labelsAndPredictions.saveAsTextFile('file:///home/hadoop/prediction.txt')

sc.stop()
```

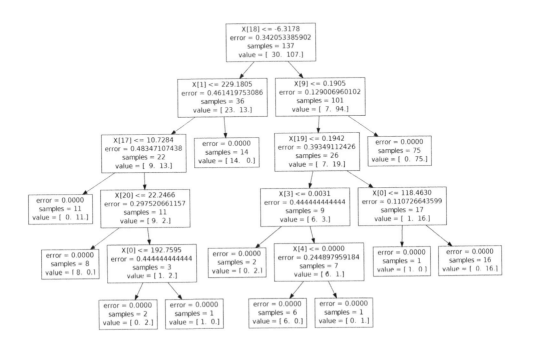

Figure 11.32: Example of a generated decision tree

Figure 11.32 shows an example of a decision tree generated for the Parkinsons dataset. The tree shows the attributes on which splitting is done at each step and the split values. Also shows are the error, total number of samples at each node and the number of samples in each class (in the value array). For example, the first split is done on the 19th column (attribute X[18]) and the total number of samples in the training set is 137. On the first split, there are 30 samples in first class and 107 samples in the second class.

11.4.5   Random Forest

Random Forest is an ensemble learning method that is based on randomized decision trees [38]. Random Forest trains a number decision trees and then takes the majority vote by using the mode of the class predicted by the individual trees. The Random Forest algorithm (Breiman's algorithm) is shown in Box 11.17.

■ Box 11.17: Random Forest algorithm

1. Draw a bootstrap sample (n times with replacement from the N samples in the training set) from the dataset
2. Train a decision tree
    - Until the tree is fully grown (maximum size)
        – Choose next leaf node
        – Select m attributes (m is much less than the total number of attributes M) at random.
        – Choose the best attribute and split as usual
3. Measure out-of-bag error
    - Use the rest of the samples (not selected in the bootstrap) to estimate the error of the tree, by predicting their classes.
4. Repeat steps 1-3 k times to generate k trees.
5. Make a prediction by majority vote among the k trees

Let us look at an example of Random Forest classification using H2O framework. For this example, we will use the Wine dataset. Import and parse the dataset file in the same way as done in the example for k-means clustering (as shown in Figure 11.5 and Figure 11.6). With the data imported and parsed, let us now build a Random Forest model. Click the Build Model button in the actions of the parsed frame or choose the Build Model option from the menu. Figure 11.33 shows the various options for the model. Select the algorithm type to be Distributed RF, the training frame, and the response column as C1. After specifying the model options, click the Build Model button to build the model.

Figures 11.34, 11.35 and 11.36 show the details of the Random Forest model built from the Wine dataset.

🗍 Build a Model

Select an algorithm: Distributed RF ▼

PARAMETERS

model_id	drf-3cfd7e40-b938-4ea5	Destination id for this model; auto-generated if not specified
training_frame	wine_data_txt_.hex ▼	Training frame
validation_frame	{Choose...} ▼	Validation frame
nfolds	0	Number of folds for N-fold cross-validation
response_column	C1 ▼	Response column
ignored_columns	Search...	

Showing page 1 of 1.

☐ C4 REAL
☐ C5 REAL
☐ C6 INT
☐ C7 REAL
☐ C8 REAL
☐ C9 REAL
☐ C10 REAL
☐ C11 REAL
☐ C12 REAL
☐ C13 REAL
☐ C14 INT

☑ All   ☐ None

Only show columns with more than ⃝ % missing values.

ignore_const_cols	✔	Ignore constant columns
ntrees	50	Number of trees.
max_depth	20	Maximum tree depth.
min_rows	1	Fewest allowed (weighted) observations in a leaf (in R called 'nodesize').
nbins	20	For numerical columns (real/int), build a histogram of (at least) this many bins, then split at the best point
nbins_cats	1024	For categorical columns (enum), build a histogram of this many bins, then split at the best point. Higher values can lead to more overfitting.
seed	-711231048995561500	Seed for pseudo random number generator (if applicable)
mtries	-1	Number of variables randomly sampled as candidates at each split. If set to -1, defaults to sqrt(p) for classification and p/3 for regression (where p is the # of predictors
sample_rate	0.632	Sample rate, from 0. to 1.0

ADVANCED

score_each_iteration	☐	Whether to score during each iteration of model training
fold_column	{Choose...} ▼	Column with cross-validation fold index assignment per observation
offset_column	{Choose...} ▼	Offset column
weights_column	{Choose...} ▼	Column with observation weights
balance_classes	☐	Balance training data class counts via over/under-sampling (for imbalanced data).
max_confusion_matrix_size	20	Maximum size (# classes) for confusion matrices to be printed in the Logs

Figure 11.33: Building a Random Forest model using H2O Flow UI

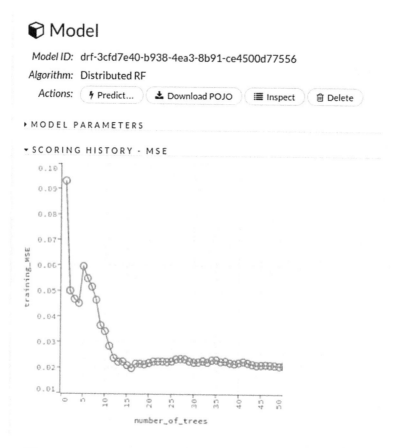

Figure 11.34: Viewing details of the Random Forest model

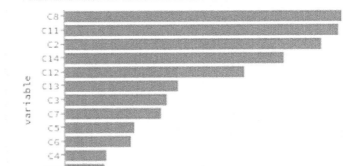

▾ TRAINING METRICS - CONFUSION MATRIX

	1	2	3	Error	Rate
1	59	0	0	0	0 / 59
2	0	70	1	0.0141	1 / 71
3	0	0	48	0	0 / 48
Total	59	70	49	0.0056	1 / 178

▾ OUTPUT

cross_validation_models	·
cross_validation_predictions	·
model_category	Multinomial
validation_metrics	·
cross_validation_metrics	·
status	DONE
start_time	1441793541073
end_time	1441793541789
run_time	716
init_f	0

Figure 11.35: Viewing details of the Random Forest model

▾ OUTPUT - MODEL SUMMARY

```
      number_of_trees  150
   model_size_in_bytes  24301
            min_depth  3
            max_depth  9
           mean_depth  4.6467
           min_leaves  4
           max_leaves  18
          mean_leaves  8.4867
```

▸ OUTPUT - SCORING HISTORY

▾ OUTPUT - TRAINING_METRICS

```
              model  drf-3cfd7e40-b938-4ea3-8b91-ce4500d77556
     model_checksum  -7230121784556874752
              frame  wine_data_txt_.hex
     frame_checksum  -1597625842813973760
        description  Metrics reported on Out-Of-Bag training samples
     model_category  Multinomial
       scoring_time  1441793541774
        predictions  ·
                MSE  0.021024
                 r2  0.964802
            logloss  0.101696
```

▾ OUTPUT - TRAINING_METRICS - TOP-3 HIT RATIOS

k	hit_ratio
1	0.9944
2	1.0
3	1.0

Figure 11.36: Viewing the model summary and training metrics

Next, import and parse the test dataset in the same way as we imported and parsed the training dataset. To make the predictions for the test dataset, enter the *predict* command or choose the predict option from the menu, then select the model and test frame, and then click the Predict button. Figure 11.37 shows the prediction summary.

```
cs  predict model: "drf-3cfd7e40-b938-4ea3-8b91-ce4500d77556", frame: "wine_test.hex",
    predictions_frame: "prediction-4f4b3701-339c-4569-8c82-5d5ec191cd6a"
```

48ms

⚡ Prediction

Actions: ≣ Inspect

▾ PREDICTION

model	drf-3cfd7e40-b938-4ea3-8b91-ce4500d77556
model_checksum	-7230121784556874752
frame	wine_test.hex
frame_checksum	3950704747095732224
description	·
model_category	Multinomial
scoring_time	1441793660262
predictions	prediction-4f4b3701-339c-4569-8c82-5d5ec191cd6a
MSE	0.001000
r2	0.998380
logloss	0.026279

▾ PREDICTION - TOP-3 HIT RATIOS

k	hit_ratio
1	1.0
2	1.0
3	1.0

▸ PREDICTION - CM

▾ PREDICTION - CM - CONFUSION MATRIX

1	2	3	Error	Rate
2	0	0	0	0 / 2
0	3	0	0	0 / 3
0	0	4	0	0 / 4
2	3	4	0	0 / 9

Figure 11.37: Viewing the prediction results

Box 11.18 shows a Python implementation of the same example using H2O's Python library.

■ **Box 11.18: Python program for Random Forest classification using H2O**

```
import h2o

h2o.init()
```

```
train = h2o.import_frame(path=h2o.locate("/home/ubuntu/wine.data.txt"))
test = h2o.import_frame(path=h2o.locate("/home/ubuntu/wine.test.txt"))

train[0] = train[0].asfactor()
test[0] = test[0].asfactor()

model = h2o.random_forest(x=train[1:], y=train[0],
validation_x= test[1:],    validation_y=test[0], seed=12, ntrees=10,
   max_depth=20, balance_classes=True)

model.show()

prediction = model.predict(test)

prediction.head()

perf = model.model_performance(test)
perf.show()

print 'Confusion Matrix:  '
print (perf.confusion_matrix())

print 'Precision:  '
print (perf.precision())

print 'Accuracy:  '
print (perf.accuracy())

print 'AUC: '
print (perf.auc())

h2o.download_csv(prediction, 'prediction.csv')
```

Box 11.19 shows the output of program for Random Forest classification using H2O.

■ **Box 11.19: Output of program for Random Forest classification using H2O**

```
model.show()
Model Details
=============
H2OMultinomialModel :  Distributed RF
Model Key:  DRF_model_python_1441787876875_28

Model Summary:

 number_of_trees model_size_in_bytes min_depth max_depth mean_depth min_leaves max_leaves mean_leaves
 ----------- --------------- ------- ------- -------- -------- -------- ---------
  30       4805        3     9    4.86667  5     15    8.4


ModelMetricsMultinomial:  drf
** Reported on train data.   **

MSE: 0.0242244865001
R2:   0.963923431738
LogLoss:  0.383920432907
```

```
Confusion Matrix:

1 2 3 Error  Rate
-- -- -- ------ -----
70 0  0  0    0 / 70
0 66 2 0.0294118 2 / 68
0 1 68 0.0144928 1 / 69
70 67 70 0.0144928 3 / 207

Top-3 Hit Ratios:

k hit_ratio
-- -------
1 0.985507
2 0.995169
3 1

ModelMetricsMultinomial:  drf
** Reported on validation data.  **

MSE: 0.0110899144456
R^2:  0.982034338598
LogLoss:  0.0536092821889

Confusion Matrix:

1 2 3 Error Rate
-- -- -- ----- ----
2 0 0 0  0 / 2
0 3 0 0  0 / 3
0 0 4 0  0 / 4
2 3 4 0  0 / 9

Top-3 Hit Ratios:

k hit_ratio
-- -------
1 1
2 1
3 1

Variable Importances:

variable relative_importance scaled_importance percentage
-------- ------------------- ----------------- ----------
C13    310.435    1       0.266665
C2     197.323    0.635635    0.169502
C14    165.101    0.531839    0.141823
C11    99.1768    0.319477    0.0851934
C8     72.4592    0.233412    0.0622428
C3     59.1769    0.190626    0.0508333
C12    53.6374    0.172782    0.0460749
C10    44.0346    0.141848    0.0378259
C6     43.2904    0.139451    0.0371867
C5     41.5202    0.133749    0.0356661
C7     40.4724    0.130373    0.034766
C9     21.3045    0.0686277   0.0183006
C4     16.2047    0.0521999   0.0139199

perf = model.model_performance(test)
>>> perf.show()
```

```
ModelMetricsMultinomial:   drf
** Reported on test data.   **

MSE: 0.0110899144456
R²:  0.982034338598
LogLoss:   0.0536092821889

Confusion Matrix:

1 2 3 Error Rate
-- -- -- ----- ----
2 0 0 0   0 / 2
0 3 0 0   0 / 3
0 0 4 0   0 / 4
2 3 4 0   0 / 9

Top-3 Hit Ratios:

k hit_ratio
-- -------
1 1
2 1
3 1
>>>
>>> print 'Confusion Matrix: '
Confusion Matrix:
>>> print (perf.confusion_matrix())

Confusion Matrix:

1 2 3 Error Rate
-- -- -- ----- ----
2 0 0 0   0 / 2
0 3 0 0   0 / 3
0 0 4 0   0 / 4
2 3 4 0   0 / 9
```

Let us now repeat the same example using Spark MLlib with the Wine dataset. Box 11.20 shows the python program for Random Forest classification using Spark MLlib. This program can be run in the PySpark shell. In this program we implement a *parseLine* function which takes each line of the input file, splits the line into individual columns separated by commas, converts the values to floats and returns LabeledPoints. In this function, we also change the wine labels from 1.0, 2.0 and 3.0 to 0.0, 1.0 and 2.0 as the Spark expects the labels from 0 to N-1 where N is the total number of classes in the data. The *RandomForest* class of the MLlib classification module is used to build a Random Forest model. After the model has been built, the *predict* method is used to make the predictions. Finally, we compare the labels in the test dataset and the predicted labels and compute the test error. The predictions can be saved to a text file using the *saveAsTextFile* function.

■ **Box 11.20: Python program for Random Forest classification using Spark MLlib**

```
import sys

from pyspark.context import SparkContext
from pyspark.mllib.tree import RandomForest, RandomForestModel
from pyspark.mllib.linalg import Vectors
```

```
from pyspark.mllib.regression import LabeledPoint

def parseLine(line):
   parts = line.split(',')
   label = float(parts[0])
   if label==1.0:
      label =0.0
   if label==2.0:
      label = 1.0
   if label==3.0:
      label = 2.0
   features = Vectors.dense([float(x) for x in parts[1:]])
   return LabeledPoint(label, features)

sc = SparkContext(appName="RandomForestExample")

trainingData = sc.textFile('file:///home/hadoop/wine.data.txt').map(parseLine)

testData = sc.textFile('file:///home/hadoop/wine.test.txt').map(parseLine)

model = RandomForest.trainClassifier(trainingData, numClasses=3,
      categoricalFeaturesInfo=,
      numTrees=3, featureSubsetStrategy="auto",
      impurity='gini', maxDepth=4, maxBins=32)

predictions = model.predict(testData.map(lambda x:  x.features))

labelsAndPredictions = testData.map(lambda lp:
lp.label).zip(predictions)

labelsAndPredictions.take(10)
#[(0.0, 0.0), (0.0, 0.0), (1.0, 1.0), (1.0, 1.0), (1.0, 1.0), (2.0, 2.0),
(2.0, 2.0), (2.0, 2.0), (2.0, 2.0)]


testErr = labelsAndPredictions.filter(lambda v_p:
v_p[0] != v_p[1]).count()/float(testData.count())

print('Test Error = ' + str(testErr))
#0

labelsAndPredictions.saveAsTextFile('file:///home/hadoop/prediction.txt')
```

11.4.6 Gradient Boosting Machine

Gradient Boosting Machine is an ensemble learning algorithm like Random Forest. When Decision Trees are as used as prediction models in Gradient Boosting, the model is called Gradient-Boosted Trees (GBT). In Random Forest, each tree is built independently from a random (bootstrap) sample, whereas in GBT a decision tree is trained at each step which corrects and compliments the previously built trees. While in Random Forest, the ensemble is built from a random sample of data, in GBT the ensemble is built on the residuals (errors of the previous trees).

Gradient Boosting is the process which combines weak learners into strong learners by sequentially improving upon the learner at each step by adding a new estimator which is trained on the residual at each step [45]. Let $f_m(x)$ be the model at the step m. In the step $m+1$ the model is improved as follows:

$$f_{m+1}(x) = f_m(x) + h(x)$$

where $h(x)$ is the new estimator trained on the residual, i.e., $h(x) = y - f_m(x)$.

Let us look at an example of GBM classification using H2O framework. For this example we will use the UCI Adult dataset [41] also called the Census Income dataset. This dataset includes census income data with attributes such as age, education, occupation, etc. The prediction task for this dataset is to determine whether a person makes over 50K a year. Let us first import the dataset file using H2O Flow UI as shown in Figure 11.38.

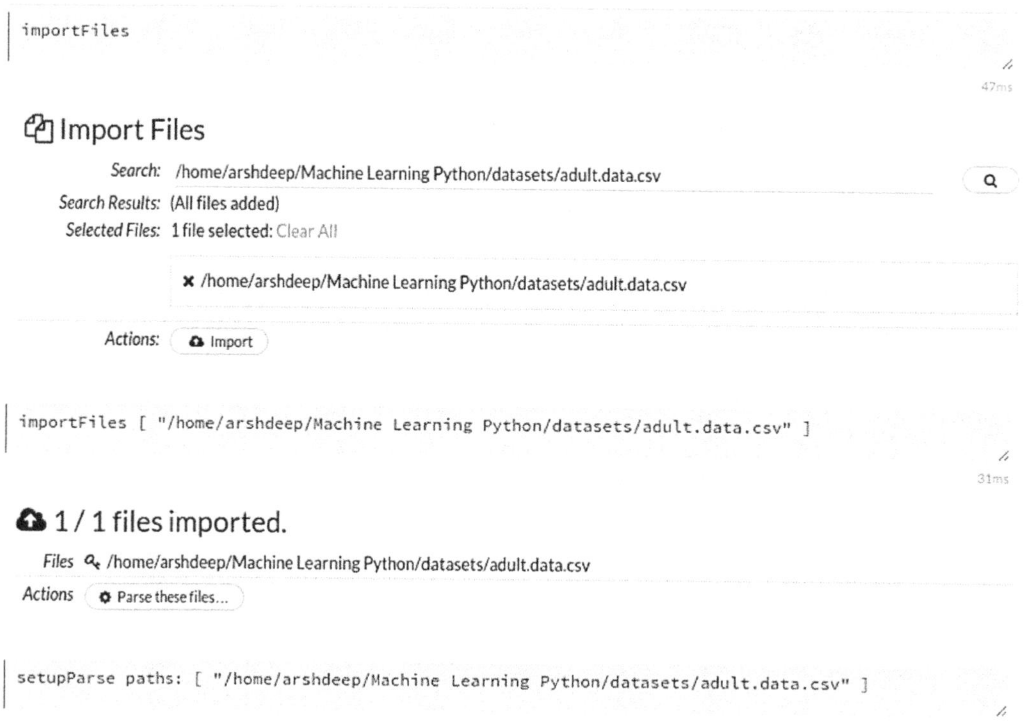

```
importFiles
```
47ms

🗐 Import Files

Search:	/home/arshdeep/Machine Learning Python/datasets/adult.data.csv
Search Results:	(All files added)
Selected Files:	1 file selected: Clear All

    ✖ /home/arshdeep/Machine Learning Python/datasets/adult.data.csv

Actions: ☁ Import

```
importFiles [ "/home/arshdeep/Machine Learning Python/datasets/adult.data.csv" ]
```
31ms

☁ 1 / 1 files imported.

Files 🔍 /home/arshdeep/Machine Learning Python/datasets/adult.data.csv

Actions ⚙ Parse these files...

```
setupParse paths: [ "/home/arshdeep/Machine Learning Python/datasets/adult.data.csv" ]
```

Figure 11.38: Importing dataset file from the H2O Flow UI

Next step is to parse the dataset file. Figure 11.39 shows how to set up the parser. After selecting the parse options, click the Parse button to parse the file. The data from the parsed file is stored in an H2O frame. Figure 11.40 shows the H2O frame created by parsing the dataset file.

With the data imported and parsed, let us now build a GBM model. Click the Build Model button in the actions of the parsed frame or choose the Build Model option from the menu. Figure 11.41 shows the various options for the model. Select the algorithm type to be Gradient Boosting Machine, the training frame as adult_data.hex, the response column as C15 and the number of trees to be 50. After specifying the model options, click the Build Model button to build the model.

Figure 11.39: Parsing the imported dataset file using H2O Flow UI

Figure 11.42 shows the details of the GBM model built from the Wine dataset. The model summary shows the various model statistics such as mean squared error (MSE), coefficient of determination (R^2) and area under the curve (AUC).

Next, import and parse the test dataset in the same way as we imported and parsed the training dataset. To make the predictions for the test dataset, enter the *predict* command or choose the predict option from the menu, then select the model and test frame, and then click the Predict button. Figure 11.43 shows the prediction summary including the ROC curve.

Figure 11.40: Viewing the H2O frame created from the parsed dataset file

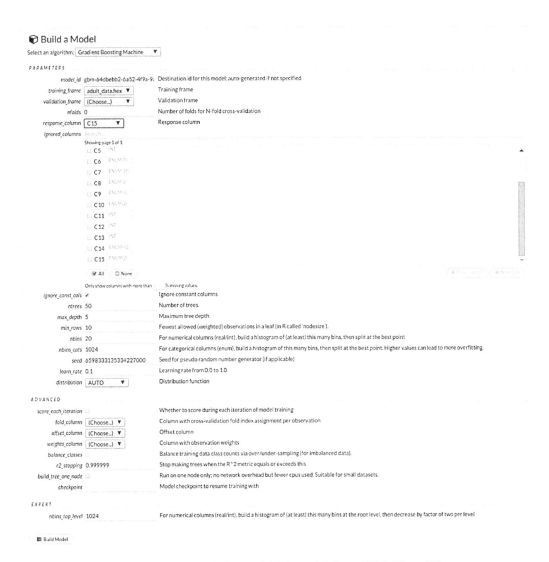

Figure 11.41: Building a GBM model from H2O Flow UI

▾ OUTPUT - MODEL SUMMARY

            number_of_trees 50
        model_size_in_bytes 20416
                  min_depth 5
                  max_depth 5
                 mean_depth 5.0
                 min_leaves 22
                 max_leaves 32
                mean_leaves 28.8400

▸ OUTPUT - SCORING HISTORY

▾ OUTPUT - TRAINING_METRICS

                     model gbm-64dbebb2-6a52-4f9a-9ac6-f6009fd2a605
            model_checksum 6679275560750278656
                     frame adult_data.hex
            frame_checksum 2526332392997958656
               description ·
            model_category Binomial
              scoring_time 1441798729618
               predictions ·
                       MSE 0.085925
                        r2 0.530004
                   logloss 0.276624
                       AUC 0.933189
                      Gini 0.866377

▸ DOMAIN

▸ OUTPUT - TRAINING_METRICS - METRICS FOR THRESHOLDS (BINOMIAL METRICS AS A FUNCTION OF
CLASSIFICATION THRESHOLDS)

▾ OUTPUT - TRAINING_METRICS - MAXIMUM METRICS (MAXIMUM METRICS AT THEIR RESPECTIVE THRESHOLDS)

metric	threshold	value	idx
max f1	0.3901	0.7415	195
max f2	0.1745	0.8155	287
max f0point5	0.6074	0.7762	119
max accuracy	0.4605	0.8783	170
max precision	0.9822	1.0	0
max absolute_MCC	0.3932	0.6589	194
max min_per_class_accuracy	0.2752	0.8479	240

Figure 11.42: Viewing GBM model details

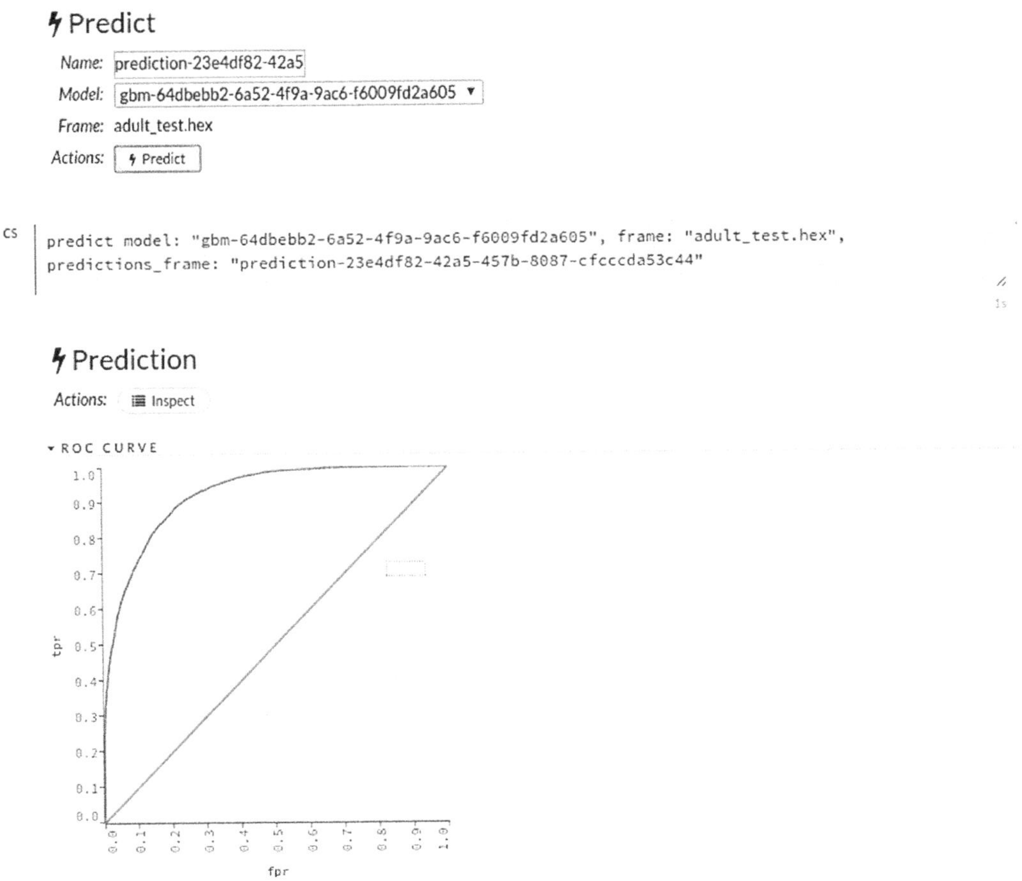

⚡ Predict

Name: `prediction-23e4df82-42a5`

Model: `gbm-64dbebb2-6a52-4f9a-9ac6-f6009fd2a605` ▾

Frame: adult_test.hex

Actions: ⚡ Predict

```
cs   predict model: "gbm-64dbebb2-6a52-4f9a-9ac6-f6009fd2a605", frame: "adult_test.hex",
     predictions_frame: "prediction-23e4df82-42a5-457b-8087-cfcccda53c44"
```

⚡ Prediction

Actions: ≣ Inspect

▾ ROC CURVE

Figure 11.43: Viewing the prediction results

Box 11.21 shows a Python implementation of the same example using H2O's Python library and Box 11.22 shows the program output.

▪ Box 11.21: Python program for GBM classification using H2O

```
import h2o

h2o.init()

train = h2o.import_frame(path=h2o.locate("/home/ubuntu/adult.data.csv"))
test = h2o.import_frame(path=h2o.locate("/home/ubuntu/adult.test.csv"))

train[14] = train[14].asfactor()
test[14] = test[14].asfactor()

model = h2o.gbm(x=train[0:14], y=train[14], validation_x= test[0:14],
        validation_y=test[14], distribution = "bernoulli",
        ntrees=50, learn_rate=0.1)
```

```
model.show()

prediction = model.predict(test)

prediction.head()

perf = model.model_performance(test)
perf.show()

print 'Confusion Matrix:  `
print (perf.confusion_matrix())

print 'Precision:  `
print (perf.precision())

print 'Accuracy:  `
print (perf.accuracy())

print 'AUC: `
print (perf.auc())

h2o.download_csv(prediction, 'prediction.csv')
```

■ Box 11.22: Output of program for GBM classification using H2O

```
>>> model.show()
Model Details
=============
H2OBinomialModel :  Gradient Boosting Machine
Model Key:  GBM_model_python_1441787876875_57

Model Summary:

 number_of_trees model_size_in_bytes min_depth max_depth mean_depth min_leaves max_leaves mean_leaves
- --------------- ------------------- --------- --------- ---------- ---------- ---------- ----------
 50      20417    5   5   5   22   32   28.84


ModelMetricsBinomial:  gbm
** Reported on train data.  **

MSE: 0.0859247340554
R²:  0.530004451115
LogLoss:  0.276624227866
AUC: 0.933188510192
Gini:  0.866377020384

Confusion Matrix (Act/Pred) for max f1 @ threshold = 0.390088332148:

   <=50K >50K Error Rate
--- ----- ---- ----- -----------
<=50K 22634 2086 0.0844 (2086.0/24720.0)
>50K 1992  5849 0.254 (1992.0/7841.0)
Total 24626 7935 0.1252 (4078.0/32561.0)

Maximum Metrics:

metric        threshold value  idx
```

```
------------------ ------- ----- ---
max f1        0.390088  0.741506 195
max f2        0.174504  0.815484 287
max f0point5   0.607379  0.776164 119
max accuracy   0.460468  0.87829 170
max precision   0.982202  1    0
max absolute_MCC   0.393242  0.658941 194
max min_per_class_accuracy 0.275248  0.847851 240


ModelMetricsBinomial:  gbm
** Reported on validation data.  **

MSE: 0.0905793133771
R²:  0.497962558845
LogLoss:  0.28949793511
AUC: 0.92284044478
Gini:  0.84568088956


Confusion Matrix (Act/Pred) for max f1 @ threshold = 0.36326916669:

   <=50K >50K Error Rate
--- ----- ---- ----- -----------
<=50K 11150 1285 0.1033 (1285.0/12435.0)
>50K 992  2854 0.2579 (992.0/3846.0)
Total 12142 4139 0.1399 (2277.0/16281.0)

Maximum Metrics:

metric       threshold value  idx
------------------ ------- ----- ---
max f1        0.363269  0.71484 211
max f2        0.172859  0.799287 291
max f0point5   0.553204  0.757278 141
max accuracy   0.514136  0.871568 155
max precision   0.9865  1    0
max absolute_MCC   0.468827  0.625792 169
max min_per_class_accuracy 0.26159  0.836973 250


Variable Importances:

variable relative_importance scaled_importance percentage
------- --------------- -------------- --------
C8   5012.7    1     0.302438
C11   3214.44   0.641258    0.193941
C4   2816.11   0.561795    0.169908
C6   1444.81   0.28823    0.0871717
C7   1423.55   0.283988    0.0858887
C12   921.112   0.183756    0.0555747
C1   780.083   0.155621    0.0470658
C13   464.666   0.0926977    0.0280353
C14   195.269   0.0389548    0.0117814
C2   184.469   0.0368003    0.0111298
C3   53.7663   0.010726    0.00324396
C10   41.7206   0.00832298    0.00251718
C5   17.0094   0.00339327    0.00102625
C9   1.61617   0.000920896   0.000278514
>>> prediction = model.predict(test)
>>>
>>>prediction.head()
First 10 rows and first 3 columns:
predict  <=50K  >50K
------  ------ ------
<=50K   0.984939 0.015061
```

```
<=50K   0.783672 0.216328
<=50K   0.703814 0.296186
>50K    0.0240078 0.975992
<=50K   0.988003 0.0119969
<=50K   0.982786 0.0172137
<=50K   0.981567 0.0184325
>50K    0.260574 0.739426
<=50K   0.985382 0.0146176
<=50K   0.911547 0.0884534


>>> perf = model.model_performance(test)
>>> perf.show()


ModelMetricsBinomial:  gbm
** Reported on test data.   **

MSE: 0.0905793133771
R²:  0.497962558845
LogLoss:  0.28949793511
AUC: 0.92284044478
Gini:  0.84568088956


Confusion Matrix (Act/Pred) for max f1 @ threshold = 0.36326916669:

   <=50K >50K Error Rate
--- ----- ---- ----- -----------
<=50K 11150 1285 0.1033 (1285.0/12435.0)
>50K 992   2854 0.2579 (992.0/3846.0)
Total 12142 4139 0.1399 (2277.0/16281.0)

Maximum Metrics:

metric          threshold value  idx
----------------- ------- ----- ---
max f1        0.363269  0.71484 211
max f2        0.172859  0.799287 291
max f0point5     0.553204  0.757278 141
max accuracy     0.514136  0.871568 155
max precision     0.9865  1   0
max absolute_MCC     0.468827  0.625792 169
max min_per_class_accuracy 0.26159  0.836973 250

>>> print 'Confusion Matrix: '
Confusion Matrix:
>>> print (perf.confusion_matrix())

Confusion Matrix (Act/Pred) for max f1 @ threshold = 0.36326916669:

   <=50K >50K Error Rate
--- ----- ---- ----- -----------
<=50K 11150 1285 0.1033 (1285.0/12435.0)
>50K 992   2854 0.2579 (992.0/3846.0)
Total 12142 4139 0.1399 (2277.0/16281.0)


>>> print 'Precision: '
Precision:
>>> print (perf.precision())
[[0.9864996454832976, 1.0]]
>>>
>>> print 'Accuracy: '
Accuracy:
>>> print (perf.accuracy())
```

```
[[0.5141359851152871, 0.8715680854984338]]
>>>
>>> print 'AUC: '
AUC:
>>> print (perf.auc())
0.92284044478
```

Let us repeat the same example of GBM classification using Spark MLlib with the Adult dataset. Box 11.23 shows the python program for GBM classification using Spark MLlib. Since some of the attributes in this dataset are non-numbers (string attributes), we use Spark's Tokenizer and HashingTF classes for feature extraction and transformation. The Tokenizer converts the input string to lowercase and then splits it by white spaces. HashingTF is a transformer which takes sets of terms (bag of words) and converts those sets into fixed-length feature vectors (term frequencies). Also note that in this example we convert the labels from <=50 and >50 to 0.0.and 1.0 as the Spark expects the labels from 0 to N-1 where N is the total number of classes in the data. The *GradientBoostedTrees* class of the MLlib classification module is used to build a GBM model. After the model has been built, the *predict* method of the GradientBoostedTrees class is used to make the predictions.

■ **Box 11.23: Python program for GBM classification using Spark MLlib**

```
from pyspark.context import SparkContext
from pyspark.mllib.tree import GradientBoostedTrees
from pyspark.mllib.regression import LabeledPoint
from pyspark.mllib.feature import HashingTF
from pyspark.ml.feature import HashingTF, Tokenizer
from pyspark.sql import Row

LabeledDocument = Row("text", "label")

def parseLine(line):
parts = line.split(',')
label = parts[-1].strip()
if label=='<=50K':
label =0.0
if label=='>50K':
label =1.0
text=line
return LabeledDocument(text, label)

lines = sc.textFile('file:///home/hadoop/data.csv').map(parseLine)

training = lines.toDF()

training.show()

tokenizer = Tokenizer(inputCol="text", outputCol="words")
hashingTF = HashingTF(inputCol=tokenizer.getOutputCol(),
outputCol="features")

tokenized = tokenizer.transform(training)
hashed = hashingTF.transform(tokenized)
```

```
hashedrdd=hashed.select('label','features').rdd

data=hashedrdd.map(lambda a:  LabeledPoint(float(a.label), a.features))

(trainingData, testData) = data.randomSplit([0.7, 0.3])

model = GradientBoostedTrees.trainClassifier(p, categoricalFeaturesInfo=,
numIterations=3)

predictions = model.predict(p.map(lambda x:  x.features))

predictions.take(10)
```

11.4.7 Support Vector Machine

Support Vector Machine (SVM) is a supervised machine learning approach used for classification and regression. The basic form of SVM is a binary classifier that classifies the data points into one of the two classes [37]. SVM training involves determining the maximum margin hyperplane that separates the two classes. The maximum margin hyperplane is one which has the largest separation from the nearest training data point. Figure 11.44 shows the margins for an SVM. Given a training data set (x_i, y_i) where x_i is an n dimensional vector and $y_i = 1$ if x_i is in class 1 and $y_i = -1$ if x_i is in class 2, a standard SVM finds a hyperplane $\mathbf{w}.\mathbf{x} - b = 0$, which correctly separates the training data points and has a maximum margin which is the distance between the two hyperplanes $\mathbf{w}.\mathbf{x} - b = 1$ and $\mathbf{w}.\mathbf{x} - b = -1$, as shown in Figure 11.45.

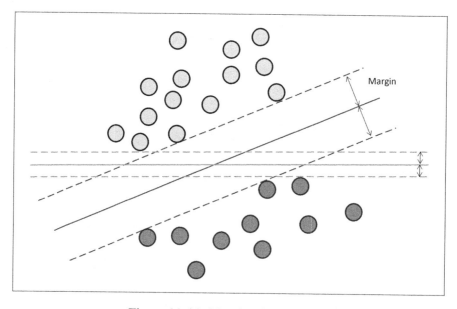

Figure 11.44: Margins for an SVM

The optimal hyperplane with maximum margin can be obtained by solving the following quadratic programming problem,

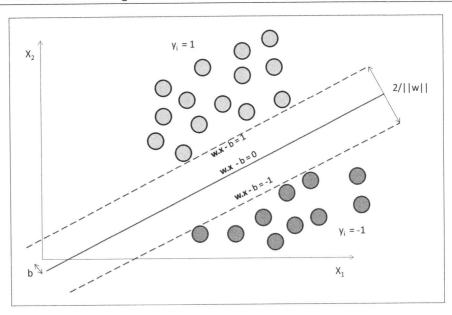

Figure 11.45: Maximum margin hyperplane

$$min_{\{w.b\}}\frac{1}{2}||w||^2 + C\sum_{i=1}^{l}\xi_i \tag{11.22}$$

subject to $y_i(w.x_i - b) \geq 1 - \xi_i$, $\xi_i > 0$, $1 < i < l$ where C is the soft margin parameter and ξ is a slack variable for the non-separable case. The optimal hyperplane is given as,

$$f(x) = sign\left(C\sum_{i=1}^{l}\alpha_i y_i K(x_i,x) - b\right) \tag{11.23}$$

where α_i is the Lagrange multiplier and $K(x_i,x)$ is the kernel function. A standard SVM is a two-class classier where the outcome is 1 or -1. When sets are not linearly separable, the data points in the original finite-dimensional space are mapped to a higher dimensional space where they can be separated easily. The performance of an SVM classifier depends on the selection of kernel, the kernel's parameters, and soft margin parameter C. The commonly used kernels include:

- Linear: $k(x_i,x_j) = <x_i,x_j>$
- Polynomial: $k(x_i,x_j) = (\gamma <x_i,x_j> + r)^d$
- Radial Basis Function (RBF): $k(x_i,x_j) = exp(-\gamma||x_i - x_j||^2)$
- Sigmoid: $k(x_i,x_j) = (tanh <x_i,x_j> + r)$

Let us look at an example of SVM classification using Spark MLlib. For this example, we will use the Wine dataset. Box 11.24 shows the Python program for SVM classification. This program can be run in the PySpark shell. In this program we implement a *parseLine* function which takes each line of the input file, splits the line into individual columns separated by commas, converts the values to floats and returns LabeledPoints. In this function, we also change the wine labels from 1.0, 2.0 and 3.0 to 0.0, 1.0 and 2.0 as the Spark expects the labels from 0 to N-1 where N is the total number of classes in the data. The *SVMWithSGD* class of the MLlib classification module is used to build an SVM model. After the model has been built, the *predict* method is used to make the predictions. Finally, we compare the labels in the test dataset and the predicted labels and compute the test error. The predictions can be saved to a text file using the *saveAsTextFile* function.

■ **Box 11.24: Python program for SVM classification using Spark MLlib**

```
from pyspark.context import SparkContext
from pyspark.mllib.tree import SVMWithSGD
from pyspark.mllib.linalg import Vectors
from pyspark.mllib.regression import LabeledPoint

def parseLine(line):
   parts = line.split(',')
   label = float(parts[0])
   if label==1.0:
      label =0.0
   if label==2.0:
      label = 1.0
   if label==3.0:
      label = 2.0
   features = Vectors.dense([float(x) for x in parts[1:]])
   return LabeledPoint(label, features)

sc = SparkContext(appName="SVMExample")

trainingData = sc.textFile('file:///home/hadoop/wine.data.txt').map(parseLine)

testData = sc.textFile('file:///home/hadoop/wine.test.txt').map(parseLine)

model = SVMWithSGD.train(trainingData, iterations=100)

predictions = model.predict(testData.map(lambda x:  x.features))

labelsAndPredictions = testData.map(lambda lp:
lp.label).zip(predictions)

testErr = labelsAndPredictions.filter(lambda v_p:
v_p[0] != v_p[1]).count()/float(testData.count())

print('Test Error = ' + str(testErr))

labelsAndPredictions.saveAsTextFile('file:///home/hadoop/prediction.txt')

sc.stop()
```

11.4.8   Deep Learning

Deep Learning algorithms are based on artificial neural networks. Artificial neural networks are inspired from biological neural networks and include a system of interconnected neurons. Figure 11.46 shows the structure of a neuron in an artificial neural network. The neuron has multiple inputs (x_i) and each input has a weight (w_i). A weighted combination of the inputs is aggregated, and the activation function (f) is applied to the aggregated inputs. A bias b is also added which accounts for the activation threshold of the neuron.

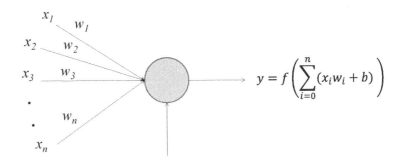

Figure 11.46: Neuron

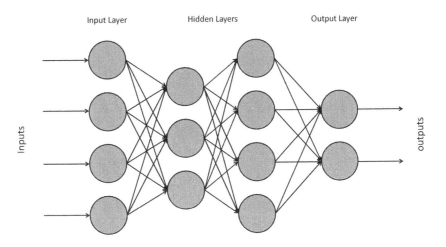

Figure 11.47: Multi-layer feed-forward artificial neural network

In this section, we will look at an example of Deep Learning using the H2O framework. The H2O's implementation of deep learning is based on a multi-layer feed-forward artificial neural network which includes multiple layers of interconnected neurons as shown in Figure 11.47. Neurons in each layer are directly connected to the neurons in the subsequent layer and there are no loops in the network. The number of neurons in the input layer is equal to the number of features in the input and the number of neurons in the output layer matches the number of outputs. In the learning process, given the inputs and the known outputs, the system adapts the weights to minimize the prediction error.

Let us look at an example of Deep Learning using H2O framework. In this example, we will use UCI breast cancer dataset [42]. The dataset consists of measurements of ten attributes each describing the features computed from digitized images of fine needle aspirate (FNA) of breast mass. The class variable has two values (2 for benign, 4 for malignant).

The first step is to import the dataset file into H2O from the H2O Flow UI as shown in

Figure 11.48.

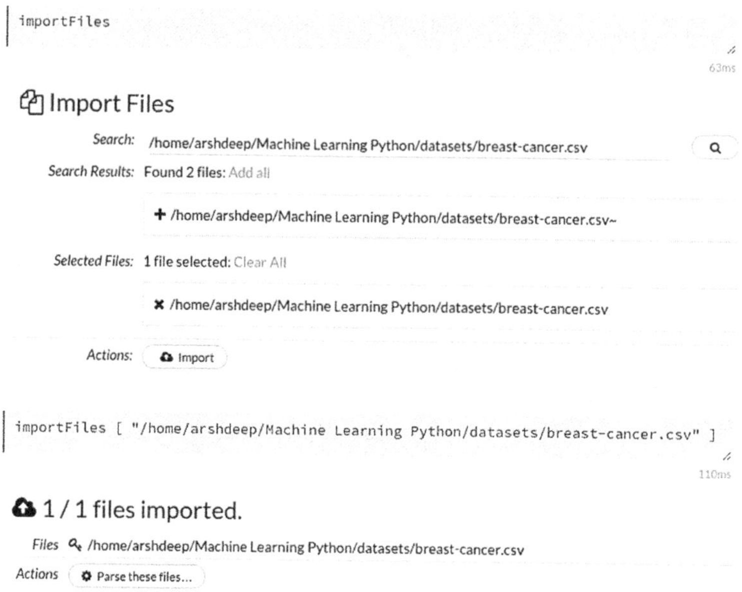

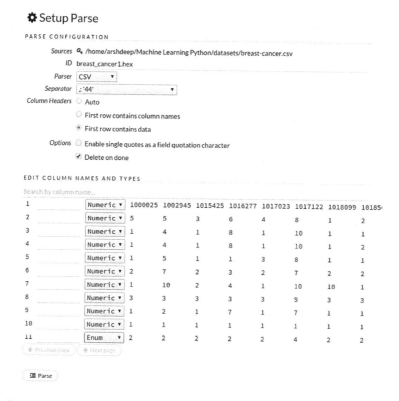

Figure 11.48: Importing dataset file from the H2O Flow UI

Figure 11.49: Parsing the imported dataset file using H2O Flow UI

Next step is to parse the dataset file. Click the Parse button after importing the file. Figure 11.49 shows how to set up the parser. In this step, you can specify various parsing options. After selecting the parse options, click the Parse button to parse the file. The data from the parsed file is stored in an H2O frame. Figure 11.50 shows the H2O frame created by parsing the dataset file. The data is split into training and test frames as shown in Figure 11.51.

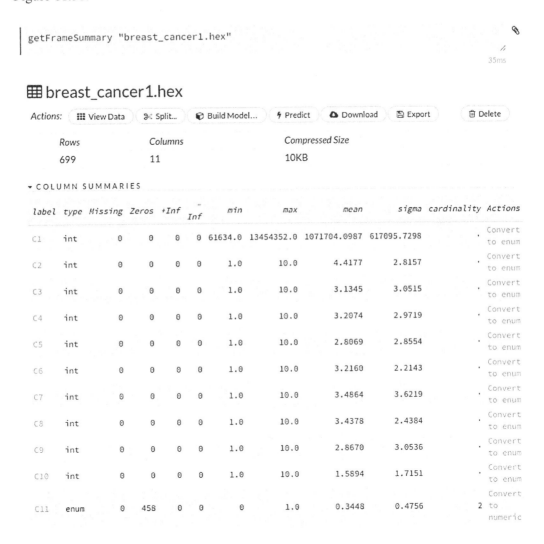

Figure 11.50: Viewing the H2O frame created from the parsed dataset file

With the data imported and parsed, let us now build a Deep Learning model. Click the Build Model button in the actions of the parsed frame or choose the Build Model option from the menu. Figure 11.52 shows the various options for the model. Select the algorithm type to be Deep Learning, training frame (frame_0.750_train), validation frame (frame_0.250_test) and response column as C11. After specifying the model options, click the Build Model button to build the model.

Figures 11.53 and 11.54 show the details of the Deep Learning model such as the training

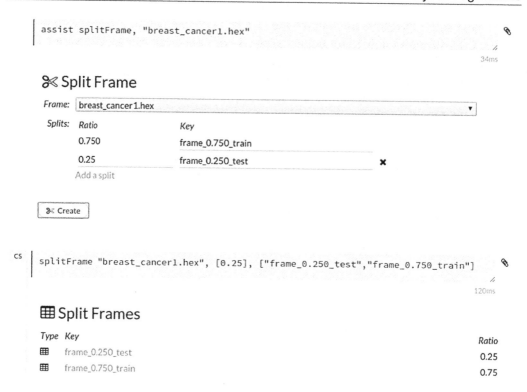

```
assist splitFrame, "breast_cancer1.hex"
```
34ms

✂ Split Frame

Frame: breast_cancer1.hex ▼

Splits: Ratio   Key
         0.750   frame_0.750_train
         0.25   frame_0.250_test   ✕
         Add a split

✂ Create

```
cs  splitFrame "breast_cancer1.hex", [0.25], ["frame_0.250_test","frame_0.750_train"]
```
120ms

⊞ Split Frames

Type	Key	Ratio
⊞	frame_0.250_test	0.25
⊞	frame_0.750_train	0.75

Figure 11.51: Splitting the H2O frame into training and test frames

and validation ROC curves, and various model statistics.

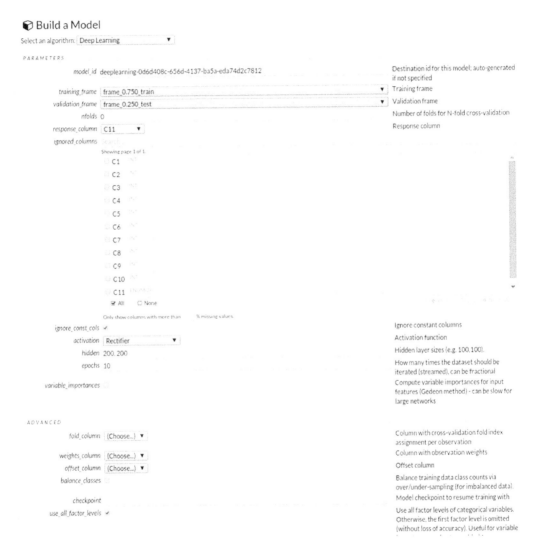

Figure 11.52: Building a deep learning model from H2O Flow UI

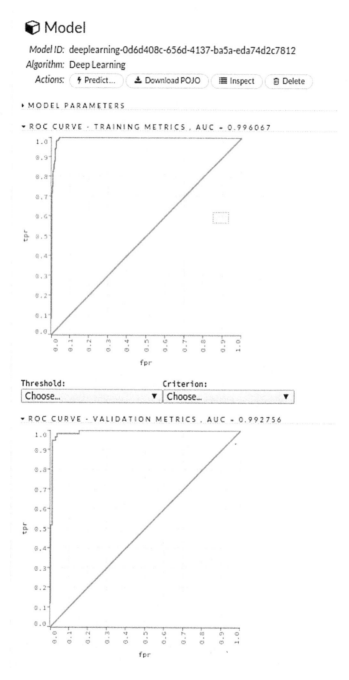

Figure 11.53: Viewing the details of the deep learning model

```
▾ OUTPUT - VALIDATION_METRICS

          model  deeplearning-0d6d408c-656d-4137-ba5a-eda74d2c7812
  model_checksum  4447524957521643008
           frame  ·
  frame_checksum  0
     description  Metrics reported on temporary (load-balanced) validation frame
  model_category  Binomial
    scoring_time  1441795605301
     predictions  ·
             MSE  0.029251
              r2  0.867228
         logloss  0.155852
             AUC  0.992756
            Gini  0.985511


▸ OUTPUT - VALIDATION_METRICS - METRICS FOR THRESHOLDS (BINOMIAL METRICS AS A FUNCTION OF
CLASSIFICATION THRESHOLDS)

▾ OUTPUT - VALIDATION_METRICS - MAXIMUM METRICS (MAXIMUM METRICS AT THEIR RESPECTIVE
THRESHOLDS)

metric                      threshold  value   idx
max f1                         0.9948  0.9649   46
max f2                         0.2392  0.9727   51
max f0point5                   0.9948  0.9752   46
max accuracy                   0.9948  0.9774   46
max precision                     1.0     1.0    0
max absolute_MCC               0.9948  0.9486   46
max min_per_class_accuracy     0.2392  0.9664   51
```

Figure 11.54: Viewing deep learning model validation results

Box 11.25 shows a Python implementation of the same example using H2O's Python library and Box 11.26 shows the program output.

■ Box 11.25: Python program for Deep Learning classification using H2O

```python
import h2o

h2o.init()

data = h2o.import_frame(path=h2o.locate("/home/ubuntu/breast-cancer.csv"))

data_split = data.split_frame(ratios = [0.8,0.2])
train = data_split[0]
test = data_split[1]

train[10] = train[10].asfactor()
test[10] = test[10].asfactor()

model = h2o.deeplearning(x=train[0:10], y=train[10],
    validation_x= test[0:10], validation_y=test[10],
    variable_importances=True, loss="Automatic")

model.show()

prediction = model.predict(test)

prediction.head()
```

```
perf = model.model_performance(test)
perf.show()

print 'Confusion Matrix:  '
print (perf.confusion_matrix())

print 'Precision:  '
print (perf.precision())

print 'Accuracy:  '
print (perf.accuracy())

print 'AUC:  '
print (perf.auc())

h2o.download_csv(prediction, '/home/ubuntu/prediction.csv')
```

■ Box 11.26: Output of the program for Deep Learning classification using H2O

```
>>> model.show()
Model Details
=============
H2OBinomialModel :  Deep Learning
Model Key:  DeepLearning_model_python_1441787876875_43

Status of Neuron Layers:

 layer units type  dropout l1 l2 mean_rate  rate_RMS  momentum mean_weight weight_RMS mean_bias  bias_RMS
 ----- ----- ------ ------ --- --- --------- --------- -------- ----------- ---------- ---------- --------

 1  10  Input  0.0
 2  200  Rectifier 0.0  0.0 0.0 0.0051586363 0.004284294 0.0   -0.0038918303 0.09932074 0.47159594  0.01983153
 3  200  Rectifier 0.0  0.0 0.0 0.042859647 0.12210885 0.0   -0.0014745063 0.06997566 0.99559456  0.007935624
 4  2  Softmax   0.0 0.0 0.0019927532 0.0024083003 0.0   -0.03239843 0.40508103 7.2054856e-05 0.0016424061


ModelMetricsBinomial:  deeplearning
** Reported on train data.  **

MSE: 0.0431564371515
R²:  0.814549813835
LogLoss:  0.287324374181
AUC: 0.99416925658
Gini:  0.98833851316

Confusion Matrix (Act/Pred) for max f1 @ threshold = 0.954812765121:

  2 4 Error Rate
--- -- -- ----- --------
2   339 14 0.0397 (14.0/353.0)
4   2 204 0.0097 (2.0/206.0)
Total 341 218 0.0286 (16.0/559.0)

Maximum Metrics:

metric          threshold value  idx
---------------- -------- ----- ---
max f1          0.954813  0.962264 63
```

```
max f2          0.913903  0.980861 66
max f0point5       0.999977  0.961945 30
max accuracy       0.992785  0.971377 59
max precision      0.999999  0.993711 9
max absolute_MCC     0.954813  0.940216 63
max min_per_class_accuracy 0.993953  0.968839 56


ModelMetricsBinomial:  deeplearning
** Reported on validation data.   **


MSE: 0.0254503614803
R²:  0.864264738772
LogLoss:  0.145122767088
AUC: 1.0
Gini:  1.0


Confusion Matrix (Act/Pred) for max f1 @ threshold = 0.999943256378:

  2 4 Error Rate
--- -- -- ----- -------
2  105 0 0   (0.0/105.0)
4   0 35 0   (0.0/35.0)
Total 105 35 0   (0.0/140.0)


Maximum Metrics:

metric          threshold value idx
----------------- ------- ----- ---
max f1         0.999943  1   14
max f2         0.999943  1   14
max f0point5      0.999943  1   14
max accuracy      0.999943  1   14
max precision     1    1   0
max absolute_MCC    0.999943  1   14
max min_per_class_accuracy 0.999943  1    14


Variable Importances:

variable relative_importance scaled_importance percentage
------- -------------- ------------- --------
C9    1       1        0.108707
C8    0.981525     0.981525     0.106698
C3    0.954005     0.954005     0.103707
C7    0.94194      0.94194      0.102395
C2    0.941813     0.941813     0.102381
C4    0.92944      0.92944      0.101036
C1    0.89463      0.89463      0.0972522
C10   0.889871     0.889871     0.0967349
C5    0.864056     0.864056     0.0939286
C6    0.801792     0.801792     0.0871601


>>> prediction = model.predict(test)
>>>
>>> prediction.head()
First 10 rows and first 3 columns:
predict    p2    p4
------ ------- -------
  2 0.985993  0.0140068
  2 0.957854  0.042146
  2 0.957854  0.042146
  2 0.999733  0.000266882
```

```
    2 0.998995   0.00100492
    2 0.979549   0.0204512
    4 5.65749e-10 1
    2 0.992313   0.0076873
    2 0.974153   0.025847
    4 2.68044e-06 0.999997


>>> perf = model.model_performance(test)
>>> perf.show()

ModelMetricsBinomial:  deeplearning
** Reported on test data.  **

MSE: 0.0254503614803
R²:  0.864264738772
LogLoss:  0.145122767088
AUC: 1.0
Gini:  1.0


Confusion Matrix (Act/Pred) for max f1 @ threshold = 0.999943256378:

   2 4 Error Rate
--- -- -- ----- -------
2  105 0 0   (0.0/105.0)
4   0 35 0   (0.0/35.0)
Total 105 35 0   (0.0/140.0)

Maximum Metrics:

metric            threshold value idx
----------------- --------- ----- ---
max f1            0.999943  1    14
max f2            0.999943  1    14
max f0point5      0.999943  1    14
max accuracy      0.999943  1    14
max precision     1    1    0
max absolute_MCC  0.999943  1    14
max min_per_class_accuracy 0.999943  1    14

>>> print 'Confusion Matrix: '
Confusion Matrix:
>>> print (perf.confusion_matrix())

Confusion Matrix (Act/Pred) for max f1 @ threshold = 0.999943256378:

   2 4 Error Rate
--- -- -- ----- -------
2  105 0 0   (0.0/105.0)
4   0 35 0   (0.0/35.0)
Total 105 35 0   (0.0/140.0)

>>>
>>> print 'Precision: '
Precision:
>>> print (perf.precision())
[[1.0, 1.0]]
>>>
>>> print 'Accuracy: '
Accuracy:
>>> print (perf.accuracy())
[[0.9999432563781738, 1.0]]
>>>
```

```
>>> print 'AUC: '
AUC:
>>> print (perf.auc())
1.0
```

11.5 Case Study: Classifying Handwritten Digits

In this section, we will describe a case study on building a system for classifying handwritten digits. For this case study, we will use the MNIST (Modified National Institute of Standards and Technology) dataset [46]. The MNIST database of handwritten digits is a collection of 60,000 images of handwritten digits which were sampled from documents written by employees of the US Census Bureau and American high school students. The digits have been size-normalized and centered in fixed-size gray-scale images of 28 x 28 pixels in dimension. Each image has a total of 784 pixels (28 × 28). Each pixel has a value between 0 and 255 (with higher numbers meaning darker pixel). The dataset file used in the example in this section can be downloaded from [47]. This a CSV file containing 60,000 rows (one column for each image) and 785 columns (columns 1-784 denoting the pixel values and column 785 has the image label - 0 to 9).

Figure 11.55 shows the components of the digit classification system We will describe two alternative implementations of the system based on H2O and Spark. The classification models are built using H2O or Spark with the training data. The web service component makes the classification system available as a web service. A Python client is used to test the system.

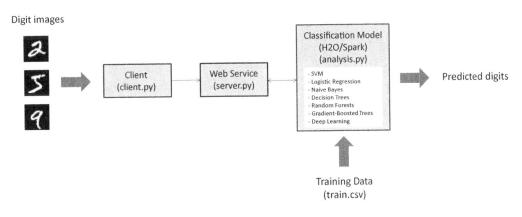

Figure 11.55: Digit recognition

11.5.1 Digit Classification with H2O

Box 11.27 shows the Python implementation of the analysis component for digit classification using H2O. In this program, we implement an *AnalysisEngine* class with methods for training a classification model and making predictions. The classification model type (Naive Bayes, Random Forest, Deep Learning, GBM) is specified in the class constructor.

■ **Box 11.27: Analysis component for digit classification using H2O - analysis.py**

```python
import h2o

class AnalysisEngine:
 def make_prediction(self, data):
  testframe=h2o.H2OFrame(data)
  prediction = self.model.predict(testframe)
  result = str(prediction[0].as_data_frame())
  return result

 def train_model(self, trainingFile, responseColumn, modelType):
  train = h2o.import_frame(path=h2o.locate(trainingFile))
  train[responseColumn] = train[responseColumn].asfactor()

  if modelType=='deeplearning':
   self.model = h2o.deeplearning(x=train[0:responseColumn],
        y=train[responseColumn])

  elif modelType=='gbm':
   self.model = h2o.gbm(x=train[0:responseColumn],
        y=train[responseColumn])

  elif modelType=='naivebayes':
   self.model = h2o.naive_bayes(x=train[0:responseColumn],
        y=train[responseColumn])

  elif modelType=='randomforest':
   self.model = h2o.random_forest(x=train[0:responseColumn],
        y=train[responseColumn])

 def __init__(self):
  h2o.init()
  trainingFile = "/home/ubuntu/h2o/data/mnistdata/test.csv"
  responseColumn = 784
  modelType='deeplearning'

  self.train_model(trainingFile, responseColumn, modelType)
```

Box 11.28 shows the Python implementation of the server component for digit classification using H2O. For the server component, we use the Flask Python web framework. When the server component is run, it creates an instance of the *AnalysisEngine* class of the analysis component. The server component exposes an endpoint (/predict). When the client sends an HTTP POST request to this endpoint with the image data, the *make_prediction* function of the *AnalysisEngine* class is called to classify the image.

■ **Box 11.28: Server component for digit classification using H2O - server.py**

```python
import json
from flask import Flask, request
```

```
from analysish2o import AnalysisEngine

app = Flask(__name__)

@app.route('/predict', methods=['POST'])
def predict():
  data = request.json['data']
  result = analysis_engine.make_prediction(data)
  return json.dumps(result)


if __name__ == '__main__':
  global analysis_engine

  analysis_engine = AnalysisEngine()

  app.run(host='0.0.0.0', port=5000, debug=False)
```

Box 11.29 shows the Python client for testing the digit classification system. This client reads an image file, converts it into a list of pixel values and makes an HTTP POST request to the server with the image data.

■ **Box 11.29: Python client for digit classification - client.py**

```
import requests
import numpy as np
import Image
import json

imgFilename = '/home/ubuntu/5.png'
img = Image.open(imgFilename).convert('L')
imga = np.asarray(img.getdata())
imgl = imga.tolist()

payload={'data':imgl}

headers = {'content-type':  'application/json'}
r = requests.post("http://localhost:5000/predict",
   data=json.dumps(payload), headers=headers)

print r.text
```

To test the system, run the server.py file first and then run the client.py file.

11.5.2   Digit Classification with Spark

Box 11.30 shows the Python implementation of the analysis component for digit classification using Spark. In this program, we implement an *AnalysisEngine* class with methods for training a classification model and making predictions. The classification model type (Naive Bayes, Decision Tree, Random Forest, GBM) is specified in the class constructor.

■ **Box 11.30: Spark analysis component for digit classification - analysis.py**

```python
from pyspark.mllib.linalg import Vectors
from pyspark.mllib.regression import LabeledPoint
from pyspark.mllib.classification import NaiveBayes
from pyspark.mllib.tree import RandomForest
from pyspark.mllib.tree import DecisionTree
from pyspark.mllib.tree import GradientBoostedTrees

class AnalysisEngine:
 def parseLine(self,line):
  parts = line.split(',')
  label = float(parts[784])
  features = Vectors.dense([float(x) for x in parts[0:784]])
  return LabeledPoint(label, features)

 def make_prediction(self, data):
  testData = Vectors.dense([float(x) for x in data[0:784]])
  result = self.model.predict(testData)
  return result

 def train_model(self,sc,modelType):
  data = sc.textFile('file:////home/hadoop/train.csv')
  header = data.first() #extract header
  data = data.filter(lambda x:x !=header) #filter out header
  trainingData = data.map(self.parseLine)

  if modelType=='naivebayes':
   self.model = NaiveBayes.train(trainingData, 1.0)

  elif modelType=='randomforest':
   self.model = RandomForest.trainClassifier(trainingData,
       numClasses=10, categoricalFeaturesInfo={},
       numTrees=10, featureSubsetStrategy="auto",
       impurity='gini', maxDepth=10, maxBins=32)

  elif modelType=='decisiontree':
   self.model = DecisionTree.trainClassifier(trainingData,
       numClasses=10, categoricalFeaturesInfo={},
       impurity='gini', maxDepth=10, maxBins=32)

  elif modelType=='gbm':
   self.model = GradientBoostedTrees.trainClassifier(trainingData,
    categoricalFeaturesInfo=, numIterations=3)

 def __init__(self, sc):
  modelType='naivebayes'
  self.train_model(sc, modelType)
```

Box 11.31 shows the Python implementation of the server component for digit classification using Spark. For the server component, we use the Flask Python web framework. When the server component is run, it creates a Spark Context and passes it to the *AnalysisEngine* class constructor to create an instance of the class. The server component exposes an endpoint (/predict). When the client sends an HTTP POST request to this endpoint with the image data, the *make_prediction* function of the *AnalysisEngine* class is called to classify the image.

■ **Box 11.31: Server component for digit classification using Spark - server.py**

```
import analysis
import json
from flask import Flask, request
from pyspark import SparkContext, SparkConf

app = Flask(__name__)

@app.route('/mnist/predict', methods=['POST'])
def predict():
 data = request.json['data']
 result = analysis_engine.make_prediction(data)
 return json.dumps(result)


if __name__ == '__main__':
 global analysis_engine
 conf = SparkConf().setAppName("MySparkApp")
 sc = SparkContext(conf=conf, pyFiles=['analysis.py'])
 analysis_engine = analysis.AnalysisEngine(sc)

 app.run(host='0.0.0.0', port=5000, debug=False)
```

To test the system, run the server.py file first (bin/spark-submit server.py) and then run the client.py (python client.py) file.

11.6 Case Study: Genome Data Analysis (Implementation)

In Chapter-1, we described the case study on analysis of genome data. The following two types of analysis were described: (1) predict the drug response based on gene expressions, (2) find correlations between expression values of all pairs of genes to find genes which have similar expression patterns and genes which have opposing expression patterns.

In this section, we will describe the implementation of the two types of analysis. For the first analysis, we will use Spark to build a regression model to predict the drug response. The target variable for the regression model is the patient drug response, and the independent variables are gene expression values. However, before we can build the regression model, we have to perform some transformations and joins to make the data suitable for building the model.

Box 11.32 shows the implementation of the program for building a regression model for predicting drug response. In this program, first, we read the four dataset files (shown in Figure 1.6) and convert them into Spark DataFrames, so that we can apply SparkSQL operations for filtering, transforming and joining the datasets. With the dataframes created, we select the genes with a particular set of functions and join the gene meta-data with patient meta-data and microarray data. Next, we pivot the results to get the expression values for each type of gene for each patient (this is table 'g2' in the code). Then we select the patient-ID, disease and drug response from the patient meta-data (this is table 'g3' in the code). Next, we join the tables 'g2' and 'g3' to get table 'g4' which has all the data in the right format to build a regression model. We use the Spark MLib's LinearRegressionWithSGD module to build a linear regression model. We described these steps with a small sample of the data in Chapter-1 (as shown in Figure 1.8).

■ **Box 11.32: Spark implementation for predicting drug response using regression model**

```python
from pyspark import SparkContext
from pyspark.sql import SQLContext, Row
from pyspark.mllib.regression import LabeledPoint
from pyspark.mllib.regression import LinearRegressionWithSGD
from pyspark.mllib.regression import LinearRegressionModel

sc = SparkContext(appName="App")

sqlContext = SQLContext(sc)

genes = sc.textFile('/home/ubuntu/GeneMetaData-10-10.txt')
header = genes.first() #extract header
genes = genes.filter(lambda x:x !=header)

gparts = genes.map(lambda l:  l.split(", "))
geneframe = gparts.map(lambda p:  Row(geneid=int(p[0]),
        target=int(p[1]), position = long(p[2]),
        length=int(p[3]), function=int(p[4])))

schemaGene = sqlContext.createDataFrame(geneframe)
schemaGene.registerTempTable("genes")


patients = sc.textFile('/home/ubuntu/PatientMetaData-10-10.txt')
header = patients.first() #extract header
patients = patients.filter(lambda x:x !=header)

pparts = patients.map(lambda l:  l.split(", "))
patientsframe = pparts.map(lambda p:  Row(patientid=int(p[0]),
        age=int(p[1]), gender=int(p[2]),
        zipcode=int(p[3]), disease=int(p[4]),
        drugResponse = float(p[5])))

schemaPatients = sqlContext.createDataFrame(patientsframe)
schemaPatients.registerTempTable("patients")

geo = sc.textFile('/home/ubuntu/GEO-10-10.txt')
header = geo.first() #extract header
geo = geo.filter(lambda x:x !=header)

geoparts = geo.map(lambda l:  l.split(", "))
geoframe = geoparts.map(lambda p:  Row(geneid=int(p[0]),
    patientid=int(p[1]), exValue = float(p[2])))

schemaGEO = sqlContext.createDataFrame(geoframe)
schemaGEO.registerTempTable("geo")
```

```
g = sqlContext.sql("SELECT p.patientid, p.disease,
        e.geneid, e.exValue, p.drugResponse FROM
        genes AS g, patients AS p, geo AS e
        WHERE g.function < 300 AND
        g.geneid = e.geneid
        AND p.patientid = e.patientid")

g.registerTempTable("responses")

g2=g.groupBy('patientid').pivot('geneid').sum('exValue')

g2.registerTempTable("gen")

g3 = sqlContext.sql("SELECT patientid, disease,
drugResponse FROM patients")

g3.registerTempTable("gen3")

g4 = sqlContext.sql("SELECT * FROM gen3, gen WHERE
gen3.patientid=gen.patientid")


def parsePoint(x):
  return LabeledPoint(x[2], x[4:])

parsedData = g4.map(parsePoint)

# Build the model
model = LinearRegressionWithSGD.train(parsedData)

# Evaluate the model on training data
valuesAndPreds = parsedData.map(lambda p:
        (p.label, model.predict(p.features)))

MSE = valuesAndPreds.map(lambda
    (v, p):  (v - p)**2).reduce(lambda x, y:  x + y) / valuesAndPreds.count()

print("Mean Squared Error = " + str(MSE))
```

For the second type of analysis, we will use Spark to compute correlations between the expression values of all pairs of genes. Box 11.33 shows the implementation of the program for this example. After loading the dataset files and converting the datasets into Spark DataFrames, we select patients with a specific disease and join the results with the microarray table. Next, we pivot the table in the previous step to get the expression values for all genes for each patient. We use this table to create the correlation matrix having correlations between the expression values of all pairs of genes. We described these steps with a small sample of the data in Chapter-1 (as shown in Figure 1.9).

■ **Box 11.33: Spark implementation for computing correlation between the expression levels of all pairs of genes**

```python
from pyspark import SparkContext
from pyspark.sql import SQLContext, Row
from pyspark.mllib.stat import Statistics
from pyspark.mllib.linalg import Vectors
#sc = SparkContext(appName="App")

sqlContext = SQLContext(sc)


genes = sc.textFile('/home/ubuntu/GeneMetaData-10-10.txt')
header = genes.first() #extract header
genes = genes.filter(lambda x:x !=header)

gparts = genes.map(lambda l:  l.split(", "))
geneframe = gparts.map(lambda p:  Row(geneid=int(p[0]),
          target=int(p[1]), position = long(p[2]),
          length=int(p[3]), function=int(p[4])))

schemaGene = sqlContext.createDataFrame(geneframe)
schemaGene.registerTempTable("genes")


patients = sc.textFile('/home/ubuntu/PatientMetaData-10-10.txt')
header = patients.first() #extract header
patients = patients.filter(lambda x:x !=header)

pparts = patients.map(lambda l:  l.split(", "))
patientsframe = pparts.map(lambda p:  Row(patientid=int(p[0]),
      age=int(p[1]), gender=int(p[2]), zipcode=int(p[3]),
      disease=int(p[4]), drugResponse = float(p[5])))

schemaPatients = sqlContext.createDataFrame(patientsframe)
schemaPatients.registerTempTable("patients")

geo = sc.textFile('/home/ubuntu/GEO-10-10.txt')
header = geo.first() #extract header
geo = geo.filter(lambda x:x !=header)

geoparts = geo.map(lambda l:  l.split(", "))
geoframe = geoparts.map(lambda p:  Row(geneid=int(p[0]),
    patientid=int(p[1]), exValue = float(p[2])))

schemaGEO = sqlContext.createDataFrame(geoframe)
schemaGEO.registerTempTable("geo")

g = sqlContext.sql("SELECT p.patientid, p.disease,
      e.geneid, e.exValue FROM patients AS p,
      geo AS e WHERE p.disease =18
      AND p.patientid = e.patientid")

g1=g.groupBy('patientid').pivot('geneid').sum('exValue')
```

```
def parseFunc(x):
  return Vectors.dense(x[1:])

parsedData = g1.map(parseFunc)

pearsonCorr = Statistics.corr(parsedData)

print(str(pearsonCorr).replace('nan', 'NaN'))
```

11.7 Recommendation Systems

Recommendation systems are used in a wide range of applications (such as e-Commerce, social networking, or content delivery applications), to recommend new products or new content to the users. The two broad categories of approaches used for recommendation systems are as follows:

- **Content-based filtering**: In content-based filtering approach, recommendations are provided to users (for items such as books, movies, songs, or restaurants) based on the features or characteristics of the items. The basic idea behind this approach is that if a user has liked an item, he may also like other similar items. In other words, this approach finds all items similar to the items a user has liked and recommends those items to the users. This approach doesn't require user ratings or implicit user preferences. While this approach works for recommending items similar to the items a user has liked, it does not recommend something new which the user may like. To find similar items, similarity measures (such as cosine similarity) or neighborhood methods (such as clustering methods) are used. This approach requires the items to have certain meaningful features which can be used for computing similarity. However, when it is not possible to extract meaningful features from the items, the collaborative filtering approach is used.

- **Collaborative filtering**: Collaborative filtering allows recommending items (or filtering items from a collection of items) based on the preferences of the user and the collective preferences of other users (i.e. making use of the collaborative information available on the user-item ratings). Collaborative filtering makes use of the ratings given by the users to various items for recommending the items to users which they have not rated. The input to any recommendation system that uses collaborative filtering is the data about user ratings for different items. Collaborative filtering approaches are of two types:

  - Memory-based approach: There are two types of memory-based approaches: user-based collaborative filtering and item-based collaborative filtering. User-based collaborative filtering finds users similar to a given user and recommends the items they have liked. Item-based collaborative filtering finds items similar to the items a user has previously liked. The similarity between users (in user-based collaborative filtering) or items (in item-based collaborative filtering) is calculated using the users' ratings of the items.

  - Model-based approach: In model-based collaborative filtering approach, a model of user ratings is built first and then the model is used to make predictions. This method adopts a probabilistic approach and predicts the user ratings for the items which the user has not rated.

The benefit of using collaborative filtering over content-based filtering is that it can discover hidden patterns and recommend something new.

11.7.1 Alternating Least Squares (ALS)

In this section, we will describe a model-based collaborative filtering approach based on Alternating Least Squares (ALS) algorithm.

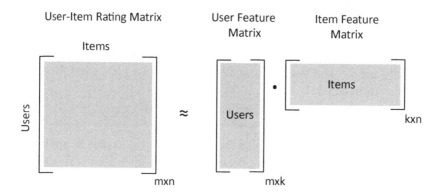

Figure 11.56: Factorizing user-item rating matrix into user feature vector and item feature vector

Let us formulate the collaborative filtering problem. Let

m = number of users

n = number of items

k = number of latent factors (or number of user/item features)

$r^{(u,i)}$ = rating given by user u to item i

$w(i, j) = 1$ if user i has rated item j and 0 otherwise

$x^{(u)}$ = feature vector for user u

$y^{(i)}$ = feature vector for item i

Figure 11.56 shows a user rating matrix where each row belongs to a user and the columns are the ratings given to items. Given the user-item rating matrix, the learning objective is to learn the user and item latent features (that represent the user preferences and item features). In other words, given an $m \times n$ dimensional user-item matrix, we want to factorize the matrix into an $m \times k$ matrix (user feature vector) and $k \times n$ matrix (item feature vector).

To learn the user features $(x^{(1)}, x^{(2)}, ..., x^{(m)})$ for all users and item features $(y^{(1)}, y^{(2)}, ..., y^{(n)})$ for all items, we can define the cost functions for $x^{(u)}$ and $y^{(i)}$ as follows:

$$J(x^{(1)}, x^{(2)}, ..., x^{(m)}) = min_{x^{(u)}} \frac{1}{2} \sum_{u=1}^{m} \sum_{i:w(i,j)=1} (x^{(u)T} y^{(i)} - r^{(u,i)})^2 + \frac{\lambda}{2} \sum_{u=1}^{m} \sum_{l=1}^{k} (x_l^{(u)})^2$$

$$J(y^{(1)}, y^{(2)}, ..., y^{(n)}) = min_{y^{(i)}} \frac{1}{2} \sum_{i=1}^{n} \sum_{u:w(i,j)=1} (x^{(u)T} y^{(i)} - r^{(u,i)})^2 + \frac{\lambda}{2} \sum_{i=1}^{n} \sum_{l=1}^{k} (y_l^{(i)})^2$$

where λ is the regularization parameter which is added to prevent over-fitting of data. The cost functions for $x^{(u)}$ and $y^{(i)}$ can be combined as follows:

$$J(x^{(1)}, ..., x^{(m)}, y^{(1)}, ..., y^{(n)}) = min_{(x^{(u)}, y^{(i)})} \frac{1}{2} \sum_{(u,i):w(i,j)=1} (x^{(u)T} y^{(i)} - r^{(u,i)})^2 +$$

$$\frac{\lambda}{2} \left(\sum_{u=1}^{m} \sum_{l=1}^{k} (x_l^{(u)})^2 + \sum_{i=1}^{n} \sum_{l=1}^{k} (y_l^{(i)})^2 \right)$$

To solve this optimization problem, the Alternating Least Squares (ALS) algorithm can be used. The ALS algorithm is summarized as follows:

1. Initialize $x^{(u)}$ and $y^{(i)}$ (user and item feature vectors) to random values.
2. Fix the item vectors ($y^{(i)}$) and solve for optimal user vectors ($x^{(u)}$) by minimizing the cost function $J(x^{(u)}, y^{(i)})$.
3. Fix the user vectors ($x^{(u)}$) and solve for optimal item vectors ($y^{(i)}$) by minimizing the cost function $J(x^{(u)}, y^{(i)})$.
4. Repeat until convergence.

Let us now look at an example of a system for making movie recommendations using the collaborative filtering approach. For this example, we will use the MovieLens dataset [48] which includes ratings given by users to movies. For development purpose, a smaller version of the dataset (MovieLens 100K) which includes 100,000 ratings from 943 users on 1682 movies, is used. For testing the working code with a big dataset, you can use the MovieLens 20M dataset which includes 20 million ratings applied to 27,000 movies by 138,000 users.

Box 11.34 shows a Python implementation of the recommendation system that uses the Spark MLlib's implementation of the Alternating Least Squares (ALS) algorithm. In this example, we first load the MovieLens dataset and split it into training and test datasets. The dataset file is tab separated with the following columns:
user id | item id | rating | timestamp

The ratings are parsed into Spark's *Rating* objects which represent (user, product, rating) tuples. The *train* function of the ALS class is used to build an ALS model. The *train* function takes input parameters such as the training data, rank (number of latent factors in the model), number of iterations and lambda (regularization parameter). The ALS model is then used to predict the ratings for a given user and product (using *predict(user, product)* function). Spark's ALS class also provides other functions such as *predictAll(user_product)* which returns a list of predicted ratings for input user and product pairs, *recommendProducts(user, num)* function for returning the top *num* products for a given user, *recommendUsers(product, num)* function for returning the top *num* users for a given product. To view the user and product features, the *userFeatures()* and *productFeatures()* functions can be used.

■ **Box 11.34: Python program for building a recommendation system based on ALS**

```
from pyspark.mllib.recommendation import ALS, Rating

# Load and parse the data
data = sc.textFile("file:///home/hadoop/ml-100k/u.data")

(trainingRatings, testRatings) = data.randomSplit([0.7, 0.3])

trainingRatings.first()
#Output:  u'196,242,3,881250949'

testRatings.first()
#Output:  u'244,51,2,880606923'

trainingData = trainingRatings.map(lambda l:
    l.split(',')).map(lambda l:
    Rating(int(l[0]), int(l[1]), float(l[2])))

trainingData.first()
#Output:  Rating(user=196, product=242, rating=3.0)

testData = testRatings.map(lambda l:
    l.split(',')).map(lambda l:
    (int(l[0]), int(l[1])))

testData.first()
#Output:  (244, 51)

# Build the recommendation model using Alternating Least Squares
rank = 10
numIterations = 50
model = ALS.train(trainingData, rank, numIterations)

#Predict rating for the given user and product.
model.predict(253, 465)
#Output:  4.5738394508197189

#Return a list of predicted ratings for input user and product pairs
predictions = model.predictAll(testData)
predictions.first()
#Rating(user=58, product=1084, rating=1.056493295594659)

predictions = predictions.map(lambda l:  ((l[0], l[1]), l[2]))
predictions.take(5)
#Output:  [((58, 1084), 1.0564932954594659),
#((316, 1084), 5.7316694387562022),
#((330, 1084), 3.5890840644277131),
#((195, 1084), 4.4394359038624369),
#((541, 1084), 5.9725270274011484)]

testRatings = testRatings.map(lambda l:
    l.split(',')).map(lambda l:  ((int(l[0]), int(l[1])), float(l[2])))
```

```
testRatings.take(5)
#[((244, 51), 2.0), ((115, 265), 2.0),
#((6, 86), 3.0),
#((200, 222), 5.0),
#((234, 1184), 2.0)]

ratingsAndPredictions = testRatings.join(predictions)
ratingsAndPredictions.take(5)
#[((105, 333), (3.0, 2.4070588034521849)),
#((109, 365), (4.0, 2.974229204549999)),
#((360, 14), (5.0, 4.5625799637027171)),
#((720, 286), (5.0, 3.9581844170381464)),
#((501, 829), (3.0, 2.4709893659891664))]

MSE = ratingsAndPredictions.map(lambda r:   (r[1][0] - r[1][1])**2).mean()
print "Mean Squared Error = " + str(MSE)
#Output:  Mean Squared Error = 1.29853954685

#Recommend the top N products for a given user
model.recommendProducts(253, 5)
#Output:  [Rating(user=253, product=1063, rating=6.7525296445231611),
#Rating(user=253, product=459, rating=6.7239131863565023),
#Rating(user=253, product=844, rating=6.643750789521941),
#Rating(user=253, product=960, rating=6.175726236721804),
#Rating(user=253, product=394, rating=6.1395628318225901)]

#Recommend the top N users for a given product
model.recommendUsers(465, 5)
#Output:  [Rating(user=519, product=465, rating=7.5049478754749002),
#Rating(user=180, product=465, rating=7.3478113160070091),
#Rating(user=217, product=465, rating=7.2194201952177766),
#Rating(user=808, product=465, rating=6.5398839496324266),
#Rating(user=93, product=465, rating=6.4988971770196038)]


#View features corresponding to a user
model.userFeatures().take(1)[0]
#Output:  (2, array('d', [-0.041698437184095383, -0.29158979654312134,
#0.60749232769012451, 0.6784324049949646, -0.12671113014221191,
#0.76399964094161987, -0.52530914545059204, 0.25506862998008728,
#0.54997712373733521, -1.3625633716583252]))


#View features corresponding to a product
model.productFeatures().take(1)[0]
#Output:  (2, array('d', [-1.2220950126647949, 0.26224410533905029,
#0.31355467438697815, 0.7695726752281189,
#0.072056755423545837, 1.233315110206604,
#0.5064246654510498, -0.024322325363755226,
#-0.10120454430580139, -0.98879802227020264]))
```

11.7.2 Singular Value Decomposition (SVD)

In this section, we will describe a collaborative filtering approach based on Singular Value Decomposition (SVD) algorithm.

SVD is a matrix factorization method that can be used to factorize a matrix X of dimensions $(n \times d)$ into matrices U of dimensions $(n \times n)$, S of dimensions $(d \times d)$ and V of dimensions $(n \times d)$ as follows:

$$X_{n \times d} = U_{n \times n} S_{d \times d} V_{n \times d}^T$$

For a recommendation system that maintains user-item ratings, the user-items matrix is typically very sparse, because the matrix may have a very large number of users and items but a given user may have rated only a small number of items. The matrix in this case would consist of most of the fields set to 0 with only a few fields consisting of the actual values, which are the ratings. Working with such a sparse matrix involves high space complexity to store the entire matrix and increased time complexity to parse the matrix and compute the relationship for an item and a user. SVD can be used for matrix dimension reduction for reducing a sparse matrix to extract the latent relationship between a user and an item. This helps in obtaining the relationship between the user and an item in a more efficient manner and helps in increasing the accuracy of the recommendation system.

11.7.3 Case Study: Movie Recommendation System

In this section we describe a case study of a movie recommendation system that uses both ALS and SVD based recommendation algorithms. For implementing ALS we have used Spark MLLib and for SVD we have used the Python-RecSys library [28].

Figure 11.57 shows the architecture of the recommendation system. The dataset used for the recommendation system is the MovieLens dataset [48]. In addition to the MovieLens dataset, additional information is added to the dataset with IMDbPY, an API to access the IMDb database [49]. From the MovieLens dataset we used the following files: movies.csv, ratings.csv and links.csv. The movies.csv has the format: movie id, title, genres. The ratings.csv has the format: user id, movie id, rating, timestamp. The links.csv the format: MovieLens movieID, IMDb movieID, TMDb movieID.

Since MovieLens movie-IDs have a one-to-one relationship with IMDb movie-IDs, IMDbPy is used to retrieve the movie object associated with a MovieLens movie-ID. The movie object contains a list of directors and a list of cast members. For the movie recommendation system, the first director in the list and the top nine cast member are added to the links.csv file. Given a movie-ID, the modified links file (links_modified.csv) can be used to retrieve more information about a movie for front end presentation. Box 11.35 shows the Python code for adding details to the links file using IMDbPY. The MovieLens dataset files and the modified links file are converted into SparkSQL DataFrames and saved as tables which are used within the recommendation engine at run time. Box 11.36 shows the Python program for saving the dataset files as SparkSQL tables.

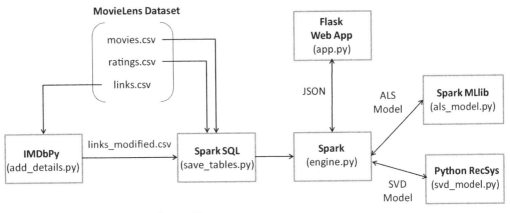

Fields in MovieLens dataset files:

movies.csv:
movie id, title, genres

ratings.csv:
user id, movie id, rating, timestamp

links.csv:
MovieLens movieID, IMDb movieID, TMDb movieID

Figure 11.57: Architecture for movie recommendation system

■ **Box 11.35: Python program for adding details to links file using IMDbPy - add_details.py**

```python
import imdb
import csv
import codecs

#Add director and cast info to the links.csv file

#Fetch from IMDB server
ia = imdb.IMDb(accessSystem='http')

file_name = 'datasets/links.csv'

old = open(file_name, 'rb')
new = codecs.open('links_modified.csv', 'wb', 'utf-8')
reader = csv.reader(old, delimiter=',')
next(reader)

new.write('movieId,imdbId,tmdId,director,cast\n')

for row in reader:
  id = row[1]
  m = ia.get_movie(id)
```

```
  director="
  cast_list=[]
  cast = []

  if m.get('director'):
   director = m.get('director')[0].get('name')

  if m.get('cast'):
   cast_list = m.get('cast')
   l = len(cast_list)
   if l >= 10:
    cast_list = cast_list[0:9]
   else:
    cast_list = cast_list[0:l]

  cast = [c['name'] for c in cast_list]
  cast_elements = '|'.join(cast)
  line = [row[0], id, row[2], director, cast_elements]
  new.write(','.join(line))
  new.write('\n')
  print id

old.close()
new.close()
```

■ Box 11.36: Python program for saving the dataset files as SparkSQL tables - save_tables.py

```
import os
import re
from pyspark import SparkContext
from pyspark.sql import SQLContext, Row

# Regex used to seperate movie movieId, name, year, and genres
RE = re.compile(r'(?P<movieId>\d+),
"?(?P<name>.+)\((?P<year>\d+))
?"?,(?P<genres>.+)')

# Initialize the Spark context
sc = SparkContext("local", "DataImporter")
# Initialize the SparkSQL context
sqlContext = SQLContext(sc)

#-----Import Movies File----------

# Read in the text file as an RDD
data = sc.textFile('movies.csv')

header = data.first() # Get the csv header
# Filter out the csv header
#data = data.filter(lambda line:  line != header)
# Split the CSV file into rows
```

```
# Formatter that takes the CSV line and
# outputs it as a list of datapoints
# Uses a regex with named groups
def formatter(line):
 m = RE.match(line) # Seperates datapoints
 if (m != None):
  m = m.groupdict()
  movieId = int(m['movieId'])
  name = m['name']
  year = int(m['year'])
  genres = m['genres'].split('|')
  return [movieId, name, year, genres]

data = data.map(formatter)
# Filter out rows that dont match
data = data.filter(lambda line:  line != None)
# Map the data into a Row data object to prepare it for insertion
rows = data.map(lambda r:  Row(movieId=r[0], name=r[1],
   year=r[2], genres=r[3]))

# Create the schema for movies and register a table for it
schemaMovies = sqlContext.createDataFrame(rows)
schemaMovies.registerTempTable("movies")
schemaMovies.save('tables/movies')

#----Import Ratings File----------

# Regex used to seperate movie movieId, name, year, and genres
RE = re.compile(r' (?P<userId>\d+),(?P<movieId>\d+),
(?P<rating>\d\d),(?P<timestamp>\d+)')

# Read in the text file as an RDD
data = sc.textFile('ratings.csv')

header = data.first() # Get the csv header
# Filter out the csv header
#data = data.filter(lambda line:  line != header)
# Split the CSV file into rows
def formatter(line):
 m = RE.match(line) # Seperates datapoints
 if (m != None):
  m = m.groupdict()
  userId = int(m['userId'])
  movieId = int(m['movieId'])
  rating = float(m['rating'])
  timestamp = m['timestamp']
  return [userId, movieId, rating, timestamp]

data = data.map(formatter)
# Filter out rows that dont match
data = data.filter(lambda line:  line != None)
# Map the data into a Row data object to prepare it for insertion
rows = data.map(lambda r:  Row(userId=r[0], movieId=r[1],
   rating=r[2], timestamp=r[3]))
```

```
# Create the schema for movies and register a table for it
schemaRatings = sqlContext.createDataFrame(rows)
schemaRatings.registerTempTable("ratings")
schemaRatings.save('tables/ratings')

#----Import Details File----------

# Regex used to seperate movie movieId, imdbId, and tmdbId
RE = re.compile(r'(?P<movieId>\d+),(?P<imdbId>\d+),
(?P<tmdbId>\d+),(?P<director>.+),(?P<cast>.+)')

# Read in the text file as an RDD
data = sc.textFile('links_modified.csv')

header = data.first() # Get the csv header
# Filter out the csv header
#data = data.filter(lambda line:  line != header)
# Split the CSV file into rows
def formatter(line):
 m = RE.match(line) # Seperates datapoints
 if (m != None):
  m = m.groupdict()
  movieId = int(m['movieId'])
  imdbId = int(m['imdbId'])
  if m['tmdbId'] != None:
   tmdbId = int(m['tmdbId'])
  else:
   tmdbId = -1
  director = m['director']
  cast = m['cast'].split('|')
  print [movieId, imdbId, tmdbId, director, cast]
  return [movieId, imdbId, tmdbId, director, cast]

data = data.map(formatter)
# Filter out rows that dont match
data = data.filter(lambda line:  line != None)
# Map the data into a Row data object to prepare it for insertion
rows = data.map(lambda r:  Row(movieId=r[0], imdbId=r[1],
 tmdbId=r[2], director=r[3], cast=r[4]))

# Create the schema for movies and register a table for it
schemaLinks = sqlContext.createDataFrame(rows)
schemaLinks.registerTempTable("detail")
schemaLinks.save('tables/detail')
```

Building ALS Model

We use Spark MLlib for implementing the ALS algorithm and for building the ALS model. Box 11.37 shows the Python code for training and saving an ALS model. The model is saved as to a file and then used within the recommendation engine. This approach is efficient since the model needs to be computed only once. Thus, the time latency of the recommendation algorithm is reduced due to this model based recommendation approach.

■ **Box 11.37: Python program for training and saving an ALS model - als_model.py**

```python
from pyspark import SparkContext
from pyspark.mllib.recommendation import ALS
from pyspark.mllib.recommendation import Rating

sc = SparkContext("local", "collaborative_filtering") #initializing sc

#Loading the data using SparkContext
ratings = "./ratings.csv"
data = sc.textFile(ratings)
ratings_data = data.map(lambda l:  l.split(','))
ratings = ratings_data.map(lambda l:  Rating(int(l[0]),
 int(l[1]), float(l[2])))

#Building the recommendation model using Alternating Least Squares
rank = 10
numIterations = 5
model = ALS.train(ratings, rank, numIterations)

#Lets save the model for future use
model_path = "./ALS_Model"
model.save(sc,model_path)
```

Building SVD Model

For building the SVD model, we use the Python-RecSys library which provides an implementation of the SVD algorithm. Box 11.38 shows the Python code for training and saving an SVD model. The model is saved as to a file and then used within the recommendation engine.

■ **Box 11.38: Python program for training and saving an SVD model - svd_model.py**

```python
import recsys.algorithm
from recsys.algorithm.factorize import SVD

#SVD Model Computation


#To obtain make the script verbose.
recsys.algorithm.VERBOSE = True

#Load the ratings file
svd = SVD()
svd.load_data(filename='ratings.csv',
    sep=',' , format={'col':0, 'row':1, 'value':2, 'ids':int})

#Now, lets compute the SVD. k = 100
svd.compute(k=k, min_values=10, pre_normalize=None,
  mean_center=True, post_normalize=True,
  savefile='movielens_model')

print("Model Computed and Created")
```

Recommendation Engine

The recommendation engine receives inputs from the web application (user-ID and movie name), and provides the recommendations using the ALS and SVD models previously trained. Box 11.39 shows the Python code for the recommendation engine.

The ALS model provides recommendations by seeking out users which are similar to the given user and then predicting the ratings for the top rated movies of the similar users. The recommended movies are basically the list of movies which have a high predicted rating amongst the top rated movies of the similar users. For this case study, the list of recommended movies is limited to five.

The SVD model provides two types of recommendations:

- Recommending movies for a particular user in the database: This produces a list of movies which are top rated by other users which are similar to the target user. This is a personalized movie recommendation and returns a list of movies which are more in line with the user's preferences.
- Recommending movies based on a particular movie: This is a type of non-personalized movie recommendation which takes in a movie as an input and predicts the ratings of other movies and returns the list of those movies.

■ **Box 11.39: Recommendation engine program - engine.py**

```python
import recsys.algorithm
from recsys.algorithm.factorize import SVD
from operator import add
from pyspark import SparkContext
from pyspark.sql import SQLContext, Row
from pyspark import SparkConf
from pyspark.mllib.recommendation import ALS
from pyspark.mllib.recommendation import MatrixFactorizationModel
from pyspark.mllib.recommendation import Rating

recsys.algorithm.VERBOSE = True

'''
This is the main file which initializes the backend and gets the machine
learning algorithms running on spark.  Use this file for running.
'''

def get_counts_and_averages(ID_and_ratings_tuple):
  nratings = len(ID_and_ratings_tuple[1])
  return ID_and_ratings_tuple[0],
  (nratings, float(sum(x for x in ID_and_ratings_tuple[1])) / nratings)

class RecommendationSystem():
  def __init__(self, sc, datapath='frontend/', model='movielens_model'):
    self.sc = sc
    self.start = True
    self.sqlContext = SQLContext(self.sc)

    self.svd = SVD(filename=datapath+model)
```

```
    self.als_model_path = datapath + 'ALS_Model'
    self.als_model = MatrixFactorizationModel.load(sc, self.als_model_path)
    self.movie_df = self.sqlContext.read.load(datapath+'tables/movies')
    self.detail_df = self.sqlContext.read.load(datapath+'tables/detail')
    self.rating_df = self.sqlContext.read.load(datapath+'tables/ratings')


# call this function to get all recommendations
def get_all_recomm(self, userid, moviename):
 movieid = self.get_movie_id(moviename)

 # all recommendation algorithms return a list of movie ids
 recom1 = self.svd_recomm(userid)
 recom2 = self.svd_similar(movieid)
 recom3 = self.als_new(userid)

 #get info about the movie based on movie ids
 brief_info1 = self.get_brief_list(recom1)
 brief_info2 = self.get_brief_list(recom2)
 brief_info3 = self.get_brief_list(recom3)

 return [brief_info1, brief_info2, brief_info3]

# get movie id based on movie name input
def get_movie_id(self, moviename):
 r = self.movie_df.where(self.movie_df['name'].startswith(moviename)).first()

 # return movie id 1 if not found
 if r is None:
  return 1

 return r['movieId']

# svd recommendation algorithm based on the user's rating history
def svd_recomm(self, userid, only_unknown):
 # output format:  (movieid, similarity value)
 similar_list = self.svd.recommend(userid, n=10,
    only_unknowns=True, is_row=True)

 movieid_list = self.get_id_list(similar_list)
 return movieid_list

# svd recommendation algorithm based on similar movie
def svd_similar(self, movieid):
 similar_list = self.svd.similar(movieid)
 movieid_list = self.get_id_list(similar_list)
 return movieid_list


# an ALS recommendation algorithm based on user rating history
def als_new(self, userid):
 recommended_movies = self.als_model.recommendProducts(userid, 10)
 recommended_movie_list = []
 for movie in recommended_movies:
```

```
        recommended_movie_list.append(movie[1])

    return recommended_movie_list

# return a list of movie id
def get_id_list(self, l):
  movieid_list = []
  for s in l:
    movieid_list.append(s[0])
  return movieid_list

# get a list of movie info given a list of movie ids
def get_brief_list(self, movieList):
  info_list = []
  for m in movieList:
    info = self.get_brief(m)
    if info['title'] != 'unknown':
      info_list.append(info)
    if len(info_list) == 5:
      break

  return info_list

# get movie info (title, direction, genres, rating, cast)
def get_brief(self, movieid):
  info = {}
  info['movieid'] = movieid
  info['title'] = 'unknown'
  info['genres'] = 'unknown'
  info['rating'] = 0
  info['director'] = 'unknown'
  info['cast'] = 'unknown'

  m = self.movie_df.where(self.movie_df['movieId'] == movieid).first()
  if m is not None:
    info['title'] = m['name']
    info['genres'] = m['genres']
    if len(info['genres']) > 3:
      info['genres'] = info['genres'][0:3]

  d = self.detail_df.where(self.detail_df['movieId'] == movieid).first()
  if d is not None:
    info['director'] = d['director']
    info['cast'] = d['cast']

  r = self.rating_df.where(self.rating_df['movieId'] == movieid)

  # default rating to be 4.6
  if r.count()==0:
    info['rating'] = 4.6
  else:
    avg = r.map(lambda row:row['rating']).reduce(lambda x, y:  x+y)/r.count()
    info['rating'] = avg

  return info
```

Web Application

Box 11.40 shows the Python code for the Flask web application. Due to space constraints, we have not included the HTML, JavaScript and CSS files for the web application. Figure 11.58 shows a screenshot of the web application. In the web interface, a user can search for a movie name in the search bar. The recommendations based on the three different algorithms are listed in the three separated columns. The movie recommendations in the left column are the outputs from SVD algorithm based on user-ID. Results from SVD recommendation based on the input movie name are listed in the middle column. The right columns are results from the ALS collaborative filtering. Brief information of each recommended movie, such as title, rating, top two genres, director, and top nine cast members of the movie, is also displayed.

The Flask web application is used to serve the static HTML, CSS and JavaScript files and act as the server, as well as connect the backend recommendation engine to the front end. The JavaScript code handles user interaction and initiates the backend processing by sending a HTTP POST request to the Flask application which in turn calls the functions for getting the recommendations using the ALS and SVD models. The JavaScript waits for a JSON response to its POST request and then parses the response and inserts the information into the HTML template.

■ **Box 11.40: Python Flask web application - app.py**

```python
from flask import Flask
from flask import request, render_template, jsonify, url_for
import json
from engine import RecommendationSystem
from pyspark import SparkContext, SparkConf

import imdb
import csv
import codecs


#Add director and cast info to the links.csv file

#Fetch from IMDB server
ia = imdb.IMDb(accessSystem='http')

file_name = 'datasets/links.csv'

old = open(file_name, 'rb')
new = codecs.open('links_modified.csv', 'wb', 'utf-8')
reader = csv.reader(old, delimiter=',')
next(reader)

new.write('movieId,imdbId,tmdId,director,cast\n')

for row in reader:
  id = row[1]
  m = ia.get_movie(id)

  director="
```

```python
  cast_list=[]
  cast = []

  if m.get('director'):
   director = m.get('director')[0].get('name')

  if m.get('cast'):
   cast_list = m.get('cast')
   l = len(cast_list)
   if l >= 10:
    cast_list = cast_list[0:9]
   else:
    cast_list = cast_list[0:l]

  cast = [c['name'] for c in cast_list]
  cast_elements = '|'.join(cast)
  line = [row[0], id, row[2], director, cast_elements]
  new.write(','.join(line))
  new.write('\n')
  print id

old.close()
new.close()
app = Flask(__name__)

conf = SparkConf().setAppName("movie_recommendation_server")
sc = SparkContext(conf=conf, pyFiles=['frontend/engine.py'])

global data
global userid

@app.route("/")
def index():
 global data
 global userid
 data = {"data":  "Empty"}
 userid = 1
 return render_template('index.html')

# change user id through url
@app.route("/<int:user_id>")
def index_id(user_id):
 global data
 global userid
 data = {"data":  "Empty"}
 userid = user_id
 return render_template('index.html')

# post movie recommendation results
@app.route("/data", methods=['POST'])
def post_data():
 global data
 global userid
 d = request.get_data()
```

```
data = json.loads(d)

# calling backend to get all movie recommendations
info = recomsys.get_all_recomm(userid, data['data'])
return jsonify({'data':  info})

if __name__ == "__main__":
 global data
 global recomsys

 # initialize backend engine
 recomsys = RecommendationSystem(sc)

 data = {"data":  "Empty"}
 app.run()
```

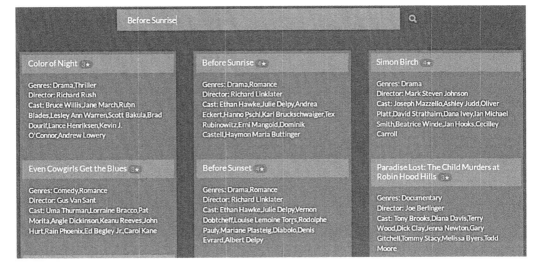

Figure 11.58: Screenshot of the movie recommendation web application

Summary

In this chapter we provided an overview of big data analysis algorithms for machine learning that include clustering, classification, regression and recommendation. Implementations and examples of applying these algorithms using Spark MLlib and H2O machine learning frameworks were provided. Clustering is the process of grouping similar data items together such that data items that are more similar to each other than other data items are put in one cluster. The k-means clustering algorithm groups data items into k clusters, such that all points in a cluster are closer to their centroid as compared to the centroids of neighboring clusters. We described various distance measures that can be used for clustering algorithms including Euclidean, Cosine, and Manhattan distance measures. Next, we described classification and regression algorithms. Classification is the process of categorizing objects into predefined categories. While in classification, the response variable is categorical and unordered, in

Regression, the response variable takes continuous values. Naive Bayes is a probabilistic classification algorithm based on the Bayes theorem with a naive assumption about the independence of feature attributes. Generalized Linear Models (GLM) are a generalization of ordinary linear regression models that allows response variables which are discrete, non-normally distributed and/or non-constant variance. In Decision Trees, the predictive model is in the form of a tree that can be used to predict the value of a target variable based on several attribute variables. Random Forest trains a number decision trees and then takes the majority vote by using the mode of the class predicted by the individual trees. In Random Forest, each tree is built independently from a random (bootstrap) sample, whereas in Gradient-Boosted Trees a decision tree is trained at each step which corrects and compliments the previously built trees. In SVM, a maximum margin hyperplane is determined, that separates the two classes. Next, we described a specific implementation of deep learning, which is based on a multi-layer feed-forward artificial neural network which includes multiple layers of interconnected neurons. Next, we provided a comparison of recommendation algorithms. While in content-based filtering approach, recommendations are provided to users based on the features or characteristics of the items, collaborative filtering makes use of the ratings given by the users to various items for recommending the items to users which they have not rated.

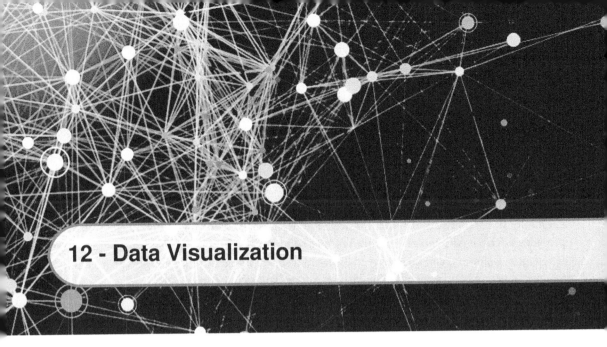

12 - Data Visualization

This chapter covers
Data visualization frameworks and libraries:

- Lightning
- Pygal
- Seaborn

In this chapter, we will describe frameworks and Python libraries for data visualization. Visualizations can help in understanding the data and the results of analysis quickly and easily. When the amount of data is massive, visualizations become important as they help us in understanding the patterns in the results or the data which may not be discernible.

12.1 Frameworks & Libraries

12.1.1 Lightning

Lightning is a framework for creating web-based interactive visualizations [67]. Lightning provides a REST API and client libraries for Python, Scala, R and JavaScript programming languages. Lightning can be deployed either in a server mode or in a local server-less mode. Lightning server can be installed and run using the following commands:

```
■ sudo apt-get install nodejs npm
sudo npm install -g lightning-server
lightning-server
```

Lightning can also be run without a server using the Python client. The Lightning Python client can be installed with the follows command:

```
■ sudo pip install lightning-python
```

To create visualizations you can either use the Lightning REST API or one of client libraries. The examples in this chapter use Lightning Python client library for creating visualizations.

12.1.2 Pygal

Since we have used Python as the primary programming language for the examples in this book, a Python charting library may be handy in visualizing the data and the analysis results. The Python Pygal library is an easy to use charting library which supports charts of various types. The charts built with Pygal can be rendered in output formats such as SVG, PNG or in the browser. The Pygal library can be installed with the following commands:

```
■ sudo pip install pygal
```

12.1.3 Seaborn

Seaborn is a Python visualization library for plotting attractive statistical plots [36]. Seaborn is built on top of matplotlib and uses data structures from Python *numpy* and *pandas* libraries and statistical routines from *scipy* and *statsmodels*. Seaborn can be installed with the following commands:

```
■ sudo apt install python-scipy python-pandas
sudo pip install seaborn
```

12.2   Visualization Examples

12.2.1   Line Chart

Line chart is one of the simplest charts that can be used to display information as a series of data points connected by a line. Let us look at an example of plotting line charts for maximum, minimum and mean temperatures recorded in the month of October 2014 in Atlanta. The data was obtained from Weather Underground [31]. Box 12.1 shows the Python code creating the line charts using Lightning and the output is shown in Figure 12.1.

■ **Box 12.1: Python program for plotting line chart using Lightning**

```
from lightning import Lightning

from numpy import random

lgn = Lightning(ipython=True,local=True)

x = range(1,32)

y1 = [30,29,25,18,21,26,27,29,29,30,28,29,
29,24,21,20,26,23,22,22,24,21,21,23,24,
28,29,25,21,19,16]

y2 = [22,22,22,13,13,17,20,23,23,23,24,23,
23,19,17,15,17,18,15,14,17,14,13,15,16,
19,19,18,15,12,10]

y3 = [14,15,18,8,4,9,13,16,18,17,19,17,
17,13,12,10,8,12,8,7,9,8,5,7,7,9,10,
11,8,5,4]

lgn.line([y1,y2,y3],thickness=6,index=x,
    xaxis='Day of Month',yaxis='Temperature (C)')
```

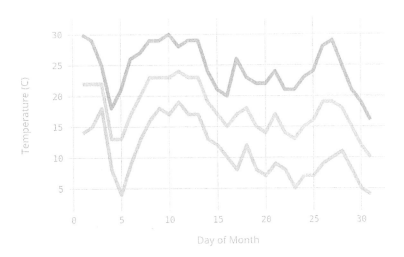

Figure 12.1: Line chart plotted with Lightning

Let us repeat the example using Pygal charting library. Box 12.2 shows the Python code creating the line charts using Pygal and the output is shown in Figure 12.2.

▪ Box 12.2: Python program for plotting line chart using Pygal

```
import pygal

line_chart = pygal.Line(fill=True)
line_chart.x_title = 'Day of Month'
line_chart.y_title = 'Temperature (c)'
line_chart.title = 'Temperature in Atlanta (Oct 2014)'

line_chart.x_labels = ['1','2','3','4','5','6','7', '8','9','10','11',
'12','13', '14','15', '16','17','18','19','20','21','22',
'23', '24','25','26','27', '28','29','30','31']

line_chart.add('Max Temp', [30, 29, 25, 18, 21, 26, 27, 29, 29, 30, 28,
29, 29, 24, 21, 20, 26, 23, 22, 22, 24, 21, 21,
23, 24, 28, 29, 25, 21, 19, 16])

line_chart.add('Min Temp', [22, 22, 22, 13, 13, 17, 20, 23, 23, 23, 24,
23, 23, 19, 17, 15, 17, 18, 15, 14, 17, 14, 13,
15, 16, 19, 19, 18, 15, 12, 10, ])

line_chart.add('Mean Temp',    [14, 15, 18, 8, 4, 9, 13, 16,
18, 17, 19, 17, 17, 13, 12, 10, 8, 12, 8, 7, 9, 8, 5, 7, 7, 9, 10,
11, 8, 5, 4, ])

line_chart.render_to_png('line.png')
```

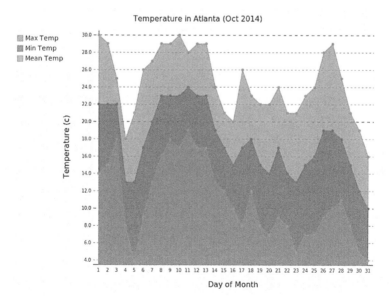

Figure 12.2: Line chart plotted with Pygal

12.2.2 Scatter Plot

Scatter plots can be used to visualize two variables along the X and Y axes. Scatter plots and are useful for identifying the relationships between two sets of data, for example fitting a regression line for bivariate data.

Let us look at examples of scatter plots for visualizing the mean temperature and mean humidity recorded in Atlanta in May 2012, May 2013 and May 2014. Box 12.3 shows the Python code creating a scatter plot using Lightning and the output is shown in Figure 12.3. The groups (shown in different colors) denote data from different years for the month of May.

■ **Box 12.3: Python program for plotting scatter plot using Lightning**

```
from lightning import Lightning

from numpy import random

lgn = Lightning(ipython=True,local=True)

#Mean Temp
x=[25,23,23,24,24,24,22,23,18,17,17,
21,18,22,21,22,21,22,21,22,23,22,22,22,24,
26,26,26,26,26,24,19,18,17,13,14,11,15,17,
20,19,20,16,13,17,22,22,21,21,19,23,24,24,
25,18,17,19,22,24,23,24,26,16,17,16,19,22,
22,21,22,22,21,23,24,24,22,15,15,14,15,18,
20,22,23,26,24,24,23,23,24,24,25,24 ]

#Mean Humidity
y=[61,62,71,76,69,66,79,79,81,62,61,66,90,
81,81,67,70,66,63,57,70,73,65,61,65,65,
60,65,70,70,61,70,78,76,84,74,81,76,70,
69,70,77,61,60,66,58,63,68,83,90,76,70,
68,66,57,61,61,64,57,67,68,63,67,53,55,
57,60,61,58,62,73,85,76,71,65,72,73,57,
70,89,77,68,62,68,65,66,69,76,79,74,71,78,71]

g=[1,1,1,1,1,1,1,1,1,1,1,1,1,
1,1,1,1,1,1,1,1,1,1,1,1,1,
1,1,1,1,2,2,2,2,2,2,2,2,2,2,
2,2,2,2,2,2,2,2,2,2,2,2,2,2,
2,2,2,2,2,2,2,3,3,3,3,3,3,3,
3,3,3,3,3,3,3,3,3,3,3,3,3,3,
3,3,3,3,3,3,3,3,3]

lgn.scatter(x,y,group=g,
    xaxis='Mean Temp (C)',yaxis='Mean Humidity (%)')
```

Lightning supports special type of scatter plot in which the size of the dots can be made proportional to a third variable. Box 12.4 shows the Python code creating a scatter plot where the size of the dots are proportional to the mean wind speed. The output is shown in Figure 12.4. The different color dots show the data from different years.

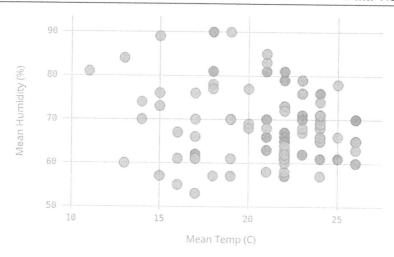

Figure 12.3: Scatter plot plotted with Lightning

■ Box 12.4: Python program for plotting scatter plot using Lightning

```
from lightning import Lightning

from numpy import random

lgn = Lightning(ipython=True,local=True)

#Mean Temp
x=[25,23,23,24,24,24,22,23,18,17,17,
21,18,22,21,22,21,22,21,22,23,22,22,22,24,
26,26,26,26,26,24,19,18,17,13,14,11,15,17,
20,19,20,16,13,17,22,22,21,21,19,23,24,24,
25,18,17,19,22,24,23,24,26,16,17,16,19,22,
22,21,22,22,21,23,24,24,22,15,15,14,15,18,
20,22,23,26,24,24,23,23,24,24,25,24 ]

#Mean Humidity
y=[61,62,71,76,69,66,79,79,81,62,61,66,90,
81,81,67,70,66,63,57,70,73,65,61,65,65,
60,65,70,70,61,70,78,76,84,74,81,76,70,
69,70,77,61,60,66,58,63,68,83,90,76,70,
68,66,57,61,61,64,57,67,68,63,67,53,55,
57,60,61,58,62,73,85,76,71,65,72,73,57,
70,89,77,68,62,68,65,66,69,76,79,74,71,78,71]

g=[1,1,1,1,1,1,1,1,1,1,1,1,1,1,
1,1,1,1,1,1,1,1,1,1,1,1,1,1,1,1,
1,1,1,1,2,2,2,2,2,2,2,2,2,2,
2,2,2,2,2,2,2,2,2,2,2,2,2,2,
2,2,2,2,2,2,2,3,3,3,3,3,3,3,
3,3,3,3,3,3,3,3,3,3,3,3,3,3,
3,3,3,3,3,3,3,3,3,3]
```

```
#Mean Wind Speed
s=[5,5,3,3,5,3,6,6,6,5,5,10,8,8,
3,3,3,5,3,3,3,5,3,2,2,2,6,13,13,
10,5,17,19,22,14,7,7,5,6,4,6,6,10,
8,5,7,4,5,7,6,3,5,7,11,15,4,3,4,
9,8,10,9,9,6,7,6,7,6,5,7,6,4,3,
6,5,9,13,11,3,2,4,6,8,10,8,4,3,
3,4,4,5,4,4]

lgn.scatter(x,y,group=g,size=s,
    xaxis='Mean Temp (C)',yaxis='Mean Humidity (%)')
```

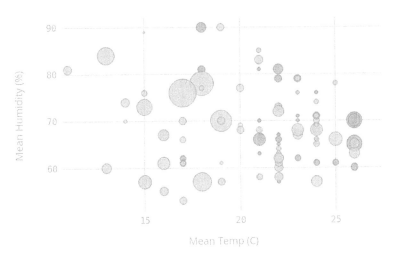

Figure 12.4: Scatter plot plotted with Lightning

Let us look at another example of a scatter plot built using Pygal library. Box 12.5 shows the Python code creating a scatter plot of mean temperature and mean humidity for the months of March and October in the year 2014 in Atlanta. The output is shown in Figure 12.5.

■ Box 12.5: Python program for plotting scatter plot using Pygal

```
import pygal

xy_chart = pygal.XY(stroke=False)
xy_chart.title = 'Mean Temp vs Mean Humidity'
xy_chart.x_title = 'Mean Temp (C)'
xy_chart.y_title = 'Mean Humidity (%)'

xy_chart.add('Mar', [(11, 62), (13, 66), (8, 79), (4, 66),
  (9, 58), (6, 61), (10, 76), (11, 66), (14, 59), (14, 58), (16, 64),
  (14, 69), (7, 44), (9, 59), (16, 56), (14, 84), (11, 93), (7, 79),
  (12, 77), (12, 57), (10, 59), (15, 61), (13, 67), (8, 58), (7, 49),
  (5, 44), (9, 51), (14, 77), (14, 79), (12, 48), (15, 48) ])

xy_chart.add('Oct', [(22, 68), (22, 70), (22, 81), (13, 55), (13, 57),
```

```
(17, 66), (20, 68), (23, 74), (23, 74), (23, 72), (24, 74), (23, 74),
(23, 72), (19, 77), (17, 68), (15, 76), (17, 65), (18, 67), (15, 67),
(14, 69), (17, 70), (14, 56), (13, 63), (15, 61), (16, 62), (19, 65),
(19, 70), (18, 73), (15, 83), (12, 61), (10, 71)])

xy_chart.render_to_png('scatter.png')
```

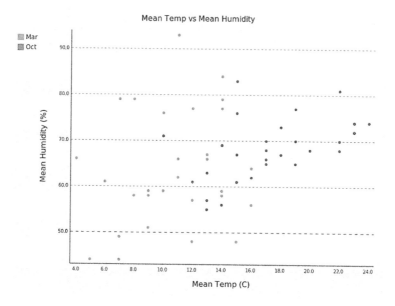

Figure 12.5: Scatter plot plotted with Pygal

12.2.3 Bar Chart

Bar chart can be used to display grouped data as bars with lengths proportional to the values represented. Box 12.6 shows the Python code for plotting a bar chart of the maximum, minimum and mean temperatures recorded in October 2014 in Atlanta. The output is shown in Figure 12.6.

■ Box 12.6: Python program for plotting bar chart using Pygal

```
import pygal

bar_chart = pygal.Bar()
bar_chart.x_title = 'Day of Month'
bar_chart.y_title = 'Temperature (C)'
bar_chart.title = 'Temperature in Atlanta (Oct 2014)'

bar_chart.x_labels = ['1','2','3','4','5','6','7', '8','9','10','11',
'12','13', '14','15', '16','17','18','19','20','21','22',
'23', '24','25','26','27', '28','29','30','31']

bar_chart.add('Max Temp', [30, 29, 25, 18, 21, 26, 27, 29, 29, 30, 28,
29, 29, 24, 21, 20, 26, 23, 22, 22, 24, 21, 21,
```

```
23, 24, 28, 29, 25, 21, 19, 16])

bar_chart.add('Min Temp', [22, 22, 22, 13, 13, 17, 20, 23, 23, 23, 24,
23, 23, 19, 17, 15, 17, 18, 15, 14, 17, 14, 13,
15, 16, 19, 19, 18, 15, 12, 10, ])

bar_chart.add('Mean Temp',    [14, 15, 18, 8, 4, 9, 13, 16,
18, 17, 19, 17, 17, 13, 12, 10, 8, 12, 8, 7, 9, 8, 5, 7, 7, 9, 10,
11, 8, 5, 4, ])

bar_chart.render_to_png('bar.png')
```

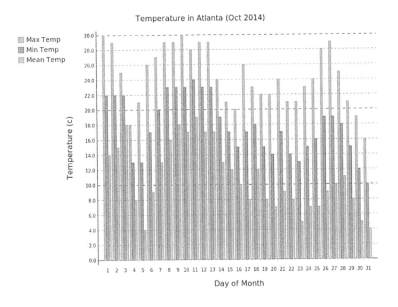

Figure 12.6: Bar chart plotted with Pygal

Let us look at another example of a bar plot plotted using Seaborn. The Seaborn bar plot shows an estimate of central tendency (mean or median) for a numeric variable (as the height of a rectangular bar) and the uncertainty around that estimate (using error bars). For plotting the box plot we will use the Auto MPG Data Set from the UCI Machine learning repository [32]. This dataset can be used for regression problems to predict the city-cycle fuel consumption (in mpg), in terms of three multivalued discrete attributes (cylinders, model year, origin) and four continuous attributes (displacement, horsepower, weight, acceleration). Box 12.7 shows the Python program for plotting bar plot using Seaborn and Figure 12.7 shows the bar plot. This plot shows the mean values for the fuel consumption (in mpg) for different number of cylinders in automobiles.

■ **Box 12.7: Python program for plotting bar plot using Seaborn**

```
import pandas as pd
import seaborn as sns
from pylab import savefig
```

```
data = pd.read_csv("auto-mpg.csv")

sns.barplot(x="cylinders", y="mpg", data=data)

savefig("bar.png")
```

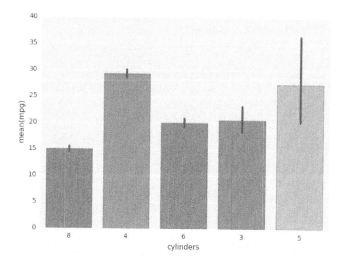

Figure 12.7: Bar plot plotted with Seaborn

12.2.4 Box Plot

Box plot can be used to display the minimum, medium and maximum for a data set. In a box plot, the whiskers denote the extremes of the dataset and the middle line is the median. The box goes from the first quartile to the third quartile of the data set. Box 12.8 shows the Python code for plotting a box plot of the total precipitation recorded in Atlanta for every month in the years 2012, 2013 and 2014. The output is shown in Figure 12.8.

■ **Box 12.8: Python program for plotting box plot using Pygal**

```
import pygal
box_plot = pygal.Box()
box_plot.title = 'Total Precipitation (mm)'

box_plot.add('2012', [67.81, 25.41 , 30.72, 78.49, 87.12,
    119.62, 98.56, 78.23 , 86.11 , 66.53, 25.65 , 149.59])

box_plot.add('2013', [28.68, 120.89, 41.90, 34.80, 81.54,
    266.70, 91.67, 46.73, 56.14 , 15.48, 69.09, 117.35])

box_plot.add('2014', [82.31, 96.01, 102.36, 82.30, 72.63,
    66.55, 116.07, 44.44, 17.77, 148.06, 133.86, 166.61 ])
```

```
box_plot.render_to_png('box.png')
```

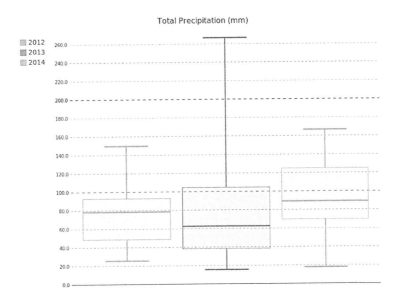

Figure 12.8: Box plot plotted with Pygal

Let us look at another example of a box plot plotted using Seaborn. The Seaborn box plot shows the quartiles of the dataset with whiskers denoting the extremes and dots denoting the points that are determined to be outliers. For plotting the box plot we will use the Wine dataset from the UCI Machine learning repository [39]. This dataset has results of a chemical analysis of wines grown in Italy. The chemical analysis determined the quantities of 13 constituents (such as alcohol, malic acid, magnesium, etc.) found in three types of wines. Box 12.9 shows the Python program for plotting box plot using Seaborn and Figure 12.9 shows the box plot. This plot shows the distribution of the alcohol content in three types of wines.

■ **Box 12.9: Python program for plotting box plot using Seaborn**

```
import pandas as pd
import seaborn as sns
from pylab import savefig

data = pd.read_csv("wine.csv")

sns.boxplot(x="Wine Type", y ="Alcohol", data=data)

savefig("box.png")
```

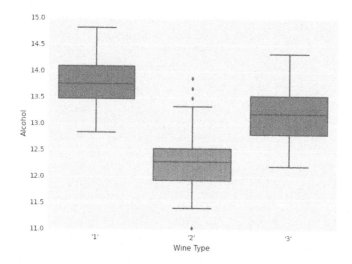

Figure 12.9: Box plot plotted with Seaborn

12.2.5 Pie Chart

Pie chart is used to display numerical proportions on a circle where the arc length is proportional to the quantity represented. Box 12.10 shows the Python code for plotting a pie chart of the total populations of the continents. The output is shown in Figure 12.10.

■ **Box 12.10: Python program for plotting pie chart using Pygal**

```
import pygal

pie_chart = pygal.Pie()
pie_chart.title = 'Population of Continents (in millions)'

pie_chart.add('Asia', 4397)
pie_chart.add('Africa', 1171)
pie_chart.add('Europe', 742)
pie_chart.add('South America', 630)
pie_chart.add('North America', 357)
pie_chart.add('Oceania', 40)

pie_chart.render_to_png('pie.png')
```

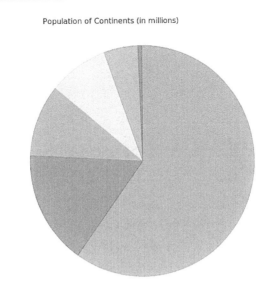

Figure 12.10: Pie chart plotted with Pygal

12.2.6 Dot Chart

Dot charts are used to display different datasets where the size of the dots are proportional to the values represented. Box 12.11 shows the Python code for plotting a dot chart of the January mean temperatures recorded in Atlanta in the years 2012, 2013 and 2014. The output is shown in Figure 12.11.

■ **Box 12.11: Python program for plotting dot chart using Pygal**

```
import pygal
dot_chart = pygal.Dot(x_label_rotation=30)
dot_chart.title = 'January Mean Temperatures'
dot_chart.x_title = 'Day of Month'
dot_chart.y_title = 'Temperature (C)'

dot_chart.x_labels = ['1','2','3','4','5','6','7', '8','9','10',
    '11','12','13','14','15', '16','17','18','19','20','21','22',
    '23', '24','25','26','27','28','29','30','31']

dot_chart.add('Jan 2012', [11, 3, -2, 2, 8, 8, 12, 11, 14, 14, 13,
    7, 0, 3, 6, 7, 12, 7, 6, 11, 13, 10, 10, 10, 10, 17, 10, 8, 6, 7, 9] )

dot_chart.add('Jan 2013', [9, 7, 4, 4, 3, 7, 6, 7, 14, 17, 17,
    18, 19, 13, 11, 14, 7, 7, 6, 7, 6, 2, 6, 7, 4, 8, 8, 11, 14, 14, 5])

dot_chart.add('Jan 2014', [2, -1, -6, -7, -1, -2, 6, 7, 11, 13, 10,
    -1, -3, -4, 0, -1, 7, 1, -3, 7, 8, 7, 7, 4, 1, 12, 4, -1, 0, -3, -1])

dot_chart.render_to_png('dot.png')
```

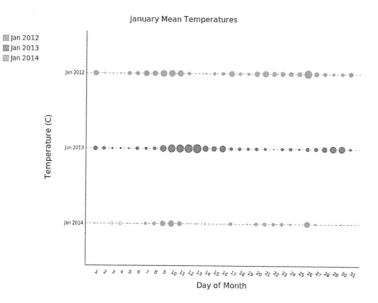

Figure 12.11: Dot chart plotted with Pygal

12.2.7 Map Chart

Let us look at some example of plotting world map charts using Lightning and Pygal. Box 12.12 shows the Python code for plotting world map chart using Lightning showing the top 20 most populated countries. The output is shown in Figure 12.12.

■ **Box 12.12: Python program for plotting map using Lightning**

```
from lightning import Lightning

from numpy import random

lgn = Lightning(ipython=True,local=True)

countries = ['CHN','IND','USA','IDN','BRA',
    'PAK','NGA','BGD','RUS','JPN',
    'MEX','PHL','ETH','VNM','EGY',
    'DEU','IRN','TUR','COG','THA']

values = [1393783836,1267401849,322583006,
252812245,202033670,185132926,178516904,
158512570,142467651,126999808,123799215,
100096496,96506031,92547959,83386739,82652256,
78470222,75837020,69360118,67222972]

lgn.map(countries,values,colormap='Pastel1',width=900)
```

Box 12.13 shows the Python code for plotting world map chart using Pygal showing the top 20 most populated countries. The output is shown in Figure 12.13.

Figure 12.12: Map plotted with Lightning

■ **Box 12.13: Python program for plotting map chart using Pygal**

```
import pygal

worldmap_chart = pygal.maps.world.World()
worldmap_chart.title = 'Top 20 most populated countries '
worldmap_chart.add('Population',
'cn':   1393783836,
'in':   1267401849,
'us':   322583006,
'id':   252812245,
'br':   202033670,
'pk':   185132926,
'ng':   178516904,
'bd':   158512570,
'ru':   142467651,
'jp':   126999808,
'mx':   123799215,
'ph':   100096496,
'et':   96506031,
'vn':   92547959,
'eg':   83386739,
'de':   82652256,
'ir':   78470222,
'tr':   75837020,
'cg':   69360118,
'th':   67222972
 )
worldmap_chart.render_to_png('map.png')
```

Top 20 most populated countries

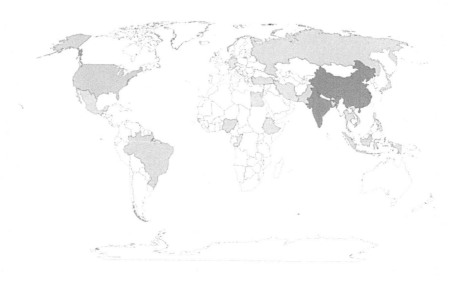

Figure 12.13: Map plotted with Pygal

12.2.8   Gauge Chart

Gauge charts display data on a circular gauge (as in automobile speedometers) where different needles represent different values. Box 12.14 shows the Python code for plotting a gauge chart of the total precipitation recorded in Atlanta in the years 2012, 2013 and 2014. The output is shown in Figure 12.14.

■ **Box 12.14: Python program for plotting gauge chart using Pygal**

```
import pygal

gauge_chart = pygal.Gauge()
gauge_chart.title = 'Total Precipitation (mm)'
gauge_chart.range = [0, 1000]
gauge_chart.add('2012', 765)
gauge_chart.add('2013', 860)
gauge_chart.add('2014', 962)

gauge_chart.render_to_png('gauge.png')
```

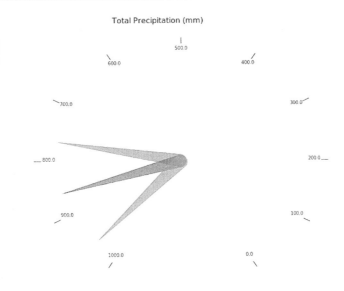

Figure 12.14: Gauge chart plotted using Pygal

12.2.9   Radar Chart

Radar chart (also called Kiviat diagram) is used to display multivariate data on a two-dimensional chart with the zero point in the middle. Box 12.15 shows the Python code for plotting a radar chart of the total precipitation recorded in Atlanta in every month of the years 2012, 2013 and 2014. The output is shown in Figure 12.15.

■ Box 12.15: Python program for plotting radar chart using Pygal

```
import pygal

dot_chart = pygal.Radar()
dot_chart.title = 'Total Precipitation (mm)'

dot_chart.x_labels = ['Jan','Feb','Mar','Apr','May',
    'Jun','Jul','Aug','Sep','Oct','Nov','Dec']

dot_chart.add('2012', [67.81, 25.41 , 30.72, 78.49, 87.12,
    119.62, 98.56, 78.23 , 86.11 , 66.53, 25.65 , 149.59])

dot_chart.add('2013', [28.68, 120.89, 41.90, 34.80, 81.54,
    266.70, 91.67, 46.73, 56.14 , 15.48, 69.09, 117.35])

dot_chart.add('2014', [82.31, 96.01, 102.36, 82.30, 72.63,
    66.55, 116.07, 44.44, 17.77, 148.06, 133.86, 166.61 ])

dot_chart.render_to_png('radar.png')
```

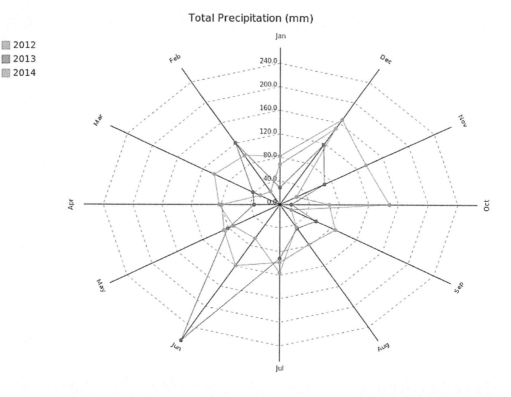

Figure 12.15: Radar chart plotted using Pygal

12.2.10 Matrix Chart

Matrix chart can be used to display data in a grid format. Box 12.16 shows the Python code for plotting matrix chart using Lightning showing a matrix of ratings given by users to different items. The output is shown in Figure 12.16.

■ Box 12.16: Python program for plotting matrix using Lightning

```
from lightning import Lightning
from numpy import random

lgn = Lightning(ipython=True, local=True)

rows = ['User-' + str(x) for x in range(1,11)]
columns = ['Item-' + str(x) for x in range(1,11)]

mat = (random.rand(10,10) * 10).astype('int')
lgn.matrix(mat, row_labels=rows,
    column_labels=columns, colormap='Reds', numbers=True)
```

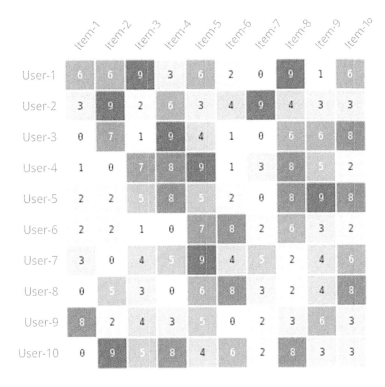

Figure 12.16: Matrix plotted with Lightning

Circle Plot

Circle plots show groups of nodes as points around a circle with the connections between the nodes represented by lines between the points. Box 12.17 shows the Python code for plotting circle plot using Lightning showing direct flights between cities (for a random synthetic dataset) in three different countries (shown as three groups in a different color). The output is shown in Figure 12.17.

> **■ Box 12.17: Python program for plotting circle chart using Lightning**
>
> ```
> from lightning import Lightning
> from random import randint
> from numpy import random
>
> lgn = Lightning(ipython=True, local=True)
>
> #Nodes denoting cities
> nodes = range(50)
>
> #Links denoting direct flights between cities
> links = [ ]
> for i in range(20):
>    x= [randint(0,50),randint(0,50)]
>    links.append(x)
> ```

```
labels = ['City-' + str(x) for x in range(50)]

#Groups denoting countries
groups = []
for i in range(50):
    groups.append(randint(0,2))

lgn.circle(links, group=groups, labels=labels)
```

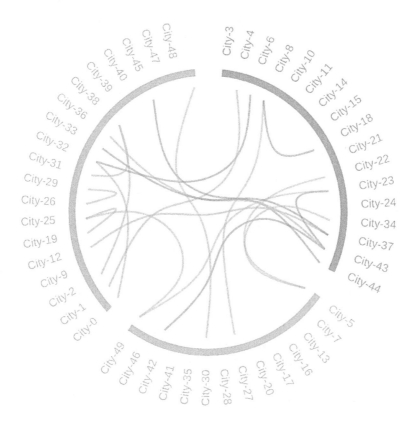

Figure 12.17: Circle chart plotted using Lightning

12.2.11 Force-directed Graph

Force-directed graphs are used to display data in an aesthetically pleasing graph. The edges represent connections between the nodes and are of more or less equal length. The layout of the nodes in the graph is such that there are as few crossing edges as possible. Box 12.18 shows the Python code for plotting force-directed graph using Lightning showing direct flights between cities (for a random synthetic dataset) in three different countries (shown as nodes in a different color). The output is shown in Figure 12.18.

■ Box 12.18: Python program for plotting force-directed graph using Lightning

```python
from lightning import Lightning
from numpy import random
from random import randint

lgn = Lightning(ipython=True, local=True)

#Nodes denoting cities
nodes = range(50)

#Links denoting direct flights between cities
links = [ ]
for i in range(20):
    x= [randint(0,50),randint(0,50)]
    links.append(x)

labels = ['City-' + str(x) for x in range(50)]

#Groups denoting countries
groups = [ ]
for i in range(50):
    groups.append(randint(0,2))


lgn.force(links, group=groups)
```

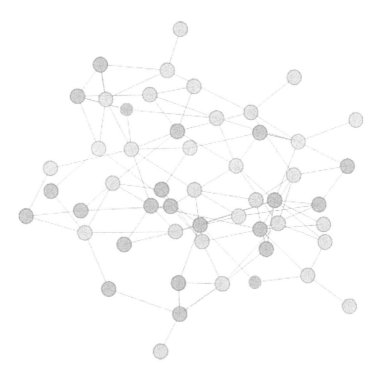

Figure 12.18: Force-directed graph plotted using Lightning

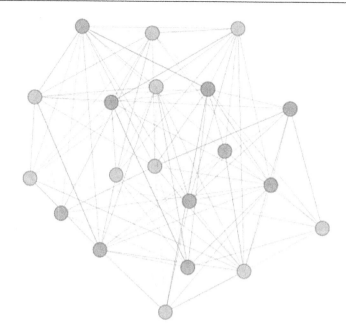

Figure 12.19: Force-directed graph plotted using Lightning

Box 12.19 shows the another Python example for plotting force-directed graph with a random dataset. The output is shown in Figure 12.19.

■ **Box 12.19: Python program for plotting force-directed graph using Lightning**

```
from lightning import Lightning
from numpy import random
from random import randint


lgn = Lightning(ipython=True, local=True)

mat = random.rand(20,20) mat[mat>0.40] = 0
group = (random.rand(20) * 4).astype('int')

lgn.force(mat, group=group)
```

12.2.12 Spatial Graph

Spatial graphs can be used to display nodes with fixed spatial positions, and the links between them. Box 12.20 shows a Python example for plotting a spatial graph with a random dataset. The output is shown in Figure 12.20.

■ **Box 12.20: Python program for plotting spatial graph using Lightning**

```
from lightning import Lightning
from numpy import random
```

```
from random import randint

lgn = Lightning(ipython=True, local=True)

x = random.randn(20)
y = random.randn(20)
mat = random.rand(20,20)
mat[mat>0.50] = 0

lgn.graphbundled(x, y, mat)
```

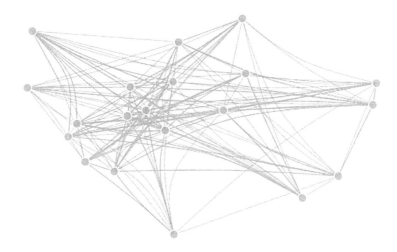

Figure 12.20: Spatial graph potted using Lightning

12.2.13 Distribution Plot

Distribution plots are used to visualize the univariate distributions of the observations. Box 12.21 shows the Python program for plotting distribution plot using Seaborn and Figure 12.21 shows the distribution plot. This plot shows the kernel density estimate and histogram for the fuel consumption (mpg) values in the Auto MPG dataset.

■ **Box 12.21: Python program for plotting distribution plot using Seaborn**

```
import pandas as pd
import seaborn as sns
from pylab import savefig
import numpy as np

data = pd.read_csv("auto-mpg.csv")

x=np.array(data.ix[0:,0])

g = sns.distplot(x)

savefig("dist.png")
```

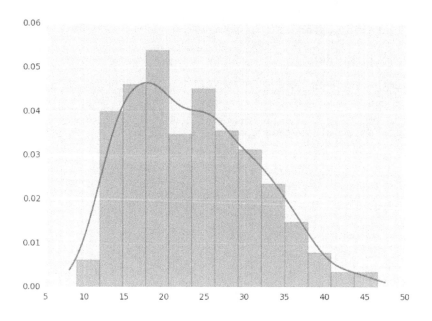

Figure 12.21: Distribution Plot

12.2.14   Kernel Density Estimate (KDE) Plot

The KDE plot can be used to plot univariate or bivariate kernel density estimates. Box 12.22 shows the Python program for plotting KDE plot using Seaborn and Figure 12.22 shows the KDE plot. This plot shows the bivariate density for the fuel consumption (mpg) and displacement variables in the Auto MPG dataset.

■ Box 12.22: Python program for plotting KDE plot using Seaborn

```
import pandas as pd
import seaborn as sns
from pylab import savefig
import numpy as np

data = pd.read_csv("auto-mpg.csv")

x=np.array(data.ix[0:,0])
y=np.array(data.ix[0:,2])

g = sns.kdeplot(x, y, shade=True)

savefig("kde.png")
```

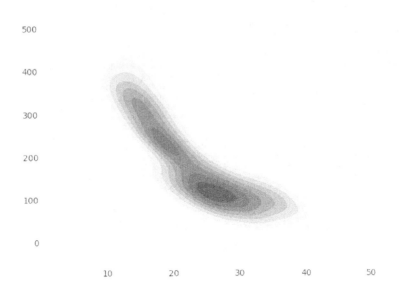

Figure 12.22: KDE Plot

12.2.15 Regression Plot

Regression plot can be used to plot the data and a linear regression model fit. Box 12.23 shows the Python program for plotting regression plot using Seaborn and Figure 12.23 shows the regression plot. This plot shows the displacement versus the fuel consumption (mpg) data in the Auto MPG dataset and a linear regression model fit line.

■ **Box 12.23: Python program for plotting regression plot using Seaborn**

```
import pandas as pd
import seaborn as sns
from pylab import savefig
import numpy as np

data = pd.read_csv("auto-mpg.csv")

#extract mpg column
x=np.array(data.ix[0:,0])

#extract displacement column
y=np.array(data.ix[0:,2])

sns.regplot(x="displacement", y="mpg", data=data, color="g")

savefig("regplot.png")
```

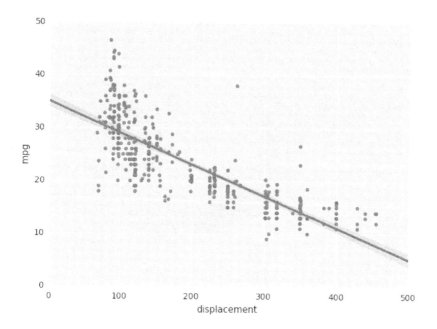

Figure 12.23: Regression plot

12.2.16 Residual Plot

Residual plot can be used to plot the residuals of a linear regression. Box 12.24 shows the
Python program for plotting residual plot using Seaborn and Figure 12.24 shows the residual
plot. This plot shows the residuals of a linear regression between the displacement and the
fuel consumption (mpg) variables in the Auto MPG dataset.

■ **Box 12.24: Python program for plotting residual plot using Seaborn**

```
import pandas as pd
import seaborn as sns
from pylab import savefig
import numpy as np

data = pd.read_csv("auto-mpg.csv")

#extract mpg column
x=np.array(data.ix[0:,0])

#extract displacement column
y=np.array(data.ix[0:,2])

# plot the residuals after fitting a linear model
sns.residplot(x="displacement", y="mpg", data=data, lowess=True,
color="g")

savefig("resi.png")
```

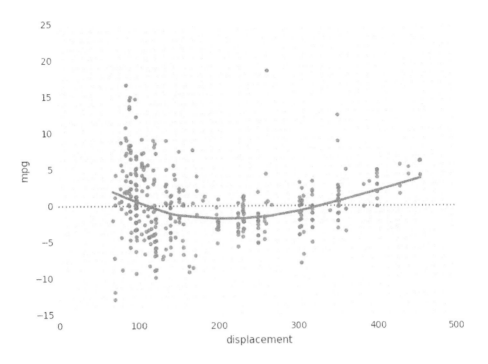

Figure 12.24: Residual Plot

12.2.17   Interaction Plot

Interaction plot can be used to visualize a continuous two-way interaction with a contour plot. Box 12.25 shows the Python program for plotting interaction plot using Seaborn and Figure 12.25 shows the interaction plot. This plot shows the two-way interaction between two independent variables (displacement and horsepower) and the dependent variable (mpg) in the Auto MPG dataset.

■ **Box 12.25: Python program for plotting interaction plot using Seaborn**

```
import pandas as pd
import seaborn as sns
from pylab import savefig
import numpy as np

data = pd.read_csv("auto-mpg.csv")

sns.interactplot("displacement", "horsepower", "mpg", data)

savefig("interactplot.png")
```

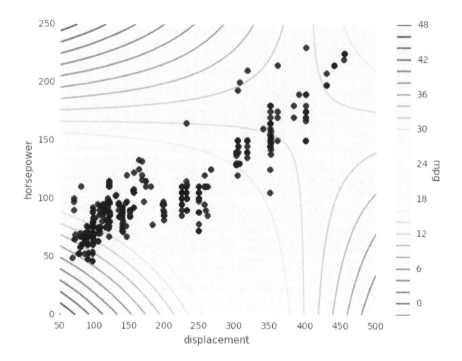

Figure 12.25: Interaction Plot

12.2.18   Violin Plot

Violin plot can be used to plot a combination of box plot and kernel density estimate.
Box 12.26 shows the Python program for plotting violin plot using Seaborn and Figure 12.26
shows the violin plot. This plot shows the distribution of fuel consumption (mpg) data for a
different number of cylinders (which is the categorical variable).

■ **Box 12.26: Python program for plotting violin plot using Seaborn**

```
import pandas as pd
import seaborn as sns
from pylab import savefig

data = pd.read_csv("auto-mpg.csv")

g = sns.violinplot(y="mpg", x ="cylinders", data=data)

savefig("violin.png")
```

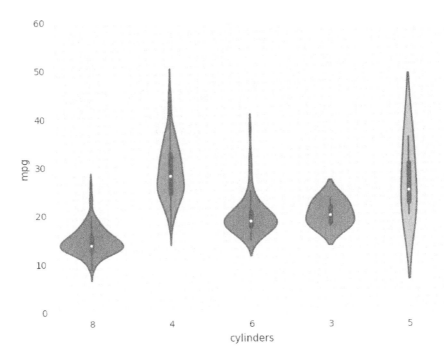

Figure 12.26: Violin Plot

12.2.19 Strip Plot

Strip plot can be used to plot a scatter plot where one variable is categorical. Box 12.27 shows the Python program for plotting strip plot using Seaborn and Figure 12.27 shows the strip plot. This plot shows the scatter plot of fuel consumption (mpg) data for a different number of cylinders (which is the categorical variable).

■ **Box 12.27: Python program for plotting strip plot using Seaborn**

```
import pandas as pd
import seaborn as sns
from pylab import savefig

data = pd.read_csv("auto-mpg.csv")

sns.stripplot(x="cylinders", y="mpg", data=data, jitter=True)

savefig("strip.png")
```

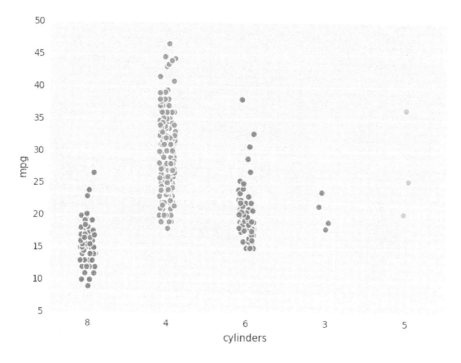

Figure 12.27: Strip Plot

12.2.20   Point Plot

Point plot can be used to plot an estimate of central tendency (e.g. mean) for a numeric variable (as scatter plot points) and uncertainty around that estimate (using error bars). Box 12.28 shows the Python program for plotting point plot using Seaborn and Figure 12.28 shows the point plot. This plot shows the mean fuel consumption (mpg) for a different number of cylinders for the Auto MPG dataset.

■ Box 12.28: Python program for plotting point plot using Seaborn

```
import pandas as pd
import seaborn as sns
from pylab import savefig

data = pd.read_csv("auto-mpg.csv")

sns.pointplot(x="cylinders", y="mpg", data=data)

savefig("pointplot.png")
```

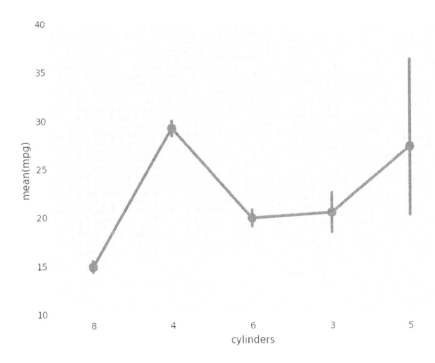

Figure 12.28: Point Plot

12.2.21   Count Plot

Count plot can be used to plot the counts of observations in each categorical bin using bars. Box 12.29 shows the Python program for plotting count plot using Seaborn and Figure 12.29 shows the count plot. This plot shows the count of observations for the three types of wines in the Wines dataset.

■ **Box 12.29: Python program for plotting count plot using Seaborn**

```
import pandas as pd
import seaborn as sns
from pylab import savefig

data = pd.read_csv("wine.csv")

sns.countplot(x="Wine Type", data=data)

savefig("count.png")
```

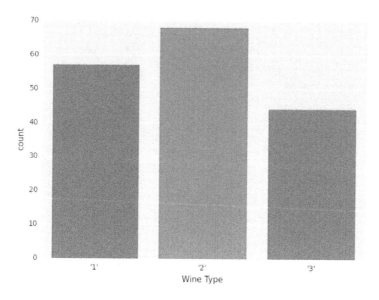

Figure 12.29: Count Plot

12.2.22 Heatmap

Heatmap can be used to plot a color-encoded matrix. Box 12.30 shows the Python program
for plotting heatmap using Seaborn and Figure 12.30 shows the heatmap. In this heatmap
the index (month) and column (year) information is used to label the rows and columns and
the values (total precipitation) are used for color coding. In this example, we use the pivot
function of the Python pandas library for reshaping the data.

■ **Box 12.30: Python program for plotting heatmap using Seaborn**

```
import pandas as pd
import seaborn as sns
from pylab import savefig

data = pd.read_csv("data.csv")
data_to_plot = data.pivot(index="Month", columns="Year",
values="Total Precipitation")
sns.heatmap(data_to_plot)

savefig("heatmap.png")
```

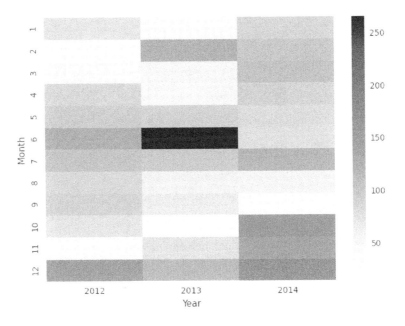

Figure 12.30: Heatmap

12.2.23   Clustered Heatmap

Clustered heatmap can be used to plot a hierarchically clustered heatmap. Box 12.31 shows the Python program for plotting clustered heatmap using Seaborn and Figure 12.31 shows the clustered heatmap.

■ **Box 12.31: Python program for plotting clustered heatmap using Seaborn**

```
import pandas as pd
import seaborn as sns
from pylab import savefig

data = pd.read_csv("data.csv")
data_to_plot = data.pivot(index="Month", columns="Year",
values="Total Precipitation")
sns.clustermap(data_to_plot)

savefig("clustermap.png")
```

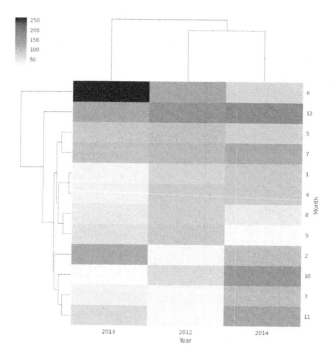

Figure 12.31: Clustered Heatmap

12.2.24   Joint Plot

Joint plot can be used to plot two variables with bivariate and univariate graphs. Box 12.32 shows the Python program for plotting joint plot using Seaborn. The joint plot in Figure 12.32 shows a scatterplot of weight vs mpg (for the Auto MPG dataset) and the regression and kernel density fits. The joint plot in Figure 12.33 shows the density estimates for cylinders and mpg.

■ Box 12.32: Python program for plotting joint plot using Seaborn

```python
import pandas as pd
import seaborn as sns
from pylab import savefig

data = pd.read_csv("auto-mpg.csv")
#g = sns.jointplot("weight", "mpg", data=data, kind="scatter", color="r")
g = sns.jointplot("cylinders", "mpg", data=data, kind="kde", color="b")

savefig("joint.png")
```

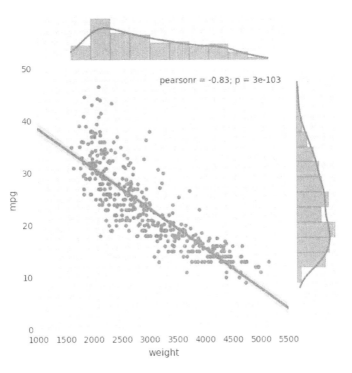

Figure 12.32: Joint Plot

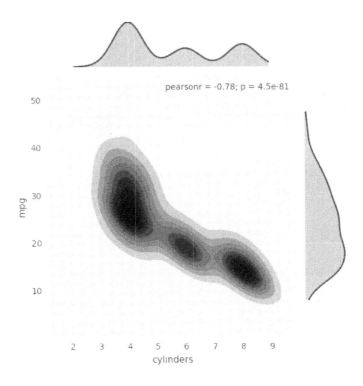

Figure 12.33: Joint Plot

12.2.25 Pair Grid

Pair grid is used for plotting pairwise relationships in a dataset. Box 12.33 shows the Python program for plotting pair plot using Seaborn and Figure 12.34 shows the pair plot. This plot shows scatter plots for each pairwise relationship between the Alcohol, Malic acid, Ash and Alkalinity of ash variables in the Wines dataset.

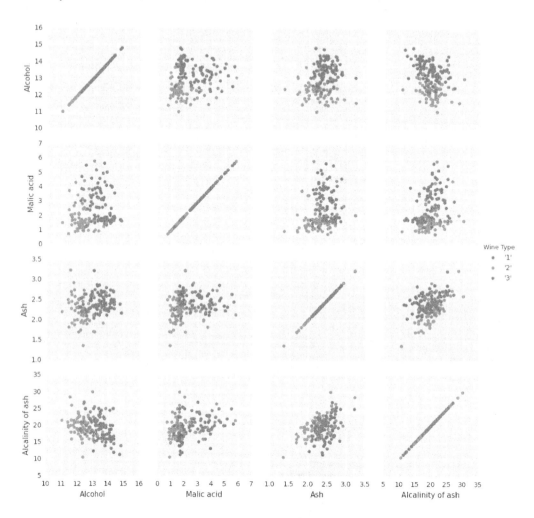

Figure 12.34: Pair Grid

■ **Box 12.33: Python program for plotting pair grid using Seaborn**

```
import pandas as pd
import seaborn as sns
from pylab import savefig
import matplotlib.pyplot as plt

data = pd.read_csv("wine.csv")
features_to_plot = ['Wine Type','Alcohol','Malic acid','Ash','Alkalinity
```

```
of ash']
df_to_plot = data.ix[:, features_to_plot]

g = sns.PairGrid(df_to_plot, hue="Wine Type")
g = g.map(plt.scatter)
g = g.add_legend()

savefig("pair.png")
```

12.2.26 Facet Grid

Facet grid is used for drawing a grid of plots with upto three dimensions where *row* and *column* variables produce an array of axes and the *hue* variable acts as the third dimension. Box 12.34 shows the Python program for plotting facet grid for the Automobile dataset from the UCI machine learning repository [33]. Figure 12.35 shows the facet grid which uses two dimensions (Drive-wheels for column and Body-style for hue). The facet grid shows the scatter plot of the wheel-base and price.

■ **Box 12.34: Python program for plotting facet plot using Seaborn**

```
import pandas as pd
import seaborn as sns
from pylab import savefig
import matplotlib.pyplot as plt

data = pd.read_csv("imports-85.data.csv")

g = sns.FacetGrid(data, col="Drive-wheels",
hue="Body-style", margin_titles=True)
g = g.map(plt.scatter, "Wheel-base", "price")
g.add_legend()

savefig("facet.png")
```

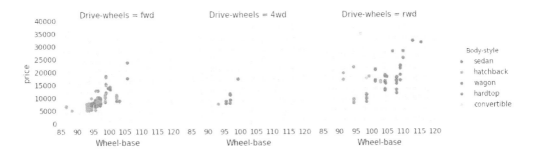

Figure 12.35: Facet Plot

Box 12.35 shows the Python program for plotting facet grid showing the point plots for the wheel base and the highway-mpg and Figure 12.36 shows the plot.

■ **Box 12.35: Python program for plotting facet plot using Seaborn**

```python
import pandas as pd
import seaborn as sns
from pylab import savefig

data = pd.read_csv("imports-85.data.csv")
g = sns.FacetGrid(data, col="Engine-type",
col_wrap=3, margin_titles=True)
g = g.map(sns.pointplot, "Wheel-base", "Highway-mpg")
g.add_legend()

savefig("facet.png")
```

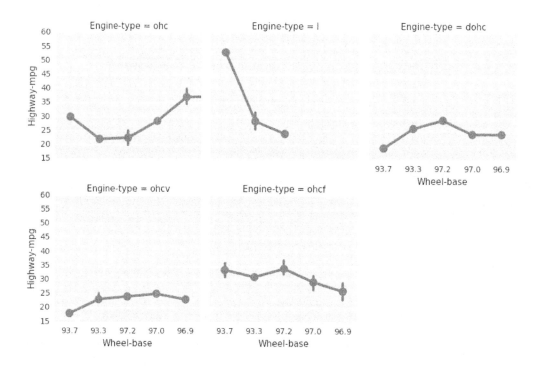

Figure 12.36: Facet Plot

Summary

In this chapter, we described the Lightning, Pygal and Seaborn frameworks for data visualization. These visualizations can be used either in a standalone manner or inside a web application built with a web framework such as Django.

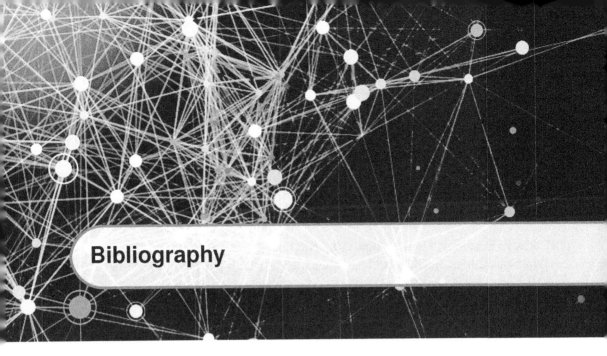

Bibliography

[1] National Research Council, *Frontiers in Massive Data Analysis*, The National Academies Press, 2013.

[2] R. Taft,M. Vartak,N.R. Satish, N. Sundaram, S. Madden, M. Stonebraker, *GenBase: a complex analytics genomics benchmark*, SIGMOD '14 Proceedings of the 2014 ACM SIGMOD International Conference on Management of Data, 2014.

[3] OpenRefine, http://openrefine.org/, Retrieved 2016.

[4] Stanford DataWrangler, http://vis.stanford.edu/wrangler/, Retrieved 2016.

[5] A. Bahga, V. Madisetti, *A Cloud-Based Approach to Interoperable Electronic Health Records (EHRs)*, IEEE Journal of Biomedical and Health Informatics, Vol. 17, Iss. 5, Sep 2013.

[6] A. Bahga, V. Madisetti, *Cloud-Based Information Integration & Informatics Framework for Healthcare Applications*, IEEE Computer, 2013.

[7] Hortonworks HDP, http://hortonworks.com/hdp, Retrieved 2016.

[8] Cloudera CDH 5 Installation Guide,
http://www.cloudera.com/documentation/cdh/5-1-x/
CDH5-Installation-Guide/CDH5-Installation-Guide.html, Retrieved 2016.

[9] What is Big Data, https://www-01.ibm.com/software/in/data/bigdata/, IBM, Retrieved 2016.

[10] Josh James, Data Never Sleeps 3.0,
https://www.domo.com/blog/2015/08/data-never-sleeps-3-0/, DOMO, 2015.

[11] Amazon Elastic Compute Cloud, http://aws.amazon.com/ec2, 2012.

[12] Google Compute Engine, https://developers.google.com/compute/, Retrieved 2016.

[13] Windows Azure, https://azure.microsoft.com, Retrieved 2016.

[14] Google App Engine, http://appengine.google.com, 2012.

[15] Apache Ambari, https://ambari.apache.org/, Retrieved 2016.

[16] Apache Ranger, http://ranger.apache.org/, Retrieved 2016.

[17] Apache Knox, https://knox.apache.org/, Retrieved 2016.

[18] AFINN Sentiment Lexicon, Finn Arup Nielsen,
      http://www2.imm.dtu.dk/pubdb/views/publication_details.php?id=6010, Retrieved 2016.

[19] Leslie Lamport, *The Part-Time Parliament*, ACM Transactions on Computer Systems
      16, 2 (May 1998), 133-169.

[20] Leslie Lamport, *Paxos Made Simple*,
      http://research.microsoft.com/en-us/um/people/lamport/pubs/paxos-simple.pdf, 2001.

[21] S. Ghemawat, H. Gobioff, S. Leung, *The Google File System*, SOSP 2003.

[22] J. Dean, S. Ghemawat, *MapReduce: Simplified Data Processing on Large Clusters*,
      OSDI 2004.

[23] Apache Storm, http://storm-project.net, Retrieved 2016.

[24] The Python Standard Library, http://docs.python.org/2/library/, Retrieved 2016.

[25] Roy T. Fielding, Richard N. Taylor, *Principled Design of the Modern Web Architecture*,
      ACM Transactions on Internet Technology (TOIT), 2002.

[26] Mark Devaney, Bill Cheetham, *Case-Based Reasoning for Gas Turbine Diagnostics*,
      18th International FLAIRS Conference, 2005.

[27] Harry Timmerman, *SKF WindCon Condition Monitoring System for Wind Turbines*,
      New Zealand Wind Energy Conference, 2009.

[28] Python-RecSys, http://ocelma.net/software/python-recsys/build/html/quickstart.html,

[29] Google NGram Dataset,
      http://storage.googleapis.com/books/ngrams/books/datasetsv2.html, Retrieved 2016.

[30] Employees Database, https://launchpad.net/test-db/, Retrieved 2016.

[31] Weather Underground, http://www.wunderground.com/, Retrieved 2016.

[32] Auto MPG Data Set, http://archive.ics.uci.edu/ml/datasets/Auto+MPG, Retrieved 2016.

[33] Automobile Data Set, http://archive.ics.uci.edu/ml/datasets/Automobile, Retrieved
      2016.

[34] E.F. Codd, *A Relational Model of Data for Large Shared Data Banks*, Communications of the ACM 13 (6): 377–387, 1970.

[35] OpenWeatherMap API, http://openweathermap.org/api, Retrieved 2016.

[36] Seaborn, https://stanford.edu/ mwaskom/software/seaborn/, Retrieved 2016.

[37] Corinna Cortes, Vladimir N. Vapnik, "Support-Vector Networks", Machine Learning, 20, 1995.

[38] Leo Breiman, "Random Forests", Machine Learning 45 (1): 5–32, 2001.

[39] Wine Data Set, https://archive.ics.uci.edu/ml/datasets/Wine, Retrieved 2016.

[40] Wine Quality Dataset, https://archive.ics.uci.edu/ml/datasets/Wine+Quality, Retrieved 2016.

[41] Adult Dataset, https://archive.ics.uci.edu/ml/datasets/Adult, Retrieved 2016.

[42] UCI Breast Cancer dataset, http://archive.ics.uci.edu/ml/datasets/Breast+Cancer+Wisconsin+(Diagnostic), Retrieved 2016.

[43] UCI Parkinsons Data Set, https://archive.ics.uci.edu/ml/datasets/Parkinsons, Retrieved 2016.

[44] Thierry Bertin-Mahieux, Daniel P.W. Ellis, Brian Whitman, and Paul Lamere. The Million Song Dataset. In Proceedings of the 12th International Society for Music Information Retrieval Conference (ISMIR 2011), 2011.

[45] Hastie, Trevor, Robert Tibshirani, and J Jerome H Friedman. The Elements of Statistical Learning. Vol.1. N.p., page 339: Springer New York, 2001.

[46] MNIST Dataset, http://yann.lecun.com/exdb/mnist/, Retrieved 2016.

[47] MNIST Dataset File,https://s3.amazonaws.com/h2o-public-test-data/smalldata/ flow_examples/mnist/train.csv.gz, Retrieved 2016.

[48] MovieLens dataset, http://movielens.org, Retrieved 2016.

[49] IMDbPY, http://imdbpy.sourceforge.net, Retrieved 2016.

[50] Apache Hadoop, *Fair Scheduler*, http://hadoop.apache.org/docs/ r1.1.1/fair_scheduler.html, 2013.

[51] Arun C. Murthy, *The Hadoop Map-Reduce Capacity Scheduler*, http://developer.yahoo.com/blogs/hadoop/posts/2011/02/capacity-scheduler/, 2011.

[52] National Climatic Data Center (NCDC) Weather Dataset, ftp://ftp.ncdc.noaa.gov/pub/data/uscrn/products/daily01, Retrieved 2016.

[53] A. Bahga, V. Madisetti, *Rapid Prototyping of Advanced Cloud-Based Systems*, IEEE Computer, vol. 46, iss. 11, Nov 2013.

[54] AutoBahn, http://autobahn.ws/, Retrieved 2016.

[55] Amazon Web Services, http://aws.amazon.com, Retrieved 2016.

[56] Google Cloud Platform, https://cloud.google.com, Retrieved 2016.

[57] Microsoft Windows Azure, http://www.windowsazure.com, Retrieved 2016.

[58] boto, http://boto.readthedocs.org/en/latest/, Retrieved 2016.

[59] Scikit-learn, http://scikit-learn.org/stable/, Retrieved 2016.

[60] Apache Tez, http://tez.apache.org/, Retrieved 2016.

[61] Django, https://docs.djangoproject.com/en/1.5/, Retrieved 2016.

[62] Apache Spark, http://spark.apache.org, Retrieved 2016.

[63] http://code.google.com/p/modwsgi/, Retrieved 2016.

[64] Apache Hadoop, http://hadoop.apache.org/, Retrieved 2016.

[65] Storm, http://storm.incubator.apache.org/, Retrieved 2016.

[66] Zookeeper, http://zookeeper.apache.org/, Retrieved 2016.

[67] Lightning framework, http://lightning-viz.org/, Retrieved 2016.

Index